CAROLINA IN CRISIS

CAROLINA

IN CRISIS

CHEROKEES, COLONISTS,

and SLAVES *in the* AMERICAN

SOUTHEAST, 1756–1763

Daniel J. Tortora

THE UNIVERSITY OF NORTH CAROLINA PRESS

Chapel Hill

Set in Utopia and Bodoni types
By Westchester Publishing Services
Manufactured in the United States of America

The University of North Carolina Press has been a member
of the Green Press Initiative since 2003.

Cover illustration: British military gorget in gilt with royal coat of arms.
Photo by John Warner, courtesy of the Museum of the Cherokee Indian.

Library of Congress Cataloging-in-Publication Data

Tortora, Daniel J.
    Carolina in crisis : Cherokees, colonists, and slaves in the American southeast, 1756–1763 /
Daniel J. Tortora.
        pages cm
    Includes bibliographical references and index.
    ISBN 978-1-4696-2122-7 (pbk   ) — ISBN 978-1-4696-2123-4 (ebook)   1. Cherokee
Indians—Wars, 1759–1761.   2. Cherokee Indians—Government relations—History—
18th century.   3. United States—History—French and Indian War, 1754–1763—Campaigns.
4. South Carolina—History—Colonial period, ca. 1600–1775.   I. Title.
    E83.759.T67 2015
    975.7'01—dc23   2014034900

CONTENTS

MAPS & IMAGES

ACKNOWLEDGMENTS

This book is the product of several years of reading, research, on-the-ground investigations, group tours, presentations and discussions, and many solitary moments of pondering, writing, and rewriting. I am grateful for the assistance and enthusiasm I have met with along the way.

Numerous people offered research leads, suggestions, and opportunities: Tyler Boulware, Greg Brooking, Al Bullman, Ashley Chapman, Jefferson Chapman, Doug Cubbison, Scott Douglas, Graham Duncan, Debra Dylan, George Frizzell, Charlie Gray, Fritz Hamer, Eric Hughey, Buck Kahler, Angie King, Will Kinton, Clayton Lewis, Christopher Lyttelton, 12th Viscount Cobham, John Maass, Ronan MacGregor, Doug MacIntyre, Jim Moore, David Neilan, Lon Outen, Freeman Owle, Lisa Parrish, Jim Piecuch, Walt Powell, Tom Powers, David Preston, Joyce Purnell, Robert Rambo, John Robertson, Tammy Sarver, Cheney Schopieray, Lynn Shirley, Robert Shook, Bullet Standingdeer, Tim Stone, Wade Stoner, Steve Tuttle, Greg Urwin, Jeff Wells, Martin West, Scott Withrow, and Doug Wood. This book is better for the patient and thorough attention of Mark Simpson-Vos and others at the University of North Carolina Press.

I also appreciate the aid of the staffs at the Beinecke Library at Yale University, Camden Archives & Museum, Charleston Library Society, Colby College Libraries, David Library of the American Revolution, Duke University Libraries, the East Tennessee Historical Society, Gilcrease Museum, Hunter Library at Western Carolina University, the Museum of the Cherokee Indian, the Scottish Tartans Museum, South Carolina Department of Archives and History, the South Carolina Historical Society, South Caroliniana Library, and the William L. Clements Library. My several visits to Fort Loudoun State Historic Area in Tennessee proved awe-inspiring as well as helpful. I also thank the many others who helped me locate documents and images at libraries and archives in Great Britain and the United States.

The following people and organizations invited me to present my work in progress: Bruce Venter and his tour group at America's History LLC, the Backcountry Revolutionary War Roundtable at Wofford College, the Braddock Road Preservation Association, Duke University Department of History, Fort Loudoun State Historic Area, the Kershaw County Historical Society,

Ninety Six National Historic Site, the Society for Military History, the South Carolina State Museum, and Southern Campaigns of the American Revolution.

Generous support from the following sources enabled extensive travel and research: Colby College and its Wiswell Research Fund, David Library of the American Revolution, Duke University Graduate School, the Institute for Southern Studies at the University of South Carolina, and the North Caroliniana Society's Archie Davis Fellowship.

People at Duke University and in North Carolina helped in the making of this book, especially Ted Brooks, David Brown, Barry Gaspar, Doug James, Max Krochmal, Wayne Lee, David Long, Jacob Remes, John Thompson, Susan Thorne, and Peter Wood. I owe much to Elizabeth Fenn. In reviewing countless drafts and helping me sharpen my work, she made my journey through graduate school fun. I'm grateful for the friendship and intellect of this outstanding bunch.

Many of my favorite memories associated with this project come from times spent in South Carolina with John Allison, Lisa Cheeks, Don Doyle, Walter Edgar, Dean Hunt, Elena Martínez-Vidal, Marjorie Spruill, and John Tompkins. Luke Reuwer, David Reuwer, George and Carole Summers, Charles and Judy Baxley, Matt Stevenson, and Eric Cheezum also provided friendship and cheer. Colleagues at Colby and friends in Maine sustained me in the later stages of this project, particularly Sherry Berard, Jim Fleming, Elizabeth Leonard, Dave and Sharon Page, Jim Webb, Robin Wiggin, and my students.

I thank my family most of all, especially Mike and Annie, Ted and Wanda, Ruth, Mike, Brian, Bill, and Diane. It is their humor and endless support that has meant the most.

CAROLINA IN CRISIS

INTRODUCTION

"The Concerns of this Country are . . . closely connected and inter-woven with *Indian* Affairs," Governor James Glen informed the South Carolina Council in 1746. Three years later, in his report to Britain's Lords Commissioners of Trade and Plantations (the Board of Trade), Glen elaborated, writing that "not only a great Branch of our Trade, but even the Safety of this Province, do so much depend upon our continuing in Friendship with the *Indians*." South Carolina, he concluded, was deeply "connected in Interest" to its Indian neighbors. The future of the American colonies, and their divergence from Great Britain, was deeply linked to the West and to the Indians who lived there. For South Carolina, those Indians were Cherokees. "Their Country is the Key of Carolina," Glen wrote.[1]

The most authoritative eighteenth-century trader and ethnographer in the Southeast, James Adair, summed up the South Carolina–Cherokee relationship during the mid-eighteenth century: "In brief, we forced the Cheerake to become our bitter enemies, by a long train of wrong measures, the consequences of which were severely felt by a number of high assessed, ruined, and bleeding innocents."[2]

This book chronicles how the mid-eighteenth century was an unmitigated disaster for the Cherokee people, a watershed moment for them. The British had long recognized and coveted Cherokee military and economic power. But from 1758 to 1761, in a series of clashes known as the Anglo-Cherokee War, Cherokees went from British allies to enemies to neglected nuisances. The process was devastating and disruptive. According to North Carolina's governor, Arthur Dobbs, "upon account of the War Sickness and famine," the Cherokee population declined by a third from 1758 to 1761.[3] In the Anglo-Cherokee War, Cherokees lost the position of strength that they had once enjoyed.

In addition, this book shows that Indians greatly destabilized the South Carolina colony in a way that threatened the livelihoods of coastal elites and raised their social and political anxieties to a fever pitch. South Carolina shared in the burdens and trials of empire to a considerable degree. With a devastating Indian war on its frontier, a slave conspiracy, a smallpox epidemic, and widening tensions between colonists and British officials, South Carolina was a critical theater of action, not just a sideshow.

Challenged by Indians from without, by slaves from within, and by British policy from afar, members of the merchant-planter class eventually took matters into their own hands. Thus, this book also argues that the Anglo-Cherokee War also was an important factor influencing conservative, slaveholding South Carolinians to throw in their lot with the resistance movement that emerged close on the heels of the 1763 Treaty of Paris. The war also had implications for the Revolutionary era.

From 1754 to 1763, the major European powers clashed over the fate of their empires, with action in Europe, North America, India, Africa, and the Caribbean. The struggle marked a significant moment: for the first time in history, war spanned the globe. In the North American theater, the French and their native allies fought the British in a conflict termed the French and Indian War. This was the epicenter of the Seven Years' War. When the conflict in North America ended, Canada became the crucial chip that fell to the British, removing France as an imperial contender on the continent. Because of the scope and repercussions of these events, the Seven Years' War has attracted considerable attention from amateur and professional historians alike. In the brief period since 1999, several book-length studies of the French and Indian War have appeared, including Fred Anderson's formidable and impressive *Crucible of War*. Yet this scholarship has little to say about developments further to the south. In *Crucible of War*, for instance, Cherokee affairs cover about 15 of 750 pages, or 2 percent of the text.[4]

Many people often react with surprise, for example, when told that South Carolina forces were present at Fort Necessity in 1754 for the opening shots of the French and Indian War. On an even more important level, many are unaware that South Carolina and the Cherokee Indians were even at war from 1759 to 1761. As Philadelphia merchant Ephraim Biggs put it in 1759, "When a man stands with his face to the North, his Back is Consequently to the South. . . . I fear but Little Notice is taken of the Situation of things in the South Quarter."[5]

In fact, in 1760, when British victory was all but assured and hostilities in the northeastern colonies of North America had ended, the future of the southeastern colonies was not nearly so clear. British authorities in the South still faced the possibility of a local French and Indian alliance and clashed with Cherokees who had complaints and cultural considerations of their own. In historians' accounts, these tensions and events usually take a backseat to the climactic proceedings farther north. Many people are familiar with the novel and film *The Last of the Mohicans*. They know of the fighting on the New York frontier. They may have heard about the surrender and aftermath of the

British defeat at Fort William Henry in 1757, but not the dramatic siege, surrender, and violence involving the Cherokees and the garrison of Fort Loudoun. Perhaps they learned about the turmoil in the South a decade and a half later during the Revolution, from the highly imaginative film *The Patriot*. But they probably overlook its few passing references to the French and Indian War, and thus fail to grasp that war's full influence and reach. Both recent scholarship and popular films have contributed to a lack of awareness of the no less dramatic events that transpired in the southern theater during the French and Indian War, including the Anglo-Cherokee War.

Perhaps, then, it may come as a revelation to many to find out that the Cherokees and the Anglo-Cherokee War so destabilized South Carolina society. In South Carolina imperial dynamics intersected with the complexities of a triracial slave society. Historians have illuminated slave life and the nature of slave societies.[6] They have also written extensively on the African American experience during and after the Revolutionary War: the formative generation of black Americans who shaped the birth of the United States.[7] Tension over race and slavery did more than shape the American Revolution.[8] It also helped shape the Seven Years' War era in the South, I argue. I show how Cherokee Indians forged the institution of slavery in South Carolina, and how slavery influenced Indian affairs, a component missing in previous scholarship on enslaved South Carolinians.

Although some historians have written about Charles Town (today Charleston) during the Anglo-Cherokee War era, the internal and external pressures influencing the city's inhabitants in these years remain only vaguely understood. This book demonstrates how events on the frontier reverberated along the coast.

The Anglo-Cherokee War contributed to and, in many ways, drove some of the tensions between colony and metropole leading to the American Revolution. Scholars have long understood that the expense of fighting the French and Indian War caused Britain to press new financial levies on American colonists. Recently, historians have also begun to explore the deeper consequences of the war on the local stage. Some have written about political discord among South Carolina whites in the 1760s, but our understanding of the conditions that created this discontent remains sketchy.[9] Other scholars have suggested links between the Anglo-Cherokee War and the Regulator movement that followed it, but here too our understanding remains incomplete.[10]

This book aims to build a bridge to the rich scholarship on the southern campaigns of the American Revolution. It introduces readers to a cast of characters, many of whom hold important roles in the Revolutionary era. The war created a generation of leaders in both the colonial assembly and the provincial military and shaped the outlooks of the British, provincials, Indians, and slaves alike.[11]

In a second way, this book reveals many connections with the Revolutionary era, complementing recent scholarship on the motivations and efforts of white, black, and native populations in the South during the Revolution. Readers will notice parallels with the pioneering *Three Peoples, One King* by Jim Piecuch. Like *Three Peoples*, this book offers a synthetic approach to white, black, and native populations in the South—but a generation earlier. The similarities are many. In both eras, Indians and blacks contributed to British military efforts, but the British failed to adopt effective policies to utilize those services. In both eras, the British neglected to understand that, as Piecuch put it, "Indians were independent allies who preferred to fight . . . on their own terms." In both eras, animosity was rife between frontier settlers and Indians, complicating British plans. African Americans "refused to remain idle during [each] struggle" but rather weighed their options and their opportunities, some contributing in valuable ways, others doing whatever it took to secure freedom. In both eras, South Carolinian elites constituted "a frightened" yet "dominant" minority surrounded by "two exploited colored majorities." In each struggle, the British had a poorly coordinated strategy in the South. Finally, in each conflict, South Carolinians often appear in a less flattering light than their British, Indian, or African American counterparts. This book also provides background for scholarship on the Revolutionary era. It shows that, in many ways, little changed from 1776 to 1783, and reveals just how little the British absorbed from their French and Indian War era experiences in the South.[12]

While studies of the French and Indian War have left out a southern component, studies of Cherokee campaigns in the Revolutionary era often omit the earlier component.[13] In addition, expanded attention to the South yields a fuller understanding not only of the French and Indian War era, but also of the genesis of the American Revolution as a struggle, driven by western expansion, that could be, as Patrick Griffin put it, "genocidal" in nature.[14]

In addition, the book has some secondary findings. First, it reveals wide divisions between groups. British settlers and soldiers often displayed great cruelty and treachery against the Cherokees, but such violent acts were often criticized by their fellow British subjects. Not all whites at the time were uniformly racist. At the same time, the Cherokee "Nation" was rarely one entity. Cherokee people had diverging viewpoints based on age, geography, gender, and other factors, making unity often elusive.

Another secondary finding of this book is the extent of cultural imperatives on Cherokee motivations. Through the lens of the white media in the eighteenth century, wars seem like expressions of gratuitous Indian violence. But, as Wayne Lee and other scholars have shown, warriors act within parameters that suit their own conceptions of appropriate behavior. Cherokees were neither benevolent nor malicious. They used their best judgment to ensure their survival in difficult circumstances. Recent scholarship encourages a more thorough discussion of Cherokee cultural mores.[15] This book offers insights into Cherokee women and their social, economic, and political roles in the eighteenth century. In more detail than previous works, this book looks to and beyond the battlefield to explore Cherokee motivations, divisions, and decisions. My research examines the ways in which those variables shaped white fears, tensions, and plans.

Three main book-length studies helped me unravel the history of Anglo-Cherokee trade, diplomacy, and war during the mid-eighteenth century, although each adopted different approaches and reached different conclusions than this book. In 1962, David Corkran's *The Cherokee Frontier* provided a detailed account of the Anglo-Cherokee War based primarily on eighteenth-century newspaper accounts. It did not make connections with slavery and with the coming of the Revolution. Instead it followed internal Cherokee divisions and offered a military-focused account of Anglo-Cherokee hostilities. *The Dividing Paths* by Tom Hatley covered a broader period of time and lacked this book's detailed focus on the Anglo-Cherokee War. Hatley considered the ways in which Cherokees and South Carolinians coexisted, collided, and ultimately separated from the 1670s to the 1780s. He believed that South Carolina revolutionaries emerged because they defined themselves against the Cherokee "other." My book argues that disagreements engendered by the Anglo-Cherokee War divided the provincials and the British. Similarly, I reach different conclusions than John Oliphant's *Peace and War on the Anglo-Cherokee Frontier.* Writing in 2001, Oliphant focused on British diplomatic and military policy, portraying British officials in a sympathetic light. Oliphant's work invites the opportunity to adopt a more bottom-up approach as well as to build connections to the Revolution.[16]

More recently, Tyler Boulware's impressively researched *Deconstructing the Cherokee Nation* focused on the evolution of the Cherokee geopolitical landscape over time and informed my understanding of Cherokee regionalism and identity. It encourages a thorough examination of wartime events and their consequence not only for Cherokees but also for Crown and colonist. While Paul Kelton's 2012 article highlighted connections between

Cherokees and Ohio Valley Indians in the Fort Duquesne campaign, it illustrated an important point that historians have often overlooked: "Cherokees indeed changed the equation of the war." Many historians "have missed the Cherokees' role in a crucial turning point in this global conflict." I write with Kelton's reminder that "natives shaped the Seven Years' War in complicated and indelible ways."[17]

I build on the exceptional and engaging work of these previous scholars and many others, and draw inspiration from the living history community, reconceptualizing key moments in the conflict and clarifying cause and effect during the war years and beyond. In a chronological, narrative-driven approach, I also place events into a broad geographical context. In doing so, I rely on several sets of sources. I incorporate voluminous eighteenth-century newspaper accounts, military and diplomatic correspondence, and the speeches and dictations of Indian peoples, transcribed by trusted interpreters or compared to other accounts. Among the most revealing of these sources are the only recently catalogued and seldom used James Grant Papers. I also use rarely seen diaries and letters from South Carolinians, including those written by preachers and women. In addition, I consult the work of eighteenth-century ethnographers and modern scholars who shine light on Cherokee culture in the eighteenth century. Finally, on-the-ground investigations helped me make sense of the battlefields and the historical geography.[18]

The first two chapters show how the coming of the French and Indian War and intercolonial competition undermined the potential for a long-lasting Cherokee-British alliance. French solicitations and British trade abuses soon tested the fragile accord that had tentatively emerged by 1750. Then, when Cherokees were drawn into the French and Indian War from 1756 to 1758, the alliance unraveled. Numerous delays and a series of misunderstandings created a crisis in Anglo-Cherokee relations; at least thirty-seven Cherokees died as a result. Cherokee law, custom, and family obligations required small-scale military operations to satisfy the families of the dead and posturing to attempt to reshape the broken relationship. But British officials ignored Cherokee culture, and this provoked a much larger crisis. Cherokee unrest stirred internal tensions in South Carolina. African Americans planned a revolt. In a province already in upheaval, a challenge to race slavery threatened social stability, undermined military readiness, and exacerbated white anxieties. This thematic thread connects my narrative.

South Carolina's governor imposed a peace and, with it, unreasonable expectations on the Cherokees, which resulted in further hostilities in 1760. At the same time, smallpox, carried to Charles Town by returning soldiers, heightened racial fears and political turmoil in the provincial capital. The narrative takes readers into the villages of Cherokee country and explains how a sense of unity developed as Cherokees attempted to free their hostages. Driven by cultural obligations, conceptions of war and justice, and a desire to drive back the South Carolina frontier, Cherokees launched an offensive in early 1760. Gripped by fear and self-pity, poor frontiersmen blamed coastal elites. Elites in turn blamed Great Britain.

The last third of the book demonstrates the problems that resulted when British troops and British authorities attempted to bring calm to the frontier. Cherokee forces scored stunning, but pyrrhic, victories in the summer of 1760. The year 1760 was the height of Cherokee power. They defeated an invading British army and seized the garrison at Fort Loudoun, and then looked for peace. War continued in 1761 because some Fort Prince George soldiers exaggerated their circumstances, and many British and provincial leaders called for vengeance. Facing starvation and ruin, a small contingent of Cherokees negotiated a treaty with British authorities after a destructive military campaign destroyed fifteen villages. Yet some South Carolinians claimed that the expedition had not gone far enough. In examining the British military campaigns of 1760 and 1761, the book offers new insight using the James Grant Papers and on-the-ground battlefield investigations among other sources. Scholars have seldom looked at the tensions created by military campaigns in the South, and their ripple effect. I show how the Anglo-Cherokee War and its conclusion drove a wedge between South Carolina and Britain. South Carolinians and British regulars viewed each other with contempt during the campaigns, and during peace negotiations, and that carried over to the postwar era. The postwar settlement brought a new, centralized Indian policy that seemed to institutionalize Britain's disregard for her colonial subjects. To white South Carolinians, rich and poor alike, it appeared that the British had abandoned them, and then sided with the Cherokee Indians rather than their own colonists.

When hostilities ended, the Cherokees had no place in the plans of western settlers and speculators. In 1761, a British printer published Glen's 1749 report without the author's name or consent. But the account that readers absorbed was a dated one. The Anglo-Cherokee War was a seminal moment after which, to paraphrase Glen, the concerns of the country were no longer so centrally about Cherokee affairs. The war began to disconnect and disentangle the colony from Indian affairs and set it on its future course of Cherokee dispossession and expansion. And as Indian relations diminished in importance, internal tensions within Carolina became even more pronounced. Much had changed.[19]

The British ostensibly protected Indian lands through the Proclamation Line of 1763, but the reality was different. Picking up where previous studies left off, I explain that settlers and speculators scooped up Indian lands, further jeopardizing the sovereignty, survival, and dignity of Indian peoples in Appalachian region. The stage was set for future conflict. African Americans, too, found themselves worse off than before, but they turned white divisions to their own advantage. The number of maroon communities increased, adding to the panic of white elites. The end of the Anglo-Cherokee War in 1761 and the end of the wider Seven Years' War two years later masked deepening fissures in the colonial world. One such fissure was between colonists and the London metropole, but there were fissures among South Carolinians themselves. When the great imperial struggle ended, African Americans found themselves worse off than in previous years. So, too, did the Cherokee Indians, now disillusioned and divided. The colony's backcountry farmers resented the political and economic power of lowcountry Anglican elites. While the elites emerged victorious, they squabbled among themselves and directed a seething resentment toward Great Britain's political and economic power, as new policies seemed to favor Indians over British subjects. The war era reshaped South Carolina.[20]

This work simultaneously cuts across many topics and genres and offers insights on many threads. It is at once a study of South Carolina–Cherokee affairs, Carolina society and politics, the deerskin trade and intercolonial diplomacy, the effects of smallpox, the possibilities that war opened to African slaves, the military campaigns of the French and Indian War in South Carolina, the meaning of the war through Cherokee eyes, and the political origins of the American Revolution. The geographical range of the book is also broad, for while it focuses on South Carolina, much content on Virginia and even Pennsylvania appears.

The era of the Seven Years' War was a historically significant, transformative time for African Americans, Indians, and whites in the Southeast. Involving Cherokees, colonists, redcoats, and slaves, the war was a violent, devastating, and significant moment in its own right. It fueled tensions between inhabitants of the South Carolina backcountry and residents of the lowcountry, produced unrest among the colony's slave population that unsettled planter society, and helped forge unity and a sense of identity among the Cherokee villages. The experience of waging war against the Cherokees from 1759 to 1761 created disagreement and animosity between the colonists and the British imperial government. This disconnect was a major source of tension between British officials and the leaders of South Carolina's provincial government and thus contributed to the development of the Revolutionary movement against Britain. Within a generation of the end of the Seven Years' War, the elites moved, albeit reluctantly, toward full separation from England. In a land now more bitterly divided by geography, race, and class, the stage was set for a perfect conflagration.

JOIN'D TOGETHER

The Anglo-Cherokee Alliance, 1730–1753

1

In 1729, an eccentric Scottish baronet named Sir Alexander Cuming sailed to Charles Town, the capital of the British colony of South Carolina.[1] He was inspired by his wife, who dreamt that he would find wealth in America. Cuming spent five months in Charles Town, where he established a loan office and a mercantile firm. Then, he cajoled a coterie of traders into following him up the Cherokee Path to Indian country. His motives remain elusive to this day. Scholars have suggested he was slightly unbalanced.[2]

In the forty years before Cuming hatched his scheme, the French and British (and their North American allies) had clashed in two major wars. Tensions had flared again, and Cuming now inserted himself in the mix. He understood that a Franco-Cherokee alliance would devastate commercial profits and endanger British interests.[3] With no credentials from the British government, he undertook an enterprise of incomprehensible hubris: he would convince Cherokees to declare their submission to the King of Great Britain and would forge an enduring Anglo-Cherokee military and commercial alliance. He would escort a delegation of Cherokees to tour England and formally seal the deal. The British Crown, Cuming hoped, would appoint him the first "minister to the Cherokees," and he would become rich and famous.[4] A member of the Royal Society, he would search for undiscovered medicinal roots and prospect for rocks and minerals. He might even lay the groundwork for a pharmaceutical or mining enterprise.[5]

The three-hundred-mile journey to Cherokee country carried Cuming toward several clusters of historically, culturally, and linguistically similar villages. Most villagers still identified strongly with their matrilineal clans. The seven Cherokee clans—Bird, Blue, Deer, Long Hair, Paint, Wild-Potato, and Wolf—corresponded at one point in time to seven "mother towns" where the Cherokee people originated.[6] Beyond clans and villages, there was no Cherokee nation-state. It existed only in the imagination of Cuming and other Britons.

Some fifty settlements housed about three hundred inhabitants each, fifteen thousand Cherokees in all. Each village was autonomous. Geography, international relations, economic connections, and dialects grouped these villages in clusters identified by British traders as early as 1715: the Lower, Middle, Out, Valley, and Overhill Towns. Each settlement cluster was independent and, by virtue of proximity to different outsiders, each pursued different economic and foreign policies.[7]

The Cherokee Path headed northwest from Moncks Corner, about twenty miles northwest of Charles Town. It followed a road now beneath the waters of Lake Marion, then passed through Eutaw Springs, St. Matthews, and into present-day Cayce—"The Congarees." From there it ran along the southwest bank of the Congaree River, then parallel to the Saluda River and through Saluda Old Town. It passed through the future site of Robert Gouedy's trading post at Ninety Six (1751) and then through present-day Anderson, Pendleton, and Clemson before entering Keowee and the Lower Towns. These villages stood in the valleys of the Keowee and Tugaloo Rivers and on the headwaters of the Savannah in present Pickens and Oconee Counties, South Carolina. Prominent villages included Toxaway, Tamassee, Keowee, and Oconee. Villagers spoke the now-extinct Elati (Lower) dialect.[8]

From the Lower Towns, the trail then headed west, over mountains and across streams, approximately along present Highway 76. In present Clayton, Georgia, it forked. A northern fork headed to the Cherokee Middle Towns. They lay on the headwaters of the Little Tennessee River and along the Tuckasegee River, nestled among the Cowee and Balsam Mountains. Watauga, Joree, Ellijay, Cowee, and Echoe were among the larger Middle Towns, but political life centered on Nequassee (now spelled Nikwasi), in what is now Franklin, North Carolina.[9]

The Out Towns, the oldest of the Cherokee settlements, sat northeast of the Middle Towns, deep in the Smoky Mountains over Leatherman Gap. They lay off the main trade routes, unapproachable from the north and difficult to reach from the south. The Out Towns included Kituwah, Stecoe, Oconaluftee, Tuckaleetchee, and Tuckasegee. In time, the descendants of Out Townsmen and those who avoided removal in the nineteenth century would

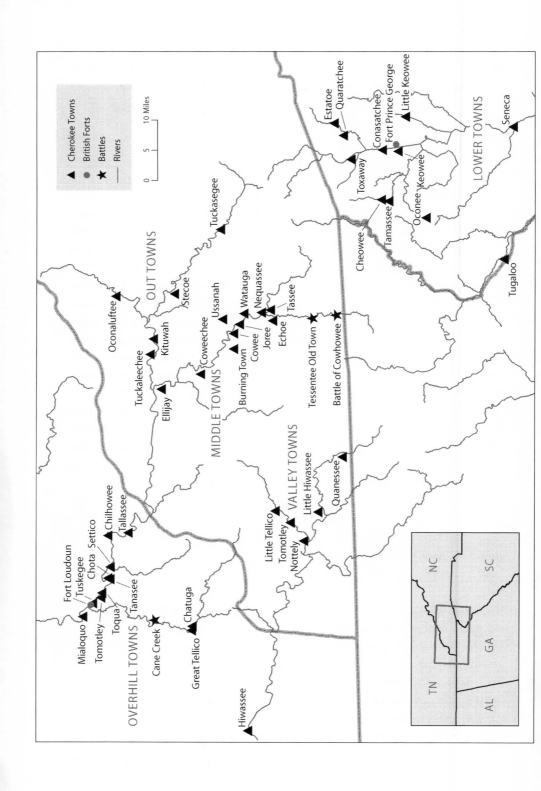

form the Eastern Band of Cherokee Indians. Both the Middle and Out Towns spoke the Kituwah dialect; the Eastern Cherokee Nation and the United Keetoowah Cherokee Nation of Oklahoma still speak it today.[10]

To the west of the fork at the Dividings in present Clayton, Georgia, and to the west of the Middle Towns, lay the Valley Towns, situated on the Hiwassee River and its tributaries. Hiwassee (or Great Hiwassee), renowned for its fierce warriors and its Natchez Indian inhabitants, was the chief village of the Valley. Other Valley Town settlements included Nottely and Tomotley.[11]

The same trail led northwest across the Unicoi Mountains to the Overhill Towns in present Monroe County, Tennessee. From there one path headed north to the Cherokee hunting ground in present Kentucky. Another followed the Blue Ridge and Shenandoah Valleys and connected the Overhills to western Virginia. Along the way, a road split off and led east to Williamsburg (sometimes spelled Williamsburgh), which lay 500 miles from the Overhills. The wide, verdant valleys along the Tellico River and the lower reaches of the Little Tennessee embraced villages such as Great Tellico, Chota, Tanasee (today spelled Tanasi), Toqua, Chatuga, Settico (Citico today), and Tallassee. Both the Overhills and the Valley spoke the same Atuli dialect. It later blended with Kituwah to form the Western dialect spoken by the Cherokee Nation of Oklahoma.[12]

While the origins of the word "Cherokee" remain fuzzy, villagers called themselves "Tsalagi," "Jalagi," or "Tsaragi." White traders commonly rendered the "ts" sound as "ch." They thus applied the term "Charakee," or "Cherokee" to the Lower Towns as they encountered those villages first, then applied the term to the people in each of the settlement clusters. The Spanish and French coming from the other direction—where the Creek Confederacy populated the area to the west—knew them as Chalaque or Chalagee.[13] But for the English, the term "Cherokee," sometimes spelled differently but with the same pronunciation, stuck.

On March 23, 1730, Sir Alexander burst into the Keowee townhouse with a cutlass at his side and two pistols in his hands. He told the Indians he would torch the building and kill those inside if any "endeavoured to make their Escape." Cuming proclaimed himself an agent of King George II. At Cuming's orders, or perhaps just to humor him, the Cherokees knelt in allegiance to the King. Cuming demanded that they send runners to invite the headmen of each village to meet him at Nequassee on April 3. Whether the Cherokees feared the economic consequences of ignoring Cuming's bizarre display remains unclear. These tribal people may also have been swayed by the kilt-wearing Cuming's use of Highland—tribal—garb.[14]

Cuming traveled through the Cherokee towns, shaking hands and memorizing names. In Great Tellico, he befriended a local leader named Moytoy. Then, Cuming and his entourage proceeded to the Middle Towns to Nequassee. Situated atop a fifteen-foot-high conical mound, that village's townhouse was the center of village life. By Nequassee legend, Nunnehi, "the immortals," lived under the mound and had come out to fight off an invading tribe, assisting local warriors. Centrally located within Cherokee country as a whole, the village of Nequassee lay in the heart of the Middle Towns. It was a "peace town," a place of refuge, in which no living thing could be killed. Cherokee houses, orchards, and fields formed a picturesque panorama, with mountains in the backdrop. Here, on April 3, as Alexander Cuming ordered, Cherokees from each of the settlement clusters converged.[15] "Such an Appearance as this, never was seen at any one Time before in that Country," the adventurer wrote in his journal.[16]

The days that followed brought with them a series of ceremonies that English and Cherokee each viewed through culturally distinct lenses. Cherokees apparently assumed that the festivities were no more than mutual displays of friendship and peace. After a day of singing and dancing, Sir Alexander convinced the Cherokees to name Moytoy the "emperor" of the Cherokee Nation. The Cherokees, unaware of the meaning of that declaration, lifted the Scotsman onto Moytoy's seat. They performed the Eagle Tail Dance for him and "stroak'd him with 13 Eagles Tails." In a rousing speech, Sir Alexander "represented the great Power and Goodness of his Majesty King *George*." He bade "all his Subjects" to "do whatever the great King ordered them." When the Cherokees then knelt, he assumed their unflinching obedience to the Crown and to himself. The next day, Moytoy presented Cuming with the Crown of Tanasee—a wig of possum hair—"with five Eagles Tails and four Scalps of their Enemies," imploring him to lay these items at George II's feet. Cuming believed that the Cherokees had given him markers of sovereign power and status to bring back to Britain. However, this was a sign of friendship, not allegiance; none of the Cherokees interpreted the events as a ceremony of subjection.[17]

Sir Alexander then assembled a delegation of Cherokees to accompany him to England to prove that this had all happened and to conclude a treaty. He had already booked passage on the *Fox*, and it would leave in just a few weeks. Cuming targeted Ouconecaw, "a young warrior of Tannassy," to join him. If the King knew "We were so poor & naked & so much Want of everything," Cuming told the warrior, "He would take pity on our condition & would give us Some Cloaths." The young Cherokee related later that his friend, the trader

Eleazar Wiggan, "pressed" him that night. Finally, Ouconecaw relented and agreed to make the trip.[18]

Young Ouconecaw, or "White Owl," was born in 1710. By some accounts, he was actually a captive from Canada. He went by many names, including the "young warrior of Tannassy" and Chuconnunta. By 1756, he answered to Attakullakulla, "the Little Carpenter." He became one of the most influential but controversial Cherokees of all time. As a child, his Wolf Clan uncles trained him in the traditions of his people. He fished and fired blow darts along the Little Tennessee and its tributaries in the Cherokee Overhills. He was groomed for greatness.[19] Young Attakullakulla witnessed a sequence of events that set the disparate peoples of the Southeast on a collision course.

By the time of Attakullakulla's birth, Cherokee warriors had raided their neighbors and sold slaves to Charles Town for a generation. European diseases and the Indian slave trade depopulated the coastal tribes. The Tuscarora and Yamasee Wars of 1711 and 1715 took a further toll on the native peoples of eastern Carolina. The Indian slave trade declined, and the once-ready supply of deerskins and hunters near the coast evaporated. By 1715, the position of the Cherokees in the deerskin trade—and that of the Creek Confederacy and other nations to their south and west—changed dramatically.[20] In 1711, trader Eleazar Wiggan had set up the first permanent trading houses among the Cherokees. By 1716, South Carolina established a public monopoly. Traders, many of them adventure-seeking Highland Scots, some of them exiled after the Jacobite Rebellion, rushed into the Cherokee country. South Carolina dominated the trade and its governor came to direct Anglo-Cherokee affairs. Charles Town was the largest and most navigable North American port below Philadelphia. From the Cherokee towns, traders sent their wares down the Savannah River and north by sea to Charles Town. Later they carried their trade overland as well.[21]

London merchants credited dealers in Charles Town, who in turn credited Indian traders with their season's stock of goods. The traders advanced supplies to the Indians, whom they expected to repay them in peltries from the years' hunt. In the winter, after several weeks of hunting, Cherokee men returned with deer. Women then cleaned and scraped the skins, since "dressed" skins fetched a higher price. In a time-consuming process, the skins were stretched on frames and dried, soaked, scraped, removed of hair, and treated with pulverized animal brains to create soft and supple leather. Cherokees also supplied ginseng root, snakeroot, and other plants to colonial markets for use as medicines. By the late spring or early summer, traders, with packhorsemen, servants, and slaves, arrived with an ever-expanding array of British goods. They brought English woolens in bright colors—strouds, duffels, striped shirts, coats, blankets, match-coats, hats, shirts, stockings, and anklets. They carried hoes, hatchets, knives, adzes, bells, kettles, scissors, and mirrors. They brought vermillion paint, guns, powder, bullets, gunflints, and tomahawks. The traders also delivered salt, liquor, and live poultry. And they established a permanent and visible presence in or near the Cherokee villages, marrying Indian women and introducing mixed-race offspring into Indian society.[22]

The deerskin trade was the vortex that sucked in the Cherokees. With gardens to tend, deer to hunt, and skins to tan, little time remained to manufacture household items and clothing. In these changed circumstances, the Cherokees needed British goods to replace things they no longer made themselves. But there were new items as well, readily incorporated into daily life. The Cherokees took pride in personal appearance, and the array of available merchandise was mesmerizing. Beholden to the merchants on the coast, traders kept the Indians in perpetual debt, or close to it.[23] Thus they became more dependent on manufactured items. By 1753, Skiagunsta of Keowee, then the most prominent warrior in the Lower Towns, claimed that "every necessary Thing in Life"—clothes, guns, blankets, and more—"we must have from the white People." He continued, admitting, "my People . . . cannot live independent of the English."[24]

By the 1750s, the Cherokee were not just dependent upon European trade goods. They were embroiled in a territorial dispute with their neighbors to the south: the loose confederacy of Indian peoples known as the Creeks. They were also in the middle of the rivalry between France and Britain. The Cherokees refused to be pawns on the imperial chessboard. Though they played the French and British against each other, Cherokees generally favored the British, thanks to their superior economic resources.

The French nevertheless posed a legitimate threat to British influence. French agents, spies, and soldiers treated Cherokees with respect. They doled out goods from outposts at Mobile, New Orleans, and Fort Toulouse, the "Alabama Fort" near present Montgomery.[25] French settlers lived farther away, in Canada and Acadia, and in much smaller numbers than the British. Cherokee leaders remained receptive to French overtures, especially during times of war between France and England. Whether the French could deliver on their promises, or what would happen if the British drove the French from North America remained unknown.

France and Britain needed the Cherokees, too. Deerskins were coveted in Europe and made into clothing, gloves, saddles, and footwear. The eighteenth-century deerskin trade was vital to the economy of South Carolina, for whom rice and indigo constituted the only other significant exports. Indigo cultivation was only just catching on. Some 150 Carolina traders and packhorsemen operated solely among the Cherokees by 1756. Enslaved frontiersmen, backcountry farmers, soldiers, merchants, and factors on both sides of the Atlantic—even boatmen and sea captains—depended upon Cherokee deerskins. Cherokee Indians thus wielded considerable geopolitical power. By the 1750s, though diminished by disease, they had 2,500 warriors. White residents lived in fear of slave rebellions, too. Sparsely settled Georgia and North Carolina could offer little aid. Cherokees could block British or French imperial expansion—if the price was right.[26]

Attakullakulla's decision to go to England in 1730 was partly to satisfy his curiosity and to appease Eleazar Wiggan. But more importantly, it was a political and economic calculation. Six of the seven Indian travelers hailed from the Overhills, and all six belonged to the Wolf Clan. A Lower Townsman named Ounakannowie joined them on the way to Charles Town. Here, the seven Indians boarded the man-of-war *Fox* on May 4, 1730. The ship landed a month later; Cuming traveled ahead with the Crown of Tanasee.[27]

For three and a half months, Attakullakulla and his companions toured the greater London area and absorbed British culture. On June 18, the Indians attended an installation ceremony for the Knights of the Garter at St. George's Chapel, Windsor Castle. Afterward they met and kissed the hands of King George II, Frederick the Prince of Wales, and the Duke of Montagu.[28]

Four days later, with Sir Alexander present, they met the king again. They streaked and spotted their faces and shoulders with red, blue, and green paint. They carried bows and wore feathers on their heads. Sir Alexander laid the Crown of Tanasee—to the Cherokees little more than a token gift—"at his Majesty's Feet." The Cherokees presented eagle's tails and the scalps of four of their Indian enemies. Dressed in flowing court clothing, "rich Garments laced with Gold," they posed for a group portrait.[29]

The Cherokee diplomats visited popular attractions, including the Tower of London. They watched "tilts, feats of acrobats, sham-fights, and miracle plays" at the Bartholemew Fair in Smithfield. They visited the Bethlem psychiatric hospital, a popular tourist attraction. A theatrical performance followed: Thomas Doggett's "Mad Tom of Bedlam; or the Distress'd Lovers, with the comical Humour of Squire Numscull." They soaked in hot baths at Richmond Wells. They socialized with London merchants involved in the trade with Carolina. They watched military drills and performed with the Society of Archers. But the rounds became stressful for the Cherokees. Thieves

IMAGE 1.1 *Cherokee Embassy, 1730, engraved by Isaac Basire after painting by Markham. Courtesy of the South Caroliniana Library, University of South Carolina, Columbia, S.C.*

robbed them of a sword and two rings. They scuffled with each other at their lodgings. After a play called *The Tragedy of Oronooko*, two of the Indians briefly vanished. So, too, did their friend; to save money, Cuming did not accompany them on their rounds.[30]

On September 7, under military escort, the Cherokees departed from their quarters in an undertaker's basement on Kingstreet in Covent Garden. They arrived a short distance later at the headquarters of the Lords Commissioners of Trade and Plantations (the Board of Trade) in Whitehall. The Lords "acquainted" them with a treaty—termed "Articles of Friendship and Commerce." The Lords then dazzled the Cherokees with a room full of presents and trade goods, much of it weapons and ammunition. But there was a catch. The Board and the Secretary of State, the Duke of Newcastle, had colluded on a scheme. "Words may easily be inserted," the Board of Trade had written, "acknowledging their Dependence upon the Crown of Great Britain," which would "Strengthen our Title in those parts, even to all Lands which these People now Possess." The interpreter then translated the document inaccurately for the Cherokees.[31]

Two days later, the Cherokees returned for the formal signing ceremony. They sang four or five songs when they entered the chamber. The Board of Trade was eager to secure a Cherokee economic and military alliance so that the Spanish and French would not draw off Cherokee deerskins and warriors. "The Chain of Friendship" extended from His Majesty King George II to the Cherokee Indians, the Board said. "As there are no Spots or Blackness in the Sun, so is there not any Rust or Foulness in this Chain." Thus, "fasten'd together by the Chain of Friendship," King George ordered "the English in Carolina" not just to trade with the Indians and to furnish them with trade goods but also to build homesteads of their own from Charles Town to "behind the Great Mountains." Sir William Keith, the former lieutenant governor of Pennsylvania, not only drafted the Articles, he also wrote the Cherokee reply. The "Articles" insisted that "the King has given his Land on both Sides of the great Mountains to his own Children the *English*." He now gave the Cherokees "the Privilege of living where they please."[32] The agreement required the Cherokees to go to war against Britain's enemies. They also agreed to protect British traders, to trade only with the British, to prohibit the settlement of non-British Europeans in their territory, to return runaway slaves, and to live under British law. In return the British sent the Cherokees home with a dazzling stockpile of guns and ammunition, cloth, hatchets, knives, kettles, belts, and wampum.[33]

None of the Indians had the authority to speak or to sign on behalf of the nonexistent "Cherokee Nation," let alone their individual villages. They saw this just as a ceremony, not as a binding agreement. Kettagusta replied through a translator on behalf of the Cherokee visitors. He thanked the Board for the kind treatment they had received. He promised to bring the "Chain of Friendship" home. He assured the Lords of Trade that "our Hands and Hearts are join'd together."[34]

According to the Cherokees, the meeting with the King was simply a military and diplomatic alliance. Eighteenth-century deerskin trader and ethnographer James Adair and another Cherokee trader, Ludovick Grant, later reported that a delegate had asked, "Is it true?" when the King claimed dominion of Indian lands. The interpreter had translated those words not as a question but as a statement—"It is true"—and the deed was done. When the

Cherokees got a full translation and explanation of the "Articles," they were furious. They nearly killed both the interpreter and Kettagusta, but cooler heads eventually prevailed. They were, after all, stuck in England. For twenty-two days, they deliberated and convinced themselves that the language was figurative and, in any event, that they had no authority to cede land or make binding agreements.[35]

On September 29, the treaty signing finally took place. For reassurance, the Cherokees visited Sir Alexander Cuming. He talked them into signing and scrawled his own name on the document. The Cherokee representatives assented, and all six Overhill delegates signed their names. South Carolina's newly appointed governor Robert Johnson looked on.[36]

In the early morning of October 2, Attakullakulla and his colleagues, laden with goods, set out for Portsmouth, where they re-embarked with governor-appointee Johnson aboard the *Fox* on October 7. Reports indicated that several of the Cherokees shed tears upon departing. Attakullakulla reportedly grasped the last person's hand that met his, an old fisherwoman's. Wringing it hard, tears welling up in his eyes, he repeated, "I tank you, I tank you, I tank you all."[37]

Although historian J. P. Brown argued that this treaty initiated the death knell of Cherokee independence, his conclusion misses the mark. As Alden T. Vaughan puts it, the Cherokee visit highlighted one of British America's most powerful and important Indian nations. "Their nation was out of the diplomatic shadows" and became a major player in the evolution of British America.[38] Attakullakulla's visit left a lasting impression on him. The English had cemented a lifelong friendship and provided him with a claim to political relevance. The Anglo-Cherokee relationship, like all relationships, rested upon reciprocity. As the Cherokees saw it, the relationship would be fluid, shaped not just by the British but also by Cherokee diplomats, French overtures, and when necessary, Cherokee warriors.

In formalizing an alliance and an exclusive trade agreement with the British, Cuming hoped he had squelched French competition in the Southeast. But the treaty did not reflect the wishes of the majority of Cherokees. And French influence remained strong. In 1733 some Overhill Cherokees renewed the agreement in Charles Town. The following year, however, any enthusiasm Cherokees had for an alliance with the British turned to pessimism and doubt. A council held at Great Tellico disavowed the treaty and rebuked its signers. The trans-Atlantic emissaries renounced the treaty they had signed. The Cherokees "say we are all slaves to the Great George," a letter writer from

South Carolina informed Georgia governor James Oglethorpe. One hundred Cherokees then plundered a trader's store at Keowee. "The Principal actors in this Affair," Oglethorpe's correspondent noted, "was those Indians that Sir Alexander Cummings lately carried over to England."[39]

In 1736, Christian Gottlieb Priber arrived at Great Tellico. British officials firmly believed that he was an undercover French agent. A gentleman of German birth, he held a doctorate and had practiced law in Europe. Priber ate, drank, danced, and slept with the Indians. The "little ugly man," one British report said, "trimm'd his hair in the indian manner & painted as they did going . . . almost naked except a shirt & a Flap." Priber befriended Moytoy and the Tellico warriors. He married an Indian woman and fathered a child with her. After learning the Overhill dialect, he compiled a dictionary.[40]

Proclaiming himself "His Majesty's Principal Secretary of State," Priber opened a correspondence with South Carolina officials. He laid out his plans for the "Kingdom of Paradise" in a manuscript that he intended to publish in Europe. He envisioned a community among the Cherokee, where "all things should be in common amongst them," including their wives. The public would share child-rearing responsibilities. "All Colours and Complexions"— Indians, Europeans, Africans, all those who adhered to the principles of the Society—were welcome. He also planned a "City of Refuge for all Criminals, Debtors, and Slaves who would fly thither from Justice or their Masters."[41]

According to trader James Adair, Priber impressed upon the Cherokees "a very ill opinion of the English, representing them as a fraudulent, avaritious, and encroaching people." The visitor convinced the Indians that the English coveted their lands and insisted that they had deliberately infected the Cherokees with smallpox in 1738. Under the visionary German's influence, more Cherokees, including the influential Overhill war chief Oconostota, broke with Attakullakulla in support of the French. As trader Ludovick Grant later said, British officials chafed at Priber's presence. They attempted twice, unsuccessfully, to take him captive.[42]

In 1743, Creek Indians and traders waylaid and seized Priber near the village of Tallapoosa, on his way to Fort Toulouse. He died in British custody in a Frederica, Georgia, jail in 1744. His utopian manifesto and Cherokee dictionary disappeared.[43] If the British had not interfered, the Cherokees might have established an independent state in the Southern Appalachians. Priber had opened their minds to possibilities, and he had confirmed their inclination to chart their own course, and not to acquiesce to British authority without a fight.

In 1740, during Priber's stay among the Cherokee, a band of Ottawa Indians captured Attakullakulla and took him to Canada, where they detained him until 1748. Moytoy died in battle in 1741. The British selected Moytoy's thirteen-year-old son, Amouskosite, to succeed his father as emperor. His birth had given him the role, but he lacked the support of other Cherokees. A struggle for power and influence raged among Overhill Cherokee headmen. In *The Cherokee Frontier*, David Corkran perhaps exaggerates this tussle. But during the late 1740s and early 1750s, Chota, one of the "mother towns," gradually asserted itself, and its anti-British leaders held considerable political and military influence.[44]

War raged between Britain and France in the 1740s. South Carolina's governor, James Glen, negotiated unsuccessfully with the Cherokees and other southeastern Indians in 1745. Glen told the Board of Trade that "if we had a Fort in these Overhill Towns," it would "bar the door against the French, & be such a Bridle in the Mouths of the Indians themselves, that would for ever keep them ours."[45] The following year, to curry South Carolina's favor and to prevent illegal expansion, a few Lower Towns headmen ceded a massive swath of land between Ninety Six and the east bank of Long Cane Creek in northwest South Carolina. It was a divisive move. Outraged Cherokees united under Connecorte, the spiritual and political leader of Chota. As a young man, he had sustained a battle wound that left him permanently disabled. The British called him "Old Hop."[46]

Also in 1746, Iroquois, Shawnees, and Nottowegas launched raids on South Carolina colonists and Catawbas. They enjoyed the full support of the Chota Council and the disaffected Lower Townsmen. The invaders carried off and eventually killed trader George Haig. Carolina rebuilt Fort Moore at the western gateway to South Carolina and established a palisaded fort at the Congarees, but the violence continued. Eventually, these Northern invaders and their Lower Towns allies turned against the Creeks, revitalizing the intermittent conflict between Creeks and Cherokees. Lower Cherokee villagers scattered to the Overhills for refuge. The Chotas cultivated their pent-up animosity over traders' abuses, prompting the refugees to threaten traders. Some joined northern Indians in assaults on the Carolina frontier. By 1751, a serious crisis raged.[47]

Traders abandoned the Cherokee country. Settlers scattered to private forts or fled to the northern colonies. All sides spread rumors and prepared for a war that didn't come—the "Panic of 1751" never evolved into large-scale violence. Pressed by the Commons House, Governor Glen held the Lower Towns

responsible for not stopping the "Norward" invaders. Northern Indian dep-
redations ranged from the Cloud homestead on the Saluda River to the sea-
side settlements in Christ Church Parish. Cherokee warriors killed just one
trader, who was trying to defuse a Creek-Cherokee skirmish, and wounded
three others. Still, in June, Glen halted the Cherokee trade and planned a military campaign.[48]

In the midst of this crisis, Attakullakulla, who had returned from captivity and moved temporarily from Tomotley to Chota, saw an opportunity.
With several dozen companions, he ventured to Williamsburg, Virginia,
arriving in August 1751. Vying for power among the Cherokees while retain-
ing his ties to the English, he hoped to bypass South Carolina. He aimed to
open trade with Virginia, undermining Glen's diplomacy and breaking the
South Carolina monopoly. Much to Glen's chagrin, Virginia's acting governor, Lewis Burwell, promised to encourage traders to visit the Cherokees. He
sent Attakullakulla home with a generous supply of presents. When Glen
pressed Burwell, claiming that the move encroached on Carolina's traditional
sphere of influence, the Virginia official backpedaled, insisting that he had
made no such promise. His about-face had little practical effect.[49]

His hand forced, Glen invited Cherokees from every village but Chota to
Charles Town. They signed a treaty on November 29, 1751, to reopen the trade,
but the accord was full of promises that neither side would honor. Glen reaffirmed his plans to build forts in the Lower and Overhill Towns. He also attempted to better regulate the trade by fixing prices to the goods commonly
exchanged. In New York, the Catawba and the Iroquois met, with colonial
officials present; the "Norward" raids subsided and peace returned to the
Southeast. The horrors predicted during the "Panic of 1751"—forecasts of alliances dashed, of Cherokee attacks on the frontier, of a slave uprising in
Charles Town, and of European and Indian warriors marching on the Cherokee settlements—had not proven true. Yet.[50]

Cherokees had heard the British propose since 1729 to build a fort in their
villages. Both sides could see many advantages. A fort offered protection for
South Carolina traders and Indian women and children from northern and
French-allied Indian attacks. It would give British colonists in South Carolina a foothold from which to secure and maintain Cherokee loyalty. This was
increasingly important given Virginia's attempt to enter the Cherokee trade.
In theory, a fort could also provide a steady stream of goods through a well-
regulated trade. With a fort nearby, the Lower Towns would gain power among
the Cherokee settlement clusters due to their increased ability to shape

foreign policy. Finally, a fort would encourage the resettlement of Lower Townspeople displaced by northern enemies and Creek expansion, further increasing the influence of the Lower Towns in the Southeast.[51]

In autumn 1753, Glen advanced his own funds to the project, in expectation of future kickbacks. Construction began in October at a site that commanded the ford on the east bank of the Keowee River and lay opposite—and below—the Cherokee Lower Town of Keowee. Six weeks later, the project was complete. The governor left a detachment of Independent Companies troops to garrison the outpost, named Fort Prince George after the fifteen-year-old heir to the British throne, later George III. The fort established a permanent British presence in the region, but it did not meet Cherokee expectations.[52]

The shaky South Carolina–Cherokee alliance now faced challenges not just from the French but from Virginia as well. Virginians had already attempted to siphon off the Cherokee trade; now, Virginia hastened a war between Britain and France. The war unwittingly drew South Carolinians—black, white, and Cherokee, into a regional referendum on the future of their relationship with Britain. The "Chain of Friendship" would be tested.

A GENERAL CONFLAGRATION
The French and Indian War Begins

2

By 1753, the French had begun to assert their claim to the Appalachian region of North America, stirring up Indian allies and jeopardizing the plans of wealthy white investors. Virginia's acting governor, Lieutenant Governor Robert Dinwiddie, sent twenty-one-year-old Major George Washington northwestward with several guides to investigate. Washington's destination was Fort LeBoeuf in the Ohio Country. The French commander Captain Jacques Legardeur de Saint-Pierre declined to withdraw. Dinwiddie then sent more militia to build a small fort at the Forks of the Ohio at present-day Pittsburgh. By April 18, French troops rushed in, forced the Virginians to abandon the post, and then erected Fort Duquesne at the same location.[1]

When Dinwiddie again dispatched Washington, now a lieutenant colonel, to the Ohio Country the next year with two undermanned, undersupplied, and poorly trained companies of Virginia provincials, South Carolina's governor, James Glen, urged caution. But Dinwiddie ignored him. Under orders from the British secretary of state, Glen reluctantly sent a third of South Carolina's Independent Companies under Captain James Mackay, to join Washington's force. The Independent Companies, commanded by colonial governors until the Crown stipulated otherwise, consisted of British regulars whose charge was to man and maintain fortifications.[2] The departure of the Independent Companies allowed slaves to intimidate and frighten coastal elites, firing weapons "to the great Terror of many Ladies," the *South Carolina Gazette* reported.[3]

By the time Mackay arrived, Washington and a detachment of his men had already clashed with a French party. To avoid conflict, the commander of the composite force graciously exercised a joint command with the Virginian. In haste, the combined forces built a small stockade, Fort Necessity, at the Great Meadows.[4] Developments in the Ohio Country "greatly alarmed" Governor Glen. "A small Spark may kindle a great Fire," he wrote to British Secretary of State Sir Thomas Robinson, and "if the Flame bursts out all the Water in the Ohio will not be able to extinguish it, but that it may soon spread and light up a general Conflagration." Glen predicted an imperial war.[5]

On July 3, 1754, six hundred French soldiers and one hundred Native allies surrounded the three hundred Virginians and South Carolina Independents at Fort Necessity. "From the numbers of the enemy and our situation we could not hope for victory," Mackay and Washington wrote. Firing from all sides for nine hours in the pouring rain, the French drubbed the Anglo-Virginian army, forcing the commanders to surrender.[6] The battle launched the imperial war that Glen had predicted. And it drew the Cherokees into it.

South Carolina, Virginia, and the French all contended for Cherokee affections. Which side would the Indians choose? That answer depended upon a variety of factors including geography and village politics.[7]

The Lower Towns leaned toward South Carolina for its proximate trade goods. Yet they feared settler encroachment, and they were politically divided due to the recent death of a prominent warrior. The Valley Towns leaned to the British but, as newer settlements, had little influence. The Middle and Out Towns were isolated due to treacherous roads and were buttressed by Cherokees to the south, west, and east. Therefore they were less significant to the British. The Overhills had been, for several decades, a military and economic force. French and Indian attacks threatened to disrupt the trade with South Carolina. With a clear path between Virginia and the Overhills, an alliance with that colony might secure villagers a more beneficial trade. But Virginia was distracted. The Overhills had Creek neighbors to the south and French neighbors to the west. And anti-British Chota headman Connecorte had much influence. Eventually many Cherokees favored South Carolina and sought a fort in the Overhill villages. But mired by the abuses of traders and the activities of French spies, the already precarious Cherokee-Carolina relationship teetered further toward collapse.

Again in 1755, developments in the imperial struggle put the Cherokees at center stage. The British hatched a strategy to attack the French on three fronts. In one of the three theaters, Major General Edward Braddock marched hurriedly against Fort Duquesne with British and colonial troops. Glen and

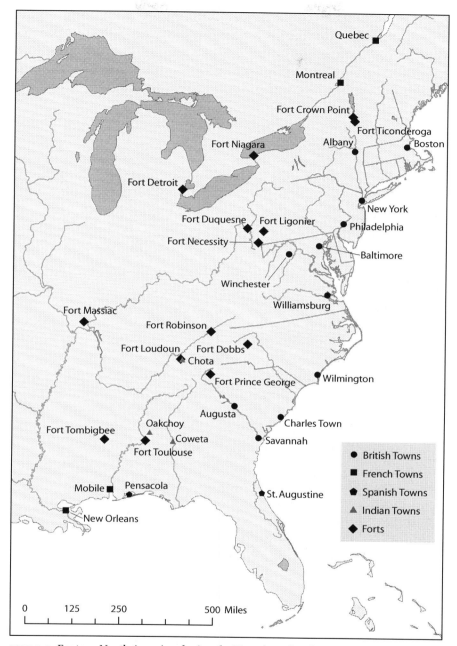

Quebec

Montreal

Fort Crown Point

Fort Ticonderoga

Fort Niagara

Albany

Boston

Fort Detroit

New York

Fort Duquesne

Fort Ligonier

Philadelphia

Fort Necessity

Baltimore

Winchester

Williamsburg

Fort Massiac

Fort Robinson

Fort Loudoun

Fort Dobbs

Chota

Fort Prince George

Wilmington

Augusta

Oakchoy

Charles Town

Fort Tombigbee

Coweta

Savannah

Fort Toulouse

Mobile

Pensacola

St. Augustine

New Orleans

● British Towns
■ French Towns
⬟ Spanish Towns
▲ Indian Towns
◆ Forts

0   125   250   500 Miles

MAP 2.1 *Eastern North America during the French and Indian War Era*

the South Carolina Assembly criticized Dinwiddie and Braddock's aggressiveness and blocked funds for the campaign. "Mr. Glen," Dinwiddie wrote to North Carolina governor Arthur Dobbs, "appears to do every Thing in his Power to obstruct" the expedition. Dinwiddie needed the help of southeastern Indians, but Glen blocked his efforts. "I cannot conceive his Conduct, as it appears quite contrary to the Int't of the Nation."[8]

To Dinwiddie's chagrin, Overhill Cherokee warriors did not rush to Virginia's aid. Instead, hoping to cultivate a military and economic alliance with the Carolinians, they accepted Glen's invitation to a peace conference. Five hundred Cherokee warriors traveled from the Cherokee Overhills, some carrying the frail Connecorte. An equally impressive contingent of the South Carolina Rangers, the Independent Companies, and militiamen from Dorchester and Charles Town made the trip up the Cherokee Path. So, too, did several members of the Charles Town elite.[9]

They met on the banks of the Saluda River near Saluda Old Town in early July 1755. Enveloped by hundreds of soldiers and warriors, Glen and Tomotley headman Attakullakulla sat on chairs under a makeshift arbor. The Indians heard Glen boast of the British Crown's power and of the benefits of an economic and military partnership. He offered forts and protection against their enemies in exchange for land and loyalty. And he vowed once more that South Carolina traders would provide them with their every material need. Speaking for the ailing Connecorte, Attakullakulla laid a bag of soil, a bag of corn, and his bow and arrows at the governor's feet. "We are brothers to the people of Carolina," he said. He introduced Glen to a Cherokee boy, probably one of his sons, "that when he grows up he may remember our agreement."[10]

No one can know for sure what delegates agreed to at Saluda. In a little-known document dated 1761, the Commons House reported, "There are Incorrectnesses" in the treaty, "for it was written by Doctor [Alexander] Garden upon his knee and Dictated by the Governor amidst the noise & Din of a thousand People."[11]

No deed exists. Some, citing the *South Carolina Gazette*, have argued that through Attakullakulla, the Cherokees surrendered all of their lands and became vassals of the British Crown.[12] But surely Connecorte would not have condoned the cession of land, no matter how small. Historian Alexander Hewatt, who knew whites present at the treaty signing, wrote in 1779 that the headman offered "part of our lands."[13] Others believe that Cherokees intended only a symbolic gesture of alliance. Glen, in search of laurels at a time of political failure, exaggerated to Lieutenant Governor Dinwiddie and to the South Carolina public and misrepresented this gesture.[14]

Just days after the Saluda Conference, French forces and their Indian allies clashed with another Anglo-Virginian expedition not far from the site of Washington's defeat the year before. Washington miraculously survived this battle though bullets whizzed by him. But the campaign's commander, Major General Edward Braddock, fell wounded and died a few days later. Hastily buried under the road as his men retreated, a third of his expedition joined Braddock among the dead. Another third fell wounded. With Braddock's Defeat, a greatly outnumbered French and Indian army trounced a numerically superior British and provincial army. The French retained Fort Duquesne and remained firmly entrenched in the Ohio Valley.[15]

Dinwiddie informed Glen of the "fatal Stroke" to the British colonies. And he blamed the South Carolina governor for keeping Cherokee warriors from aiding Virginia. If Glen had not taken a "preposterous, irregular, and inconsist't Step" at Saluda, "we sh'd not in all probability have been defeated." The purchase of Indian land, he added, "appears to me wrong." Instead the British should "cherish them with Pres'ts and regulate the Price of Goods sold to them."[16] To some Cherokees, the Saluda Conference was nothing more than a Cherokee diversion to pit the French against the British, and it had, as they intended, set Virginia against South Carolina.[17] In any event, Braddock's Defeat would have far-reaching implications.

As tensions flared on the Virginia frontier, Cherokee warrior Ostenaco went north to help. Born in the Valley Town of Hiwassee in 1703, he distinguished himself in battle and became a prominent civil and military leader. Colonial authorities also recognized this authority. Though he helped to negotiate the 1751 treaty with South Carolina, he had lost faith in Governor Glen. Eager to boost his popularity among the Overhills and with Virginia alike, the warrior headman moved to Tomotley and courted a military and economic partnership with Virginia.

After Braddock's Defeat, "French Indians," particularly Shawnees, reduced the Virginia frontier to "blood and violence." It was "a land of horror and desolation," the *Pennsylvania Gazette* described. Hundreds of settlers fled southward to the Carolinas. A preemptive Cherokee strike against the Shawnees, inveterate enemies of both Virginia and the Cherokees, would protect the Overhills. And it would rescue Virginia, which would no doubt respond with gratitude and a generous trading partnership with the Overhill Cherokees. Ostenaco acted quickly, though other Cherokee leaders wavered. In November 1755, he led 130 Cherokee warriors to Virginia for a top-secret winter campaign against the Shawnees along Sandy Creek in present-day West Virginia.[18]

Virginia was so eager to please Ostenaco and so admired the Indian's skills that the warrior and Major Andrew Lewis commanded the secret expedition jointly. Ostenaco and the Round O of Stecoe were commissioned captains. But the mission, which took place during three and a half weeks in February and March 1756, failed. Canoes ferrying supplies overturned at an icy river crossing. Provisions ran low. Starving Cherokees ate their horses. On the return trip, they took horses and supplies from settlers in the Virginia backcountry. A white frontiersman lured some of the starving warriors with food. Then he sent a ragtag group of vigilantes to ambush them. Several Indians died.[19]

While most of the survivors returned to the Overhills, Ostenaco proceeded to Williamsburg with a smaller delegation to be feted. The Cherokee and his wife (suggesting that she had joined him on the expedition) toured the Virginia capitol at Williamsburg and rode in Dinwiddie's coach. Flanked by local militiamen, the Cherokee led a parade. He dined with the family of thirteen-year-old Thomas Jefferson. He may have watched as the College of William and Mary conferred an honorary degree on publisher and inventor Benjamin Franklin for his experiments with electricity.[20] The visit flattered Ostenaco. It showed that Virginians coveted Cherokees as military allies. It also convinced many Cherokees that Virginia might be a preferable partner to South Carolina.

In December 1755, Dinwiddie dispatched Virginia councilmen Peter Randolph and William Byrd III on a diplomatic mission. First, after a surprising show of humility, they signed a treaty of military alliance with King Hagler at Catawba Town, North Carolina, on February 20. A few weeks later, on the Broad River of North Carolina, Byrd, Randolph, and some North Carolinians met with Attakullakulla and other Overhill leaders. The Indians declined to send warriors north "unless we have a Fort built for the Protection of our Wives and Children." Glen had promised to build a fort in May 1755 in Charles Town and again that July at Saluda. But he had not "made the least Preparations towards performing his Engagement," Attakullakulla complained. "I must again repeat it," he said; Glen "has forfeited his Word."[21]

Attakullakulla presented a bundle of deerskins to the Virginians as he again called for trade with the colony. Dinwiddie again asked the Cherokees to pledge warriors to serve in another Virginia campaign against the Shawnees. As they had for generations, young Cherokee warriors saw war as a path to social and political mobility. And many Cherokees hoped that a military alliance with Virginia would lead to an economic one. On March 17, the two sides finalized a treaty. The Cherokees would send four hundred warriors

IMAGE 2.1 Portrait of Syacust Ukah, 1762, by Sir Joshua Reynolds. *0176. 1017.*
Courtesy of Gilcrease Museum, Tulsa, Okla. Many believe that this is a likeness of
Ostenaco.

against the French and their Indian allies within forty days. But they would do so only after Virginia built a fort at the site the Cherokees chose. The Cherokees would block French overtures in the region. Byrd and Randolph showered the Cherokees with presents and vowed to keep the warriors well supplied.[22]

While Byrd and Randolph negotiated with the Indians, the South Carolina Council planned that colony's rival fort construction project.[23] Cash-poor and sparsely settled North Carolina had no traders among the Cherokee. It constructed its frontier outpost far from the Cherokee towns, to protect settlers from French and Indian raids. Fort Dobbs, erected in 1755, was nestled in the North Carolina Piedmont at present-day Statesville. It sat on a tributary of the Yadkin River. The "Oblong Square," fifty-three by forty feet, was a three-story oak building. It had small holes for muskets interspersed at regular intervals in the wall. Captain Hugh Waddell, a friend of Governor Dobbs's family, subsequently garrisoned the post with North Carolina militiamen and, at times, North Carolina provincials.[24]

For many years, Governor Glen had viewed the construction of a fort in the Overhills as a way to ensure Cherokee loyalty to the British. A British outpost might curb French expansion and covert activity among the southeastern Indians. A fort could serve as a base to recruit Cherokee warriors for British military campaigns. Finally, as a central location for the exchange of goods and information, it served the interests of British traders. Glen had proposed a fort as early as 1746, and he did so again in 1748. But lack of money and other distractions derailed the project.[25]

For the Cherokees, a fort was crucial. Though it brought more outsiders, they believed the benefits outweighed the costs. As allies of the British, warriors could affirm their manhood, against their enemies. While they were away, the fort would offer refuge for their families. Cherokee women stood to benefit, by selling their crops, produce, and craftwork to the men stationed among them. At the same time, a fort would bring a ready supply of trade goods and access to a blacksmith. Above all, a fort promised to give the Cherokees leverage to ensure that British traders treated them respectfully. The mere threat of a siege might be enough to secure trade and diplomatic concessions. If push came to shove, they could seize it or deliver it to the French. A fort might help them persuade the British to live up to decades of empty promises.[26]

If Glen did not move quickly, he might lose his Cherokee allies. These Indians now had another option: the French. A detachment of thirty-one French soldiers had traveled up the Tennessee River to within 150 miles of the Cherokee Overhills. "After viewing the Country," Glen learned, they "marked some of the trees and nailed a plate of lead upon them to take possession for the King of France." The Frenchmen promised that "they would return very soon in order to build a Fort there."[27]

This would leave South Carolina's frontier exposed to the French and French-allied Indians, and to disgruntled Cherokees. The deerskin trade and plans for westward expansion were at stake. Glen tried to start his own fort construction project in early 1756. In February, Attakullakulla and 120 followers visited Charles Town. Glen offered them a tour and some presents. And he sent a surveyor and a skilled engineer to plan a fort in the Overhills.[28] With a Virginia post among the Indians and with the French knocking at the door, private investors in Charles Town rallied their resources. By May, they had pooled enough money for a fort. Glen set out for the Cherokee country on May 19, 1756. With him were eighty men from the Independent Companies. South Carolina had also raised two provincial companies of sixty men to build the fort.[29]

As Glen and the troops marched to the Cherokee Overhills, William Henry Lyttelton arrived in Charles Town to replace him as governor. Lyttelton initially pleased crown and colonist alike, but by 1760 his boldness had backfired and he slipped out of town. "Billy" Lyttelton was a thirty-one-year-old bachelor, Oxford-educated lawyer, and former Member of Parliament. Family connections propelled his rise to prominence. His grandfather had been governor of Jamaica. His brother George, a famous poet, sat on the Privy Council. His friend Lord Halifax was president of the Board of Trade. William Pitt, another family friend, became secretary of state in 1756.[30]

In 1755 Lyttelton sailed for South Carolina. As a French squadron captured the ship, he threw all his instructions overboard. He was taken prisoner but soon released. Fearing for his life, he traveled under an assumed name to Brussels and then embarked for England.[31] While recovering from his ordeal and awaiting a new set of instructions, Lyttelton impregnated his brother's housekeeper. Without making any arrangements for the woman and her child, Lyttelton sailed once again for Charles Town, leaving some people to wonder if his brother was the father.[32]

Charles Town lay on a small, one-mile-wide peninsula, bordered by the Ashley River to the west and the Cooper River to the east. Patterning itself after London, it enjoyed a reputation as a place of refinement, fashion, and hospitality, but it was hardly a city by most Britons' standards. It was, in 1756, a bustling seaport of four thousand whites and four thousand slaves, the fourth-largest city in British North America. Slave labor made the town run.

At that time South Carolina had about thirty thousand whites and seventy thousand slaves. By comparison, in 1750, London had seven hundred thousand inhabitants.[33]

Lyttelton reached Charles Town aboard the *Winchelsea*, a twenty-four-gun naval vessel. As the ship navigated the shallow bar in Charles Town Harbor, he saw Fort Johnson on a high bluff jutting into the harbor on James Island. Its cannons sat at water level. It had barracks and ramparts above. He may have looked out to the starboard, several miles distant, to see shackled and emaciated Africans disembarking from squalid ships for two weeks of quarantine on Sullivan's Island and a lifetime of misery in a land far from home. Enslaved South Carolinians toiled as craftsmen and laborers, and as pilots and oarsmen. More frequently, they suffered on the South Carolina plantations in the brutal work of lowcountry rice and indigo cultivation.[34]

If Lyttelton looked toward the city itself, he might have seen that the hurricane of 1752 had left the city's fortifications in ruins. But several bastions dotted the waterfront, connected by a high wall. As the *Winchelsea* drew nearer, the skyline of the seaport town came more clearly into view. Two-story brick and stucco buildings, with storefronts below and residences above, dazzled in a palette of bright colors. Most had balconies and verandas. The steeples of the city's several churches rose high above the skyline. One of these, St. Michael's, was under construction. The ship docked at one of the several large wharves lining the Cooper River.[35] William Henry Lyttelton had at last arrived safely in his new home.

Public celebrations marked the arrival of the province's new governor, as Charles Town residents greeted Lyttelton with "Respect and unfeigned Joy," according to the *South Carolina Gazette*. Private and public readings of Lyttelton's commission followed. That evening, Charles Town elites attended an elegant ball at John Gordon's inn and tavern at the corner of Broad and Church Streets. Candles placed in upper-floor balconies lit up the night sky along Bay Street. Like many inhabitants, Peter Timothy, editor and publisher of the *Gazette*, expected much of the new governor. After all, much had "been mentioned of him in numberless Letters," Timothy said.[36]

Lyttelton inherited a political system in shambles and disrupted by debate over Crown prerogative versus the rights of elected provincial representatives. He hoped to reverse the gridlock that had characterized Glen's final year in office. He soon learned how contentious the colony's politics could be. Glen and his council had clashed repeatedly with the Commons House. They had feuded over the transparency of council proceedings and the right to appoint government officials. They had also disagreed over the fate of the

IMAGE 2.2 *William Henry Lyttelton, by Benjamin Wilson, ca. 1755–60. Private Collection, Trustees of Antony, Cornwall, UK. National Trust Inventory Number 353068.*

Acadians. Twelve hundred of these disadvantaged and despised French-speaking refugees, forcibly deported from their homes in Nova Scotia in late 1755, had landed in South Carolina's capital city. The Commons House had stalled on funding for fortifications, particularly the new project in the Cherokee Overhills, until just before Lyttelton's arrival. A fierce conflict had emerged, pitting the assembly against Glen and his unofficial spokesman, the polarizing councilman William Wragg.[37]

The new chief executive set to work right away. In June he halted Glen's Fort Loudoun expedition.[38] By this point, the Virginia commissioners had returned. The House of Burgesses allocated Crown funds to build a fort. Dinwiddie dispatched a construction crew under Major Andrew Lewis to the Overhills.[39] On June 28, 1756, Lewis's party and some Cherokee Indians selected a site across the river from the village of Chota. In six weeks, the Virginians completed "a meer bubble constructed to humour the Indians . . . a square of 30 Paces," 105 feet on a side. A ditch and an earthen wall two feet high and four feet wide surrounded the palisaded fort. "Two little bastions" rose just seven feet skyward. To the Cherokees' dismay, however, Dinwiddie did not garrison the fort. The empty edifice thus failed to provide the leverage that the Indians anticipated.[40] Misled, if not betrayed, only thirteen warriors and five women journeyed with Lewis and trader Richard Pearis to fight in Virginia that fall. The irritated Virginia commander, Lewis, wrote, "They are like the Devill's Pigg they will neither lead nor drive." Invited to stay for the Green Corn Dance, the annual community celebration, Lewis declined, and departed in a huff.[41]

Back in Charles Town, Lyttelton carried out his orders and addressed the Acadian "threat." Their arrival portended, for many coastal elites, impending doom. Acadians would "tamper with our . . . Indians, and draw them . . . to the French interest." They might use their navigational skills and knowledge of Charles Town to aid a French invasion. They might revolt, finding accomplices among the Catholic slaves, whom they might encourage "to run away to [St.] Augustine." On June 17, a "hellish" fire swept through Beale's Wharf in Charles Town—allegedly set by an Acadian arsonist. Lyttelton was first to arrive on the scene and the last to leave. Five days later, despite William Wragg's objections, Lyttelton insisted upon legislation directed against the Acadians "to prevent their being burthensome or dangerous" to South Carolina. Lyttelton later secured Wragg's dismissal, much to the delight of the assembly.[42]

By July 16, the assembly passed legislation for "disposing of" the Acadians. Militia and Independent Companies troops then promptly disarmed the controversial refugees. Churchwardens enumerated the exiles. Then the troops shackled and removed 645 of the 784 Acadians from Charles Town and dispersed them throughout the province. Acadian orphans were forced into indentured servitude. With their familial ties weakened, the exiles struggled in their new communities. Workers' wages were garnished to fund services for the ill and unemployed. By 1759 many Acadians returned to Charles Town in search of work, exacerbating wartime tensions in the city. The assembly's treatment of the Acadians previewed the neglect that awaited poor frontiersmen in 1760.[43]

The Acadian "problem" seemingly solved, Lyttelton next turned his attention to military matters. He launched a program to renovate and expand the fortification system in Charles Town and along the coast. He oversaw militia reorganization and retraining.[44] With a fresh plan and money from the assembly, Lyttelton sent a military expedition in July 1756 to construct a fort in the Cherokee Overhills. He sent engineer John William Gerar (or Gerard) De Brahm—who went by "William De Brahm"—to design the fort. Lyttelton sent two newly raised companies of South Carolina provincials to build the fort. He also sent Captain Raymond Demere (sometimes spelled Demeré), with eighty troops from the Independent Companies to garrison the fort and defend the surrounding territory against French plots.[45] By late August, an expedition left Fort Prince George. At Tomotley on September 21, the leading chiefs in the Overhills and two hundred warriors, painted and finely dressed, greeted Demere, the provincial officers, and the engineer. The British and Carolinians and their slave laborers set up the "English Camp Tennecy River." Construction began on October 4.[46]

On July 30, 1757, after bickering with the engineer and alienating the Indians, Demere reported that "our fort is entirely completed and in a posture of defense." The captain had completed his task. Their work done, the provincials declined his offer to enlist in the Independent Companies and departed "in a great hurry." Thereafter, British regulars of the South Carolina Independent Companies manned the fort, joined two years later by provincial reinforcements.[47]

Lyttelton named the new outpost Fort Loudoun after John Campbell, fourth Earl of Loudoun. At the time, Loudoun oversaw British military operations in North America. The elaborate, European-style fort on the banks of the Little Tennessee River sat on a rocky ledge that sloped upward from south to north. A low-lying meadow rolled away to the southeast, with the village of Tuskegee within it. Palisaded walls, three hundred feet on a side, enclosed the fort. Bastions projected from each corner with gun ports and cannons in each one. The fort commanded the river, but with an unnavigable stretch of the Little Tennessee a few miles downstream, that proved immaterial.[48]

A dry moat and a dense hedge of honey locusts surrounded the entire fort. The shrubs had three- to four-inch thorns and, in engineer William De Brahm's view, rendered the fort "impregnable at least against Indians who

IMAGE 2.3 *The Little Tennessee Valley of 1757, by Chester Martin, 1973.
Courtesy of the Fort Loudoun Association.*

always engage naked." Dirt from the ditch built an upward-sloping earthen breastwork. Heavy square logs, sharpened at the top, protruded from the parapet at an angle, forming a treacherous abatis around the fort. Inside, a row of barracks lined the western wall. The fort included a powder magazine. A large blacksmith shop doubled as a chapel, council house, and a temporary guardhouse. Soldiers dug a well and added several additional storehouses and structures.[49]

A replacement for the "sick and infirm" Captain Raymond Demere arrived on August 6, 1757. Eight days later, Demere ordered the garrison to arms and formally turned over command to Captain Paul Demere, his brother (sometimes spelled Demeré). Paul Demere, a career military officer, had served in Gibraltar, in Georgia, and at the Monongahela under General Edward Braddock. Raymond left the fort on August 19 and returned to his post at Georgia's Fort Frederica. He never saw his brother again.[50]

As Demere soon found out, the construction of Fort Loudoun planted the seeds for further conflict between the Overhill Cherokees and South Carolina. As the most isolated British fortification, Fort Loudoun lay, depending upon the path taken, 450 or 500 miles from Charles Town and about 500 miles from Williamsburg, Virginia. It was 200 miles from Fort Prince George and 320 from the Congarees. De Brahm noted that the Cherokees might easily hold the garrison hostage. He cited "the Difficulty in sending Ammunition, Stores, Relief, and Reinforcement to a Fort at so great a Distance through impregnable Defilee's and a savage People, easily offended and revengeful." Indeed, in late 1756, the construction crew had run out of supplies and nearly starved.[51] Why Lyttelton built no fort in the Middle Towns remains unclear. Lacking both money and foresight, perhaps he did not realize that such a supply base would be helpful.

Ensconced near the fort, French agents, enemy Indians, and disgruntled Cherokees threatened Captain Paul Demere's success. For over a year, French provocateurs had circulated in the Cherokee villages. On Demere's march to assume command, a Canadian-born agent known as French John, a Savannah (southern Shawnee), and a party of Great Tellicos killed and scalped the mentally ill wife of a Fort Loudoun soldier as she followed the redcoats' column near Cane Creek. French John and the others would continue to work to undermine British activities.[52]

The principal French operative was Antoine Adhémar de Lantagnac. Formerly a French deserter turned British trader in Great Tellico, he had returned to the French fold. He had extensive connections with Overhill Cherokees, including an Indian wife.[53] By 1756, Lantagnac distributed presents and spouted anti-British rhetoric, stirring up Cherokees, Savannahs, and Creeks. He attempted to turn the Overhills against the English. Those farthest from South Carolina were easily swayed since they were poorly supplied by English traders.[54] A Cherokee war party reportedly attacked British settlements along the North Carolina frontier that summer. Along the Broad River and the South Catawba River, settlers reported "Several abuses and Robberies."[55] Rumors swirled that the French might build a fort at Hiwassee. Lantagnac brought the Mankiller of Great Tellico and two dozen other Cherokees to Fort Toulouse on October 18, 1756. They continued to New Orleans, where they agreed to preliminary terms for a treaty of alliance.[56] What would it take for all the Cherokees to turn against the British?

In many ways, Fort Loudoun functioned just as the Cherokees hoped it would. Indian visitors frequented the post regularly. Indian men brought broken guns and tools to the blacksmith. Indeed, they kept him so busy that he could do no other work. Women exchanged fish, wild berries, and vegetables for trade goods. They traded and interacted with "their sisters the White women," Demere wrote. European contact had incrementally marginalized female participation in Cherokee politics, since white men preferred to deal with male leaders.[57] Though the political prominence of

Cherokee women declined, they exercised new economic and social power at Fort Loudoun.

The fort nevertheless brought frustrations. It had not, as the Cherokees hoped, guaranteed an ample or fair trade with South Carolina. The 1751 regulations on the trade went largely unenforced. Nor had Cherokees received the abundant trade goods that Governor Glen had promised at Saluda in 1755. Cherokee grievances against Carolina traders grew more frequent. Glen had never addressed his 1753 promise to reduce trader fraud. On more than half a dozen occasions, Cherokee leaders voiced their concerns at Fort Loudoun, but nothing changed. The longstanding lack of a British response fueled Cherokee resentment and made French overtures all the more appealing in 1757.[58]

Captain Raymond Demere sympathized with the Cherokees. The traders "will be the ruin of this Nation if proper Measures are not taken by your Excellency and the Council," he wrote. They were "for the most Part a Sett of Villains who studdy Nothing but their own narrow Views and private Emoluments without having the least Regard to Justice or to the public Weel." Without decisive action on the governor's part, there would "always be a Discord" among the Cherokees.[59]

In a lengthy letter to Governor Glen in 1755, trader Ludovick Grant outlined "many and greivous Complaints" of the Indians. Cherokees carried "a seeming Hatred and Grudge" against the Carolina traders. His contemporaries, he stated confidently, were "cheating the Indians in the Prices of Goods." In 1757, four years after Governor Glen had promised to send the Indians accurate scales and yardsticks, Cherokees confirmed their suspicions. They informed Governor Lyttelton that "what weighs twelve pounds on the new Stillards, weighs but ten" in trader John Elliott's, "and his yard [stick] is a good deal Shorter than you Sent." Other traders extended "extravagant" credit. Cherokees also despised the trade "on account of the Debts they owe." Some traders deliberately instituted shortages to keep prices high. This, Grant believed, explained "why the Indians covet and are fond of a Trade from other Places." He feared that the Indians might murder the British traders and defect to the French. Yet, as Daniel Ingram points out, neither travel nor violence would bring cheap goods to the Cherokee villages directly.[60]

In this tense environment, "lawless and contemning" unlicensed traders peddled rum to the Indians, despite prohibitions against it. John Williams from Augusta's Rae and Barksdale firm brought "considerable Quantities of Rum and Spirits." Williams allegedly sold it in the Lower Towns at exorbitant prices in underfilled containers, according to the Estatoe trader James

Beamer. This "always . . . and now does breed great Disturbances, Quarrels and even Murders between the White People and Indians," Beamer argued.[61]

Cherokees also complained about mistreatment. Attakullakulla urged Lyttelton to replace the traders among the Overhills with men "that will use them with Justice." The Mankiller of Great Tellico frequently visited Fort Loudoun, each time to gripe about the trade. He brought his wife with him, but the officers ignored her. "He sayd that he had met with a great Deal of ill Usage" by the white traders, Raymond Demere reported. They had taken his horses and insulted him and thrown things at him "as if he had been a Dog out of Doors." The abuses, he added, made him receptive to French overtures.[62]

The Mankiller also noted that his town had no resident licensed trader. Robert Gouedy, licensed to trade at Great Tellico and Chatuga, instead sold goods on the South Carolina frontier to subcontractors "at so much per cent Profit," Demere wrote to Lyttelton. Then, "those Fellows comes with few Goods to those Towns and imposes so much on the Indians," the captain added. The Indians sometimes took matters into their own hands and seized the goods they believed should belong to them.[63]

In February, 1757, Chotas came to the fort with fresh complaints about trader John Elliott. The Indians produced paint that Elliott had sold them and griped about its inferior quality. Elliott confessed to Demere that he had sold them "Shirts, Linnings, &c." at "a most exorbitant Price." He admitted that he and others had scammed the Indians with faulty scales. Connecorte produced a paper Glen had signed at Saluda regulating the prices of several articles. The traders "had no regard to that Paper." His anger building, the headman said that the Indians now "looked upon that paper to be Nothing but Lies as they did all the rest of the Papers that came from Carolina." Charles Town, he seethed, "was a Place where Nothing but Lies came from."[64]

At the same time, another delegation led by Attakullakulla took Indian complaints directly to the governor. Lyttelton gave the visitors presents and promised to deal with the fraud in the deerskin trade. While Attakullakulla had remained strongly tied to the British, Connecorte drifted further away, carrying a growing group of followers with him.[65] Trade grievances remained unresolved despite Lyttelton's promises.

By 1757, despite the construction of Fort Loudoun in the Cherokee Overhills, Cherokee frustration with the trade, regulated and based out of South Carolina, was building, especially in Great Tellico and Chota. But the French had yet to demonstrate that they could provide a reliable supply of trade goods, weapons, and ammunition. The promise of wealth and status lured many warriors northward. Cherokee men answered Virginia's call to serve in British campaigns against the French at Fort Duquesne and in the Ohio Country.[66] Circumstances had not yet pushed the Cherokees to break with the English, but constantly being misunderstood and mistreated caused their resentment and frustration to slowly build. Indian anger simmered as the war between France and England escalated. The American Southeast inched closer to open war.

KILLED ON THE PATH

Cherokees in the Campaigns against Fort Duquesne

3   In early April 1757, 148 Cherokees, primarily from the Lower Towns of Keowee and Estatoe, traveled north to Virginia. The Indians included Wawhatchee, Keera-rustikee, Youctanah, and the Swallow. "Not finding the Presents which they expected," wrote Superintendent of Indian Affairs for the Southern Department Edmond Atkin, they ransacked local farms. They finally obtained some trade goods at Bedford Court House. A Halifax County justice ushered them to Winchester, where no presents, and more disappointments, awaited.[1]

The Indians were disenchanted. For eighteen months, the Swallow said, Virginia had promised many things: a fort in the Overhills, generous compensation, and a trade alliance that might break South Carolina's near-monopoly. Virginia had failed to meet Cherokee ex-pectations and had denied them the benefits that they expected. Cherokees told Virginia officer George Mer-cer that "the Govr knew not how to treat Indians." The Swallow promised his warriors "great Rewards." But, he told Mercer, "the Govr had made him a liar." Because Cherokee leadership depended upon results, and lead-ers had redistributive duties, the Swallow's future was on the line. As David Preston explains, natives were not the "subservient auxiliaries" that white officials would have wished. They were "autonomous warriors" fight-ing for their own goals.[2]

In the summers of 1755 and 1756, Shawnees, Dela-wares, and Ohio Valley Indians had attacked Virginia plantations, particularly on the Holston and New Riv-ers. These forays proved resounding successes, driving back the frontier 150 miles. British and colonial officials longed to end these raids. They also looked to capture Fort Duquesne on the Forks of the Ohio, avenging General Edward Braddock's defeat in 1755. These campaigns were part of an expanding French and Indian War strategy. Indian allies, particularly Cherokees, proved essential to achieving these goals. As Preston explains, Indian allies were indeed both "a consistent presence" and a "formidable threat" to the French and their Indian allies. From 1755 to 1758, eight hundred Cherokees and more than two hundred Catawbas, Meherrins, Nottoways, and Tuscaroras participated, while hundreds of other Cherokees operated in the Mississippi and Ohio Valleys.[3] No one disputed the value of these services. "Without Indians to oppose Indians," George Washington wrote in 1756, "we may expect but small success."[4]

Cherokees and others served vital and often underappreciated roles. From British forts on the Virginia, Maryland, and Pennsylvania frontiers, they scouted enemy operations in and around Fort Duquesne. They raided French posts along the Venango Path leading north from Fort Duquesne to Lake Erie. They captured prisoners for questioning. They intimidated the French and their allies and deterred attacks on frontier settlers. They trained non-Indian soldiers in wilderness tactics and strategies and developed close bonds in the process. They shared their beliefs, their customs, and their medicines. And they participated in vital behind-the-scenes diplomacy with other tribes, to the benefit of all.[5]

In 1756, despite Dinwiddie's numerous invitations, only thirteen Cherokee warriors and five women fought in the British-provincial campaign against Fort Duquesne. Governor Dinwiddie attributed the Cherokees' reluctance to one cause: "naturally they are la[zy]."[6] Later that year, George Mason wrote, "I stedfastly believe they have no Thoughts of giving themselves any further Trouble than to get what they can from us."[7] Overhill Cherokees had just fought a war with the Creeks. They were waiting for the benefits Virginia and South Carolina had promised. And they were gauging larger geopolitical considerations.

In 1757, 230 Cherokees answered Virginia's call to arms. Early frustrations aside, Wawhatchee and his warriors took four scalps and two prisoners in May. A few weeks later, Cherokees ranged thirty-five miles beyond Fort Duquesne. They engaged a party of ten Frenchmen, killing two and wounding two. They captured the French officer who had coordinated Indian attacks on the Virginia frontier in 1756. But their success came at a cost: the Swallow died in battle, and his son was wounded. For four consecutive days, the Indians carried him on their backs, 115 miles to Fort Cumberland, eating nothing but wild onions.[8] Later in June, Cherokee parties scouted Fort

Duquesne and took two more scalps. Cherokees had proven their mettle and their merit.[9]

The spring and summer, however, were marred by tension and chaos. Wawhatchee and Youctanah bounced from one fort to the next in search of the goods the Cherokees had been promised, as Superintendent Atkin and various officials squabbled over who had jurisdiction over Cherokee affairs. Youctanah grew frustrated and left. Not even the arrival of decorated Sandy Creek campaign veterans made a difference. Both the Round O from the Out Town of Stecoe and Ostenaco offered similar services but faced familiar frustrations. After a summer of disarray in Indian affairs, Atkin made another misstep. Lacking an interpreter, he detained a party of Cherokees from Chota and some Mohawks. He suspected them of being French spies, but they were actually diplomats. Several of the detained Indians became violently ill.[10]

The events of 1757, Colonel George Washington observed, had shown two things. First, "the friendship and assistance of the Cherokees are well worth cultivating." In fact, "they are indispensably necessary." Second, though the Cherokees had demonstrated their commitment "beyond the most distant doubt," they had endured "a train of mismanagement," ingratitude, disorganization, and delay. Some Indians stayed through the winter, but many returned home "without any kind of reward or thanks—or even provisions to support them on their march." They were "justly fired with the highest resentment." He feared that "our Interest with those Indians is at the brink of destruction."[11]

In the spring of 1758, Indians once again went out to war against French forts and French-allied Indians. During the winter, 180 warriors from the Overhill Towns went by water to the lower Ohio. Their destination was a French fort later known as Fort Massiac, and subsequently anglicized to Fort Massac.[12] Other Cherokees turned their eyes to Virginia and Pennsylvania. From April to August, at least 17 parties of Cherokees ranged from British forts to points west of the Allegheny Mountains, again scouting, skirmishing, training white soldiers, sharing their culture, and deterring Indian attacks.[13]

The proposal for Cherokee involvement in a larger push toward Fort Duquesne in 1758 seemed straightforward. But it unraveled, with tragic consequences for everyone involved. With the massive influx of warriors, the gap widened between Anglo and Cherokee expectations, alienating warriors who had offered campaign-changing contributions. The alliance collapsed not under the weight of the Cherokees' economic demands or expectations related to gift giving. Nor did it stem from officers' racism. Rather, endless delays drove Cherokees to depart in bitter frustration. On the way home, frontier skirmishes claimed the lives of at least thirty-seven warriors, creating a crisis of epic proportions.[14]

By May 4, 1758, as many as eight hundred Indians had made the five-hundred-mile trek to Virginia's Fort Loudoun, strategically located in the broad swale of the Shenandoah Valley near the site of Winchester today. Seven hundred of them were Cherokees.[15] At the same time, British and provincial agents continued to recruit Indian troops. The South Carolina Assembly allotted £20,000 in trade goods and sent Colonel Probart Howarth, who held a joint commission in the Independent Companies and also commanded South Carolina's provincial regiment, to the villages. British authorities sent Virginia's William Byrd III—soon made a colonel in the 2nd (2d) Virginia Regiment—and trader George Turner.[16]

The events of 1757 gave the Cherokees pause. The mismanagement of Indian affairs disenchanted and deterred many. Dinwiddie still had not garrisoned the Virginia fort in the Overhills. Nor had he sent the goods authorized by the Virginia House of Burgesses. Nonetheless, the lure of a long-term trade agreement, and expectations of victory, wealth, and status, propelled many Indians northward.[17]

South Carolina's Colonel Howarth returned to Charles Town without gaining a single recruit from the Middle Towns or the Overhills. The Overhill warriors had been deceived before. They therefore agreed to join the army only after trade goods arrived.[18] Byrd struggled as well. Not until he bribed the Estatoe trader James Beamer and paid his half-Cherokee son, Thomas, to serve as an interpreter did a party of sixty Lower Townsmen make the trip to Virginia. They left on March 1. Seven more men traveled separately.[19]

The warriors who remained at home had good reason to hesitate. Deerskin traders with their own interests at heart reminded the Indians of what they already knew: if the fighting extended through the summer of 1758 and into the fall and winter hunting season, the result would be widespread hardship and indebtedness for Indians and traders alike. Estatoe trader James Beamer warned the Cherokees that Virginians would "give them no Presents to cloath their Wives and Children." In the village of Joree, trader James May reportedly told local warriors that the journey was "so far that you will dye or be killed." He also issued a vague but ominous admonition. According to trader and interpreter Ambrose Davis, "There was a great many White People coming from Virginia and likewise from Carolina" May said, "and what they were after he could not tell." With menacing uncertainty in the offing, May "desired them all to stay at Home, and guard their Towns."[20]

What of James May's enigmatic warnings? Behind them lay a kernel of truth. A string of French victories in the North had put a deep-seated fear into British officials, especially those in the South. The southern colonies might be the next French objective. With this in mind, the governor of South Carolina proposed a preemptive strike, thinking that perhaps a British campaign against France's southern strongholds could stave off the looming threat. Lyttelton's proposed targets included the coastal settlements of New Orleans and Mobile and the inland outposts at Fort Toulouse and Fort Tombigbee. The plan hinged on Native American help. One scenario involved a British-provincial invasion starting at Chota and striking down the Tennessee River. What might this mean for the Cherokee Towns? The hazy details of Charles Town's worst-kept secret gave some warriors good reason to opt out of the Fort Duquesne enterprise.[21]

The hundreds of Cherokees and Catawbas who gathered at Virginia's Fort Loudoun had doubts from the start. On April 23 they listened to Captain Abraham Bosomworth of the Royal American Regiment. He said little to inspire them. The officer delivered a rambling address from a prepared script. In it, he appealed to the Cherokees to defend their families and "property" from French encroachment. Given the reality of English, not French, usurpation, this made no sense to them. But, eager to accomplish what they had set out for, the warriors at Fort Loudoun agreed to Bosomworth's proposals. However, they also issued a caution. The "great Warriors Troops" must "be assembled" as quickly as possible, they said, so "that our young men may not be tired with waiting."[22]

Timing was everything. The fighting men who journeyed to Virginia for the Fort Duquesne campaign intended to return to their villages for the Green Corn Festival, the yearly celebration of the fall harvest. They needed to be home in time to undertake their winter hunts. Their families depended on it. Without deerskins to trade, the clothing and other trade goods that had supplanted traditional handicrafts were out of reach. The hunt was especially crucial for the war parties that had served continuously since spring 1757, given the large number of hunters who had gone north to fight.[23]

From the outset, few signs pointed to a speedy campaign. Cherokee recruits streaming northward in 1758 observed but a handful of Pennsylvania and Virginia provincials. It would take time to assemble and supply seven thousand British regulars and colonial troops. Clothes, food, weapons, and ammunition—the supplies they required to carry out their end of the Bosomworth bargain—were nowhere to be found. To make matters worse, Brigadier

General John Forbes, the commander of the expedition, would have to co-ordinate the campaign from his sickbed. He was suffering from a terminal stomach ailment. Once Forbes provisioned and armed his men, he had to carve a path over the undulating ridges of the Alleghenies, creating a chain of fortifications on the way, in order to safely reach Fort Duquesne. Thousands of French soldiers and their Indian allies stood between the British and their goal. Forbes did not arrive on the Pennsylvania frontier until early July. Only then did his army reach full strength, with sufficient supplies.[24]

The white men did the best they could to allay the warriors' anxieties, but Indian angst was cumulative as delay compounded delay. In June, Colonel Henry Bouquet led an advance detachment with many Indians to scout the prospects ahead. But Forbes's army did not begin its final march on Fort Duquesne until early November. By then, nearly all of the Cherokee warriors had given up in disgust. Incrementally, they set out for home, a journey that soon gave them more reason to turn away from their British allies.[25]

Home invasions, horse thefts, and armed robberies happened daily during the summer of 1758. Impatience and language barriers contributed to other altercations in a pattern of conflict that dated to 1756. But with the Fort Duquesne campaign in the offing, the stream of Cherokees coming and going along the Great Indian Warpath did little to cultivate amity. By the end of May 1758, at least six Indians and one white man were dead, and several white men and women were badly beaten.[26]

The party of Cherokees with William Byrd III's hired escort observed the situation firsthand. The warriors traveling to and from the Winchester rendezvous point were destitute. They needed to protect themselves from their Shawnee enemy and to guard against the frenzied frontiersmen. The frontiersmen, for their part, coveted Virginia's generous bounty on Shawnee scalps and captives. The colony had instituted payment for enemy Indian scalps in August 1755, and had upped the reward in April 1757. Plus, a new wave of French-sponsored Indian raids in late April had killed or captured more than sixty settlers in southwestern Virginia. Settlers did not trust any Indian. To make matters worse, most Cherokees spoke no English and often had no translators. The Cherokees thus did not understand the words of the armed men they encountered.[27]

To some degree, the conflict also stemmed from horse stealing on both sides. British officials frequently reported that Cherokee war parties had returned home with stolen horses. The Catawbas' agent and guide, Samuel Wyly, heard that one group of warriors had "14 Horses packed with Mostly plunder." Fort Prince George's commander, Lachlan McIntosh, reported that

Estatoes brought forty horses back to the Lower Towns. North Carolina's governor, Arthur Dobbs, claimed that Overhill warriors had sixty horses with them when they passed through the Moravian settlements. From the warriors' perspective they were only defending themselves after reclaiming the horses that had strayed from them while in the British service, horses for which they received no reimbursement from Forbes. However, Virginians also stole Cherokee horses, according to traders and interpreters James and Thomas Beamer, who accompanied Cherokee parties.[28]

At times, miscommunication was also to blame. In one instance in mid-May, the Cherokees tried to solicit the aid of a frontier militia unit against the Shawnees. In this incident and many others, confusion led to chaos and tragedy. The Indians continued, "clapping their Hands, on their Breasts, and making signs," and "signifyed to them, there was a great many Shawanees all about them." Then, according to the militiamen, the Cherokees purportedly robbed the leader of the militia party, stripped him naked, and beat him with their tomahawks, cutting him "thro the upper Lip." Cherokees often stripped nearly naked in preparation for battle. What the militiamen saw as an assault may actually have been a frustration-laden invitation to joint enterprise, steeped in long-established Indian ritual. In the end, the parties separated. The Cherokees, unable to recover their clothes and horses, went on to plunder several homesteads.[29]

The next, and most controversial, incident involved thirty Cherokees led by the Raven of Settico. By some accounts he and his young warriors became disenchanted by the slow pace of the campaign and the lack of supplies.[30] By other reports, he left Winchester in shame. British authorities and warriors from a rival village alleged that he had attempted to collect two bounties on one scalp.[31] Jealous Cherokee rivals distanced themselves from him.

Frontiersmen, unaware of these allegations, killed five of the Raven's thirty warriors in mid-May. The victims had just taken seven scalps and five prisoners in a dangerous scouting mission; some had been wounded. But the frontiersmen "scalp'd them & left them on the Road" in Halifax County for the other Cherokees to see. When news of the atrocities reached Winchester, Quartermaster General Sir John St. Clair feared that the Cherokees might "revenge themselves." With "great Difficulty" the Virginian William Byrd III "prevented my men from going back to take immediate Revenge."[32]

Forbes's subordinates doled out trade goods and supplies. They increased Cherokee rations. But, the general observed on May 19, the Cherokees grew "weary, and languish[ed] after their own homes, complaining that they see no appearance of our Army" and that they had been out "many months"—time enough.[33] They "are now no longer to be kept with us neither by promises nor presents," Forbes wrote on May 29. Then Cherokees learned of the frontier skirmishes in Halifax and Bedford counties. Seeking restitution, some went "so farr as to seize the presents design'd for them, and divide it among themselves according to their own Caprice," Forbes said.[34] A few parties still scouted Fort Duquesne. But, as St. Clair reported on May 31, "all the Cherokees are gone or a[re] going home."[35]

The situation became tense. Forbes was still in Philadelphia. Though he and his top officers grumbled in frustration, the general knew that the Cherokees were vital to his campaign's success. "I think the Cherokees of such consequence," he wrote, "that I have done every thing in my power to provide them in their necessarys." Additional supplies arrived from Philadelphia in mid-June, and Forbes's subordinates doled those out in batches. But his army was still not ready.[36]

Only Indians closest to Fort Duquesne and in the thick of the action seemed content. Bouquet, who called the Indians a "damned Tanny Race," nonetheless knew how to appeal to the warriors. In a flowery speech at Raystown on June 16, Bouquet offered Indians the opportunity to take scalps, to prove their "Virtue and Courage," and to make their wives and children proud. While some Indians guarded the expedition's encampments, others advanced ninety miles to the French stronghold. In early June they got close enough to observe French troop strength and activities.[37]

Those at a distance were less enthusiastic. Captain Bosomworth swayed few minds at Winchester. He complained on June 9 that "after an Infinity of Labour, Slavery and unwearied Importunity," the Indians departed nonetheless. Colonel Byrd noted two weeks later that the Cherokees had "all grown very impatient," and "behave[d] with the greatest Insolence."[38] George Washington similarly griped that the Cherokees grew "tired of waiting." In vain, he begged Forbes to send an officer to the Cherokee villages to resolve all grievances; "Indians to us, are of the Utmost Importance."[39]

In the Cherokee villages, in an atmosphere of disgruntled uncertainty, Attakullakulla struggled to recruit. He had gone to war earlier in the year against the French fort on the lower Ohio River. He delivered two scalps to Charles Town in April, and he promised Governor Lyttelton and Colonel Byrd he would lead a large war party to join Forbes. But then he stalled. Overhill warriors refused to take up the hatchet. The most eager fighters had already taken part in the campaigns to Louisiana and the Illinois Country. Others had assisted Virginia the previous year, but Virginia still had not paid them. Ostenaco still resented Superintendent Atkin for detaining the

Cherokee diplomats.[40] All awaited the latest news from the Virginia and Pennsylvania frontier.

Attakullakulla, Virginia trader George Turner, and a Presbyterian missionary from Virginia named John Martin had escorted a caravan of trade goods to South Carolina's Fort Loudoun. The headman distributed them to Cherokee recruits. At Fort Loudoun on June 21, Turner loaded his horses to head north, expecting a large number of Cherokee warriors to follow. But Attakullakulla approached at the eleventh hour with an announcement.[41]

It was not uncommon for a war effort to be delayed or thwarted by bad omens. As one white observer put it, Cherokees "depend on their conjurers to foretell to them what success they'l have in Hunting & in all their Concerns."[42] Chota's conjurer had warned the warriors that if they went to war "after Two moons there wou'd be a Great Sickness amongst them." As a result, "they should lose a great many of their Men." Going anyway, against the advice of the conjurers, would subject the community to affliction. Plus, Attakullakulla added, "it was very hot weather." And no one had sent them wampum belts. He wondered aloud if Turner legitimately represented Virginia. Despite Turner's protestations, "in Short [they] positively refused to stir." Attakullakulla offered to depart in the fall with three hundred men. For once, longstanding roles were reversed as Attakullakulla now made promises to the white men that he could not keep.[43]

Attakullakulla was playing many cards at once—keeping the British in his orbit, appeasing reluctant fighting men at home, and chastening the disgruntled warriors who had departed Forbes's army. In council with the British, the headman disavowed the returning men. He called them "Rogues who under the Pretence of Assisting their Brethren the English went in to Rob the Out Settlers and murder them." He offered to order the killing of the Raven of Toxaway, whom he accused of improprieties along the path.[44] If he put off his march to Virginia by promising to raise more men, he might secure more compensation and trade goods. Thus he could buy time to gain the affection of his Cherokee followers.

Back in Pennsylvania, Cherokees soon spotted former South Carolina governor James Glen. In an effort to restore his damaged reputation and to help his cousin, Forbes, Glen had sailed with Montgomery's Highlanders from Charles Town to Philadelphia at his own expense. Meeting with Forbes, he touted Lyttelton's proposed southern campaign against Louisiana. Then Glen traveled westward along the chain of forts. He tried to help Forbes manage the Cherokees. But the warriors took little notice of Glen's efforts. By July 10, only two hundred Cherokees remained with the expedition. "No method was left untried to detain them," Forbes said; "but they are like Sheep, where one leaps, all the rest follow." Glen and Bosomworth left Fort Cumberland for Raystown on July 17.[45]

By this time, the ailing brigadier general finally reached Carlisle. He traveled in a hammock slung between two horses. The sight was disconcerting to the Indians. Cherokee warriors led by example, on the front lines. To see the "Great Warrior" in a feeble state inspired little confidence. Forbes's officers failed to convince them "that he was so fierce and of an explosive disposition that they thought it safe only to let him out on the battlefield."[46]

Forbes failed to acknowledge why Cherokees were leaving. He blamed their departures not on the expedition's slow pace but on several other factors. He blamed the absent superintendent, Edmond Atkin. He attributed the mass defection to Cherokee greed yet overlooked the services Cherokee scouts had rendered, the warriors that had died, and the hunts they had missed. Though he did call the Cherokees "Scoundrells," Forbes was fair. He ensured that the Indians received their goods. He demanded that the governors provide "safe passage for the Indians" but they did not.[47] Lieutenant Governor Francis Fauquier, who had assumed office in June and would serve as acting governor for the next decade, begged Forbes "to let none return . . . without proper Escorts." Forbes lacked the manpower to implement the suggestion. Colonel Washington recommended sending "a proper person" to the Cherokee country to make amends, but nothing came of the idea. Events would show, however, that not even an escort of white men could guarantee the safety of the Cherokees, and no one could smooth over Cherokee heartache.[48]

While at least three parties were still out scouting, more Cherokees returned home. Additional skirmishes took place along the Virginia frontier, with frontiersmen leaving yet another Cherokee corpse on the road. Fort Loudoun's commander Captain Paul Demere blamed the frontier clashes on Cherokee horse thieves. Though some Cherokees were still in Virginia, and some had returned home with fine clothing, there were "some wounded, and others have been killed on the Path." Fort Prince George commander Ensign Lachlan McIntosh concurred. "By all Accounts," he wrote, "there is a good Deal of Mischief done upon the Frontiers of Virginia betwixt white People and Indians." Captain Bosomworth wrote that British officers had fitted Indian allies with "a yellow Badge, or Fillett which they wear round their Heads, or tye about their Arms or Breast, as they think fit and are very conspicuous, & easily seen at a distance in the woods." Indians also carried Union flags. If

Cherokees displayed these symbols while returning home, they were being intentionally targeted.[49]

More departures followed. Many Catawbas returned home in July. Accompanied by white translators, the Catawbas reached their homelands safely by a route through the Virginia Piedmont.[50] More Cherokees soon left, too; they would not be so lucky.

By August 3, Colonel Byrd reported that "every one of my cursed Indians has left me, their Excuse was they were tired of waiting." He continued, "I make no doubt but that they will shortly revolt from our Interest."[51] Another fifty Cherokees stationed at Raystown left Colonel Bouquet on August 10. Forbes detached Major James Grant and two hundred Highlanders from the 77th Regiment to, "in moderate terms," scold them. The major obeyed Forbes's orders. At Shippensburg on August 16, he asked the Indians to stay, but they declined. Grant took care to note that the Indians "committed no Disorder, did not even ask for Rum." They merely claimed the "Bundles" of "Goods" they had collected thus far. "They were so anxious to get home," Grant reported, that "they went of[f] very quietly, without waiting either for Talk or Dinner, and took a few horses with them." Grant was rather sympathetic.[52]

As Colin Calloway explains, Highlanders and Indians discovered that they had much in common. Both were tribal societies living on the edges of empire. Both were deeply linked to the land. Both valued war as a path to status. Both shared a love for family, for the supernatural, and for dance. Highlanders adopted moccasins, wore leggings, and carried powder horns on a quillwork strap. No one could have imagined that in two short years, the "cousins" of the Cherokees would be sent to burn and destroy the villages of their friends and comrades.[53]

As the summer progressed, the death toll mounted. Only one war party returned home without people killed or robbed on the way. On September 2, the remaining Estatoe warriors, accompanied by messenger James Holmes and the Beamers, set out from Winchester, Virginia. They woke the morning after their first encampment to find six of their horses stolen. As they proceeded southward, at Bedford Court House, Virginia settlers warned Beamer "if I did not take Care I should have some Indians killed." Beamer sent word ahead that the three white men in the party would keep the Indians under control. Nonetheless, the next morning, near Goose Creek in Bedford County, eighty white men "rose up" suddenly, without provocation, on both sides of the road. They ordered the Indians to ground their firearms, which they did.

According to Beamer, the frontiersmen "positively say, that it is the Governor of Virginia's orders to kill and robb" the Cherokees. Likewise, James Beamer insisted, "The Governor of Virginia . . . has Given these people orders to kill them, and take away what Presents they Got there." The frontiersmen opened fire, killing three Indians and wounding one. When the Cherokees then picked up their weapons, a three-hour standoff ensued. The Beamers convinced the Cherokees, who lacked numbers and ammunition, not to take revenge. The warriors continued to Estatoe, arriving on September 8.[54]

On September 10, a warrior returned to the Valley Towns "very much wounded and not a Rag on him." The journal of a Virginia militiaman reveals that on August 20, frontiersmen had detained the Cherokee's party of five as it journeyed home with five horses and several enemy scalps. The next morning, the captain released the captives. But he sent a detachment to ambush the warriors. The Virginians opened fire from a peach orchard that overlooked a river crossing, and killed and scalped four of the Indians, presumably to collect the scalp bounty. Afterward, the captain ordered his men to swear "not to tell that we Ever heard them say that they were Cherokees."[55]

News of additional bloodshed arrived just days later in the Lower Towns. On September 15, wounded warriors reached Quaratchee and revealed some tragic news: white people had killed six of their townsmen on the path. And on September 17, the Lower Towns learned of yet another skirmish in Bedford County. White assailants killed six Cherokees and wounded seven more. Then they allegedly pursued and killed the wounded.[56]

Because Cherokee society was a matrilineal society, women called on their male relatives to take revenge. To appease the "crying blood" of those captured or killed, male relatives of the fallen had to go to war. If the avengers failed, the relative's ghost would loom nearby, subjecting the community to illness or bad luck. Therefore, an equivalent number of white men, members of the offending clan, had to die. As one white observer remarked, "Such is their Custom, that they will have Man for man, if not the guilty, another." But this was a decision that no Cherokee family, clan, or village took lightly.[57]

The Indians carefully considered the timing, logistics, and potential consequences of retribution. Some prominent headmen from the Overhills and the Lower Towns had proposed an alternate implementation of the law to Governor Lyttelton: to atone for the deaths of both the Virginians with a blood gift of sorts—a strike "without delay" against the French. Lyttelton never responded. Meanwhile, more Cherokee warriors died on the path from Virginia.[58]

For the first time, a pan-Cherokee unity began to emerge. Village leaders from the Valley, Middle, and Out Towns gathered to discuss retributory action. The Round O of Stecoe in the Out Towns, formerly a British ally, "Jump'd on a Corn-house Scaffild." In traditional fashion, he beat a drum and summoned the men of the village. He sang war songs and reminded warriors of their duty of retaliation. The war leader collected forty volunteers and the village spent the night dancing. "I make noe Doubt," James Beamer wrote, "he will Be Joyn'd By three times that Number."[59]

"All the warriors of the lower Towns" converged on Fort Prince George on September 17. According to Wawhatchee and Seroweh—whom the British called "the Young Warrior of Estatoe"—the Virginians had slain thirty-seven Cherokees that spring and summer. Another account placed that figure at forty. The Indians could bear it no longer. "Every thing is turned the Indians Quite Mad and they talk Nothing Now but of Revenge," Ensign McIntosh observed. The visitors demanded a response from Governor Lyttelton in fourteen days.[60]

On September 21, a total of three dozen warriors from Quaratchee, Toxaway, and Estatoe departed in search of revenge. Indian trader John Elliott was "bringing up a fresh Cargo of rum," McIntosh added. He predicted bleakly: "we shall have still more Trouble than Ever."[61] James Beamer reported that in his thirty years as a Cherokee trader, "I Never In my Life Beheld the Indains Look upon white men as they Doe or talk Soe hard of them." They say, he reported, "There will Be a Great many white people kill'd Before they are all Gone." Likewise, his son Thomas worried, "I am afraid many hundred poor Souls in the back Inhabitants will be massacred, which I pray God may not come to pass."[62]

When he received the letters from McIntosh and the Beamers on September 26, Lyttelton sent a threatening dispatch to the headmen and warriors of the Lower and Middle Towns. On the basis of reports from Virginia's lieutenant governor, Francis Fauquier, Lyttelton concluded that "the Cherokees were the first aggressors."[63] In his message to the Indians, he insisted that the frontiersmen had acted without official sanction. He offered "presents" to the families of the slain, "sufficient to hide the Bones of the dead Men and wipe away the Tears from the Eyes of their Friends." But, he threatened, if the warriors shed the blood of frontiersmen in revenge, "you will remember my Words and repent your Rashness when it is too late." Relatives sometimes accepted a blood gift as restitution for the dead person and called off plans for revenge. But if a non-Cherokee had taken a Cherokee life, family members were less likely to accept blood gifts. Lyttelton did not acknowledge, and perhaps did not care, that only the relatives of the deceased could decide whether or not to take revenge. The decision was not based on a broad consensus.[64]

The Virginia House of Burgesses repealed the scalp bounty on enemy Indians on September 28, and Fauquier gave his assent on October 12. Fauquier ordered militia captains to "act on the defensive only, and to avoid as possible doing any Injury to the Cherokees." But it was too little, too late. The Virginia lieutenant governor blamed the Cherokee deaths on "the Rashness of a few disorderly" Virginians. He urged the Cherokees to "call back their Parties . . . to prevent the Effusion of more Blood." He vowed, vaguely, that Virginia would "do every Thing to recover and preserve a mutual good understanding and inviolable Friendship." With some skepticism the Virginia Council hoped that he could "effect a Reconciliation."[65]

Though the details remain sketchy, some of the Lower or Middle Towns sent runners to the Savannah River Chickasaws and the Upper Creeks, begging them to send warriors for a wave of retaliatory attacks. The Savannah River Chickasaws were British allies and profited by assisting the still active Creek and Chickasaw trade. They therefore gave the Cherokees "a very cold reception." The Upper Creeks showed interest, sending diplomats to Estatoe. But when intoxicated Cherokee visitors "beat and abused" their Creek hosts in the Creek town of Okfuskee, circumstances changed. The Creeks killed and scalped two of the Cherokees. At the very least, deerskin trader Lachlan McGillivray wrote, "it will nevertheless keep them shy, and at a distance from one another for some time." The Creeks therefore declined to ally with the Cherokees, at least for now.[66]

By mid-October, in the absence of Creek and Chickasaw support, many Cherokees were recalling their revenge-seeking war parties, likely anticipating "blood gifts" from Fauquier in the form of trade goods. The Estatoes seemed "altered for the Better," the elder Beamer reported. Some were even planning to smooth things out with Lyttelton in Charles Town. It was too late. Blood had already been shed. Nottely warriors reportedly killed and scalped a white man in the "Irish [Quaker] settlement" at Pine Tree Hill near the Catawbas.[67]

From his station at Fort Loudoun in the Cherokee Overhill Towns, Captain Paul Demere somehow prevailed upon Ostenaco, Oconostota, and a few dozen warriors to set out against French forts in the Illinois Country and the Ohio Country in mid-September 1758. They left just before runners from the grief-stricken Cherokee towns brought word of the carnage on the Virginia frontier. The Overhills had lost no warriors in the most recent conflicts, but some of their kinfolk had died. Given the strength of clan ties, tensions rose just as French agents toured the Overhill Towns. On October 15, Captain Demere sent Lyttelton a despairing plea: "if we had any good Success to the North you would let me know it, for I begin to think that I am now in another world."[68]

In late August, four months later than he had promised Colonel Byrd, Attakullakulla had departed for Virginia with just thirty warriors.[69] They stopped first in Williamsburg to meet with the lieutenant governor. They proceeded northwest to Winchester and then westward to Raystown, ninety miles shy of Fort Duquesne. There they found General Forbes on October 13. They saw no more than eighty Indians with the expedition. Forbes hoped that Attakullakulla could halt Cherokee departures for the final push to the French fort. Instead, the headman and others upped what the British saw as "avaritious" and "extravagant" demands for more goods. Forbes was incensed. He failed to understand three things. First, as the season progressed, the Indians lost more of their hunting time. Second, as they performed dangerous—and fruitful—scouting missions, they expected compensation. Third, they had lost relatives and townsmen on the Virginia frontier and naturally sought atonement. Oblivious and frustrated by the further departure of Indians at a critical juncture, Forbes dubbed the Cherokee "as great a Rascal to the full as any of his companions."[70] Attakullakulla later recalled that he "was prevailed on to go out to Warr & accordingly proceeded" forty more miles to Loyalhanna (later Fort Ligonier), just fifty miles from Fort Duquesne. There Bouquet and two thousand troops manned the expedition's most advanced post. "I took one Scalp, & should have been longer out had not my Young Men deserted me," Attakullakulla said. When Forbes began his final advance on October 30, he had "not now left with me above fifty" Indians, many of them Catawbas.[71]

Forbes knew the importance of Indians to his campaign and was determined to keep what few of them remained. With anti-British fervor rising in the Cherokee villages to the south, Lyttelton and Fauquier wanted Attakullakulla to visit Williamsburg to broker an end to the crisis. Attakullakulla wished "to return to my own Nation, on account of some disturbances there." Without telling Forbes, the Cherokee gathered an escort of nine men and set out for the Overhill villages. To Forbes's benefit, Attakullakulla first met with Iroquois warriors and urged them not to help the French. He had conducted a valuable service, part of what Paul Kelton describes as a "complicated and largely hidden diplomacy." But as Forbes saw it, a high-ranking officer had absented himself without leave.[72] "To prevent him from harming any of the settlers," on November 19, Forbes unnecessarily dispatched

Pennsylvania troops to disarm the Indians. Attakullakulla and his followers were humiliated, though treated delicately. The demoralized Cherokee did not blame Forbes. He said he "blame[d] no person but Mr. Glen" for putting Forbes up to it.[73]

Governor Lyttelton still held out hope for a British-provincial invasion against French Louisiana, governed by Louis Billouart, Chevalier de Kerlérec. As Admiral Edward Boscawen wrote, Kerlérec "has not received a Letter or Order from the ministry for 3 years past, nor even a Recruit. It is astonishing," he continued, "how much that Colony is neglected, of which he complains in the strongest Terms." Unfortunately, few French letters made it to Paris, and fewer survive today, giving a fuzzy and at times misleading view of Governor Kerlérec and other officials' activities.[74]

As Cherokee-British relations unraveled in September, the Indian superintendent, Edmond Atkin, had slowly wandered southward to Charles Town from a gout-induced convalescence on the North Carolina coast. In October he headed west to begin a mission to the Creek Indians. Atkin sought to ensure Creek loyalty by better regulating the Creek deerskin trade. He also wished to lay the groundwork for Creek cooperation in the proposed invasion of Louisiana.

Atkin arrived in Augusta on October 24. Few had confidence in his abilities. Georgia governor Henry Ellis found him arrogant and incompetent.[75] Charles Town elites also expressed skepticism. Dr. Alexander Garden wondered "how far the design and import" of His Majesty's "appointment will be answered, by a man whose sole business is to cook good dinners for himself in Charlestown." Garden predicted "the defection of some or other of these nations." Atkin's activities among the Indians of the Southeast and the fate of Lyttelton's grandiose Louisiana expedition deeply and immediately affected any decisions that Cherokees would make. But as 1758 came to a close, Atkin remained in Augusta.[76]

Back in Charles Town, twenty-three Cherokees from the Valley and Lower Towns arrived on November 8. They met on November 14 and 15 with the governor. Lyttelton read his September 26 letter aloud and warned them again not to seek retribution. The visitors assured the governor that runners had recalled the warriors that had set out on the vengeful path. Among the Indians in the delegation were Conjurer Jamie and Tistoe (sometimes spelled Tiftoe) of Keowee. Jamie had lost two cousins and Tistoe had lost his nephew in the frontier violence. But in a traditional sign of peace and friendship, Tistoe presented a string of white wampum to the governor. Challenging Attakullakulla's authority, Tistoe claimed that he too had journeyed to England in 1730. Tistoe offered to spread a message of peace upon his return. Lyttelton pledged to send goods and ammunition to their villages. It was not clear that the peace would last or that the Cherokee visitors spoke for all the villages.[77]

On November 25, Forbes's army entered the abandoned and charred ruins of Fort Duquesne. The British had captured the fort at last. They avenged the disastrous British loss at Braddock's Field, where an attempt on Duquesne had failed three years earlier. But the 1758 Fort Duquesne campaign had shattered the Anglo-Cherokee military alliance. Over a three-year period, one thousand Cherokees had served as British military allies. Some had traveled nearly three thousand miles and had provided valuable assistance. Yet thirty-seven warriors had died—not fighting their Indian enemies but at the hands of those who they thought were their allies: the Virginia frontiersmen. Maligned, misunderstood, and murdered, despite their military and diplomatic contributions, the Cherokees were more disaffected than ever.

TILL SATISFACTION SHOU'D BE GIVEN

The Crises of 1759 and the Lyttelton Expedition

After provincial troops had detained his party at Winchester for a few weeks, Attakullakulla and a few dozen supporters visited Williamsburg in late January and early February 1759. Attakullakulla hoped to secure the elusive trade alliance with Virginia, swinging the pendulum of power among the Overhills his way. But when he returned to Fort Prince George on March 14, he carried only Lieutenant Governor Francis Fauquier's promise that Virginia would send trade goods in the spring. Worse, a mob of white frontiersmen in North Carolina "insulted and persued" his entourage on the way home. "I suppose by the number they intended to kill some of us," he concluded. On March 15, representatives from the Valley, Middle, and Lower Towns gathered in Keowee, where Attakullakulla delivered a speech. According to Fort Prince George commander Ensign Lachlan McIntosh, he informed them "that they were to Blam and not the White People." Announcing that he had "made up all Differences" in Virginia, he promised death to any who should do "Mischief to the White People."[1]

British officials liked to view the pliable Attakullakulla as a political figure with great influence over other Cherokees. In general, Indian governance was decentralized. Coercive power was weak. As the Fort Loudoun engineer William De Brahm explained, they did not "pay any Obedience unto their head-Men, unless when they go out upon a warlike Expedition." Attakullakulla hoped to improve the trade or to negotiate an effective peace. If he did so, he thought he could win his people's respect, and perhaps increase his influence. By 1759, however, most Cherokees rejected Attakullakulla's diplomacy. The ineffectual headman could not assuage Cherokee dissatisfaction; many Cherokees disagreed with his conciliatory approach.[2]

When he then rushed off to Charles Town, pent-up frustration exploded. Cherokees launched small-scale operations and threats out of cultural necessity. They also pressured the British to mend the Anglo-Cherokee relationship. But British officials did not take into account Cherokee culture and circumstances. As James Adair, the eighteenth-century deerskin trader and ethnographer put it, "Tyrants are obstinately deaf, and blind." And, he continued, they "instead of redressing the grievances of the people, have sometimes openly despised and insulted them," for modestly seeking "a restoration of their rights and privileges." Thus, the crisis escalated between South Carolina and the Indians, and tensions rose within South Carolina as a result.[3]

Cherokees remained mindful of their obligation to avenge the "crying blood" of the kin killed or captivated. The winter hunting season had put war on hold. And some clan mothers had accepted blood gifts. But "kindred duty" of retaliation could be ignored no longer.[4]

Most young men anticipated, if not embraced, the call to war. Men saw war as a matter of duty and honor. War also offered the opportunity to win status and respect. As William Fyffe, a doctor and planter from Georgetown, South Carolina, put it, "their greatest Ambition is to distinguish themselves by military Actions." Indeed, "it is by scalps they get all their war-titles," Adair explained. According to William De Brahm, Cherokee warriors earned titles like Raven and Mankiller, and displayed their status through tattoos. War had a similar function for women. Women occasionally accompanied men into war. Usually they carried water and prepared food. Sometimes they helped load weapons in battle. But some women also saw combat. Nanyehi—later known as Nancy Ward—Attakullakulla's niece, replaced her husband when he was killed in a battle with the Creek Indians in 1755. Cherokee women, like men, gained social and political status through war.[5]

But this is only part of the story. The Cherokees had other reasons to act. Land encroachment was one of them. From December 1758 to February 1759, villagers urged visiting missionary William Richardson to consider their plight. "The English have encroached very much upon them of late," Richardson observed. In direct violation of the 1746 Cherokee–South Carolina conveyance, the interlopers threatened Cherokee survival, poaching deer thirty or forty miles west of South Carolina's Long Cane Creek. "We steal their Land, their Bear, Elk, Dear, Beaver," the evangelist concluded. The preacher failed to impress the Indians with his teachings, but he pitied the "great Injustice" they daily faced. Richardson wished that "the government would take it into their Consideration & remedy this Evil, & make these People remove as I am afraid it will occasion a War." His analysis was prophetic. Though his journal reached Williamsburg, Lieutenant Governor Fauquier never took action. Even the *South Carolina Gazette* criticized the "great Number of lawless Vagabonds" who had "obtruded themselves" upon the Cherokees, but its report inspired no governmental action.[6]

Unresolved complaints about the deerskin trade constituted another major source of Cherokee bitterness. Trade goods remained scarce and trader fraud ran rampant. On March 5, Keowees urged Lyttelton to recall John Elliott, who, they noted, "not only steals our Horses and Bells, but also our Skins by his false Stilyards [scales]." The ongoing skirmishes in Virginia had taken Cherokee hunters away from the Southeast. As a result, Cherokees had no skins to trade. Their clothes were in tatters and they fell further into poverty and indebtedness.[7]

In the face of such complaints, traffic in one item still boomed. Opportunistic, unlicensed traders from Georgia, Virginia, and South Carolina peddled rum to the Indians. In the winter of 1758–59, the Lower Towns drank "upwards of Twenty Caggs" of it, James Beamer complained. One trader was an African American pioneer, John Chavis. The colonial governments failed to stop the illicit trade. Once consumed, rum often led to violence spurred by frustration or bravado. "It is a Pity there is not a stop put to the carrying so much Rum among them who when sober in general behave well," Richardson noted.[8]

George Milligen, a surgeon in the Independent Companies, summed up the situation. He called the traders "a Shame to Humanity, and the Disgrace of Christianity; by their iniquitous and foolish Conduct." They turned Indian respect for the English "into a general Contempt and Dislike." Cheated, disrespected, and "corrupted" by the English, "*French* Emissaries among them . . . took much Pains, with Success enough, to alienate their Affections from the *English*."[9] Though some traders had cultivated the alliance, married into Cherokee clans, and enjoyed a reputation as fair and friendly, the ongoing level of dishonesty and fraud was alarming.

French and Creek agents indeed emboldened disgruntled Cherokees. Connecorte held "private Correspondence with the French," Captain Demere noted. White traders among the Creeks reported that a French boat traveled from Mobile to Fort Toulouse, laden with brandy and ammunition. In late March, the Mortar—war chief of the Upper Creek town of Oakchoy—traveled through the Overhill Towns. He established three Creek settlements along the southeastern Cherokee frontier. These villages served as bases for French, Creek, and Cherokee diplomacy. Demere sent men to investigate. Would the Mortar and others drive a wedge deeper between the Cherokees and the English?[10]

In early April, as reports of Cherokee unrest reached Charles Town, Attakullakulla brought fifty men, women, and children to meet with the governor and council. A series of three conferences, spread over two weeks, took place. In the first meeting, Attakullakulla defended his actions in the Forbes campaign. In the second conference, he vowed to keep French agents out of Cherokee towns and pledged to restrain the warriors "of my Nation." Though he lacked the authority to do so, he reportedly offered the English the right to "plant Corn any where in the Nation they please." Lyttelton responded approvingly.[11] The governor sent Attakullakulla home with a string of wampum and a paltry amount of trade goods. To impress the governor and secure the trade goods Cherokees wanted, Attakullakulla would have to produce results. The *Gazette* said that Attakullakulla left on April 28, "thoroughly satisfied."[12] Whether or not this was true, many other Cherokees were far from content.

On April 25 and 26, while Attakullakulla was in Charles Town, three war parties set out from the Overhill Town of Settico. They marched to the sparsely settled North Carolina Piedmont. They struck unsuspecting homesteads between the Yadkin and Catawba Rivers. The Setticos "put all our Frontiers in sad Confusion," wrote Colonel Nathaniel Alexander of the North Carolina Rangers. Letters and newspapers reported nineteen killed. White inhabitants fled their farms. Some retreated into private forts. Another 120 took refuge in the Moravian villages of Bethabara and Bethania. "There is great fear all through the land," reads the "Bethabara Diary" for 1759.[13]

North Carolina had given the Cherokees no cause for concern. In fact, North Carolina Moravians had hosted warriors traveling to and from Virginia the previous year. Many of the Cherokee deaths in Virginia had come at the hands of German Virginians. Perhaps Cherokees associated all Germans as one clan. Regardless, the Setticos took justice into their own hands—and Governor Lyttelton intervened. In a speech to the South Carolina Council, he reasoned that the Cherokees were "more immediately connected and dependent upon this government." The killings were the act of a few, but Lyttelton held all Cherokees responsible and demanded "satisfaction." He demanded that Cherokees hand over those responsible for the "murders," in equal proportion to the white settlers killed. To the Cherokees, "murderers" were family members fighting for the honor, and the soul, of the fallen. But Lyttelton and colonial officials saw any Indian act of violence as a declaration of war. The governor demanded a "national" response by Cherokees who made their decisions on a clan, village, or family-by-family level. And he did not address other Cherokee grievances that, for some Indians, further justified the killings. The governor escalated the conflict before the Cherokees had fully avenged their dead.[14]

Lyttelton also alerted his Native American allies: the Catawbas, led by King Hagler, and Pyamingo's Savannah River Chickasaws. Now Cherokees faced enemy attacks.[15] Cherokee leaders in the Middle, Out, and some of the Lower Towns disavowed the actions of the incensed Cherokee minority. All thirteen Middle and Out Town chiefs, to show their loyalty, placed their hands on a medallion, and then sent it to the governor as a token that "the Chain [of Friendship] always as usual be kept clear and bright as the day."[16] But other towns were not so complacent. Overhill runners journeyed northward and to the French, inviting interested parties to a conference at Tanasee. The question at hand was whether to kill more white people.[17]

When Attakullakulla returned from Charles Town in late May, debate continued among the Overhills. Delivering the accused "murderers" was problematic. Not only would it undermine the avengers' intent—to honor their obligation to the Cherokee dead—but if they acquiesced now, Lyttelton would surely not address Cherokee concerns more generally. Settico's young warriors had experienced the worst of the violence in western Virginia in 1758. It would be difficult to restrain them. Such a scenario was unacceptable to South Carolina. Attakullakulla somehow collected eight of the scalps the Setticos had taken, advancing gifts to the families who had requested the scalps in the first place. The soldiers at Fort Loudoun buried them inside the fort.[18]

Many Cherokees embraced the French and the Creeks. Lieutenant Richard Coytmore (who in April, 1759 had replaced Ensign McIntosh as commander of Fort Prince George) and Fort Loudoun's Captain Paul Demere urged warriors to attack the fledgling Creek villages "to nip them in the bud." But to do so would risk starting a war with other Creek towns, and it would endanger the safety of Cherokee emissaries among the Creeks.[19] By now, Demere's spies had returned from their investigations. They saw five French boats, "loaded" with guns, ammunition, and rum, at the Creek settlement on the Coosa River. Attakullakulla offered to lead an expedition to remove the settlement. But he gained few supporters. In fact, the Slave-Catcher of Chota instead led a massive delegation of Cherokee men and women to Oakchoy and then to Fort Toulouse to meet with Creek and French representatives. The French did not expect a supply of trade goods for four months. A larger joint Cherokee-Creek-French campaign was on hold.[20]

As tensions with the Cherokees heightened, a millenarian preacher predicting the end of the world took to the streets of Charles Town. For the colony's enslaved black majority, the combined crises were an opportunity in the making. For African Americans, with militiamen drawn off to face outside enemies, and with Spanish governors offering freedom in St. Augustine, wartime was the best time to seek a change in relationships with Anglo-Americans.

The Cherokees were one catalyst of hope for African Americans. Richard Clarke, the highly esteemed rector of Charles Town's St. Philip's Church, was another. Clarke wielded considerable influence on black and white South Carolinians alike. As one Anglican missionary put it, "His abilities as a Divine were so great, and his piety so strict, that he gained over many" converts. He directed the school for black children at St. Philip's, and seventy new pupils enrolled under his watch.[21]

Clarke was influenced by a millenarian tract that he had read a few years earlier. The tense situation with the Cherokee Indians and the worldwide dimensions of the Seven Years' War inspired him to act. "The Clergyman of much Learning but of an overheated imagination" delivered some controversial sermons in February 1759, just as reports of Cherokee hostility reached Charles Town. Clarke "asserted that the World wou'd very soon be at an end." And, Governor Lyttelton continued in his letter to the Board of Trade, the rector predicted that in September "some great calamity wou'd befall this province." Clarke's "Enthusiasm" soon "rose to such a height" that, in the likeness of John the Baptist, "he let his beard grow and ran about the streets crying, Repent, Repent for the Kingdom of Heaven is at hand."[22] In early March, Clarke published a wildly popular book in which he calculated and predicted the end of the age. Then, according to plan, he resigned his benefice and sailed for England.[23]

The minister "made an impression upon some weak minds," wrote Lyttelton, unwilling to fathom what followed. Not long after Clarke's departure, a free man of mixed-race descent from St. Helena Parish named Philip John (also spelled Johns and Jones) reported a vision of his own. In September, the same month mentioned by Richard Clarke, "the white People shou'd be all underground, that the Sword shou'd go thro' the Land, and it should shine with their blood, that there should be no more white King's Governors or great men, but the negro's should live happily & have Laws of their own." In April,

John gave a "secret paper" to two slaves, Tom and Trane, and asked them to "carry it to all the Negroes." Tom and Trane reported John to the authorities. He was tried, whipped, and branded "for endeavouring to stir up Sedition among the Negroes" of St. Helena Parish.[24]

John was not done. The prophet retreated into the woods for a week. When he returned he told his wife that he had experienced visions. He traveled and recruited "among all the Slaves wherever he came." Soon, "a spirit of Cabal" allegedly "began to shew itself among them," Lyttelton wrote. The ferment was strongest in Prince William Parish, a predominantly black district in southern South Carolina. On June 17, 1759, "officers of the publick Justice" interrupted church service at Stoney Creek, a Reformed Presbyterian congregation twenty miles northwest of coastal Beaufort. They "siezed and carried of[f]," Pastor Archibald Simpson reported, "a Negro . . . on suspicion of his being concerned in some evel designs."[25] According to local leaders Thomas Drayton and Stephen Bull (the nephew of Councilman William Bull II), Philip John had been plotting his conspiracy. John Pendarvis, a wealthy free man of mixed-race descent, provided £700 in South Carolina currency and purchased weapons. Caesar, an enslaved black carpenter, planned the uprising. According to John, "the Indians were then to be sent to and they would come and assist in killing the Buckraas [white men]." With vastly different hopes and aspirations, white and black residents all wondered the same thing: had Philip John met with any Indians?[26]

Cherokee unrest had encouraged slaves to plot a revolt. The tips from Drayton and Bull spread fear in Charles Town and spurred officials to action. On June 20, Chief Justice Peter Leigh signed warrants for the arrest of Philip John, John Pendarvis, Caesar, and several co-conspirators for "promoting and encouraging an insurrection of the Negroes against the white people." Lyttelton alerted the militia colonels in the lowcountry and ordered them to "cause the Laws to be attended to and pointedly executed in their several Districts." Caesar was soon apprehended. Stephen Bull sent the prisoner and three witnesses—one of them the congregant in Simpson's church—to Charles Town.[27]

In July, Philip John and John Pendarvis were captured. Throughout July and August, Lyttelton interrogated blacks detained "some Time in our Jail for seditious Practices," the *South Carolina Gazette* reported. The governor uncovered "their Scheme." In a plot that bore a striking resemblance to the Stono Rebellion exactly twenty years earlier, they planned to seize "some Arms & Ammunition" from a storehouse in the country. But this time, "with what force they could collect," the co-conspirators planned to march on

Charles Town. With many white residents gone to their summer homes, the rebel army could gain new recruits and wreak havoc in the city. Lyttelton, who tried to project an air of calm, dubbed the plot a "crude, ill-digested project." But a report in the *Gazette* pointed to something more substantial. John and the others had "widely communicated" their conspiracy to "the most sensible Fellows throughout the Province, and even in *Charles-Town*." According to the paper, the frightening plot extended still further. John told many "that the *Indians* were to be concerned in the extirpation of the white People from the Face of this Earth." The possibility of an interracial alliance horrified South Carolina elites.[28]

Philip John and John Pendarvis stood trial in Prince William Parish for "seditious and treasonable Practices." The governor dismissed the others who testified against the leading conspirators. On the day of the trial, Pendarvis escaped from custody and was never heard from again. The court sentenced Philip John to death, and he met the hangman's noose two days later. The plot fueled lingering "suspicions and apprehensions" among whites, especially south of Charles Town. Sheer numbers made slave insurgency a possibility at any time, but several factors converged in 1759 to heighten white anxieties. A severe drought and a decline in the rice and indigo harvests meant that black Carolinians had more mobility and free time than in typical seasons. War with France—and the French privateers along the Carolina coast—gave slaves a viable if distant ally. And an incipient war with the Cherokees gave them an ally closer to home. Similar dynamics shaped the calculations of South Carolina's ruling class for weeks, months, and even years to come.[29]

For white elites, the Philip John revelations seemed terrifying. Until the Indians were pacified, people like Clarke could stir up chaos, making blacks more likely to capitalize on white distraction and revolt. As slave unrest heightened, Cherokee warriors also made their move, killing eight white settlers in June and July. In mid-June, a small war party that included Youctanah of Estatoe took three scalps on South Carolina's Pacolet River.[30] Lower Townsmen reportedly killed two more men on the Broad River on June 22. Before the end of the month, Cherokees killed two and captured two on the North Carolina frontier. Governor Arthur Dobbs sent 140 provincials to reinforce Fort Dobbs.[31] Cherokee violence reached the Virginia frontier, where Overhills killed and scalped a man in early July.[32]

The Setticos made a half-hearted effort to mollify the British by turning over the other eleven scalps their warriors had taken. But neither they nor any other Cherokees intended to fulfill Lyttelton's demand for satisfaction.

Rather than work to mend the broken relationship between Cherokees and colony, Lyttelton exacerbated Anglo-Cherokee tensions. He imposed economic sanctions by removing and transferring Settico's trader on July 12. The next day the assembly funded two troops of rangers to patrol the frontier.[33]

On July 21, Attakullakulla traveled by canoe to the Illinois Country with a small group of family members. He intended to collect French scalps and placate the British. Attakullakulla's trip—which took three months—proved unsuccessful. He took two French prisoners and four scalps in a raid on Fort Massiac, but he lost two dead and one wounded in the process. This poor showing further discredited him among his own people, who now feared that the raid might spur revenge attacks.[34]

By early August, four war parties from the Lower Towns were out on the South Carolina frontier. They returned on August 12 to Fort Prince George with the scalps of a white woman and child from the Enoree or Broad River in South Carolina. This was different than the targeting of Germans in North Carolina and Virginia. They informed Coytmore, "It is now War with the white People who they can kill like Fowls." At Fort Prince George, Lower Townsmen accosted soldiers, "taring their cloaths and shaking Hatchets over their Heads," Coytmore reported. The Slave-Catcher of Chota once again journeyed to Oakchoy and Fort Toulouse, returning with inflammatory letters from French officers. Coytmore had not "the Least hopes of a change of affairs in these Parts." The Cherokees had now killed thirty-three whites since the previous fall. It was still fewer than they had lost in Virginia. Coytmore invoked some instructions the governor had sent him in May. On August 14, he stopped the guns and ammunition headed to the Cherokee villages. This proved to be a critical mistake.[35]

Coytmore's embargo put the Cherokees "in an uproar," Captain Demere reported. They believed that the English "wanted to Starve them." As Oconostota explained, his people had missed the last year's hunts because of the Forbes campaign. They needed clothes, and they needed food. The Green Corn Dance ended in late August, two weeks after Coytmore halted the munitions supply. Then hunting season began. Without powder, shot, and working weapons, the onset of winter looked grim. In the current environment some Cherokees expected to continue normal trading relations even though other Cherokees were raiding the frontier. From a European perspective, Coytmore's move made perfect sense: British military and political brass thought that the embargo would cause all Cherokees to fall into line with British expectations. It was a bold move by an inexperienced commander.[36]

Meanwhile, Wawhatchee journeyed from the Lower Towns to Georgia's Broad River on his own initiative. At John Vann's trading post, he dictated a letter to Georgia's governor, Henry Ellis. The letter protested that "the People of South Carolina have made Encroachments upon their Lands & have Settled so near to their Nation That it of Course makes Deer scarce, so that they are not able to Support their Wives & Children with Meat & Cloaths." This, Wawhatchee claimed, "is the great Grievance they have to complain of." He begged Ellis to remove the encroaching settlers. The warrior requested a meeting with Georgia's governor, vowing that the Cherokees' greatest desire was "to preserve Peace."[37] Many Cherokees anticipated Ellis's involvement as a path to peace. Indian diplomacy often used neutral third parties. The British generally did not. Ellis offered to mediate, but Lyttelton forbade him from doing so.[38]

Unaware of Coytmore or Wawhatchee's adventures, on August 15, 1759, Lyttelton detached eighty-eight South Carolina Provincials under Captain John Stuart to reinforce Fort Loudoun, raising the number of soldiers there to nearly two hundred. Their arrival put the Cherokees into a heightened state of alarm. Not only were more troops marching; many had new red uniforms, reminiscent of the formidable Virginia Regiment.[39]

The arrival of Stuart's detachment struck many Cherokees as a clear sign of British aggression. As Coytmore put it, Cherokee hunters threatened that "if they did not get ammunition, they had nothing to do but kill the white People here, & carry their Scalps to the French," who would provide for them. Yet he and Demere dug in their heels. They refused to release the ammunition until Cherokees provided satisfaction. Cherokees refused to deliver those who had fulfilled Cherokee blood law. And no coercive power existed to force clans to deliver the purported "murderers." A stalemate ensued. Coytmore exaggerated matters in his reports. Demere determined never to write a good word about an Indian "till satisfaction shou'd be given."[40]

The Cherokees brought their own pressures to bear on British officials, and news of Cherokee activities worked the *South Carolina Gazette* into a frenzied state. Warriors took six scalps on the Broad and Saluda Rivers. Militiamen responded in kind, killing two Cherokees and wounding two more.[41] The agitation was at its highest in the Lower and Overhill Towns. Desperate for ammunition, a Lower Townsman fired at a trader near Fort Prince George on August 30. A few days later in the Overhills, Setticos killed a packhorseman who was escorting a supply convoy to Fort Loudoun.[42]

Ostenaco had traveled three thousand miles in service to the Anglo-Cherokee alliance. Now recovered from shooting himself through the foot in a hunting accident, he led Cherokee opposition in the Overhills. Warriors "block'd up" the roads and vowed to kill white travelers on sight. Opportunistic Cherokees struck soldiers and traders. On September 7, four Setticos killed soldier Samuel Simmons when he ventured out of Fort Loudoun to gather grapes. Not coincidentally, warriors targeted the men who would call in Cherokee debts at a time when Cherokees could not repay them, and who had clothes, arms, and ammunition. On September 12, a Chilhowee killed that town's trader. Nottely Cherokees blockaded the road leading to their town in the Valley and fired on traders and packhorsemen headed to resupply Fort Loudoun. The garrison slaughtered and salted livestock "as fast as we can," storing up food for an expected siege.[43]

Meanwhile, trade goods from Virginia were finally on the move. Lyttelton, however, would have none of it. Anxious to keep his embargo in place, he asked Virginia lieutenant governor Francis Fauquier to halt the shipment. Fauquier complied. The supply train stood still at Salisbury, North Carolina, on orders to remain there until the Cherokees acquiesced to South Carolina's demands.[44]

Traders abandoned their possessions and their wares to Cherokee freebooters and streamed into Fort Prince George. By the time Stuart's detachment reached the fort on September 22, he had lost a fourth of his men to desertion and was forced to await reinforcements.[45] Cherokees welcomed Creek envoys in the Lower Towns on September 24, but records do not reveal what transpired. Facing hunger, exposure, and debt, the next day, Ostenaco, Oconostota, and eighteen Indians went to Fort Prince George to demand the ammunition. Coytmore and Stuart refused to release it. "Affairs here are blacker than my Pen is able to paint them," the panicked commander wrote.[46]

Despite the recent presumed slave conspiracy, Lyttelton moved swiftly in sending troops and resources to the frontier. Back in Charles Town, on October 1, the governor and the council ordered the commanders of the three backcountry militia regiments to fire the alarm, assemble their men, and draft half of them into temporary service. Lyttelton also placed nearly all of the troops in Charles Town on standby. He secured the aid of the Savannah River Chickasaws and Catawbas. He informed British officials of his preparations. And he convened the Commons House to fund a military campaign.[47] Without meeting with Cherokee delegates or consulting other British officials, he had determined to go to war.

Most Cherokees wished to avoid full-fledged armed conflict. Four Overhill villages decided against war. They sent the Prince of Tanasee to Fort Loudoun with strings of wampum. But they still would not hand over the men

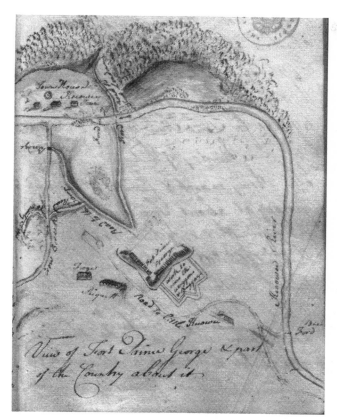

IMAGE 4.1

"View of Fort Prince George [in 1761] & part of the Country about it." From the Journal of Captain Christopher French, page 95. Library of Congress, Washington, D.C. Manuscripts Division, MMC-1869.

who had killed white settlers according to Cherokee blood law. Captain Demere refused to accept the gesture.[48] Negotiations got nowhere. Two separate parties, one under Oconostota and Ostenaco, and the other under the Round O of Stecoe, failed to convince Stuart and Coytmore to release the ammunition. On October 2, Oconostota and Ostenaco led fifty-five Lower, Valley, and Overhill Towns Cherokees to Charles Town to ask the governor in person. Three days later, The Round O led more than forty Middle and Out Towns men, women, and children. The presence of women and children indicated their peaceful intentions. And, Captain Stuart noted, they were "not concerned in the Dissorders committed." Ostenaco apparently had second thoughts. Along the way, he turned back and returned home.[49]

The South Carolina militia draft took place on October 12, while the Cherokee diplomats were still en route. Pastor Archibald Simpson described the day's events from Prince William Parish: "Early this Morning an Alarm was fired by the discharge of three muskets at every dwelling place in this

Province." Men grabbed their firearms and rushed to designated muster grounds. There, Simpson added, "the one half were draughted and ordered to be in readiness at an hours warning to march against the Indians." The draft and the impending war confirmed the millenarian spirit of the times. "We seem a people ripe for Judgement," Simpson added.[50]

Many in the Commons House opposed the impending war. Speaker Benjamin Smith reported, "Some think there was no necessity for the Expedition." Lyttelton might have kept the embargo in place "till ample Satisfaction was made." Christopher Gadsden predicted war would "be attended with the greatest Evils and Calamities, and be productive of the most dangerous and even fatal Consequences." The Commons House did not fund all of Lyttelton's requests. It provided pay for the troops only until January 1. With provincial taxes skyrocketing, they prohibited the governor from leaving the colony's borders. Lyttelton responded by praising his supporters for their "Love of Country." The action foreshadowed similar disputes in the years to come. Many in the assembly doubted that a Crown-appointed governor and council had their best interests at heart. Lyttelton drafted two versions of a declaration of war, but, for fear of further alienating the legislators, chose not to read either version.[51] Lyttelton secured £45,000 South Carolina currency in loans from private firms and individuals—many of whom had a vested interest in supplying a costly campaign and who would profit from the restoration of the deerskin trade that would ostensibly follow.[52]

Since early July, southern Indian superintendent Edmond Atkin had been touring the Creek villages. As the tribes came to realize that the French had few trade goods, weapons, and ammunition, Atkin resolved disputes and reformed the Anglo-Creek deerskin trade. But his progress soon slowed. Then, on September 28, an unexpected event sealed the success of his mission. As he spoke to 150 influential headmen from all the Creek towns, Atkin said, a Cussitah warrior called the Tobacco-Eater crept up from behind, "with a Pipe Hatchet fell on me & by repeated Blows brought me to the Ground." The dazed Atkin staggered, bleeding "immensely" from the head and shoulder. His secretary, stepping in to help, sustained severe wounds. Atkin shouted to the white men to take up arms. Traders and Indians scattered, while "*Molton*, a Half-Breed," and other Indians seized the Tobacco-Eater. If this was to be the "first blow" disaffected Cherokees were waiting for, they were sorely disappointed.[53]

Unfortunately for the Cherokees, British authorities proved responsive to Creek concerns. On October 10, a large delegation of Lower Creeks visited Governor Ellis and the council in Savannah. They too disliked Atkin's threats and his "very uncommon and provoking language" but insisted that the assault on Atkin was a scripted event. White frontiersmen had settled their hunting grounds and "wander[ed] all over the Woods destroying . . . Game." Ellis and the Lower Creeks struck a deal. The Indians agreed to deter the Cherokees from attacking Georgia and to stay out of Georgia and South Carolina. Ellis then ordered settlers "illegally occupying Indian hunting grounds to remove from those lands by January 1. He concluded that the Creeks would not fight against the English, even if the Cherokees did.[54] A general Indian war looked doubtful.

After the hatchet attack, Atkin and the Creeks also signed a treaty. The document opened the Choctaw trade and smoothed out disagreements in British-Creek trade on terms favorable to the Creeks. The Choctaws ratified their own treaty, in the Creek village of Waulyhatchy, on November 10. Goods flowed freely to both peoples. For the time being, Atkin and Ellis had neutralized the Creek and Choctaw "threat" to the British. With trade goods at their disposal, and with a responsive Georgia governor at the helm, the Creeks and Choctaws had less incentive to join the Cherokees.[55]

On October 19, fifty-five Cherokees crowded into the council chamber along with Governor Lyttelton and several of his advisors. "I am a Warriour but want no War with the English," Oconostota said. He sought peace and the restoration of trade and the embargoed ammunition. The "Great Warrior" laid a pile of deerskins at the governor's feet as a sign of magnanimity and friendship. The Cherokees felt insulted when Lyttelton refused to take the skins.[56]

Then, several other Indians explained Cherokee discontent. Tistoe mentioned fraud and the dearth of supplies in the deerskin trade. "They have used us Ill and the Officer says he is not afraid of us," he said. Ill treatment drove the Keowees "to do what they have done." Tistoe turned to another major Cherokee concern: soldiers were raping Cherokee women. Lieutenant Coytmore "gets Drunk, he goes to our Houses, and draws our Women from us . . . and has to do with our Women at his own Pleasure." James Adair, a deerskin trader among the Creeks, was well acquainted with events in the Southeast. He wrote that "three light-headed, disorderly young officers of that garrison"— identified by Indians as Coytmore, Ensign Alexander Miln of the Independent Companies, and the Provincials' Ensign John Bell—had "forcibly violated some of their wives" lately, "while their husbands were making their winter hunt . . . and which infamous conduct they madly repeated." Adair continued: "No wonder that such a behaviour, caused their revengeful tempers to burst forth into action." The problem was not new. Agent Daniel Pepper had alerted the governor in 1757 to widespread reports that soldiers took Cherokee women "in the Fort before their Husbands' Faces and used" them.[57]

In Cherokee culture, women were respected as social and political equals. Women chose their husbands and sexual partners. Some women went to war. British officials excluded women from their military and diplomatic councils and often from their records. Attakullakulla once wondered aloud to Governor Lyttelton why the white people did not include women in politics. Was that not "the Custom of the White People also," he wondered. "White men as well as red were born of Women," he said. Lyttelton responded that white men "do place a Confidence in their Women and share their Counsels with them," but only "when they know their Hearts to be Good." British officers and politicians viewed women as objects, as passive observers, as unreliable snitches whose loyalty could be purchased for a trifle. Their marginalization and mistreatment posed challenges for them and their husbands. But neither male nor female Cherokees accepted white expectations.[58]

One by one, a series of Cherokees spoke after Tistoe. Each expressed peace and goodwill. For the diplomats, the violence reflected blood revenge but also came in response to multiple snubs and longstanding mistreatment. Despite their complaints, the visitors sought a cessation of hostilities and the restoration of the trade. As one Cherokee had said a year earlier, "they Cant Doe as they used to doe formerly in old Times for they have Bin soe long used to the White people that we should all Dye without them." Creek and French aid looked doubtful, and few wished to invite a war from the west. Short on guns and ammunition, Cherokees needed to hunt, and the Virginia trade goods alone would alleviate much of their want. The Head Warrior of Estatoe and the Valley headman Killianaca, the Black Dog of Hiwassee, invoked the Chain of Friendship and hoped trade and business would resume as usual. Killianaca promised, "None of my boys [have] hurt a white man." When asked by the governor, the other Cherokees present responded, "We all agree."[59]

It made no difference. The South Carolina Council met twice to review accounts of Cherokee violence. After conferring at length, the eight men divided equally. Four voted to conduct the expedition "as proposed." The four others voted "for keeping a certain number of Indians now in Town as Hostages till the Cherokee Nation should make the satisfaction to be demanded."[60] That afternoon, the governor summoned the Cherokees. He harangued them for the violence of the past eleven months. Peace would be restored, and trade goods would flow again, but first he would march to Cherokee country to secure the "murderers." Oconostota attempted to speak, but Lyttelton abruptly terminated the conference. In so doing, he ignored not just the Cherokee but also one of his own: Councilman William Bull II. Bull had extensive experience in Indian diplomacy and was also the commander of the Charles Town Regiment of Horse. He urged Lyttelton to hear Cherokee "Proposals for Satisfaction, which the Indians then in Town were contriving to propose." Lyttelton instead sent the Indians away under an armed guard. The Cherokees would march with the army—as hostages.[61]

The South Carolina governor, in trying to secure the frontier and calm the unrest reverberating through the province, blatantly disregarded Cherokee culture and expectations. As James Adair, the eighteenth-century trader and ethnographer wrote, "he failed, by not knowing aright the temper and customs of the savages."[62] He also mistakenly thought that what Attakullakulla said was, or could be, the general will. Further, the *South Carolina Gazette* distorted the efforts of peace-seeking Cherokees. Only Councilman Bull, it seems, and some of the South Carolina Commons House, had some discernment.[63]

Charles Town's troops, with gentleman volunteers that included future revolutionaries Christopher Gadsden, Francis Marion, and Thomas Lynch, Sr., left the city on October 23 and 26. The Round O of Stecoe and his more than forty peace-seekers arrived from Cherokee country and encountered them at Moncks Corner just outside Charles Town. They offered "to war to the very last, against all the enemies of Carolina. This they told me on the spot," trader James Adair said. Lyttelton brusquely insisted that the delegation accompany his army back to the Cherokee country. They followed the army to the Congarees, where Lyttelton joined militia battalions under Colonel Richard Richardson and Colonel John Chevillette on October 31. Colonel George Gabriel Powell, the disgraced and hot-tempered former governor of St. Helena Island in the South Atlantic, led a third militia battalion, "300 of the sadest Dogs that were ever got together," which soon arrived from northeast. Many of the militiamen were shoeless, unarmed, and poorly disciplined. They deserted in droves to protect their families. There can be no doubt that the Cherokees among Lyttelton's men noticed this.[64]

No sooner had the army left Charles Town than a group of lowcountry slaves took advantage of the military vacuum. Peter Timothy, editor of the *South Carolina Gazette*, reported to the governor on November 3 that "The Militia of St. Andrew's, Stono, and Wadmalaw have been twice out in Quest of a Gang of violent arm'd run-away negroes." They took only two. African American prisoners wounded a sentinel at the Charles Town guardhouse. In the confusion another sentinel was shot. Alexander Garden, an Anglican minister in Christ Church Parish, summed up the situation: the province teetered on the precipice of a dangerous Indian War. Half of the men aged sixteen to sixty were "drawn out to march at an hours Warning . . . Whilst the other half of the militia is employed in Guarding [against] the Insurrections of our numerous Slaves."[65] The Cherokees had reignited internal divisions and created an opportunity for black residents. Lyttelton's outgoing letters during the campaign are missing. Perhaps he urged Timothy not to publish the news of slave unrest.

Several Indians—one from each of the Cherokee settlement clusters—slipped off under the cover of darkness on November 7. The governor placed the rest of the Round O's party under armed guard although he had previously promised not to do so.[66] Lyttelton now held ninety Indians, among them women and children. As historian Alexander Hewatt, a friend of William Bull II, later wrote, "The breach of promise an Indian holds an atrocious crime." This, "they with reason deemed an unpardonable injury." Five more Cherokees escaped and returned home with news of the governor's betrayal. With the assembly disbanded, Lyttelton ordered more militia companies to reinforce Ninety Six. Then he asked the council to amend its minutes to make it look as if they initiated the reinforcements. The council refused.[67] Drawing militiamen from the coastal regions of the province further exposed the white inhabitants to slave unrest.

After ten days the army passed Saluda Old Town, site of the controversial treaty negotiated by Attakullakulla and Governor James Glen in 1755. Men sickened. Others abandoned the service, "10 and 12 at a Time," according to the *South Carolina Gazette*. Settlers, too, fled their homes.[68] The army reached Robert Gouedy's trading post at Ninety Six on November 21. Here, soldiers, local militiamen, volunteers, and slaves toiled for a week. They built a stockade fort around Gouedy's barn. Engineer Richard Dudgeon observed that the fort "has neither the Strength nor advantages Requisite for a Post of Consequence." The Cherokees with Lyttelton knew it. Though no one realized it then, Fort Ninety Six became a strategic outpost on the South Carolina frontier.[69]

Cherokee spies reconnoitered the camp, observing the motions and size of the army. Sickness and desertion continued. Soldiers contracted measles, influenza, and pleurisy. The governor's glorious march to Cherokee country looked more and more like a debacle, yet the Cherokees could not capitalize on it. Lyttelton still had the hostages. And South Carolinian reinforcements arrived—among them Savannah River Chickasaws and more gentleman volunteers.[70] Lyttelton left the sick soldiers at Fort Ninety Six and set out for Fort Prince George on November 29. The terrified hostages looked on as the army practiced deploying into lines of battle on both sides of the

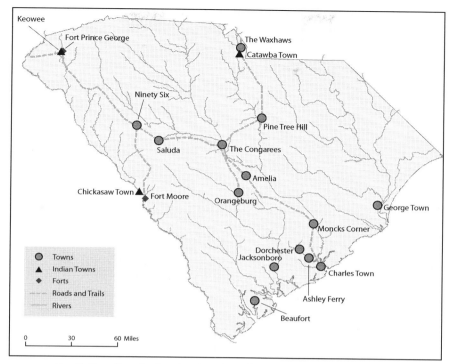

MAP 4.1 *South Carolina during the French and Indian War Era*

rugged, narrow road approaching Twelve-Mile Creek. The Cherokees who had escaped knew the governor's army was poorly trained, poorly armed, and afflicted by disease and desertion. But the Cherokees feared that if they attacked, Lyttelton would kill the hostages. Captain John Grinnan's rangers sounded the alarm. The troops rushed to their posts, but no enemy appeared, and the two-mile-long train continued unopposed.[71]

Two days later, "many" Cherokees gathered on the high hills of Keowee that overlooked Fort Prince George. They watched in dismay as Lyttelton's army approached. The fort and the incoming army saluted each other in a symbolic welcome. "Above 200 Indians," a soldier observed, "appeared on the Hills and gave two running Fires after their Manner." Some soldiers "looked upon [it] as a Salute." But others saw it "as bidding Defiance, and to shew that they had Ammunition to spare." Lyttelton's army camped in the windswept plain below Keowee and outside of the fort. The governor dismissed all but twenty-eight of the hostages, whom he considered headmen of note. Many of these men came from towns that had nothing to do with the revenge killings.

The Crises of 1759 and the Lyttelton Expedition : 77

Indians from four Lower Towns—the only four whose kin had taken white scalps—gathered that afternoon in the Keowee townhouse. Lyttelton met only with the conciliation-minded Second Man of Conasatchee and summoned Attakullakulla from the Overhills.[72]

For all parties, developments were ominous. For the Cherokees, smallpox was rampant in Keowee. Two hundred more militiamen and six Catawba warriors joined the army on December 9. Though Cherokees did not know it, the governor could go no further and his power was slipping. The troops were paid only through the end of the month. Measles was "rife." Fearing smallpox, the Chickasaws fled. A muster on December 12 totaled just 1,105 men fit for duty. The Virginia House of Burgesses refused to send troops. Hugh Waddell's North Carolinians were finally on the march from Fort Dobbs. They numbered just fifty provincials and fifty militiamen and "Every Night Deserted," the frustrated officer reported. They mutinied on the way and never reached Lyttelton's army.[73]

On his way home, Ostenaco escorted Stuart from Hiwassee, and the captain finally reached Fort Loudoun on October 27. In his early life, the red haired Scotsman had been a clerk in Spain. He had circumnavigated the globe in a British naval expedition. And he had been a struggling merchant in Charles Town. In 1756, the socially and politically active Stuart received a captain's commission in the South Carolina Provincials. He helped to construct Fort Loudoun and befriended Attakullakulla. Since then he had overseen construction of a tabby fort, Fort Lyttelton, at Port Royal. Now, Stuart (known by the Cherokees as Oonodutu, or "Bushyhead") returned to the Overhills and would become a major player in an unfolding drama.[74]

When Attakullakulla received the governor's invitation to come treat for peace, the Indian first visited Fort Loudoun. There he met with Captain Stuart. Attakullakulla "shed tears" at the notion of "Delivering up their Countrymen," Stuart wrote. Instead, the Cherokee again proposed joining white soldiers against the French "as the properest way of making up matters." Stuart and the officers declined. Instead, they offered him power and status if he would "heartily fall in" with Lyttelton's demands. If not, he would "Loose the good character he has acquired." This "made a deep impression," Stuart wrote. "I Expect he will heartily fall into any measures your Excellency will propose."[75]

Motivated in part by spite, Attakullakulla proceeded to Fort Prince George with a few loyal supporters from the Overhills. The rivalry between Connecorte and Attakullakulla had reached "an open quarrel," Stuart reported. Connecorte accused his rival "of being an Enemy to his Country and a servil dependent upon the English." He also made light of Attakullakulla's poor showing in his raid on French Fort Massiac. Attakullakulla was "Greatly incens'd," Stuart reported to Lyttelton. Though he might object at first, "The Little man," would "fall in to all your Excellency's measures," the captain wrote. Stuart added that in this "present Emergency," Attakullakulla sought power and influence.[76]

When Attakullakulla arrived at Fort Prince George with a French prisoner on December 19, the governor treated him as the voice not only of the Over-hills but of the entire Cherokee people. The headman was neither. "So small was his influence among the Cherokees at this time," historian Alexander Hewatt noted, "that they considered him as no better than an old woman."[77]

The next day, Attakullakulla, Willenawa of Toqua, and a few other Indians met with the governor. Several hostages joined them. In a show of friendship, Attakullakulla cited the metaphorical "Chain of Friendship" that extended from the king to the Cherokees. He presented a string of white wampum. Ocayulah of Chota did the same. He hoped that "people and goods may pass as before." For most Cherokees and for Indians in general, peace was less a formalized arrangement than a temporary mollification of feelings. Attakullakulla and Ocayulah simply asked the governor to agree to a truce.[78]

The governor responded sternly that "in order to prevent that chain [of friendship] from contracting rust, and at last being broken, certain conditions must be observed." Citing the controversial 1730 "Articles of Friendship and Commerce," he demanded that the Cherokees surrender twenty four "murderers" without delay.[79]

"It would now be difficult" to get them, Oconostota interjected. The Indians conferred privately. The next day, Keowees delivered two of the accused. In exchange, Attakullakulla secured the release of hostages Tistoe and the Warrior of Estatoe. Then, for a few days, he disappeared. If he planned to wait for Lyttelton's army to unravel, claim favorable terms, and return home a hero, things did not work out as he intended.[80]

December 24, 1759, was Lyttelton's thirty-fifth birthday. He was unaware that on November 14, the Board of Trade had appointed him to the governorship of the empire's most profitable colony, Jamaica.[81] His plans for invading France's southeastern possessions had not materialized. His demands for "satisfaction" looked like empty threats. Some saw this campaign as a defining moment for the colony. Though it would have been the right solution, Lyttelton would not relent from his incendiary demands.

The next day, Lyttelton dispatched Coytmore with two traders to confront the headman. They found him camped outside Tamassee, cast off by the

Lower Towns. If Attakullakulla did not settle matters to the governor's satisfaction the next day, Lyttelton vowed to "lay waste" to Estatoe. More Berkeley County militiamen arrived later that day. This, he said, "occasioned a very great consternation among the *Indians*."[82]

The Indians had surrendered just two "murderers." Lyttelton demanded twenty-two more to match the number of white colonists that the Cherokees had allegedly slain since the peace conference in Charles Town in November 1758.[83] Lyttelton's aide drafted a treaty. To save lives, Attakullakulla and Oconoeca signed it. In exchange for freedom to carry on the struggle, the hostages Oconostota, Killianaca, Kettagusta of Chota, and Ottacite also signed. The treaty renewed the 1730 Treaty of Whitehall and stated that "a firm peace and friendship" existed between the Cherokees and the British. Twenty-two hostages remained in British custody, to be replaced by twenty-two "murderers" whom the British would "put to death or otherwise [dispose] of." Only then would Lyttelton restore the trade. Cherokees had to use their "utmost endeavours" to capture or kill Frenchmen among them. The treaty said nothing about white land encroachment. It stipulated no trade regulations. And it addressed none of the sexual assault allegations against the garrison of Fort Prince George.[84]

Two days later, on December 28, the Keowees delivered another accused murderer, Youctanah of Estatoe, a veteran of the Fort Duquesne campaigns. The governor permitted "that such as were afraid of smallpox" could "move away," and seven hundred militiamen left immediately. The rest of Lyttelton's army scurried back to Charles Town with just three Indian prisoners. Charles Town was astir, as a rash of robberies overwhelmed the skeleton crew of militia and regulars remaining there.[85]

Meanwhile, four Cherokee hostages returned home. But twenty-one innocent Cherokee leaders remained in a small, dark hut at Fort Prince George. The *Gazette* predicted "public rejoicings" when the governor returned. After several months of Cherokee raids and Anglo-Cherokee negotiations, which triggered slave unrest, Lyttelton's expedition "has terminated *honourably*," it continued, if not "*happily*, for ourselves; for the neighbouring Provinces, and for Posterity." But the governor had not forced "a very numerous, powerful, treacherous and insolent nation of SAVAGES" to "submit," as the *Gazette* reported. Quite the opposite. Lyttelton had "patch'd up a hasty peace," one South Carolinian later recalled. The Cherokee response in the wake of this unpopular treaty would foster discord and disarray among the South Carolinians he governed.[86]

A SITUATION TOO TERRIBLE FOR US

Smallpox and Social Upheaval

5 On Tuesday, January 8, 1760, Charles Town residents awoke suddenly as three cheers and three volleys of gunfire sounded in the crisp night sky. The noise marked the return of Governor Lyttelton's army from the Cherokee country. Residents poured into the streets to greet the soldiers as the celebration moved on to Governor Lyttelton's mansion. The next day, cannons boomed from the forts and from vessels in Charles Town Harbor, and local troops regaled the governor "with a general Volley." Fireworks, bonfires, "and other Demonstrations of that Satisfaction and Joy" later lit the night sky. All marked the apparent success of the expedition.[1]

Jubilation soon turned to frustration. In the ensuing weeks and months, white Carolinians found little cause to rejoice. Cherokees attacked Fort Prince George and the southern Appalachian frontier. And a fearsome epidemic took hold in Charles Town. "Our Governor returned from the Cherokee country in January, as we then thought crowned with laurels," physician and naturalist Alexander Garden wrote, "but, alas," he griped, "bringing pestilence along with him, and having the war at his heels."[2] Indeed several simultaneous crises unfolded in the coming months. One of them was a smallpox epidemic.

Smallpox first appeared in Charles Town six days before the troops came home. An African American boy contaminated on a ship from Philadelphia left quarantine during the incubation period. In a few days, smallpox struck at Mr. Duvall's house on the southern tip of the peninsula at White Point.[3]

Scholars have already chronicled the symptoms, transmission, and treatment of the disease. They have discussed its effects on native populations and have offered general analyses of its impact in early America. But the social and political consequences of smallpox deserve further attention, particularly in South Carolina in the year 1760. The epidemic demoralized, debilitated, and destroyed Indian communities. It exacerbated race and class tensions, exposing a colonial government unprepared, reluctant, and unwilling to deal with the contagion effectively. As Charles Town elites questioned Lyttelton's leadership, seeds of doubt took root for what would soon become the Revolutionary generation. The transition was stunning. On January 8, Charles Town greeted Governor Lyttelton "as a Conqueror," George Milligen recalled, "such as the Intrepidity of a *Wolfe*, or the gallant and exemplary Behavior of a Lord *Howe*, or such-like, could only deserve."[4] It took only a month to demolish the conqueror's reputation.

South Carolinians faced epidemic disease regularly. Yellow fever, malaria, dysentery, diphtheria, and mumps took many lives. Measles, whooping cough, and respiratory ailments lingered for much of 1759. But everyone feared the worst disease of all: smallpox.[5] A common killer in Europe and Africa, it appeared in the American colonies with sporadic regularity. South Carolina withstood five mild epidemics from 1698 to 1732 and then suffered a severe outbreak in 1738.[6] The smallpox-infected troops sent to the colony under Henry Bouquet's command in 1757 somehow avoided spreading the illness to local residents.[7] The next year, Lyttelton sent an armed guard of militiamen to quarantine the DeSaussure plantation and tavern outside the city until an outbreak there ran its course.[8] Smallpox confers immunity on those who survive it, but in 1760, six thousand of Charles Town's eight thousand inhabitants had never contracted the disease.[9] The population had doubled due to immigration and natural growth since the last epidemic. The city had no public health laws or disaster relief plans.

For the residents of Charles Town, January 1760 was a frightening month. Returning soldiers arrived daily with measles, "pleurisies," and, worst of all, smallpox. It took just "two or three weeks," Dr. Garden reported, for the pox to travel "furiously" through the town. By January 26, it broke out "at the New Barracks, out of Town." Guards kept watch at the Duvall House and the army barracks. Doctors fumigated the homes on White Point. On February 2, the *Gazette* tried to soothe its readers' fears. The "Distemper will spread no farther," the paper opined, and the outlying settlements at Moncks Corner and Ashley Ferry remained smallpox-free. But other signs were ominous. Two people had already died. By February 7, the pestilence appeared at several more homes. Finally, on February 9, the *Gazette* conceded that containment efforts had failed: "all Hopes of its being prevented spreading are over."[10] For the first time, the assemblymen began discussing how to deal with the epidemic.

Smallpox had spread through Indian country for months before it arrived in Charles Town. Catawba warriors brought it home from the Pennsylvania frontier in early 1759 when they returned from the Forbes campaign against Fort Duquesne. It "raged with great violence" through December, when the *Gazette* reported that it had "carried off near one half" of the Catawba Nation. The missionary William Richardson, who visited the Catawbas after his short stint with the Cherokees, described the epidemic and its outcome. "The Smallpox spread among them surprisingly," he wrote, "on which they fled to the woods, and died in great numbers; which, with the present disturbances, have made them leave their towns, so that they are at present out of my reach."[11] By 1760, fewer than sixty warriors remained. The Catawba population now stood at just 4 percent of its number at the time of Carolina's settlement less than a century earlier.[12] Only eight warriors from the tribe joined Lyttelton's campaign. More vulnerable to their traditional enemies than ever before, Catawba warriors requested a reservation with a stockaded fort to house their women and children when they were gone. These long-term Anglo-Carolinian allies lost the influence they once enjoyed.[13]

The disease was spread by Catawba warriors raiding Cherokee villages in October 1759. It then raged for at least six weeks in Keowee. By January it swept through the Lower Towns. "The living Ones are all fled to the Woods to avoid it," reported the *Gazette*. But they unwittingly carried the infection with them. As a consequence, the paper observed, "many of them must perish as the *Catawba* did." Lieutenant Richard Coytmore, the commander of Fort Prince George, viewed the epidemic as his ally. "I cant help being so unhuman," he wrote, "as to wish it may spread through the whole nation."[14] By the end of the month, it reached the Middle Towns. By April, the *Gazette* reported, an "abundance of *Cherokees* are dead of the Small-Pox."[15] The Overhill Towns so dreaded the infection that they refused to admit "a single Person" from the Lower Towns. Because of their location, they had less contact with South Carolinians, too. The inhabitants of those towns remained largely smallpox free.[16]

Smallpox increased generational tensions and tested the authority of conjurers and healers. Interpretive accounts from the 1760 outbreak are elusive. But in the 1738 epidemic, many Cherokees had reportedly blamed smallpox on the indiscretions of their young married people, who, according to deerskin trader, ethnographer, and historian James Adair, "had in the most notorious manner, violated their ancient laws of marriage in every thicket, and broke down and polluted many of the honest neighbours bean-plots, by their heinous crimes." The treatment of victims may have served to restore balance. Since the pox "was believed to be brought on them by their unlawful copulation in the night dews," villagers isolated the victims and forced them to "lie out of doors, day and night, with their breast frequently open to the night dews, to cool the fever." The religious men "shewed their priest-craft," said James Adair, "in the fields where the infected victims had allegedly committed their transgressions." Conjurers "poured cold water on their naked breasts, sung their religious mystical song . . . and shaked a calabash with the pebble-stones." They also put patients through the intense heat and humidity of the sweat lodge. When the patient was "well soak'd" in sweat, Georgetown, South Carolina doctor and planter William Fyffe wrote, "they hurry Him to the nighest River & throw Him in." Indian medicine, like European medicine, was ineffective against smallpox, and a great many died. "The Cheerake showed," Adair wrote, "little skill in curing the small pox." The epidemic undermined unity as villagers called conjurers' abilities into question.[17]

Smallpox took a deep psychological toll on individual Cherokees. Scars showed easily. Adair recalled that, as a result, "a great many killed themselves; for being naturally proud, they are always peeping into their looking glasses." He witnessed suicides, one at the hands of a hoe-helve. As soon as they fell ill, many took their own lives by "throwing themselves into the River." Adair continued: "A death, in defence of their beloved land, and beloved things, was far preferable" to spreading the disease to others. Such Cherokees might have viewed suicide as a courageous sacrifice. Otherwise, "They were only spending a dying life, to the shame and danger of the society," Adair wrote. Lieutenant White Outerbridge, the commander of Fort Augusta, had a slightly different take. Observing the Savannah River Chickasaws in 1759, he wrote that Indians attempted to treat the smallpox by "getting drunk and Plunging into the River."[18]

Farther east, in Charles Town, most people who could afford it turned to inoculation. A practitioner inserted a bit of pus from the pox of an infected patient into an incision (usually in the upper arm) of an uninfected patient. If all went well, the inoculated patient contracted a mild, shorter-duration form of the disease. After recovery, the inoculated individual had lifelong immunity.[19]

Eliza Lucas Pinckney, a widowed plantation owner six miles upstream from Charles Town, reported the mood in Charles Town: "The people," she wrote, "were inocculation mad." They "rushed into" the procedure "with . . . presipitation." The doctors, Garden noted, "were in a state of hurry and confusion." But, Pinckney added, "The Doctors could not help it—the people would not be said nay."[20] Inoculation had risks. Not only were the inoculated contagious, but some died from their symptoms. Anne Loughton Smith, wife of Speaker of the Commons House Benjamin Smith, succumbed this way. In addition, incisions often became infected. Still, smallpox by inoculation in 1760 proved seven times less fatal than smallpox contracted naturally.[21]

Those who could not afford inoculation and contracted the disease naturally suffered severely. They turned to home remedies. They placed butchered fowls on the feet to reduce fever and slathered their throats with a honey and dried dog dung poultice. "Many poor wretches," Eliza Lucas Pinckney recalled, "died for want of proper nursing."[22]

In part because they had access to inoculation, the wealthy white inhabitants of the city fared better than those who were less privileged. But they suffered hardship nonetheless. Many white families left the city. William Hutson, pastor of the Independent Meeting (later known as Circular Congregational Church), his pregnant wife, and six small children went to James Island. The stress of the move had tragic consequences, inducing premature labor in Mary Hutson. Both newborn and mother died.[23]

Many of the city's slaves had smallpox, so whites in the country attempted to keep their slaves out of Charles Town. Whites fled Charles Town, while those on its outskirts avoided coming in. Commerce ceased between Charles Town and the surrounding countryside. Merchants and businessmen relocated to Dorchester village. A women's academy and a tavern shut down briefly and thereafter struggled for months to regain customers. Still, because of their socioeconomic advantages and mobility, fewer than 5 percent of Charles Town's white residents died of smallpox. Survivors displayed their grief by reading poems aloud from the *Gazette* and by donning mourning clothing and jewelry.[24]

Charles Town's African Americans fared worse. Nearly 15 percent of the entire black population in the provincial capital, five hundred people in all, died within two months of the virus's appearance.[25] The epidemic demoralized slaves already disappointed by the failure of Philip John's plot. In a revealing letter to the *South Carolina Gazette*, "Z. Z." reported that slave owners sought to protect their property from infection. But in so doing, they denied slaves work, and they denied them the opportunity to grieve and to bury their loved ones properly. They paid white laborers generous wages to bury African

American smallpox victims. With business stymied, urban slaves fell behind in the earnings that they needed to fulfill their obligations to their masters. Z. Z. argued that blacks "would have been very thankful" to do the work. The *Gazette* reported a grinding mortality in the black community, sometimes "12, 14, 16, and 18 buried" per day. The hastily dug graves were inadequate. Z. Z. reported many "buried not a Foot under Ground" at the Negro Burial Ground. "I do assure you," he added, "that the very Cows, by their pawing, had laid one Coffin quite bare."[26]

When they denied bondspeople the opportunity to bury their friends and family, slave owners deprived them of the chance to congregate and mourn in the presence of the deceased. When they let cattle desecrate slave corpses and graves, slave owners interfered at the spiritual level. Many South Carolinians of African descent believed that the soul traveled back across the Atlantic in the afterlife. But white authorities imposed their will whether slaves were dead or alive, with little regard for spiritual and physical consequences.[27] Dr. Alexander Garden boasted that he tested new methods of inoculation "partly by some bold trials on a negroe of his own."[28]

Since "a Principle of Humanity" did not compel the slave master "to see his Negro buried in a different Manner from his Dog," Z. Z. hoped "*Self-Preservation* would." The anonymous writer suggested that "every one may conceive . . . some Pestilence far worse than the Small-Pox."[29] On the day that the *Gazette* acknowledged the epidemic was out of control, Lyttelton issued guidelines to the assemblymen in hopes of averting a slave revolt: the men must strictly obey all laws; they must closely monitor their families and domestic affairs. Moreover, the governor urged the assemblymen to use their influence to "preserve the internal quiet of the Country from any attempts of Negroes or other Persons to disturb it." Patrols regularly kept watch over the city, especially on nights and weekends, to "intimidate the black slaves" and to nip opportunistic activities in the bud. Now, the patrols increased in frequency and strength as fears of a slave rebellion became widespread.[30]

Some concerned citizens worried that such treatment would heighten slave resentment. The epidemic had limited their financial opportunities. Charles Town's African Americans faced a food shortage. Their markets barely operated. Those whose owners allowed them to hire themselves out had no work or wages. Philip John's conspiracy still lingered in the minds of blacks and whites alike. And despite their own high mortality, enslaved Carolinians saw the ratio of black to white inhabitants increase in Charles Town as whites fled. "From one of the most flourishing provinces," Dr. Garden wrote, "we are . . . brought into a situation too terrible for us, who have a double enemy within ourselves to fear, viz. the small pox and the negroes." Outside the capital, the demographic imbalance sparked longstanding white fears. "About 70,000 negroes in our bowels!" despaired Garden. Militia rolls were down. "We muster about 8 or 9,000 men in the province," he complained, apparently unaware that the province actually mustered close to 7,000. "*This* is our happy situation."[31]

As hundreds of African Americans died, whites feared for their own financial and physical well-being. The Presbyterian pastor Archibald Simpson summarized his concerns succinctly. "Should this awful Malignancy prevail and spread" among slaves outside Charles Town, he wrote, it could ruin "numberless famelies, and prove dreadful indeed."[32] The families he worried about were not black but white.

Frontier disruptions compounded the province's ethnic and class divisions. Wealthy whites failed to mobilize the resources needed to support a dislocated and destitute populace. Thousands of Scots-Irish Presbyterians fled the frontiers for fear of the Cherokee Indians. They carried the virus with them. They lost their homes and their families. Pastor Simpson peered out of his parsonage at the "most deplorable state of complicated misery & distress." "No Description can surpass its Calamity," a Charles Town resident wrote to a friend in Philadelphia. "What few escape the Indians, no sooner arrive in Town, then they are seized with the Small-Pox, which generally carries them off." Simpson discerned "with much grief" that in Charles Town "these poor distressed famelies" received "little Sympathy, pity or assistance, yea are abused because they were overpowered by the enemy." Their treatment rubbed old wounds raw, convincing them of the indifference of the Anglo-Carolinian elite.[33]

South Carolina's Acadian exiles, all of them poor, suffered a more miserable fate. Several hundred of the one thousand who landed in Charles Town in 1755 still remained.[34] With smallpox spreading through the city in early February, a Commons House committee met to "inquire into the present state of the French Acadians" and to address other matters of concern. The committee issued a report with ideas on how to accommodate the unwelcome strangers as it also made recommendations for "preventing the Small-Pox from spreading" further. The Acadians, 340 in all, lived in four dilapidated buildings. "These several Houses are insufficient," the report stated. Their derelict condition might "produce Contagious and Malignant Distempers, dangerous in their Consequences to the health of the Inhabitants of this Town." And it threatened to create "the most direful Effects to [the Acadians] shou'd the Small-Pox spread amongst them." The assembly converted an old school building and the army barracks into temporary shelters. Five days later, it granted a mere £2,000 and hired a single doctor for the 340 refugees. These measures came too late.[35]

Charles Town had no poorhouse or public aid. Unlike northern seaport towns, the city forced its poor to rely on private charity for survival. Wealthy merchant Gabriel Manigault, the grandson of French Protestants, coordinated the Acadian relief effort. Volunteers inoculated some of the exiles in a gesture toward preventive care. But they put a greater effort into alleviating the suffering of those who fell ill. The expense ran to £5,235, a price that vastly exceeded the £2,000 allotted by the assembly and the charitable contributions from concerned citizens. About 34 percent of the Acadians died of smallpox. Another 4 percent succumbed to other ailments. By July 15, only 210 remained alive. A Commons House report acknowledged that the French-speaking refugees "suffered extremely in the late Calamity." Some "lost their Limbs, some their Eyes and others their Lives for want of proper Care, Necessaries, and Attendance."[36]

When the costs of caring for the Acadians rose, the assembly mercifully covered those expenses. The deportees also appreciated the private charity they received. But it did not keep them from becoming "disaffected and discontented." Their sufferings had made them wholly averse to living under an English Government," reported another Commons House committee. In May, the committee proposed deporting the "burthensome and useless" Acadians to "prevent any Mischief being done." Britain's Board of Trade nixed the plan. Charles Town's Acadian community stayed where it was, miserable and impoverished, depleted by 38 percent in just a few months.[37]

In mid-April 1760, the *Gazette* reported that the pestilence was "happily abated or attended with much less malignant circumstances, and by June or July only isolated cases remained.[38] But the toll of the 1760 smallpox epidemic was not merely physical and demographic but political and psychological as well. "This is truely the most awful time ever I or the oldest person in these parts ever saw," Archibald Simpson wrote.[39] For black Carolinians, the scourge only confirmed the dominance of a merchant-planter class that tried to control every dimension of slave life. Coming on the heels of the Philip John conspiracy and Cherokee attacks, the epidemic reinforced white awareness of the colony's internal instability. But the scourge also undermined white confidence in British authority and benevolence. On February 7, a month after his triumphal return from Cherokee country, Governor Lyttelton conceded failure on two fronts: he announced the renewal of hostilities with the Indians as well as the epidemic status of smallpox. The men of the

Commons House responded with a public rebuke. They also "omitted the common form of giving thanks for the Speech." Lyttelton noticed the gesture and promptly reported it to higher authorities.[40]

On February 13, Lyttelton received an official letter dated November 27, 1759. It informed him that he was now the governor of Jamaica. The Board of Trade appointed William Bull II as South Carolina's lieutenant governor, to serve in an executive capacity until Thomas Pownall, transferred from Massachusetts, assumed the reins. But Pownall resigned without ever filling his post, so Bull remained in office until Pownall's successor, former New Jersey governor Thomas Boone arrived.[41] With smallpox raging, Lyttelton withdrew from public affairs. "We have been for this month past in a state of suspense," Garden wrote on March 21, 1760, "our old governor embarrassed and taken up in settling his private affairs, and our Lieutenant-governor cannot act till the power regularly devolve upon him."[42]

On April 4, Captain John Lindsay navigated the naval gunship the *Trent* over the bar. At noon, Lyttelton took his berth. The town where he had spent the past four years disappeared on the horizon two days later. The *Trent* and several other ships set sail under convoy "with a fair Wind." But a tempest raged in the Southeast with no end in sight. Dr. Garden blasted Lyttelton, arguing, "We are, by a fatal piece of ambition, brought into a situation too terrible for us."[43] As smallpox ravaged Cherokee country and Charles Town, another crisis unfolded at Fort Prince George.

PUT TO DEATH IN COLD BLOOD

The Fort Prince George Massacre

6

Cherokee villagers weighed matters of import in their townhouses, the centers of community life. A townhouse was a conical rotunda, as large as sixty feet in diameter. The roof's central high point stood some thirty feet above the ground. From there, it sloped down and out, extending to low, wattle-and-daub walls at the building's perimeter. The roof consisted of layered poles, cane, bark, soil, and grass, all supported by eight interior posts. On the south side, a narrow, winding entryway led to a small door, which in turn opened into a large, circular amphitheater. This was where village politics unfolded. As many as six hundred tribespeople could congregate here, seated by clan on benches, mats, or carpets woven from ash or oak splints. A large fire burned at the center of the room for such gatherings, the smoke venting through an opening in the roof. War and peace chiefs sat near the fire, and to their left and right, all other men and women of rank, whose opinions carried equal weight.[1]

Villagers crowded into their townhouses in the winter of 1759–60 to discuss the budding crisis all Cherokees faced. Women and men alike, according to custom, discussed the kidnapping of innocent and unsuspecting delegates now called "hostages" by the British. They rejected the hastily imposed "treaty" signed on December 26, 1759, without the consent and ratification of the Cherokee people. They discussed the hostages' confinement at disease-infested Fort Prince George in a cold hut unsuitable for a fourth of that number. As Captain John Stuart noted, "Indians know no Difference between a prisoner and a slave, to which they prefer Death, it's impossible to give them an Idea of any confinement that is not Igno-

IMAGE 6.1 *Cherokee Townhouse at Chota, by Thomas Whyte, ca. 1982.*
Courtesy of the McClung Museum of Natural History & Culture,
University of Tennessee, Knoxville, Tenn.

minious."[2] Village by village, sometimes alone, sometimes in tandem, the Cherokees organized to take action.

In the weeks after the Treaty of Fort Prince George, negotiations to free the hostages failed and the outcry from the various Cherokee regions grew louder. Using violence and siege tactics in place of ineffective diplomacy, Cherokee villagers burst into action against the British. The hostage crisis did not create a singular Cherokee nation. Cherokees still identified first with their villages or clans, then with their settlement clusters. But the hostage crisis did alter Cherokees' sense of themselves. It galvanized villages throughout the Cherokee settlements. And it pushed them toward unified stands not just on retributive justice but on other matters as well. Henceforth, they tolerated neither betrayal nor imperial arrogance.

As 1760 began, Lieutenant Richard Coytmore of Fort Prince George perceived "a Universal uneasiness" in Cherokee country. The Lower Towns exchanged Scalp Jack of Toxaway for a hostage. Cherokee spokesmen from each of the settlement clusters negotiated in vain at the frontier forts for the release of the hostages. Their frustration only grew. When Tistoe of Keowee urged Coytmore to free the hostages because their families were "very un-easy at their Confinement," the officer responded by reading the treaty aloud and haranguing the Indians present. The Round O of Stecoe then "declared that he was ignorant of the contents" of the treaty that "he was inadvertently persuaded to sign." A flummoxed Coytmore, noting that the Out Town head-man's two adult sons were hostages, dismissed the objection as a mere ex-pression of "Paternal affection." Meanwhile, Oconostota, Chota's head war-rior by affirmation, and his brother, the Raven of Chota, scurried back to that village to consult with Connecorte. On the way they passed through Esta-toe, where they urged the Lower Towns not to exchange accused murderers for hostages. The situation called for more drastic measures.[3]

On January 6, the hostage Chistannah of Estatoe took matters into his own hands and tried to escape. He "rushed precipitately by the Sentry," who grasped desperately for the Indian's blanket. A soldier outside the fort chased him toward the riverbank and fired a shot that missed its target. Moments later, Coytmore promised the hostages kind treatment—though he never de-livered on it—and ordered his sentries "to Fire on any of them that shou'd offer to Pass by them."[4]

By January 7, Cherokee warriors from the Lower, Middle, Out, and Valley Towns, "much Chagreen'd at the Confinement of their People," set out for the British posts. Their intent, Coytmore learned, was to use "every method to redeem them, if not by fair means, by force." Overhill warriors soon followed. A week later, Seroweh announced that he would arrive soon at Fort Prince George with three or four murderers to exchange for hostages.[5] The garri-son waited tensely, unaware that the proposed exchange was a ruse intended to launch the Cherokee offensive.

On January 17, three traders arrived at the banks of the Keowee with news to report. Some Indian women had warned them "to make their Escape directly." The women whispered that the people of the Lower Towns "were determined to . . . kill the White Men, first at Keowee," then at trader John Elliott's nearby hamlet. After that, they would "try what they could do at the Fort." Coytmore placed his soldiers on alert and vowed to the hostages that "if One of my Garrison was hurt" by the Indians, he "would put every One of them to the Sword directly."[6]

On January 19, seventy to eighty Cherokee men and a few women from all of the Lower Towns assembled at Estatoe. Their leaders were Seroweh and Tistoe. They convinced Thomas Beamer to accompany them as interpreter. Unbeknownst to the half-Cherokee trader, they were all secretly armed and they had the support of additional men hiding nearby. They planned to rush the fort, kill the soldiers, and liberate the hostages.[7]

Thirty warriors split off from the larger group. The other forty or fifty, clad in blankets, arrived at the fort in a downpour at 4:00 P.M. The Cherokees sought admittance into the fort "to see their friends, and choose which of them to [exchange]" for two murderers. Coytmore, afraid that the Indians planned "to surprise the fort," would admit no more than three or four at a time, and ordered his soldiers to remain in their barracks with weapons trained. "I took every precaution to guard against any Strategems they might Endeavour to practice," he wrote. The hills overlooking the fort teemed with Indians. One soldier counted 115 men.[8]

After much negotiation, Seroweh agreed to enter the fort with three or four companions as well as the purported murderers. But twelve men, none of them accused murderers, pushed their way inside. Coytmore ordered the gate shut. Inside, he and Seroweh had a "friendly" talk. The latter "went out to fetch the Murderers." A hubbub ensued, and two of the hostages—Tullatahee of Toqua and the Yellow Bird of Watauga—escaped. Seroweh returned empty-handed. A soldier escorted the Cherokee visitors out. Anticlimactically, the Cherokees dispersed and Beamer went home.[9]

While these events unfolded at Fort Prince George, Cherokee warriors vented their frustration nearby. The thirty warriors who had split off on the way to Coytmore's outpost marched to trader John Elliott's home and trading post at Little Keowee, just a mile and a half from the fort. They killed Elliott and thirteen more, including the interpreter for the treaty signing, and took two prisoners. They drove off cattle and divided Elliott's goods and rum among themselves. Later that day, Coytmore sent out the Round O of Ste-coe, who, in hopes of freeing his sons, gathered intelligence confirming the reports. Soon Thomas Beamer heard the same story from a Keowee boy. As Fort Prince George grasped what had happened at Elliott's, several Indians hidden in the woods fired at three soldiers cutting firewood near the fort, killing one and wounding another.[10] Warriors weakened and demoralized the garrison by picking off its soldiers one by one.

Beamer, a close observer of Cherokee activities, "would not pretend to say" that the British had alienated all Cherokees. But he speculated that it might be so. Cherokees attacked traders, they besieged Fort Prince George, and they cut off all communication between the British garrisons and Charles Town. A few hundred warriors surrounded Fort Prince George. The Lower Towns courted assistance from the Creek Indians, and two war parties from Cussitah in the Lower Creek towns arrived to consider whether to offer their assistance against the English. At the end of his bimonthly report, Coytmore summed up his situation succinctly: "Surrounded and Shut up (like Birds in a Cage) both Day & Night."[11]

Desperation spread throughout Cherokee country. Those Cherokees at a distance from the forts targeted the traders. Traders demanded Cherokee payment. But with the embargo in place, ammunition ran low. And the traders had supplies and goods that the Cherokees needed. The Cockeyed Warrior of Nottely, a Valley Town, enraged that his son was among the hostages, "gave a talk to his people, to kill all the white men." Traders scattered. Those with Indian friends or good luck reached safety. When another Nottely headman told Isaac Atwood "that he would not kill him then, but that he would never spare a white man for the future," the trader fled to Hiwassee. The next night, he learned "that there was a party then coming to kill him." Accordingly, he set off for Fort Prince George, where he arrived with a fellow trader on January 19.[12]

Other traders lost their lives as they attempted to escape. Hiwassees and Nottelies dispatched Nottely trader John Kelly, a long-reputed swindler and cheat, whose body they dismembered and put on public display. Two others met a similar fate in Watauga and Nequassee. Nequassee warriors "confin'd" five other traders. In the Lower Towns, two more died at Cheowee and another three narrowly escaped. A dozen more white men lost their lives in other episodes. Other traders were beaten and threatened.[13]

At Fort Loudoun, as at Fort Prince George, the Cherokees tried negotiations first. The failure of negotiations caused the Indians to turn to the same sorts of violence they used at the other post. Throughout the month of January, two familiar guests frequented Fort Loudoun: Attakullakulla and Oconostota. Both were rivals for power among the Overhills. The physical contrast between them was stark. As naturalist William Bartram later described him, Attakullakulla was "a man of remarkable small stature, slender, and delicate frame." Another contemporary observed that "his ears were cut and banded with silver, hanging nearly down to his shoulders." He was mild-featured, brilliant and witty—a gifted statesman.[14] Oconostota was a "large man," barrel-chested, "a man of extraordinary physical prowess." He towered half a foot over his contemporaries and weighed perhaps two hundred pounds. He had a large head and a face that bore the scars of smallpox. A leader by example and not one for words, he was pensive, terse, and intense.[15]

On January 6, Attakullakulla had arrived at Fort Loudoun and told its commander, Captain Paul Demere, to expect peace. The next day, the conciliatory Cherokee spoke in the Chota townhouse to the Overhill headmen. He "spoke very severely to them all for their late behavior" and publicly called out Connecorte for instigating them. The lecture had little effect. The next day a "young fellow" fired upon soldiers cutting firewood outside Fort Loudoun, though he missed his mark. Attakullakulla nevertheless convinced Demere of his loyalty when he visited again on the ninth. Oconostota, on the other hand, appeared dour when he arrived four days later. He warned "that there will be some disturbances." The murderers' relatives refused to give them up. By Cherokee law and custom, there was no recourse. "We cannot take them away from them by force," Oconostota said.[16]

Trudging through snow so deep that "no Indian ever remembered to have seen the like," the two men visited Demere again on January 23. When the captain asked if they had any murderers to deliver up, "they were several minutes without saying any thing." At last, Attakullakulla confessed that anti-British fervor had spread throughout the Cherokee settlements, and that "the consequences will be worse than before." Villagers complained of the lengthy confinement of their people, and readied to strike. Attakullakulla demanded that Demere write a letter and promised that his brother would carry it to Fort Prince George. The letter, the headman said, should contain the following terms: the British would free the hostages. In exchange, Overhill warriors would set out against the French in the spring and would return with French or Indian enemy scalps equal in number to the settlers killed in 1758 and 1759. Demere refused. He knew that warriors had already departed to seek an alliance with the French. He held a different conception of justice, and he understood his place within the imperial system's hierarchy. But beyond this, he believed, British gentlemen, not Indian subjects, should make the rules.[17]

If he secured the release of the hostages, Attakullakulla might cover for his complicity in the Fort Prince George treaty that kept them confined. He might bolster his tenuous claims to political authority. He thus assured Demere that it was not too late. An express "with a painted stick, and a White mans scalp" had arrived from the Lower Towns, but to no effect, he reported. Oconostota knew this was not true. His own people had lied to Attakullakulla. Standing by as the conversation between Demere and Attakullakulla unfolded, Oconostota "seem'd to be very cross." Throughout the month of January, runners from all corners of the Cherokee settlements had streamed into Chota, "complaining that their Friends were still confined."[18] Oconostota felt personally responsible. He too had signed Lyttelton's treaty. Frustrated, aggrieved, and mindful of his own recent captivity, he concluded that diplomacy had failed. The Great Warrior would take a different route than Attakullakulla.

The men at Fort Loudoun, like those at Fort Prince George, felt the direct effects of changing Cherokee tactics. Communication eastward was impossible—at least for white travelers, "as all the Indians, are resolved to kill any Body, that go on the Path, and are watching it," Demere said. Overhill warriors intercepted two dispatches. The captain exhorted his men and offered money, but "all in Vain." They refused to attempt the trip. In desperation, Demere "fixed upon a Negro fellow," Abram, "and promised him his freedom, if he wou'd undertake it." During the next several months, Abram repeatedly risked his life for his white masters. He undoubtedly knew that heroic acts were one of the few routes to manumission in late colonial South Carolina.[19]

Abram had the skills of a frontiersman. Although it was illegal to employ slaves in the deerskin trade, the penalty was a fine, and it was rarely enforced. Numerous bondsmen toiled for traders as packhorsemen, blacksmiths, and boat pilots. Abram knew the five-hundred-mile stretch from outpost to colonial capital as well as anyone. Cherokee emissaries had agreed in 1751 to return runaway slaves to South Carolina authorities, although they sometimes adopted runaways. Perhaps Abram did not wish to take his chances. He now seized his opportunity for freedom.[20]

Abram left Fort Loudoun for Fort Prince George on January 26, 1760, and made the 150-mile trek in just over a week. The news he carried showed the grim situation at Fort Loudoun. Demere expected a siege. With only ten weeks' worth of corn and "four Months meat provision" remaining, the captain had cut rations. Yet the soldiers remained "in high spirits," and they kept busy by repairing the fort. Having delivered his news, Abram waited at Fort Prince George for Lieutenant Coytmore to send him on the next leg of his journey.[21]

By late January, the Middle Towns and the Overhills were mobilizing for war. Middle Townspeople met at Echoe and sent numerous war parties down the path. Among the Overhills, Connecorte blocked all efforts at diplomacy. Demere learned that Overhill warriors agreed to detain "any White People" that "shou'd pass by" and to execute any whites found with letters.[22] Overhill representatives also headed for Fort Prince George "to demand the Hostages belonging to their Parts."[23]

Within the next few days, repercussions of another event rippled throughout the Cherokee settlements. Connecorte, whom most Cherokees saw as the principal spiritual and political figure in the Overhills and beyond, died. The demise of "Old Hop" left a leadership void at a critical period. His death also further galvanized a single anti-British mindset. Villagers as far away as Keowee sang the death song. As a faithful supporter of Connecorte, and with military prowess to boot, Oconostota gained influence among the Overhills. Connecorte's nephew, Conocotocko (sometimes spelled Kanagatucko)—and known as Standing Turkey in the historical record—rose to prominence as well.[24] The tug of war for political power between Attakullakulla, who cast his lot with the British, and Oconostota, who advocated a stance that better preserved Cherokee sovereignty, continued. The British recognized Attakullakulla as the "emperor" of the Cherokees, but the Indians themselves did not. They fed him false intelligence and ignored his counsel.

Oconostota filled the political vacuum left by Connecorte. At Fort Loudoun on January 29, he met with Captain Stuart. Soon thereafter, the headman also went to Fort Prince George to secure the release of the four Overhill hostages. Coytmore had orders from the governor "to not set the hostages free (except as the Treaty directs) without fresh Orders from me." The captives, Oconostota insisted, were innocent of murder. And neither he nor Attakullakulla could deliver up the true culprits. By Cherokee law, only "their Relations" had the "power to punish them." But the families could "not be prevailed upon to Deliver them." Aside from this, the Overhills would agree to all the other articles of the treaty. Had Coytmore freed the Overhill hostages, "these Towns may in all probability remain Quiet," Stuart thought. Oconostota misled Stuart. He did not tell him that war parties from Settico, Great Tellico, and Chota had already set out for the frontier settlements.[25]

As new negotiations failed at Fort Prince George, disaffected Cherokees came together in a show of force. Cherokees from several settlement clusters visited in late January, but to no avail. Eight hundred Cherokee warriors—from the Middle Towns, Lower Towns, and Hiwassee—converged on the fort. These Cherokee freedom fighters, dubbed "Rascals" by Coytmore, besieged the fort and intimidated its inhabitants. Inside the post, five hostages had died, four of them from smallpox. Coytmore expected this news to further "enrage" the Cherokee people. "We are always expecting an attack," he wrote. Hoping to liberate his sons, the Round O of Stecoe visited several of the Lower Towns to encourage peace but found reluctance everywhere.[26]

The growing aggregation of disaffected Cherokees outside Fort Prince George frightened Coytmore enough. But inside, the garrison faced desperate conditions. Soldiers detained an inebriated Conasatchee man who visited the fort. When he boasted of killing four men at Elliott's trading post and tried to incite the hostages to revolt, he was shackled and guarded night and day. Soldiers did not dare to "go [one] Hundred Yards from the Fort" to fetch firewood, though "Not a Stick" remained. Heavy rains collapsed the well. Four soldiers had died of smallpox and eighteen were "dangerously ill of it." Coytmore and others also complained of a "Disorder seemingly of as bad a Nature" consisting of "a violent pain in the Head, Loyns, and Back, with a Vomiting." The officer again dispatched Abram with a plea for reinforcements for his garrison, "now like Birds in a Cage."[27]

On February 6, under the cover of darkness, Abram went from Fort Prince George to Keowee and "brought off a Horse that was tyed under a Corn House in the middle of Town." He attempted to gather intelligence. The next morning, he departed with Coytmore's journals and a letter to the governor. By the fourteenth, the day Abram arrived in Charles Town, the members of the South Carolina Commons House had already concluded that "Fort Loudoun . . . cannot be reliev'd by this Government." Though they agreed to pay for provincial troops through July 1, they had little expectations it would attract enlistees. South Carolina's demographic disparity discouraged white men from enlisting. The assemblymen held out hope for Fort Prince George and sent supplies for its relief.[28]

Lyttelton sent a letter to the commander in chief of the British Army in North America, General Jeffery Amherst, begging for British regulars and for a second military expedition to quell the Cherokee uprising and rescue the garrison at Fort Loudoun. Amherst obliged, but the new troops took months to arrive. In the meantime, in Charles Town, Abram came down with smallpox.[29]

At noon on February 14, Oconostota, his brother, and interpreters Charles McLemore and John Calwell arrived at the Keowee riverbank beside Fort Prince George with several letters. "They were come for their Hostages," they explained. They also brought Demere's warning that the Overhills "wou'd soon go with the Flood" and take to the warpath. Coytmore gave the same curt response he had given to the Middle and Lower Towns: he would honor Governor Lyttelton's December 26 treaty. Oconostota "denied, that he made the least Agreement or consented to any Treaty." With his brother and McLemore, the "dissatisfy'd" headman returned to Keowee. Calwell entered the fort to report that the Overhills had now joined "with the rest having been denied their Hostages" and that Chotas and Great Tellicos were already in the area.[30]

The morning of February 16 was exactly one moon after Seroweh's failed attempt on Fort Prince George. Two Indian women who had been trusted informants appeared at the edge of the Keowee River. It was a setup. Within seconds, Oconostota arrived. He had "something of Consequence to impart" in Charles Town and needed a white man to escort him there. When Coytmore offered to provide a horse, Oconostota "carelessly" whirled a bridle three times over his head. A volley of "25 or 30 Guns" erupted from the thickets. Coytmore "was shot thro' the left Breast" and two other men also sustained wounds.[31]

Ambrose Davis rushed out to help Coytmore, escorting the weak and bleeding commander into the fort through a shower of fire. Davis then fired his rifle into a group of four or five Cherokees, dropping one. From the hills, rifle fire steadily sprayed the fort. From the fort, artillery launched heavy balls indiscriminately into Keowee. The wounded men found their way to the surgeon. Ensign Alexander Miln, whom the Indians despised as much as Coytmore, assumed command.[32]

Miln recorded the ensuing events in his journal. When the Cherokees shot Coytmore and the others, "the Men swore bitterly that they wou'd kill every Indian" hostage, and fixed their bayonets. Miln claimed he "order'd them not to attempt any such thing." But the soldiers were beyond Miln's control. He "pacified them a little" by ordering the hostages "to be put in Irons, and ty'd with Ropes." With irons and ropes in hand, one "Sergeant Parsell"— Thomas Parsell of the Independent Companies—and other soldiers approached the building the hostages occupied. Despite the absence of a translator, they called for the captives to come outside. None did. "They imagined that we intended to put them to death," Miln wrote. Miln's account then becomes subject to dispute. As the soldiers "went in to draw them out," the ensign claimed, the hostages allegedly uncovered tomahawks and knives buried in the dirt floor of their jail to defend themselves, and "began to use their Weapons." With two of their companions wounded, the soldiers "immediately fired" on the captives. Miln claimed he tried to stop them, "but before I cou'd get one to hear or answer me, they laid them all lifeless." Was Miln telling the truth? He continued, "Happy for us all, that they were destroy'd, for searching the House where they were kept, [we] found a bottle of Poison that they had hid under Ground, which we imagined was to poison the Well."[33]

In the evening, some Indians came near the fort. Firing two guns, they cried out, "Fight strong, and you shall be assisted." The men "expected a General Attack," Miln explained. Gunshots erupted from the hills surrounding the fort. Cherokees "kept a continual firing all night" but did not approach the fort. Inside, "the Men lay upon their Arms in the Angles till Day Light."[34]

The Fort Prince George Massacre : 99

In Charles Town less than two weeks later, the *South Carolina Gazette* endorsed the soldiers' massacre of the hostages. But the *Gazette*'s account of the events of February 16, 1760, was flawed. Read by literate Charles Town residents and transmitted throughout the British Empire, it omitted the details Miln provided and failed to report that he had lost control of his men.[35]

Few discerning minds in Charles Town believed the *Gazette*'s account. Alexander Garden, a physician and naturalist, believed the hostages "were, to a man, put to death in cold blood."[36] George Milligen, a physician in the Independent Companies who later served with veterans of the skirmish, blamed Miln for the massacre. In *A Short Description of the Province of South-Carolina*, penned in 1763, he dubbed the slaying an act of "revenge" for the shooting of Coytmore. The soldiers, the doctor said, "were *permitted* to kill the innocent and unfortunate Prisoners, in a Manner too shocking to relate."[37] Milligen believed the carnage was avoidable.

In 1775, ethnographer and historian James Adair, who had traversed the Southeast as an Indian trader for decades, offered yet another version of events. As Cherokee gunfire erupted from the hills, he stated, the hostages cheered their countrymen. Then, Adair described what happened next: "A white savage . . . cut through a plank, over their heads, and perpetrated that horrid action, while the soldiery were employed like warriors, against the enemy." Adair continued: "he, like the wolf in the fable, falsely accused them of intending to poison the wells of the garrison." The hills high above Fort Prince George, though out of range of gunfire, overlooked the fort. Did Cherokee observers see what happened? If so, one can only imagine how they and their compatriots felt.[38]

"By this Massacre," Milligen observed sympathetically, "for I can give it no softer Name, most of the Head-Warriors lost Relations and Friends, which fired them with an implacable Desire of Revenge."[39] Two of the fourteen dead were suspected murderers. Before the "massacre," five had died of illness, and three more had escaped to tell of their mistreatment. But after inflicting weeks of mistreatment, soldiers slaughtered the remaining Indians.

Thanks to runners carrying news far and wide on mountain trails, the villagers shared a determination to crush the British before the grim action of February 16. The massacre merely confirmed decisions made in townhouse discussions weeks before. And warriors had already left for the South Carolina frontier.

On February 25, two months after the Treaty of Fort Prince George, Lieutenant Coytmore succumbed to his wounds. Several soldiers buried the fallen commander in a shallow grave outside the fort's southwest bastion. Three days later, Cherokee snipers shot and killed a sentry. Only two artillery pieces worked. "By Death and Sickness we are really very weak, and in a very bad situation for the want of Wood," Miln wrote. He had a porthole cut out for one massive iron cannon. Lacking a better plan, soldiers sought to weaken Cherokee unity and spiritualism. Gunmen "fired through" the townhouse and the conjurer's house at Keowee, dispersing the few remaining villagers to the hills.[40]

As Miln and the garrison braced for the worst, they had no idea that the carnage and tumult at Fort Prince George paled in comparison to events in the white settlements. Affronted Cherokee warriors took to the offensive. They hoped to catch the enemy off guard. They aimed to avenge the death of their kin and to replenish their population through adoption. And they hoped to drive off encroaching settlers by inflicting fear and violence. Perhaps they could inspire the Creeks and French to come to their aid. Drawn together by the hostage crisis, they hoped to steady a world careening out of control.

THAT KINDRED DUTY OF RETALIATION

The Cherokee Offensive of 1760

In light of the recent Cherokee population decline, and the carnage at Fort Prince George, taking captives and scalps constituted a major priority. Not only did captives augment native populations, but they also assuaged survivors' grief and replaced the fallen. Thus when Cherokees took to the warpath, they did so in part to replace their dead. In lieu of holding prisoners as bargaining chips, natives assimilated them. Indian warriors preferred, rather than exempted, women and children. Through proper ritual and ceremony, anyone, regardless of race or cultural heritage, could in time become a full-fledged Cherokee. Prisoners sang songs and danced with their captors. Captives were washed, dressed, and "made over" in the Cherokee fashion through hairstyle, dress, and jewelry. And they learned the ways of their new people. Captives often bridged gaps between people in their new and former worlds. Sometimes women and children became slaves first. But for slaves, adoption and equality was possible. Connecorte's son was an escaped African American slave.[1]

Cherokees also sought scalps. They may have hoped to torture a few prisoners, too. Both scalp-taking and ritualized torture of the enemy freed a dead Cherokee's soul and lifted the grief of the community. As James Adair put it, "when that kindred duty of retaliation is justly executed, [the dead] immediately get ease and power to fly away." Scalping prevented the Cherokee dead from haunting and harming the living. They "give a slash round the top of the skull, and with a few dexterous scoops, soon strip it off," he added. They "spread [it] on a small Hoop, and carry it in Victory as a Token of their

Exploit to their Town Houses, where all the Scalps are publickly exposed during Several Weeks," William De Brahm recalled.[2]

Generally, Indians took male captives and tortured them when avenging a clansman's death that was particularly heinous. Indians tied their enemies to a tall pole. The entire community contributed by poking, burning, beating, and eventually scalping and dismembering the captive. Cherokees believed that through torture, they drew power from an enemy and transferred it to themselves. The community-based nature of ritual torture shocked British observers, though they too used torture. Britons saw torture as a state-sanctioned and state-administered punishment for crime. For Cherokees, the people and the state were synonymous.[3]

Raids on the frontier, as they always had, also offered opportunities for ambitious young men to prove their masculinity and gain social standing. In 1760, Cherokees looked to the frontier for other purposes, too: to vent their disgust with the deerskin trade, and to reclaim traditional hunting grounds. Sometimes Indians simply wished to enact violence and inspire fear. But they were unwilling to carelessly sacrifice the lives of their warriors in the process. With all these goals weighing heavily on them, they sometimes inflicted large casualties.

As smallpox raged and the hostage crisis unfolded, from February 1 to April 1, eight hundred Cherokee warriors attacked the southeastern frontier. At the end of February, the action paused briefly as some warriors returned home. Others, seeking revenge for the massacre at Fort Prince George, launched additional assaults in March. At least fifty Cherokees died in these campaigns. Several were captured. But Cherokees killed two hundred white and black South Carolinians and captured between fifty and one hundred more. In the process they sowed still more political dissension in South Carolina.[4]

Archibald Simpson, a Presbyterian preacher in coastal Prince William Parish, heard of nothing "but house burning, women & children left helpless in the woods, murders, rapine, and devastation." He heard too of "the most horrid cruelties committed" upon the living and the dead. Another eighteenth-century observer noted that the land, "once settled, is now a wilderness; some killed, others scalped, others drove far from their habitations, others carried captive, and some put to death in the most cruel manner."[5] For the Indians, scalping conformed to spiritual realities and cultural necessities. White men scalped Indians to intimidate Indians or to collect bounties. Due to cultural taboos, Cherokee Indian warriors did not rape the enemy. The damage inflicted was premeditated and deliberate.[6] In stirring up fear, suffering, and self-pity, conventional accounts showed the Cherokee offensive's psychological impact on whites, but obscured the Cherokees' understanding of events and overlooked the motivations that underlay Indian strategy.

The Cherokees accomplished some of their objectives in early 1760. In the process, they also widened the chasm between backcountry farmers and coastal elites. The farmers and their supporters saw the dearth of support from the colonial government as evidence of class bias and indifference. Elites criticized the incompetence of British colonial governance. Cherokees gained the upper ground in the conflict. They failed, however, to draw the French or the Creeks to their assistance. French Quebec fell to the British in September 1759. Some feared that the French would "Bend all their Industry and Assiduity to the south" in order to "Retrieve what they Lost in the North and to Amply Revenge Themselves." But French soldiers and civilians did not flee to the South to rally to the Cherokees. Without supplies from the French in Louisiana, Creeks focused instead on hunting and waited for a better opportunity.[7]

Motivated by clear and consistent cultural imperatives, warriors from the Middle and Lower Towns reached the uppermost South Carolina settlements on January 29. The warriors first targeted the squatters and encroachers at Long Canes. They also eyed Fort Ninety Six, the strategic trading depot and military outpost along the Cherokee Path.[8] A nineteenth-century story claims that Cateechee of Keowee rode to warn Ninety Six, where her white lover, trader Allan Francis, resided. One version of the tale has her riding into Long Canes. Whether or not that happened, scouts from Ninety Six also captured two warriors who might have leaked what they knew. And two traders arrived from the Lower Towns, revealing information about Cherokee plans. Ninety Six braced itself for an attack and alerted Long Canes.[9]

Settled in 1756, Long Canes was a Presbyterian enclave in western South Carolina populated by Scots-Irish migrants and African slaves. The white migrants had fled the frontier violence in Virginia, and also sought free land and space to practice their religion without coercion. But their settlement violated the 1746 Carolina-Cherokee agreement. They also hunted thirty or forty miles into Cherokee lands.[10] The squatters altered the environment by damming the Little River and fishing it heavily. They raised cattle in the salt licks used not long before by deer and buffalo. They also peddled liquor and household goods as unlicensed traders to the Cherokees. By 1760, 250 black and white settlers carved out a living in the region called Long Canes. But they did so at the Cherokees' expense.[11]

Harmonious coexistence was far from possible. In 1759, Connecorte had complained about the land incursions to the Presbyterian missionary William Richardson. Wawhatchee shared Cherokee concerns with Georgia authorities the same year. If not for the Lyttelton expedition, Cherokee hunters would have "broken up" the Long Canes settlement in November. British authorities took no action despite these developments.[12] As a result, Cherokees directed their first attack on the South Carolina frontier on the Long Canes squatters.[13]

In the early morning hours of February 1, 100 mounted Cherokees attacked 150 fleeing Long Canes settlers. Several men died in the first volleys. Long Canes surveyor Patrick Calhoun later recalled that the white and black refugees were soon "overpowered and scattered in every direction." Then warriors converged. Cherokees took what scalps they could. The warriors also took thirteen prisoners, mainly women and children. The captives included future South Carolina politician John C. Calhoun's cousins, Ann (also spelled Anne), age four, and Mary, age two. The skirmish lasted thirty or forty minutes.[14] The Indians then burned the woods after the struggle. By clearing the underbrush they hastened the return of deer and turkeys to hunt. And they removed cover for enemies who might ambush them in those hunting grounds.[15]

The fight proved costly for the Cherokees: twenty-one reportedly died, including two headmen. The next day, Patrick Calhoun and a party of militiamen returned to the scene. They recovered twenty-three Long Canes inhabitants' bodies and interred them in the mass grave. The Cherokees boasted that they killed fifty-six settlers.[16] In the days and weeks that followed, fifteen children were found wandering in the woods, wounded and disoriented. One teenage girl cowered in a canebrake. And still other refugees regrouped and made it to Fort Moore.[17]

In search of more scalps and adoptees, Cherokee warriors ambushed settlers fleeing Stevens Creek settlement, not far from Long Canes. Twenty-three settlers and two Cherokees died. The rest, 170 in all, crowded into Fort Moore with the Long Canes survivors.[18] White and black inhabitants of neighboring eastern Georgia "crammed" into Fort Moore, Fort Augusta, the Anglican church, Macartan's trading house, "& every other House of Security" in Augusta. Edmond Atkin lamented that "All things round here now wear a wretched Aspect." He feared "The Terrour will spread . . . far into the Settlements."[19] It already had.

War parties from the Lower Towns, led by Seroweh, arrived at the headwaters of the Saluda River on February 2. They soon fanned out along the Saluda and its tributaries. Some targeted the small trading post and garrison at Ninety Six. Capturing it would accomplish two things. First, it would

IMAGE 7.1 *Gravestone of Catherine Calhoun, killed in 1760. Author photo.*

diminish the capacity of the colony to protect the settlements nearby. Second, it would serve as a symbolic gesture of disgust toward the deerskin trade. Two Cherokee spies fell into the hands of trader Robert Gouedy and several white scouts up the path from Ninety Six. This gave the fort's defenders some warning. Soon after, forty warriors led by Seroweh fired on members of cowboy Andrew Williamson's family fleeing from their home a mile from Fort Ninety Six. "We had a struggle to save them," Captain James Francis, the post's commander, wrote. Though the Williamsons escaped injury and got inside the fort, the Cherokees captured the two slaves in the party.[20]

The next day, February 3, the same forty Indians reappeared in view of Fort Ninety Six. The garrison's men—who were demolishing all freestanding structures outside the fort in order to remove cover for the expected attackers—hastened back into the enclosure. Thirty-three white and twelve black South Carolinians defended the fort, working side by side as they often did in the deerskin trade. The warriors torched the two buildings that still stood outside the fort: Gouedy's home and an outbuilding. Their efforts in vain and their ammunition expended, they withdrew two hours later with two dead. One white man was slightly wounded. Captain Francis subsequently begged the governor to send the weakened fort "an immediate relief."[21]

On the same day—February 3—a similar scene played out at Turner's Fort, where the Saluda and Little Saluda meet thirty-six miles southeast of Ninety Six. Another Cherokee war party "fired incessantly" on occupants for four hours, the *South Carolina Gazette* reported. The Indians lost seven and wounded one settler behind the still incomplete stockade. Looking for a less risky way to take scalps and captives, the warriors pressed southeast. They attacked several houses. They captured children.[22] From February 1 to February 6, twenty settlers lost their lives along the Saluda and Bush Rivers.[23] By February 9, warriors had "destroyed" the Saluda River settlements "all below" Ninety Six. Sensationalized and gory newspaper accounts painted the scene: a tableau of devastation.[24]

Cherokee warriors then struck along South Carolina's Broad River and its tributaries, driving two hundred settlers away from their homes, livestock, and possessions. Warriors reportedly killed and captured nine on the Tyger River. They claimed over a dozen lives in the Enoree settlements nearby. Afterward, thirty poorly armed men and 125 women and children huddled fearfully in "a little post called Fort Enoree." They "Cant subsist Long in this Station," militia captains Samuel Aubrey and Edward Musgrove wrote. Some fled "with all their familys into some other Province with an Intention never to Return and we must infailably follow them," the captains said. Musgrove could recruit only seven men to scout, as the Indians were "very numerous." Aubrey rushed to Charles Town for help.[25]

From his fort twelve miles above the mouth of the Broad, John Pearson captured the panic and frenzy of the backcountry farmers on February 8. "In Short," he wrote, the Indians had "burnt & Distroy'd" everything. "How long wee may continue in Safety . . . I know not for the Tourrant hath been so Great." Of all the refugees, "hardly One Stops att the Congarees so that I may say wee Are now the back Inhabitants." Pearson begged for scalp bounties. He also sought ranger units to "pursue and Kill & Destroy" Cherokee warriors and to stop "the Tourrant" of frontier-fleeing whites and blacks.[26]

In the area called the Dutch Fork, between the Broad and Saluda Rivers, Cherokees carried off "severall" people. "All the Settlers above the Congrees are hourly coming down with their family's," Henry Gallman wrote from Congaree Creek on February 12. He saw "the road all along crowded" with refugees. He fenced in his house and yard as a fort for his neighbors. But less than a quarter of the 215 destitute people Gallman sheltered could fight. Gallman feared "the people wil be obliged by want of Subsistance to go down and be troublesome to the Settlements." Without assistance, those settlers clustered in the backcountry shipping and trade hubs might follow them, Gallman feared, leaving the frontiers "entirely Desolate."[27]

Less than one hundred miles from Charles Town, warriors killed or captured four men and women along Beaver Creek, a tributary of the Congaree. Inhabitants were frightened. "Instead of their obeying my Command," militia captain Peter Crim reported, local men "Beat me and Abused me with the Rest of the officers in a Very Grose manner." But the upstarts were right. Until the government issued Crim an official commission, he could not compel them to fight the Cherokees. While he waited for word from Charles Town, he built a small fort and took in what few settlers he could, leaving others to escape on their own or perish trying.[28]

Rather than attack the Georgia or South Carolina frontiers in a unified front with warriors from the Middle and Lower Towns, Overhill warriors targeted other areas, beginning on February 10. The strategy reflects the way the Cherokees coordinated their efforts by village clusters. Fort Dobbs, located in present Statesville, offered little protection for widely dispersed settlers in the North Carolina Piedmont. Thus the farmers on the Yadkin and Catawba Rivers made easy targets. By February 19, refugees streamed into the fledgling Moravian settlements of Bethabara and Bethania.[29]

Cherokees scouted and planned an attack on Fort Dobbs for several days. On February 27, the warriors gathered along a spring a few hundred yards below the fort to make their move. Between 8:00 and 9:00 P.M., the garrison's dogs began to bark. The commotion lured Colonel Hugh Waddell and nine others out of the fort and down the hill toward the spring to investigate. It unfolded just as the Cherokees had planned. Sixty or seventy Setticos opened fire and advanced "either to tomahawk or make us Prisoners," Waddell said. Three of his men fell dead. The colonel ordered his troops, twelve paces from the Setticos, to return fire. The volley stunned the Cherokees and bought time for Waddell's detachment to retreat back up the hill. But as they did, gunfire shattered Waddell's gun barrel and another party of warriors attacked the fort. The garrison repulsed the Cherokee attack. But one of the wounded men was scalped. Waddell guessed that his men killed "not less than 10 or 12" Cherokees. The next morning, the soldiers "found a great deal of blood" and a dead Cherokee.[30] Waddell's men lacked the numbers to engage the numerous and well-armed Indians. Nor could they leave the fort to protect or rescue North Carolina settlers.

Overhill warriors, among them Chotas and Great Tellicos, also lay siege to Fort Loudoun in what is now Tennessee. The warriors "attacked this Fort, if Firing at about 300 yards Distance for 4 days can be called an Attack," Captain John Stuart wrote. Ostenaco directed the Cherokee siege, but the captain apparently misinterpreted the Indians' objectives. The siege was a ploy to lure soldiers out of the fort for an ambush. The attempt failed, and the Indians "Dessisted, neither side having received any Dammage." But Fort Loudoun was surrounded, the paths to and from it blocked to white travelers.[31]

Cherokees sought scalps and prisoners on the Georgia frontier, too. From February 6 to 15, Indians killed at least ten Georgians in the settlements above Augusta. They wounded several others and took several captives. The fate of another fourteen backcountry Georgians remains unclear. At least two or three of the war parties hailed from Estatoe in the Lower Towns.[32]

The Georgia Assembly, unlike its South Carolina counterpart, provided a prompt and generous response. It immediately funded the construction of log forts in exposed areas and fed two hundred militiamen. Governor Ellis moved ranger troops and Independent Companies troops to the frontier.[33] Volunteers fortified Augusta. Traders and settlers retreated into private forts. Nearly all of the six hundred white and black inhabitants of northeast Georgia found shelter at James Germany's trading post fourteen miles up the Broad River from Augusta. The quick and coordinated efforts saved many lives; Cherokees took just five more scalps in Georgia in mid-February.[34]

Their plans foiled, Cherokees changed their approach. With settlers secure in forts, warriors targeted African American slaves employed in the deerskin trade. The Cherokees made no distinction between white and black. They saw them as partners complicit in exacerbating Cherokee grievances. Whites had used slaves in the corrupt trade and to clear and till lands in Cherokee hunting grounds. The Indians killed, tortured, or assimilated blacks and whites alike according to gender, age, and the clan mothers' wishes. Because their labor left them in the open and exposed, slave workers made easy targets. Along both sides of the Savannah River, Indians killed and wounded these African American bondsmen.[35] Cherokees were attacking white southerners' economic lifeline—slavery.

By venturing into Georgia, the Cherokees may have been trying to frame their Creek Indian neighbors. If they made it seem that Creeks had broken out against the English, maybe some Creeks would believe it and would take arms in kind. Either way, the action aimed to strengthen the Cherokee military situation.[36] Most Creeks, however, insisted on neutrality. They had no love for the Cherokees, with whom they had warred until the mid-1750s. The

Creek Confederacy was a loose, decentralized medley of diverse peoples and disparate languages. The French protected the western Creek villages from British-allied Chickasaw raiders without encroaching on Indian lands. Thus pro-Cherokee and anti-British Creeks were rare. Georgia governor Henry Ellis extended £1,000 from his personal fortune to Indian agents for Creek gifts. He offered £5 sterling to any Indian bringing in a Cherokee scalp. He slowly won over a handful of warriors in the Lower Creek towns, where French influence was weaker.[37]

Ellis and Indian agent Edmond Atkin begged Lower Creek warriors to attack the Cherokees. But the Indians refused to allow Atkin to manipulate them into action, and they would not strike against the Cherokees without first reaching a broad consensus among themselves. Atkin threatened to withdraw the Creek traders. He was bluffing, but the Creeks did not know it. Alleck of Cussitah and other Lower Creeks rushed to Savannah to meet Ellis.[38] Ellis found shelter for Creek women and children and sent supplies and presents to the Lower Creek towns. Most Creeks failed to buy into Ellis's plan, but several war parties agreed to take Cherokee scalps in the settlements.[39]

More might have joined if not for Atkin's antics. The superintendent paraded to Coweta in the Lower Creek towns. There on February 21, he "did not ask their help, but required it." Atkin alienated Creek leaders with his threats and demands. The Cowetas vowed that if the agent persisted in his machinations, they would attack the British garrison at Fort Augusta. "This Gentleman," Georgia governor Henry Ellis wrote, had "greatly disturbed and embarrassed" Creek affairs, and "he appears very ill calculated for the employment he is in." Atkin quieted after that.[40]

By the end of February, the Cherokees halted their operations. Warriors returned home with at least fifty prisoners. They had avenged their dead and taken enough captives to fulfill social and spiritual needs. They tortured some prisoners and sent others to the French in a sign of sympathy for French dead and in an attempt to build an alliance. Then they learned that the soldiers at Fort Prince George had killed the Cherokee hostages.[41]

The news was galvanizing. It meant that the respite from violence was short-lived, several days at most, no longer than the waiting period required for warriors to reenter society and then prepare again for war. Hundreds of Cherokees returned to the South Carolina frontier to avenge the death of the hostages. This time they were less successful. They first struck the smallpox-riddled stockade at Fort Ninety Six. Two thirds of the garrison was ill. At least fourteen had died in the previous month, leaving just twenty-five men to fight.

But "We put ourselves in the best Order we were able for their Reception," Captain Francis wrote. After sunrise the next day, March 2, 240 or 250 Indians "run up within 60 yards of the stockade," Francis recalled. Unable to lure anyone out or to find a low-risk way to capture the fort, the Cherokees withdrew after a brief engagement. Two white men were wounded.[42]

But "We had the Pleasure," Francis gloated, to kill six Cherokees and to wound "many" others. The high casualty count suggests that the Cherokees desperately wanted to capture the post, to affirm their military prowess and avenge their unsuccessful assault the month before. They also recognized the strategic and symbolic purpose of the fort. "We have now the Pleasure Sir," Francis boasted, "to fatten our Dogs with their Carcases, and to display their Scalps, neatly ornamented on the Tops of our Bastions."[43]

The display licensed the Cherokees to exact blood revenge and to release the lingering souls of the Cherokee departed to complete their journey to the afterlife. Ironically, in their efforts to drive off the Cherokees, Francis's black and white militiamen and traders caused the opposite to happen, perpetuating a vicious cycle of retribution. The captain noted soon after that the grim spectacle seemed to "irritate them, as to collect their whole Force, and make a stronger Effort if they possibly can to seek Revenge."[44]

Next, 350 Cherokees went to the Saluda River settlements and approached the farms and communities they had targeted in February. Finding few settlers nearby, they burned and destroyed cabins and "all the Grain and Fodder they could meet with." The warriors likewise "called up all the hogs in to the houses, and burnt them also," the *Gazette* reported. And they killed "all the large Cattle near" the road. This was more than an attempt to lure refugees from the forts. It was more than a rare "scorched earth" tactic. Cherokee men despised hogs and saw cattle as "white mens' deer," Tom Hatley has pointed out. Moreover, by killing these animals, Cherokee men aggressively attacked whites' means of making a living and their humanity. This was payback for poaching Cherokee deer. Cherokee warriors also intended to send a crippling blow not only to the Carolina frontier economy, but also to the provincial psyche.[45]

The hideous violence continued. In an action reminiscent of the second battle at Fort Ninety Six, militiamen killed and scalped two Cherokees at a fort on Bush River. The *Gazette* alleged that the backsettlers had gone mad in the wake of the recent Cherokee assaults. "The Bodies of the Savages," according to one report, "were cut to Pieces and given to the Dogs, so much are the Back-Settlers exasperated at their Perfidy and Barbarity." This was psychological warfare. And its effect on readers was electrifying. The message and the treatment were consistent with the way that many white South Carolinians saw Cherokees.[46]

Cherokee warriors also returned to nearby Turner's Fort, the private stockade and site of their failed February 2 assault. This time they killed two men and captured two others outside the enclosure. As they withdrew, a party of rangers under Captain John Grinnan engaged them in battle. The Cherokees drove the outnumbered rangers into the fort. Rather than lay siege, the warriors departed. Siege warfare was difficult and thus undesirable unless it fit a specific strategic objective, such as luring men out of the fort, capitalizing on a numerical advantage, seeking revenge, or saving face. Instead, they went on "burning and destroying every Thing in their Way." As always, the Cherokees strove to limit casualties to their own troops.[47]

More warriors struck along the Broad River, just as they had in February. But they met an energized militia no larger charged with helping refugees flee. The Cherokees lost thirteen men. In the Congarees, the warriors either killed or carried off just one man, rounding up horses near his home a mile from Gallman's Fort. A day later in Saxe-Gotha Township, they killed and scalped two farmers. If reports are credible, warriors may have taken twenty-five scalps in the Forks of the Edisto, less than one hundred miles from Charles Town, but that seems doubtful.[48] With the frontiers largely emptied, ammunition scarce, and the forts defensible against Cherokee attack, few easy targets remained. With prisoners in tow, they returned home. Welcoming festivities, ritual torture of prisoners, and induction rites for new adoptees awaited before the planting season began. By late March, they withdrew to their home villages.[49]

The Cherokees soon ceased their attacks on Georgia as well. Georgia's Indian allies served as a powerful deterrent. By mid-April, fifty Lower Chickasaws from their settlement at New Savannah joined the Georgia Rangers in search of Cherokee warriors. Eventually, half a dozen British-allied war parties operated on the Georgia–South Carolina border. They soon brought in several Cherokee scalps.[50] The last thing the Cherokees wanted was a war with the fierce Chickasaws or the populous Creeks. It would expose their southeastern and western borders to enemy Indians and their eastern flanks to South Carolina provincials or British troops. With this in mind they withdrew permanently from Georgia.

North Carolina was a different matter. Overhill warriors resumed their campaign in the piedmont in March. Skirmishes took place almost daily. From February 10 to April 6, Cherokees killed over two dozen settlers along the Yadkin. Half of North Carolina's frontier settlers had fled for the coast or for the fortified Moravian settlements of Bethabara and Bethania. Here, as in South Carolina, when it became too risky to kill or capture the white inhabitants, they killed and intimidated stragglers, forestalling resettlement and recovery.[51]

The initial success of the Cherokee offensive and the continued Cherokee presence on the frontier triggered a massive refugee crisis. When the attacks abated, fear, destitution, and despair remained. Nowhere was the crisis worse than in South Carolina. Settlers entrenched themselves in hastily constructed stockades "all filled with most wretched people, destitute of every thing." At least thirty scattered backcountry fortifications accommodated more than 1,500 people.[52] But when they fell ill of smallpox and measles and began to starve, the evacuees fled for communities closer to the coast. Hundreds of Scots-Irish crowded into the Presbyterian enclaves throughout the colony—Williamsburg, Stoney Creek, Jacksonboro, and the Waxhaws. Hundreds more Germans and Swiss from Saxe-Gotha and the Congarees fled to Ebenezer, Savannah, and Purrysburg. Others retreated, ironically, to Virginia, from where they had come just a few years earlier.[53]

The Cherokees had pushed the frontier more than one hundred miles southeast. Reports placed Cherokee warriors near Orangeburg—173 miles from the Lower Towns, and just 76 miles from Charles Town. Colonel George Pawley marched half of the coastal unit of George Town militia twenty miles up the Black River to respond to a panicked letter that "the Indians is now upon us."[54] As long as coastal elites took no action to either raise troops or protect and assist the colonists, the Cherokees would claim success.

The consequences rippled deeply through South Carolina society. The growing export trade was crippled. Without frontier settlers to impede them, the Cherokees brought their assaults ever closer to the coast. This hampered the plantation economy and imperiled the lifestyles and lives of the rich. Though the frontiersmen bore the brunt of Cherokee attacks, "every one suffers more or Less & will continue so till we are at peace with the Indians," attorney and plantation manager Robert Raper wrote. "Great Charges will arise." Some planters were "afraid to plant Rice, for fear of having their Negroes killed," he added. "War Time more or less stops all proceedings." As long as Cherokee violence—or the threat of it—drew off coastal militiamen, black Carolinians might also take action to improve their lot. "We have but a handful of white men and 70,000 negroes," Dr. Alexander Garden wrote. "We know not whether our Indians or negroes be our greatest enemies." Underscoring their fear of black insurgency, and perhaps shaken by the foiled

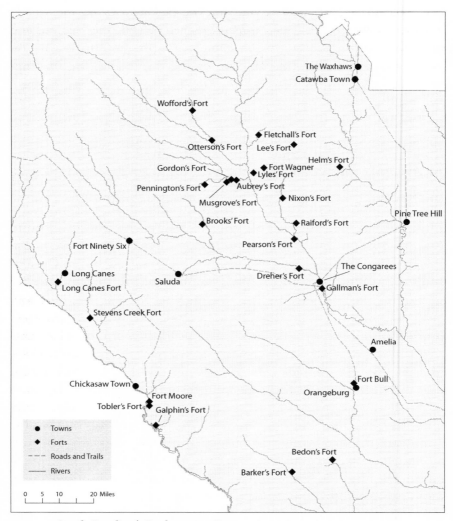

MAP 7.1 *South Carolina's Backcountry Forts, 1760*

Philip John conspiracy several months earlier, white residents of Colleton County had a new fort built on the upper Ashepoo River to defend themselves against a slave revolt. The stockade was 40 miles inland from Charles Town, and 250 miles from the Lower Towns.[55]

The accounts of Cherokee success turned backcountry settlers against elites. The slow response of British authorities and the coastal aristocracy further convinced backcountry settlers of the neglect and indifference that they had dealt with for years. George Milligen, the surgeon on Lyttelton's campaign, recalled, "Many who fled into the Woods, for Safety lost themselves and miserably perished." And "the luckiest, who escaped the Indians and gained the lower Settlements," he continued, "were reduced, from Affluence, Plenty, and Independence, to Poverty, Beggary, and Want." Though "the unhappy Sufferers" were "calling aloud for Assistance and Support," they got none from colonial elites and British officials.[56]

On February 17, Presbyterian pastor Archibald Simpson, who lived about twenty miles northwest of Beaufort, reflected on the "poor destitute famelys present with us, without habitation or dwelling place." Simpson's own congregants were "melencholy, amazed and overwhelmed with terrour," fearing that they were next in line for Cherokee hatchets and bullets. More than six weeks later, "poor famelies in droves" still fled "in the most melencholy circumstances," Simpson wrote, and the destruction was "coming nearer and nearer daily." They met "with but too little sympathy or support, among those who are safe in their habitations." The preacher observed that all signs "of pity, and compassion to the distressed," poor, non-Anglicans, "seem shut up."[57]

Newspaper coverage of the Cherokee raids had created a one-sided and misleading perspective of the events. Forts were filled "with most wretched people, destitute of every thing." The "unfortunate" backcountry inhabitants were "inhumanly butchered," their "mangled dead bodies" left to rot. Cherokees were "burning and destroying every Thing in their Way." As Peter Silver has observed in Pennsylvania, through the violence and the "rhetoric of suffering" it solidified, settlers built a shared identity. Indian violence created long-lasting "self-pity." The Cherokee offensive created, and laid the groundwork for a strengthening anti-Indian mindset among the backcountry settlers and their sympathizers. Likewise, it created a sense of mistrust, even disdain, for British policy that would, in future years, seem to side with the Indians.[58]

Fort Augusta's commander, Lieutenant White Outerbridge, wealthy enough to have bought his commission two decades earlier, took a less sympathetic view of events. He did not blame the death toll on the government's failure to respond. Instead he attributed it "in some measure to the Impudence of the White People, who go out in small Parties, & unhappily differ among themselves & divide in yet smaller Partys . . . which give the Savages a good Opportunity of Destroying them." Outerbridge ascribed their fate to disciplinary lapses, disrespect for authority, and lack of military training.[59]

The public confidence that Lyttelton had once enjoyed turned to disdain. Lyttelton had unwisely "brought upon us a war," Dr. Milligen, a surgeon in the Independents, recalled. The province, saddled with the costs of that campaign and plagued by smallpox, "was unable of itself to manage [that] War," he continued. Lyttelton checked out of public life altogether by March 1760. He was, according to Alexander Garden, "embarrassed and taken up in settling his private affairs" before departing the province.[60]

But the governor's departure did not quell the public critique. Lyttelton had, Garden lamented, "laid a design to conquer [the Cherokees] very ill, and executed it without judgment or discernment." The doctor continued: "Never was there a man more outwitted; never was there a province more abused. We have lost our money, our friends, and our character. All a sacrifice to ambition and undiscerning pride." Lyttelton's mismanagement, Milligen and Garden noted, also triggered a financial crisis. To make matters worse, the province felt neglected by the metropole. "You will laugh at me for spending so much paper on politics," Garden wrote to his friend John Ellis across the Atlantic. But "I wish they could be seriously thought of at home. War is at our door, and when I consider the general ignorance of our people of the country, where the seat of the war must be, I tremble," he said.[61] South Carolina needed British help.

But for the Cherokee Indians, the spring campaigns brought optimism and relief. By following "Governor Lyttelton at the heels, with fire, sword, and devastation," as Garden put it, the Cherokees returned home with scalps and adoptees.[62] They regained their hunting grounds and drove back the South Carolina frontier. They began to restore their world and lifted spirits in the villages. And they did so in time for the spring planting to begin. Soldiers remained among them at Fort Loudoun and Fort Prince George. Grievances were still unresolved. But the time seemed right for a peaceful settlement. Unfortunately for the Indians it did not come. South Carolina authorities sought British troops instead of negotiations.

FLUSH'D WITH SUCCESS
Cherokee Victory and the Fall of Fort Loudoun

8 On March 20, Ostenaco led a large party of warriors against Fort Loudoun. The Indians surrounded the fort and fired on it for four consecutive days and nights. They cut off the garrison from all outside communication. By April, food ran low. By May, the beef was spoiled. There was no salt. Two hundred men, women, and children were shuttered inside, with only some corn, "pease pumpkins potatoes &ca," smuggled in by Cherokee women, Captain John Stuart reported. In traditional matrilineal Cherokee society, women were the arbiters of justice. They often called for revenge and instigated war. But when revenge was accomplished and captives taken, they could call off war, too. In the three years since the fort's completion, Cherokee women had gained economic power through their ability to barter surplus crops at the outpost. "Their Women are so much used to our Commodities, Ribbands, Paint, etc.," James Mark Prevost, an officer at Fort Prince George wrote in 1764, "that they soon feel the want of it." Prevost claimed that in 1760, Cherokee women pressured the men to end the war and to reopen the trade.[1]

Cherokee women had also taken husbands and started families with the soldiers at Fort Loudoun. They had done the same with the traders who took refuge with the garrison. Those men were now part of their clans, thus under their protection. Writing in 1762, one white observer noted that Willenawa, a Toqua warrior organizing the siege of Fort Loudoun, "threatened death to those [women] who would assist their enemy." But the abettors of the beleaguered garrison "laugh[ed] at his threats" and vowed to "succor their husbands every day." If he killed their white husbands, they pledged, "their relations would make his death atone for theirs." Willenawa did not act on his threats. With the trade suspended, ammunition dwindled. So too did food and European goods. Now the Cherokee women wanted peace, and the warriors would not listen to them. By acting as intermediaries between the villages and the fort, the women tried to convince the soldiers and traders inside to reach peace terms that addressed Cherokee complaints. But since whites did not recognize the social and political equality of Cherokee women, these efforts were in vain.[2]

Like the women, though apparently independent of them, Attakullakulla too advocated peace with South Carolina. But many Cherokees blamed him for the hostage crisis and for the hostages' death. As Captain Stuart noted, "His Life was threatned and he was obliged to Fly to the woods." By mid-March, Attakullakulla moved his family to Fort Loudoun. His status was that of an exile. He "holds no manner of Communication with any of his own people," wrote Stuart. Attakullakulla hoped the British would purge his rivals, the captain reported, "and then he hopes to reestablish his Authority by becoming a mediator." Attakullakulla's political future was at stake.[3] A majority of Cherokee villagers agreed with him. After April 1, they regrouped, planted corn, and integrated their new members into Cherokee life. Smallpox still lingered in several Cherokee towns, displacing and distracting many.

A small minority of Cherokee men disagreed with the women, with Attakullakulla, and with the majority of their townspeople. They wished to remove the soldiers and to prove their mettle and their manhood in the process. To do so would rid them of the cultural, physical, and economic abuse that had become more widespread since the construction of the forts. Beyond that, they coveted the guns, ammunition, and other goods inside the forts. Some among them also feared that peace with the British would invite Creek and French attacks from the south and southwest. So some warriors continued to choke off Fort Loudoun and Fort Prince George.[4]

At the same time, some British authorities sought to end hostilities. In April 1760, former South Carolina governor James Glen, still hoping to restore his reputation, offered to broker a peace with the Cherokees. He hoped that "matters may be honorably accommodated" and called for an assimilation program afterward. General Jeffery Amherst rejected the proposal.[5]

Instead, Amherst promptly responded to Lyttelton's panicked letters. The general dispatched 1,312 battle-tested British troops, flush with recent victories over the French in New York at Ticonderoga and Crown Point, to South

Carolina. The troops included the 2nd Battalion of Royal Scots (the 1st Regiment), and Scottish Highlanders of the 77th Regiment, under Colonel Archibald Montgomery. The thirty-four-year-old Montgomery was charismatic and wildly popular with his troops. Though a Lowland Scot, he "mixed much with the people," spoke Gaelic, and had "a considerable dash of romantic enthusiasm in his composition," one contemporary observer wrote. Suffering from rheumatism, Montgomery rarely wrote letters. He delegated much of the campaign's logistics and correspondence to his opinionated and high-handed second, James Grant (now a lieutenant colonel). Amherst ordered Montgomery to take to the offensive against the Cherokees, "by Destroying their Towns, and cutting up their Settlements." Amherst granted Montgomery leeway to proceed in whatever manner "shall occurr best to You for the future Protection of the Colony, the Lives and properties of the Subjects, and the present punishment of those barbarian savages." He instructed him not to remain in South Carolina unless absolutely necessary. With the British conquest of Canada planned, Montgomery's troops would be needed to the north.[6]

Montgomery was skeptical of the South Carolina legislature's expectations. The assemblymen "are for putting all the Cherokees to Death, or making Slaves of them," he wrote. "Those Indians are Rogues, as they all are," he continued. "But I fancy they have sometimes been hardly dealt by and if they would tell their own story I doubt Much if they are so much to blame as has been Represented by the People of this Province." The colonel sympathized with the Cherokees, as Grant had at Shippensburg in 1758. Foreshadowing British sentiments in future years, Montgomery blamed the province for creating and exacerbating the crisis on the frontier. Moreover, he resented that that the province was diverting Crown resources to clean up a mess of its own making.[7]

To colonists, Cherokee resistance emboldened slaves and drew off militiamen from the province. It also disturbed the colony's economy by halting the deerskin trade. By driving off backcountry settlers, it disrupted farming and ranching on the frontier. The settlers were becoming an increasingly indispensable cog in the provincial economy. They also buffered coastal elites against Indian attack and deterred runaway slaves and maroons. South Carolina's lowcountry merchants and planters—who made up the provincial assembly—depended on British protection for safety and prosperity. Ultimately, as the war escalated instead of diminished, many colonial elites called for a harsh policy toward the Cherokees. Assemblyman Christopher Gadsden later recalled that "an entire dependence was placed on [the redcoats], that they would *certainly* do our business," which he envisioned as "getting upon [the Cherokees'] backs & cutting their throats."[8]

Montgomery agreed that "if there were no troops in the country . . . A dozen of Indians might go to Charles Town." The Highlanders, along with soldiers from the Royal American Regiment and some Virginia provincials, had spent the winter of 1757–58 in Charles Town. As Colonel Henry Bouquet had observed two years earlier in a bitter struggle with the assembly for supplies and barrack necessities, the legislators would "feel no inconveniences" for that protection. The redcoats, depleted by sickness and dismayed at their poor reception, had been redeployed to Pennsylvania just before tensions came to a head. But Jeffery Amherst, expecting another tense standoff between Crown and province, voiced his expectations for the 1760 campaign: "Men that go to defend & protect the Lives and Properties of the Subject, deserve a more gratefull Return."[9]

Montgomery and Grant arrived in a tense environment. According to attorney and plantation manager Robert Raper, Montgomery vowed "that if the Governmt here don't send them waggons immediately, he will reimbark for N. York so there is no hopes from the Ships of Rice Rising." He not only would withdraw the troops, but he would hurt the planters and merchants, too. Only through threats and coercion did Montgomery and Grant secure the carriages, wagons, and supplies they needed for the campaign. They marched on April 24 from Moncks Corner, "not very well satisfied on account of Government assistance being very tardy," Raper reported. Montgomery's army did not reach the Congarees until May 1.[10]

From May 1 to May 9, peace-seeking Indian emissaries daily arrived near Fort Prince George from the Overhills. But Ensign Alexander Miln, the fort's commander, had other plans. He sparked yet another hostage crisis on May 9. During a formal dinner, on his orders, traders and soldiers overpowered and shackled Cherokee diplomats. Miln released the Wolf of Settico with a message for Standing Turkey of Chota, Connecorte's successor. Miln demanded that Cherokees deliver all the white prisoners they had taken in recent months. A new hostage crisis was underway. Lieutenant Governor William Bull II condemned Miln's actions: "A Confidence in public Faith" must be observed "even among Enemies," he opined. Miln saved Fort Prince George from attack and bought time for the British troops then on the march. Cherokees knew what would happen to their hostages if they attacked and would not sacrifice their own people.[11]

Montgomery rendezvoused at the Congarees with a meager detachment of provincial soldiers and rangers. On May 17, after a soggy weeklong journey his army spotted the stockade at Ninety Six "and a great number of miserable people, chiefly women and children, cooped up in it," one soldier wrote.[12] As Montgomery waited for more cattle and flour, Abram, the slave messenger promised his freedom by Captain Demere four months earlier, arrived with several letters. One of the letters was from Captain John Stuart to his brother, Allan, the surgeon in Montgomery's regiment. In short, the captain predicted as he recalled what had happened since he had marched to Fort Loudoun, "I expect to be an Actor, in a scene of Great Distress." Few Cherokees wanted to negotiate for peace. Montgomery was aware that Fort Loudoun might fall to the Overhill warriors. Yet to relieve that outpost, the colonel would have to push 250 miles further with little support from South Carolina. The provincial commander, Colonel Richard Richardson, "greatly mortified" at his meager corps assembled at Ninety Six, resigned and went home. The ragtag army was now under Captain John Morrison of Amelia Township and his second, Lieutenant Patrick Calhoun of Long Canes. Montgomery grumbled that Morrison and Calhoun had "about eighty [provincials], the half of those good for nothing." In fact, he decided, "We have not a single man with us that is of any consequence in the Provincials."[13]

On May 28, the troops left Fort Ninety Six. The army now consisted of over 1,700 men, including the provincials, 300 provincial rangers, 40 Catawbas, and packhorsemen and guides. Montgomery intended "to burn a few Indian Towns and Punish some of the Most guilty, and make A treaty with them." On June 1, they reached the Lower Towns. The colonel left a small detachment to guard the cattle and carriages. Then he led his men on a thirty-six-hour rampage.[14] The army stormed through Little Keowee, bayoneting Cherokee men, seizing Indian women and children, and liberating captives. Cherokee defenders, caught by surprise, managed to kill three privates and wounded four.[15]

The troops pressed on, burning "every house and town in the Lower nation," Grant reported. The next stop was Estatoe. Those "who had not time to escape, were killed," Grant added. "I know for certain," he continued, that some Cherokees "perished in the flames." Indeed, "The surprise was compleat," a soldier wrote, "and the *Indians* so terrified" that they offered but "trifling" resistance. Cherokees killed just three; most of the Indians watched helplessly from the mountaintops as flames consumed ammunition and "astonishing" storehouses of corn and enveloped Cherokee homes full of wampum, clothes, skins, and other items. Toxaway, Quaratchee, and the newly fortified village of Conasatchee were razed. Then, the army returned to Fort Prince George, its mission accomplished.[16]

More than fifty Cherokees lost their lives in thirty-six hours. Thirty to thirty-five were British prisoners. The Cherokees "are in our power," Grant wrote, and "we are ready to give them peace." The British officers released Tistoe and the Old Warrior of Estatoe with letters to the Middle and Overhill Towns, pledging to destroy them "if they did not acquiesce." They also sent an express to Captain Demere urging him to send Attakullakulla and John Stuart to negotiate. Edmond Atkin prepared for parleys at the fort. Soldier morale ran high. Many observers in Charles Town, however, thought that Montgomery should push further and take more vengeance.[17]

By the time the troops returned to Fort Prince George, Lieutenant Governor Bull had already forwarded Montgomery the peace terms proposed by the South Carolina Council. They called for the execution of "the principal incendiaries" of the Cherokees, among them Seroweh. They required the Cherokees to deliver at least five "of the sons of the principal headmen of the Cherokee nation not under 20 years of age" to be held as hostages in Charles Town for "one year at least," until they had fully proven "their Loyalty and Subjection to His Majesty." The Cherokees were to deliver "All Prisoners" and "all the Frenchmen." Only then could negotiations begin in Charles Town between the governor and forty or fifty headmen "chosen & regularly Deputed by the whole Nation." Then Bull and the council would restore the trade on the same footing as before the war started.[18]

Perhaps unsurprisingly, Cherokee villagers refused to treat for peace. The terms were far too harsh. The idea of hostages was as incomprehensible to them in 1760 as it was the year before. As Montgomery wrote, "The unlucky affair of Hostages . . . not only prolongs the war, but in some measures makes a Peace impracticable." As Grant put it, "those savages cannot be convinced that a white man is honest." Fort Loudoun's fall seemed imminent. Only Tomotley, Attakullakulla's hometown, stood for peace.[19] The families of the dead Lower Townsmen demanded revenge. Warriors attacked rangers, packhorsemen, and soldiers. They killed four, wounded five, and captured one. As a sign of good faith, Montgomery released four more of the Cherokee hostages at the fort, including the Raven of Estatoe. The Cherokees rebuffed Montgomery's overtures and prepared to repulse Montgomery's likely invasion.[20]

Peace looked unlikely, so Montgomery planned to invade the Middle Towns. From Mount Vernon, Virginia, the retired colonel George Washington expressed doubts about the prospects of the enterprise. Montgomery should "be wary," he said; "he has a crafty, Subtil Enemy to deal with that may give him most trouble when he least expects it."[21] Short on guides and scouts and low on provisions, Montgomery had little chance of reaching Fort Loudoun. But the soldiers at Fort Loudoun and the white observers in coastal South Carolina expected him to do so. Vexed by an uncooperative assembly, a meager South Carolina provincial regiment, and numerous delays, Montgomery wished to return to the North. "I long much to get out of this Indian War and to Return to the Army," he wrote to Amherst.[22]

Amherst expected Virginia and North Carolina troops to invade the Overhills from the northeast and lift the siege of Fort Loudoun. But both failed to mobilize quickly enough. Fauquier called on a reluctant Colonel William Byrd III to lead the enterprise. Byrd called the plan "ill-concerted." It took the entire month of June for the Virginia Burgesses to recruit, clothe, arm, and supply soldiers for the expedition. And no one expected much from cash-poor and politically contentious North Carolina.[23]

On May 14, warriors in several Lower Creek towns killed fifteen white traders.[24] Word reached Charles Town on May 30, sparking fear that the Creeks would join the Cherokees in an offensive against the southeastern British frontier. Bull prepared to lead an army against the Creeks. He placed half of the militia on marching orders. He ordered Major Lachlan Shaw to abandon Fort Moore and to reinforce Fort Augusta. The Cherokee offensive had made South Carolina's military situation desperate.[25]

Though no Anglo-Creek rift actually took place, the specter of a war with Creek Indians still loomed in the minds of lowcountry elites. A strong show of force by Montgomery and Grant could "ma[k]e an impression on the Creeks." And it could also quell the possibility of slave unrest. With militiamen drawn to the frontiers, slaves might seize the opportunity to rise up against the further outnumbered coastal white minority. Alexander Garden captured the fears of South Carolina's 35,000 white colonists directly: "about 13,000 external enemies. About 70,000 negroes in our bowels! Our strength consists of 1200 men with Col. Montgomery, gone against the Cherokees; and we muster about 8 or 9000 men in the province. This is our happy situation!" White South Carolinians had done little to cultivate allies. "We know not," Garden said, "whether our Indians or negroes be our greatest enemies." Legislators also feared the influence of free blacks over enslaved African Americans. John Pendarvis, Philip John's co-conspirator in 1759, had proven that. If Montgomery could swiftly secure peace, he not only limited the possibility that Creeks might join the Cherokees to rout the British, but he also stabilized the internal situation in South Carolina.[26]

As Montgomery marched toward the frontier, news of a massive slave up-rising in Jamaica reached Charles Town. The rebellion became known as Tackey's War. Could something similar also happen in South Carolina? Black colonists surely hearkened to the possibility. If the Cherokees were "exter-minated," a vast, mountainous territory beckoned anyone who dared slip the bonds of slavery. "Those fertile Vallies, surrounded by Mountains," Lieuten-ant Governor Bull opined, "afford a secure and plentiful Refuge to the run away Negroes from this Province and Virginia, who might be more trouble-some and more difficult to be reduced than the Negroes in the Mountains of Jamaica." The construction of remote communities by runaways, or so-called maroons, had done much to fuel the Jamaican rebellion. And it was a recurring dream for South Carolina slaves. Bull hoped merely to "chastise" the Cherokees, believing that they "should be received into our favour again." He hoped that if he accomplished his goals, marronage, and African Ameri-can resistance in general, would wane. Meanwhile, to avoid heightening white fear and black resolve, the *Gazette* omitted "any Accounts of Insurrections" from Jamaica.[27]

Back in the Overhills at Fort Loudoun, Cherokee women continued to pro-cure food and intelligence to protect their white husbands. Attakullakulla still faced frequent death threats. He occasionally ventured out to find pro-visions and collect intelligence. But "the Indians hide every thing from me, & say that I am the white people's Friend." Women swayed public opinion in Toqua and Tomotley, but the other Overhill Towns supported the ongoing siege.[28]

To seek revenge for the new hostage crisis at Fort Prince George, a party of Overhills came to Fort Loudoun on June 3. Some Cherokee women in-formed the soldiers of a possible attempt "to surprise our horse-Guard." The warriors then hid in the bushes. When Lieutenant Maurice Anderson of the Independent Companies and packhorseman Thomas Smith "walked not about 50 yards," Stuart recalled, "they killed them both Dead, Scalped and mangled them." Fifty soldiers "Sallied out" but retreated hastily when they found the Cherokees "very numerous." The only casualty was a soldier "shot thro' the arm."[29]

Attakullakulla left the fort and followed the warriors back to Tomotley. In that village's townhouse, risking his life, he begged them to cease hostilities, reported Captain John Stuart. But "they Insulted" and taunted the peace-minded Cherokee, asking "where the Army was he had sent for." And they "wanted to see how he would cry for his Friend," the now-dead Maurice An-derson. Attakullakulla "boldly" shouted back, Stuart noted, that the warriors

IMAGE 8.1 *A view of the reconstructed Fort Loudoun, at Fort Loudoun State Historic Area, Tenn. Author photo.*

were cowards for killing "a man who had allways been good and kind to them." The headman returned to Fort Loudoun, where he informed Stuart of what happened and confessed that he longed "anxiously" for Montgomery's arrival.[30]

Soldiers braced for an attack when they learned that Oconostota planned to assault the fort at night, "to burn down the Puncheons, and put us every one to death." A soldier wrote from Fort Loudoun that Ostenaco "openly repeated, that if peace was made even 7 times," whether "thro' necessity or convenience . . . he would always disregard and break it." Demere complained on June 6 that the Indians "about the fort" blocked intelligence and foodstuffs from reaching the garrison.[31]

Early on June 24, Montgomery's army departed Fort Prince George. Over the next two days, it traversed dangerous mountain passes. On June 26 the army crossed what is today called Rabun Gap and reached the Dividings and camped for the night where the trail forked. One treacherous road led west to the Valley Towns; the other followed the Little Tennessee River north to the Middle Towns. At 4:00 A.M. on June 27, the troops marched again. Echoe, the southernmost village in the Middle Towns, lay eighteen miles north. Echoe was a mother town, one of the original seven Cherokee settlements in the Southeast. As such, it was also place of refuge and of peace. That was about to change.[32]

Six miles south of Echoe, the river takes a sharp, horseshoe turn to the right. The trail follows it. Here, at a narrow pinch point, on the outskirts of Tessentee Old Town, 630 Cherokee warriors awaited the invaders. Some of the warriors lay in a brushy area to the east, "so thick that one could scarce see three yards distance in some places." To the west was a steep mountain. The trail was mucky. Lower and Middle Townsmen made up most of the force. According to Montgomery's guides, a handful of Creeks and Choctaws were there as well. It was a remarkable moment: a bold statement of Cherokee unity and resolve against an invading force. Seroweh, the Raven of Estatoe, and Tistoe of Keowee led the army. Each had already figured prominently in the events of 1760. It would not be, as people might expect, an unorganized free-for-all.[33]

At 9:00 or 10:00 A.M., Cherokees ambushed Montgomery's army. From the cover of the brushy thicket, Cherokees opened fire on an advanced guard of two dozen South Carolina troops. Provincial commander Captain John Morrison fell instantly, and his men retreated to the main body. Then, they and the British troops charged forward into a shower of Cherokee bullets. Several redcoats fell dead or wounded. Heavy firing and hand-to-hand combat ensued. From the steep cliff to the west, Indians fired down on the invaders who tried to push north through the narrow pass. Montgomery's men carried makeshift carbines, "Brown Bess" muskets cut down to reduce their length and weight. The Cherokees' rifles shot farther than the redcoats' muskets, so they inflicted heavy casualties. While British troops flanked the Cherokees and gained the hilly ground, some of the Indians escaped. They would merely regroup later. In fact, a few miles north, the Indians reappeared and fired across the river from a hilly savannah. Both armies then faced each other and fired repeatedly as Montgomery drove his drawn-out column toward Echoe. Montgomery's men, in moving rapidly, attempted to prevent the Cherokees from flanking them. The army was soon spread out over several miles.[34]

The fighting lasted four or five hours. Seroweh directed the Cherokee assault, giving commands in his distinctive voice. He urged his men to "fight strong." In a form of psychological warfare, Indians whooped and jeered in English. By showing bravery, they avoided feeding the enemy's power, inspired panic in the hearts of the opposing army, and diffused any power the enemy had over them. To further intimidate the invaders, Cherokees also chattered in the Muskogean tongue.[35]

When the first of Montgomery's men reached Echoe village at dusk, Cherokees began to fire at the baggage train, cattle, and packhorsemen at the place where the river first begins to turn—six miles south.[36] Cherokee veterans of the British campaigns to the north knew how dependent European armies were on cattle and supplies. As unarmed packhorsemen and slaves scattered, Cherokees attacked "from all quarters." In constant motion, the Indians ran through the woods. They fired from the cover of bushes and trees, "in their usual way," attempting to envelop the soldiers. The British, meanwhile, lined up in squares and fought in platoons. The Cherokees later informed a white trader that the troops held rank "with uncommon steadiness and resolution." But "instead of being intimidated," he continued, the Indians "were encouraged, and shot down the men (as they express it) like turkies." The Cherokees killed dozens of horses. They shot through bags of flour. Redcoat reinforcements relieved the beleaguered rear guard, forcing the Cherokees to withdraw. British troops buried the dead under a full moon. Back at Echoe, the soldiers feared that if they entered the Cherokee huts, they would catch smallpox. So they stripped wood off Cherokee houses and made shelters. They nursed the dead. The last of Montgomery's army limped into Echoe as the sun rose the next morning.[37]

Montgomery and Grant took stock of their losses. Nineteen troops and some packhorsemen and rangers lay dead. Sixty-six were wounded, some with broken femurs and others with traumatic brain injuries.[38] Fifty Cherokees lost their lives, but only a few were wounded.[39] The following day, British troops nursed the wounded. Cherokees interred their dead—and they exhumed and mutilated the British dead. At 5:00 P.M., Cherokee warriors fired on the camp from the hills surrounding Echoe. They wounded two or three soldiers, and then withdrew unscathed when a large detachment of Montgomery's Highlanders engaged them.[40]

After this new Cherokee attack, the officers debated their options. They had traveled just sixty miles from Fort Prince George. Fort Loudoun lay ninety treacherous miles to the northwest. All agreed that with no British post in the Middle Towns, it would be "inhumane to Abandon" the wounded. Yet, they did not consider building a post. With so many horses killed and so much flour destroyed, the redcoats deemed it "impossible to Proceed." As one provincial put it, "we had not force enough to attempt the relief of fort *Loudoun*." In fact, "we must have lost Men in getting to it," Montgomery concluded. Not only had Cherokee resistance exceeded the redcoats' expectations. The

Cherokee assault on the rear guard had proven decisive. Montgomery opted to leave for New York. "Tis impossible," he wrote to General Amherst, "to extirpate" the Cherokees, "and they will not treat with us for fear of being made Prisoners." Grant echoed Montgomery's sentiments in a letter to Lieutenant Governor Bull. Yet he rather dubiously boasted that "we have succeeded in every thing we have attempted." To prevent uproar in Charles Town, Bull suppressed one of Grant's letters.[41]

Montgomery scuttled flour and corn into the river to free up horses to carry the wounded. Then, leaving campfires in the village burning, he ordered a silent midnight retreat. Cherokees had scored a stunning victory. And they had saved the Middle Towns—and the smallpox-weakened residents and refugees in them—from annihilation. The dispirited army trudged over the battlefield, encountering the disinterred, scalped, stripped, and mutilated bodies of Captain Manly Williams of the Royal Scots, and others. The men marched twenty-five miles to War-Woman's Creek, where they camped for the night.[42]

Cherokees waited, too, intending to attack the next morning at a river crossing half a mile to the south. Just after the troops began their march, fifty Highlander flankers led by Montgomery's cousin, Lieutenant Hugh Montgomery, spotted sixty Cherokees camped on a hill top. The Highlanders opened fire. More soldiers emptied a volley of shots into a group of Indians perched on another hill. The Cherokees dispersed with several dead. Cherokees then attacked the rear of the army as it forded the crossing. One Highlander was killed and another was wounded. British estimates placed the Cherokee dead at "at least A Dozen" that day. Given these casualties, and a paucity of ammunition, the Cherokees withdrew, and the army reached Fort Prince George uncontested.[43]

As fear mounted, dissension made life tense in the garrison. Rangers and provincial soldiers deserted in droves. As Gadsden later wrote, fed up with Grant's haughty treatment and disrespect on the campaign, they were further incensed to find their comrades "picked off" and the colonel "tamely submitting" to daily "scalping parties." The demoralized soldiers threatened to return to Charles Town. Montgomery left a detachment of British regulars "to strengthen the garrison and to keep the others in order." With Atkin—who would not be negotiating a peace treaty after all—and with the sick and wounded—the retreat resumed. The day after Montgomery's departure, four Cherokees killed and scalped a provincial soldier at Fort Prince George. It was an ominous sign to the British.[44]

On July 10, Abram reached Charles Town with accounts of the Cherokee victory and of Montgomery's retreat. The colonel's hasty departure had "rather inflamed, than extinguished" hostilities in the Southeast, Lieutenant Governor Bull reported. "The People here were terribly exasperated at this Retreat," Georgetown's William Fyffe remarked.[45] Cherokees stood poised to capture Fort Loudoun and Fort Prince George. They had so frightened the members of the council that some envisioned "the destruction of the British Southern Colonies." And they turned British elites against each other. Burdened by rising costs (£50,000 sterling in just nine months) and the impracticable chore of raising troops, the assembly argued that Montgomery must not leave the Cherokee country. In dispatches carried by Abram, Bull begged Montgomery to invoke the discretionary powers in his instructions and to stay.[46]

Abram returned with the commander's reply on July 23. Montgomery was determined to leave South Carolina. The colonel posted four companies of the 1st Regiment, Royal Scots, at the Congarees for defensive operations. Writing for Montgomery, Lieutenant Colonel James Grant insisted that the redcoats had humbled the Cherokees. Besides, as Grant saw it, the French posed little threat. They were "not in a Situation to the Southward to think of making Conquests."[47] Amherst told Montgomery to "not think of Coming away 'till You have most Effectually punished these Scoundrell Indians," or else it would "begin again." Had the colonel ensured, as Amherst had insisted, that "they cannot hurt the Province again soon?"[48]

The assembly doubted it. Pastor Archibald Simpson agreed. "We are to be exposed to the barbarous Indians enraged with loss of their people," he said in an unusually long journal entry. Now, "the poor men in Fort Loudoun . . . will in all probability fall a prey to that horrid Enemy." But, he allowed, "this is much owing to our own Inactivity," the "troops not having been properly supported by the country." On the retreat, Grant fired a parting shot at South Carolina's assemblymen: "Those Gentlemen might have . . . Exerted themselves a little more in forwarding the Publick Service." The redcoat criticized South Carolina's soldiers, too. He saw them as wholly incompetent and pitiful. The "few Provincials," unpaid and dressed in rags, he wrote, "seemed determined Not to serve." The South Carolina Rangers—unpaid for fourteen months—had gone home. Grant resented the colonials' sense of entitlement. The province "would never have raised a man or taken any Step for their own Security." They wished to reap the benefits of British rule but offered nothing in return. As the redcoats retreated, horses weakened and carriages broke. Three more soldiers died. And "the Sickly Season was fast come on." The redcoats boarded their still-waiting transports in Charles Town Harbor and sailed northward. They arrived too late to participate in the British conquest of

Canada. The colonel secured leave and returned home. By January 1761, the British Army officer Isaac Barré, who was severely wounded in the Battle of Quebec, then passed over for a promotion, wrote, "Montgomery is pushing, & (in Companys whose credulity is adapted to such tales,) wants to pass for the Conqueror of the Cherokees." Soon after, both Barré and Montgomery were elected to Parliament.[49]

Montgomery's departure pushed the Overhill Cherokee men closer to their goal of capturing Fort Loudoun. The Fort Loudoun garrison envisioned its demise. Now 160 men, 20 women, and 20 children languished in an "excessively weakened" state. People ate horse flesh, scraps of pork, and beans smuggled in by Indian women. And they plucked plums from trees errantly planted in a ditch. Samuel Terron, a former trader now living among the Cherokees, explained that Montgomery's retreat had emboldened the Cherokees. They saw it "as the effect of fear," he reported. The British withdrawal imbued them with "fresh spirits in their attempt upon fort Loudoun." The Indians "are afraid of no other troops than Virginians, who, they say, know how to shoot and fight them in their own way." But Virginians were nowhere to be seen.[50]

Cut off from incoming correspondence since June 4, Demere and his men renounced "every prospect or hope of seasonable deliverance from any quarter." On June 27, the captain described his situation as "miserable beyond description." Letters from the fort, the *South Carolina Gazette* reported, made Fort Loudoun seem "as if it was abandoned and forsaken by God and man." By July 7, the bread was gone, and only horse flesh remained. Soon, an express confirmed Montgomery's defeat. Indians boasted that they had "killed and scalp'd so many their hands were sore." The officers more than once proposed peace, but Oconostota refused. Parties of soldiers deserted on August 1, 4, and 5, and headed for Virginia.[51]

Could the Cherokees capture the fort before Colonel Byrd and the Virginians relieved it? Byrd collected soldiers, weapons, and supplies very slowly. He built forts every twenty-five miles along his march. On July 5, he reached Augusta County Court House. Two weeks later he camped on the Roanoke River. He was still 300 miles from Chota. He found "every article, except provisions, vastly deficient." Virginia's assemblymen differed. They charged him with unwarranted caution.[52]

Byrd had little desire to make war on the Cherokees. As a long-tenured member of the Virginia Council, his real goal was to draw off the Cherokee trade from South Carolina. Personal experience may also have contributed to his reluctance. Byrd's 1758 service in Forbes's campaign left him with enduring respect for Cherokees. But beyond this, Byrd wished to return to his

IMAGE 8.2 *William Byrd III, by unknown artist, mid-eighteenth century. Courtesy of the Library of Virginia, Richmond.*

private affairs after several years on the frontier. His finances were a mess. His indulgent mother urged him to resign. In a letter with her care package, Maria Taylor Byrd admitted, "I must divest myself of all humanity before I can injoy peace of mind." The acerbic Indian trader James Adair, who led Chickasaw raids on the Lower Towns in July, put it best: "The Virginia troops kept far off in flourishing parade." North Carolina appropriated funds for an expedition in June, though Governor Dobbs was "afraid we can spare few [men] to assist our Neighbours." Dobbs also signed legislation that incentivized the capture and enslavement of enemy Indians. The law also offered a £10 scalp bounty to private citizens, and £5 to provincial soldiers. "As a further encouragement," the province offered scalping North Carolinians "all plunder" taken within twenty miles of the Cherokee Towns.[53]

On August 6, exactly three years after Captain Paul Demere assumed command, with desperation and starvation at their apex, the officers at Fort Loudoun unanimously agreed to surrender. Captain John Stuart and Lieutenant James Adamson of the Provincials negotiated terms in Chota. The next day, Demere, Standing Turkey, and Oconostota signed the "Articles of Capitulation."[54] On August 9, the garrison surrendered its artillery, one thousand pounds of powder, two thousand pounds of ball, and eighty guns to the Cherokees. This valuable cache would support Cherokee hunting and war needs. The soldiers and families of Fort Loudoun kept arms and ammunition for hunting, drums, and personal items. Seven hundred Indian escorts led them southward. They would march through the Valley Towns, then southeast and east, to Fort Prince George. Soon afterward, Captain Demere thought, prisoners would be exchanged and the war would end.[55] The Cherokees had other ideas.

After marching sixteen miles, the parolees from Fort Loudoun camped under the stars in a meadow, where Cane Creek flows into the Tellico River. They were just two miles from Great Tellico.[56] What really happened the next morning, August 10, 1760, remains shrouded in myth, contradiction, and conjecture.

Some firsthand accounts suggest that Oconostota orchestrated an attack, much like he did when he waved the bridle to order the killing of Richard Coytmore in February. Thomas Hawkins, a white man living among the Cherokees, claimed that overzealous young warriors sought scalps and prisoners. Setticos clashed with Chotas "on account of an unequal distribution of plunder" from Fort Loudoun, he said. Additionally, Demere had violated the articles. In fact, Hawkins claimed, Demere had ordered his soldiers to bury twelve bags of gunpowder before surrendering the fort, and he had taken six kegs of gunpowder with him. Still another theory suggests that the warriors wanted to avenge the deaths of the hostages six months earlier.[57] Warriors may also have sought revenge for the deaths of kin from the Lower and Middle Towns who had died in the battle against Montgomery. Perhaps, with the winter drawing near and with the trade interrupted, they needed ammunition. Or perhaps they wished to ensure that soldiers would not return. We will never know for sure what triggered the events that happened next.

At daybreak, just after reveille, soldiers on guard spotted Indians and "gave the alarm." Several officers rushed forward to investigate, and Stuart "called to the men to stand to their arms." Two Cherokees fired from the tall grass and woods. Lieutenant Adamson returned the fire, wounding a Cherokee. The later ransomed Private John Stevens (sometimes spelled Stephens), Fort Loudoun's chief carpenter, offered further details. "Upon this the war-whoop was immediately set up, and vollies of small arms with showers of arrows poured in upon them from every side," he recalled. Most of the warriors in the Overhills—some several hundred Indians—"surrounded the whole garrison," causing "the greatest confusion." The Fort Loudoun people tried to surrender, Stevens recalled, but "the Indians rushed on them with such impetuosity." Middle Townsmen later reported that Settico warriors had wanted only to capture people. Others insisted that the warriors intended to wipe out the garrison's leadership for symbolic, cultural, and practical purposes, and then to adopt the rest. "Had they not attempted to run away, none would have been hurt."[58]

The Round O's brother, Onatoy of Toqua, whisked Stuart across the creek to safety during the fighting. The captain had a close bond with many Cherokees. "Bushyhead" also had an Indian wife—and reportedly had fathered a child—and therefore must be protected by his wife's clan. Demere was not so lucky. A warrior darted in and lifted the commandant's scalp without killing him. Others forced him to dance. Word soon reached the French in Louisiana that the Indians stuffed dirt down his throat and sneered, "Dog, since you are so hungry for land, eat your fill." Then they chopped off his limbs one by one.[59] As Captain Stuart once admitted, Demere "always has ben most heartyly hated by the Indians. Nor is he greatly Esteemed by any white man here." When taken captive, Indians generally sang and danced as they recalled their martial deeds. By making Demere do this, the Indians completed a familiar ritual. And, singling out a powerful leader like this sent a message that intended to deter future villains. According to Samuel Terron, Ostenaco next "ran to every part of the Camp, and ordered the Indians to stop their hands for that they had got the man they wanted," Captain Demere.[60]

Cherokees no doubt had spared lives at Cane Creek, but they had responded to British treachery with their own equally hostile acts. The Cherokee defense of Echoe and the capture of Fort Loudoun proved pyrrhic; they would serve only to fan the racial hatred of South Carolina elites and the resolve of British-colonial retribution. In his speech to the Commons House on October 9, Bull reported thirty-two dead. Three of the fallen were officers—Captain Demere of the Independent Companies, and Lieutenant Adamson and Ensign

William Wintle of the South Carolina Provincials. Three were white women. A few more men from a party led by Independent Companies ensign John Bogges were never heard of again. The number of Cherokee dead remains unknown.[61] Reports from the scene claimed that the Indians committed "the most shocking barbarities on the bodies" of the dead. The Indians led the survivors to the various Overhills towns. The warriors recounted their deeds to excited villagers and waved the scalps in triumph. The captives would be adopted into Cherokee society. Fort Loudoun became a temporary Cherokee settlement, hosting warriors and refugee Cherokees. Indian men moved the fort's cannons, coehorn mortars, guns, powder, and ball from Fort Loudoun to Chota.[62]

Onatoy brought Stuart back to Indian-occupied Fort Loudoun. Stuart related the news to Samuel Terron and asked him to intercede with Attakullakulla, then hiding in the woods. Oconostota reportedly threatened to torture Stuart and to burn the soldiers if he did not help them use the "great guns" against Fort Prince George. Stuart refused.[63]

On August 27, Attakullakulla ransomed Stuart and a few others. He secretly carried them toward Byrd's army on September 3. By this time, the soldiers who had deserted Fort Loudoun in early August had reached Byrd's camp, then at Reed Creek. Major Andrew Lewis and three hundred Virginians found Attakullakulla and his party a few days later. On September 14, Stuart and the others told Byrd about the fort's surrender and the attack at Cane Creek. They also reported that the Cherokees aimed to take Fort Prince George next.[64]

The news convinced Byrd to seek peace. Meeting with Attakullakulla on September 16 and 17, the Virginian proposed a flexible and open-ended treaty. He promised the Indians "His Majesty's Pardon," a prompt prisoner exchange, and the reopening of the deerskin trade. Virginia would supplant South Carolina in influence. Cherokees must return Fort Loudoun, to be garrisoned only by General Amherst's orders. And they were to recognize Attakullakulla as "emperor." Byrd left other terms open ended or unenforceable.[65]

Attakullakulla misrepresented his power and influence among the Cherokees. He pledged to bring in the leading headmen for peace talks. He would "put the French to death," return all the English prisoners, and hand over all the Cherokees accused of murder. Attakullakulla then headed home. He hoped to return in three weeks to reach favorable peace terms with Byrd.[66]

He carried with him Byrd's letter to Overhill leaders. Byrd lacked the desire or the manpower to attack, but he demanded that they "come in directly" to discuss peace. If they did, "You shall meet with good usage, and not a hair of your heads shall be hurt." The colonel swore, "I do not want to destroy your people." But if necessary he would "not leave one Indian alive, one town standing, or one grain of corn, in all your country."[67]

It was a tough sell. Attakullakulla himself admitted to Byrd that the English must "beat them into" a peace, "for [the Cherokees] are much flush'd with success," the colonel reported. Most Cherokees treated Attakullakulla with contempt. Seroweh and others still hoped that the French, or other Indian tribes, would rally to help the disaffected Cherokees. In fact, to save the Lower Towns from extermination and from further humiliation, Seroweh threatened to attack Fort Prince George if British troops did not evacuate it immediately. He also demanded that Bull release one of the accused murderers held in Charles Town—Youctanah or the Slave-Catcher of Conasatchee. They stood on the cusp of driving British soldiers from their country once and for all. And they had Fort Loudoun's weapons and powder. They needed, if not outside assistance, time to regroup and resupply. So they waited.[68]

White observers, in particular the soldiers at Fort Prince George, therefore viewed the independent proposals for peace with skepticism. Lieutenant Governor William Bull II of South Carolina worried that Byrd had made empty threats without the ability to follow through on them. By the time Byrd determined to attack, it would be too late in the year, and his soldiers' enlistments would expire. Byrd's proposed treaty also had little in common with the terms the South Carolina Council unveiled before Montgomery's retreat.[69]

A majority of Cherokees favored peace. Byrd's terms upheld Cherokee dignity while showing respect for Cherokee military culture. Fauquier agreed. The treaty, he believed, would "make them our Friends," by treating them with "Justice and Humanity," because "White, Red, or Black; polished or unpolished Men are Men."[70]

The effective Cherokee army had dwindled by more than a third since 1758, to just 1,400 men. Many Cherokees were weary, destitute, and starving. The prospect of recruiting allies faded. Smallpox now incapacitated the Upper Creeks. In the Lower Creeks, only fourteen warriors were willing to join the Mortar of Oakchoy to assist in the reduction of Fort Prince George. The corn of the Lower Towns had been destroyed. And warriors in the Middle and Lower Towns had expended ammunition against Montgomery's army. On September 22, the Wolf of Keowee, the Corn Tassel of Toqua, and two half-Cherokee traders and messengers visited Charles Town. They agreed to a prisoner exchange as a preliminary to peace negotiations. Bull and the South Carolina Council agreed to send the Cherokee prisoners to the Congarees to await an exchange at Ninety Six. Still, colonial officials worked to resupply Fort Prince George and continued efforts to raise a new provincial regiment.[71]

Voices in the Overhills called for peace as well. Oconostota, Ostenaco, and other warriors journeyed through the Cherokee towns. They spoke to massive crowds at Chota, Nequassee, and Conasatchee, and secured popular support for peace. Oconostota sent a runner through the Cherokee towns calling for a ban on torture. Villages recalled war parties and agreed to allow English people to travel freely in the Lower Towns. After crowds affirmed the warriors' message of peace, the two warriors sent an account of their proceedings to Fort Prince George.[72]

At the same time, from September 16 to October 4, a stream of Cherokee men and women came to Fort Prince George. Some brought beef, venison, and corn. Old Caesar of Chatuga delivered two soldiers from the Fort Loudoun garrison: James Holmes and James Hosfield. The Mankiller of Nequassee and his wife frequented the fort. Visitors, including an Indian woman, Nancy, smoked the peace pipe with the soldiers. The women shared news, advocated for peace, and urged the restoration of the trade. To keep faith with their visitors, the soldiers hid Chickasaw Indians paid by the colony to raid the Lower Towns.[73]

The soldiers at Fort Prince George remained skeptical. They were dissatisfied by the low number of captives the Cherokees had released. They overlooked the disarray caused by an epidemic in the Overhill, Valley, and Middle Towns. Dozens fell ill with "a violent disorder in their stomach and a flux," Holmes and Hosfield reported. And, they informed the Fort Prince George soldiers of Fort Loudoun's fate. The skeptical garrison, itself reduced to horse flesh, envisioned its own demise.[74] On October 15, Major William Thomson and 268 handpicked rangers arrived from Ninety Six. They delivered flour and salted beef to Fort Prince George and returned without incident. Thomson enabled Fort Prince George to hold out longer.[75]

Peace looked imminent. Bull sent the more than thirty Cherokee prisoners to the frontier. On October 13, another massive meeting took place in the Overhill Towns. As a result, Ostenaco and Oconostota rushed back to the Overhills a week later to raise an official delegation of men for diplomatic talks with Colonel Byrd. What happened next shocked everyone—and it triggered an unnecessary panic on the part of British and colonial authorities.[76]

In late October, Antoine Adhémar de Lantagnac, ten French soldiers, and a handful of Shawnee Indians traveled by river from the Illinois Country to Chota. The officer distributed goods. He urged the Cherokees to take up the "War Hatchet" against the English. Oconostota refused and set out for Byrd's camp nonetheless. But Seroweh journeyed to Chota and accepted the Frenchman's offer. As a soldier from Fort Prince George reported, the Indians "began the War Dance, and sent Runners to Call back the Indians who were gone on their way to Negociate with Colonel Byrd." Lantagnac left the ten French soldiers in Chota. He promised to return in three weeks with men and cannons to take Fort Prince George.[77] As Atkin put it, "The long flattering Hopes" of peace had "entirely vanished." The panicked, pessimistic reports from Fort Prince George lacked corroboration. And, even if Seroweh "took up the Hatchet," he represented just one Cherokee town out of nearly forty.[78]

Attakullakulla and Willenawa reached Byrd's camp at Alexander Sayer's mill on Reed Creek on November 3, each with a group of followers. Each side got what it wanted. The parties agreed to a cease-fire through "the New Moon in March" and agreed to resume talks in the spring. The Cherokees delivered ten Virginia captives. Byrd sent the Cherokees home with trade goods. He discharged his soldiers on November 22. Much to Fauquier's chagrin, Byrd resigned his command on December 3. He journeyed to New York to meet with Amherst, and then continued to Philadelphia. There would be no winter invasion from Virginia.[79]

But the melodramatic soldiers' reports from Fort Prince George and the news that Seroweh had taken up the hatchet convinced Lieutenant Governor Bull that any peace—declared or not—seemed unlikely. Thus, the thirty Cherokee prisoners would not return home. Instead, Bull ordered Captain Peter Gordon, who now commanded the British troops at the Congarees, to return the Cherokee prisoners to Charles Town. And he begged General Amherst for a new supply of redcoats. The Indians—he was wrongly convinced—were stalling, only to attack with redoubled vigor. Amherst immediately obliged. He readied 1,200 troops. He transferred James Grant to a different regiment but detached him to lead the new campaign.[80]

In August, the Commons House had finally raised additional provincial troops. Showing their desperation, they debated a motion to arm five hundred slaves, and to manumit any slave who killed and scalped two enemy Indians. Though dozens of slaves had been hired as militia scouts, drummers, and even boatmen in 1759 and 1760, they would not play a larger role in defending the colony. Speaker Benjamin Smith cast the decisive vote to defeat the measure.[81] As in the Revolution to follow, authorities could not agree on a coherent policy to arm slaves.

As 1760 drew to a close, Bull sent the meager provincial regiment to winter at the Congarees. He hoped to give the Cherokees "some apprehensions."

Recruiting proceeded slowly, as Lieutenant Francis Marion and other officers traversed South Carolina and North Carolina.[82]

On December 3, Major Thomson, this time with 470 rangers, again resupplied Fort Prince George. He delivered a ten-week supply of flour, clothing, salt, and cattle, providing a further disincentive for Cherokees to stray from their peaceful intentions. Rangers cut and delivered firewood, "the major setting his men the example." Morale improved. Thomson left Fort Prince George a few days later with surplus powder and guns for the provincial arsenal. He met no opposition whatsoever.[83]

Few other peace-seeking Cherokees arrived at the fort, but few Cherokees had war on their minds. The Mankiller of Nequassee and a dozen warriors came to Fort Prince George on December 8. He bore beads from seven Lower and Middle Towns. He swore that *they are tired of the war; that they love the* English *and want peace*" and trade. The Mankiller could not gather any prisoners. To Cherokees, returning prisoners made little sense: "They would lose the chance to both grieve and exult, and their enemies would live to fight them again," James Adair explained.[84]

The garrison wondered if Cherokees had gone to the Overhills to prepare for war. Actually, most Cherokees were hunting. Two Overhill delegations, intrigued by the promises of Lantagnac, went to the French forts to seek help. Oconostota led one party. The Seed of Settico led the other. Estatoe warriors also remained bitter.[85] Despite these limited exceptions, Cherokee support for peace was now overwhelming. The summer of 1760 marked the height of Cherokee power in the Southeast. After defeating and driving back an invading army, Cherokees captured Fort Loudoun. But they may have reached too far. The destruction of the Lower Towns, disease, starvation, and a lack of ammunition began to take its toll. Peace looked appealing to many. Yet the British demanded the call to be unanimous. This was nearly impossible among the decentralized Cherokee people. They desired a formal, signed peace, something alien to Cherokees. And paranoid soldiers at Fort Prince George, fresh off the misunderstood episode at Fort Loudoun, continued to stir up sensationalized reports. So the war continued. And another military expedition was imminent.

DESTROYING THEIR TOWNS, AND CUTTING UP THEIR SETTLEMENTS *The Grant Campaign*

9

On February 11, 1761, two Cherokees came to Fort Prince George with a white flag. They bore the messages of Overhill leaders Standing Turkey, Ostenaco, and Attakullakulla. All three wanted hostilities to end. Attakullakulla proposed to meet with Virginia's Colonel William Byrd III. Antipathy toward the British waned further with an unforeseen accident among a Francophile faction. The Seed of Settico, with four of the six men accompanying him to a French fort, sickened and died on the way. And Oconostota returned from his visit to New Orleans with only a beautifully embellished French captain's commission from Governor Kerlérec. French military strength dwindled without reinforcements. A personnel change at Fort Prince George also calmed many Cherokees. Grant replaced the inexperienced, unpopular, and corrupt Ensign Alexander Miln. Lachlan McIntosh, "much esteemed by the Indians," and recently promoted to lieutenant, arrived on February 20 and assumed command the next day. The Cherokees did not prevent rangers from resupplying Fort Prince George with cattle, hogs, flour, and firewood. With McIntosh's encouragement, desperate, starving, and homesick Lower Townsmen—their charred villages vacant for the previous year—settled under Tistoe of Keowee in a refugee camp east of Fort Prince George, with McIntosh's blessing. Food and clothing remained scarce after yet another year's disruption in the deerskin trade. Worse, the winter of 1760–61 had been exceptionally harsh.[1]

Hunger, destitution, and a desire to move on fueled the impulse to conciliation. As newly promoted Lieutenant

IMAGE 9.1 *A military commission given to Oconostota by the French governor of Louisiana, 1761. National Archives, Washington, D.C., ARC Identifier 6924937.*

Colonel James Grant, Montgomery's former second in command, put it, the war existed primarily "in the heated Imaginations" of a few men— Independent Companies ensign Alexander Miln and two provincial officers at Fort Prince George. Spurred on by hawkish Charles Town elites, these men "alarm[ed] the Province & the Continent with ridiculous Representations of Danger," the Scotsman opined. Moreover, Grant believed, the officers' history of rape, murder, and treachery had "in a great measure occasioned the Disaffection of the Indians."[2]

The recall of these officers and the desperate situation in the Indian villages inspired Cherokee peace overtures. Within six weeks of McIntosh's arrival, Cherokees had delivered sixty-seven prisoners to Fort Prince George in exchange for food and clothing. Ransoming prisoners, though not unheard of, showed Cherokee desperation. Attakullakulla visited and spent ten days at the fort in late March. Even Seroweh talked of peace. On April 1, the Estatoe warrior visited Fort Prince George. He had journeyed as far southeast as Ninety Six in search of sustenance, not scalps. Disrespect and ill treatment at the fort had driven his young people "mad," he said. Now, the embodiment of Cherokee resistance told McIntosh that "my heart is straight and will continue so." He kept a meager amount of beef for his starving people and delivered the rest of the cattle he had seized in the South Carolina settlements to commander McIntosh. Ostenaco also appeared contrite. In an April 19 message to Grant, he begged for the restoration of the trade. White Carolinians, on the other hand, were less sanguine. From Ninety Six, a correspondent to the *South Carolina Gazette*—probably Provincial Lieutenant Thomas Bell—hoped that "whispers here about peace" were unfounded. The Cherokees, the writer believed, should "first receive the proper reward of their perfidy and cruelty."[3] Many South Carolinians echoed his sentiments.

While Ostenaco, Attakullakulla, and Seroweh made overtures to Anglo-Carolinians, other emissaries approached Virginia. In early April, Willenawa of Toqua led eighty Overhill Cherokees northeast. General Amherst had again ordered Virginia provincials to invade the Cherokee towns. The Toqua headman wished to stall the colony's troops and to negotiate a more favorable, separate peace on the terms proposed in November 1760. He delivered sixteen Fort Loudoun prisoners to Major Andrew Lewis's advance post at Fort Chiswell. Soon, however, tragedy struck. Governor Fauquier and his agents, acting on Amherst's orders and imperial protocol, refused to negotiate the peace that Willenawa sought. Under the cover of darkness, Indian enemies from the North attacked the starving and disheartened Cherokee camp. They killed six and wounded "a great many." Willenawa's survivors left their women and wounded under Lewis's care and then rushed off in a fruitless search for the assailants. Eventually, Lewis sent the heartbroken Cherokees home with fourteen horse-loads of blankets, food, and other supplies. Willenawa believed the Virginia troops posed no immediate threat to the Overhills. Indeed, Colonel Byrd, griping that his force was inadequate and his supplies insufficient, once again headed the regiment. As in 1760, the colonel had little faith, or interest, in a Virginia-based invasion of Cherokee country.[4]

But Cherokees faced yet another campaign from the Southeast, a replay of the Montgomery campaign the year before. On December 15, 1760, General Jeffery Amherst had dispatched 1,200 British troops to Charles Town under the command of Lieutenant Colonel James Grant. Demanding "the most Exemplary Vengeance," Amherst ordered Grant to take the offensive, "destroying their Towns and cutting up their Settlements" in order "to reduce them to the absolute Necessity of sueing for Pardon." Amherst's hatred for

Indians, like that of many British elites, was palpable. He called the Cherokees "perfidious and inhuman," a "Race of Barbarians."[5] As retired Virginia provincial commander George Washington noted, the Cherokees "are the only People that disturbs the repose of this great Continent."[6] With the French threat seemingly neutralized in North America, incapacitating the Cherokees—and punishing them for their success in 1760 with a harsh and formal peace remained a key goal for Amherst and for South Carolina. To bring this about, Grant unleashed wanton destruction. Cherokees ran out of options other than to accept a formal declaration of peace.[7]

Grant gathered horses, wagons, and cattle. He griped that the colony was too slow to support him. He fretted over the "sickly" state of the Royal Scots. Five hundred rangers "were scattered up and down the face of the earth." The colonists, he sardonically noted, "will never have any share in the war and are therefore very desirous to promote it; peace is a very unfashionable topick." Grant, like Montgomery, had some sympathy for the Cherokees' plight. "If both Parties were heard," he wrote to General Amherst, "I fancy the Indians have been the worst used . . . the greatest part of them are sory for what has been done, & would be glad to make Peace." It did not matter. His orders called for him to be ruthless. Many South Carolinians expected him to be.[8]

With the grass tall enough to serve as forage for the cattle and horses, the British regulars left Charles Town on March 20. Grant augmented his army with Indian auxiliaries, including several Iroquois, "the greatest Warriours in the world," Carolina planter Eliza Lucas Pinckney wrote. Silverheels, a Seneca Mingo from the Ohio Valley, was the most feared and admired of Grant's Indians. He had already fought at Great Meadows, Braddock's Defeat, Crown Point, and Ticonderoga. Encamped thirty miles northwest of Charles Town at Moncks Corner, Grant's army drilled, organized, captured deserters, and added reinforcements for three weeks.[9]

On April 14, Grant marched his men northwest from Moncks Corner. Violence erupted thirty miles later near Eutaw Springs. A British officer recalled the ghastly scene. Without provocation and "In a fit of Drunkenness," Silverheels tomahawked a family of "Settlement Indians"—possibly Cusabos—living near the camp. And, the officer added, "Two of them was thought mortally wounded." Grant's second in command, Major Alexander Monypenny "wish'd, he had been shot" for this "outrage." Grant, however, chose not "to have it done." Silverheels was "our favorite Indian," the colonel confessed.[10] The incident was an omen of the brutality to come. And it was emblematic of the way the British utilized their Indian allies.

IMAGE 9.2 *James Grant, by Allan Ramsay, ca. 1760s.*
Courtesy of Sotheby's Picture Library.

Grant's army arrived at the Congarees on April 22. There it joined a desertion-ravaged South Carolina Regiment as well as the 2nd Battalion of Royal Scots. Lieutenant Jacob Farrington signed on too, with four Rogers' Rangers, ten Stockbridge Indians, and one Mohawk. These were not Cherokee enemies, but rather soldiers in the British Army in all but rank and regimental affiliation.[11] A day later, the army set out for Ninety Six. Indian allies from the Southeast also streamed in. Lured by the excitement of combat and by financial reward, Upper Chickasaws arrived from villages on the Mississippi and Lower Chickasaws from their town near Augusta. They had a score to settle against the Cherokees, too. In the previous year, Cherokees seeking to impress the French had attacked the Chickasaws. Three Yuchis from the Creek Confederacy joined. And Catawbas under hereditary monarch King Hagler and war chief Colonel Ayres also came to fight. Monypenny mocked these brave and steady allies. The major overlooked their faithful service against Fort Duquesne, and he failed to consider their struggles against land encroachment, war, disease, and broken promises from Charles Town. Instead, he saw them as no more than "drunks and beggars."[12]

Meanwhile, other British allies acted independently. A party of Chickasaws saw an opening when Tistoe left his starving followers at the Fort George refugee camp in order to get corn from the Middle Towns. The Chickasaws' attack was brutal. They entered Tistoe's home, where they killed a woman and wounded a boy. "This is exactly True Indian Assistance," Monypenny noted proudly.[13]

The march to Ninety Six bolstered the enthusiasm of Britain's Indian allies. With time to socialize, they bonded across tribal lines. They shared dances and goodwill.[14] The army reached Ninety Six on May 14.[15] There they found a small detachment of British regulars and two hundred more provincials with fifty slave laborers under Major John Moultrie Jr. The rangers were also assembled there. Grant and Monypenny thumbed their noses at these uncouth frontiersmen. British officers disrespected their white allies—not just in New England as Fred Anderson has demonstrated—but in the South as well. Grant and his subordinates, through their elitist and highly professionalized and precise lens, saw rangers as overpaid and unreliable. "This might be a most usefull Body of Men," Monypenny wrote, "were their officers Men of spirit & integrity. But the shamefull abuses in the Corps"— drunkenness and lack of discipline among other things—"are not to be believ'd." Such biases resembled the later development of a Revolutionary-era lack of affinity toward the British on the part of frontiersmen. This chasm widened during the campaign.[16]

At Ninety Six, camaraderie between the Indians continued. They "danc'd the War Dance" around a bonfire and shared other ceremonies "peculiar to themselves." The Indians also joined forces with a handful of white soldiers. On May 18, Monypenny and Grant formed an elite unit commanded by Captain Quintin Kennedy. The Lowland Scot, a survivor of Braddock's Defeat, had led ranger operations for five years. Now, he took charge of ninety Indians and four dozen white men dressed and painted as Indians.[17]

As the campaign siphoned white manpower inland, the racial imbalance in coastal areas only grew. War again brought crisis for whites and Cherokees, but opportunity for African Americans. Therefore, throughout 1761, slave resistance increased.

But few could capitalize on the absence of so many Carolina troops. A rash of poisonings allegedly took place on Wadmalaw Island, southwest of Charles Town, in early 1761. Brutal public executions awaited the accused slave conspirators. Ten slaves ran away from Colonel Thomas Middleton's plantations. Bondsmen fled coastal South Carolina for Spanish St. Augustine, where freedom awaited; Christopher from Horse Shoe Plantation near Jacksonboro and Peter from coastal St. Helena Parish appear in the documentary record. Reflecting recruiters' desperation to enlist men, and the generous enlistment bounties and pay that the province offered, a "mulatto" runaway named Jack reportedly enlisted in a ranger unit. Of the rangers at Ninety Six on May 16, "above ten were Negroes," provincial officer Henry Laurens later recalled. For others, like one "Philip, 16," the British lines provided an alternative to life on the plantation. For Philip and other black laborers in the army, high pay and adventure awaited, though the work was hard and the danger was great. But for meritorious service, freedom did not await as it had in wars past.[18]

In April, the Commons House finally settled the matter of Demere's promise of freedom to Abram, the slave messenger who played so prominent a role in 1760. Upon Lieutenant Governor Bull's recommendation, the assemblymen purchased Abram's freedom. He became the last of fifteen or sixteen slaves to be freed by the provincial government during the colonial period. A "mulatto slave" from Berkeley County, Joe Fleming, was not so lucky. Forced to fight in a ranger company during the Montgomery campaign of 1760, he had killed and scalped a Cherokee in battle. But heroism got Fleming nowhere. The Commons cited budgetary constraints and refused to free him.[19] The decision indicated to slaves that putting one's life on the line for white South Carolinians meant nothing.

Indeed the already high costs of the war concerned lawmakers. In May, the busiest time of year on Carolina plantations, the Commons House debated a bill addressing "the pernicious Consequence of too free an Importation of NEGROES into this Province." When an additional duty effecting "nearly . . . a Prohibition" seemed possible, the Gazette printed the proposed bill in full. It would have levied an additional forty-pound tax in Carolina currency on each slave imported into the colony. The bill passed the Commons House but fell to defeat in the council.[20]

White anxieties soared. In the twilight hours of June 15–16, a newly created watch company in Charles Town took thirteen African Americans into custody. Watchmen apprehended men "in a Disorderly house in Rapers Alley Union Street" and "in the Streets and upon the Wharrfs," some after lengthy chases. Two blacks unable to produce passes from their masters fled on horseback at 2:00 A.M. One escaped; the other was captured, carrying a bayonet. All were jailed in the guardhouse. Their fate remains unknown.[21] Surely blacks were aware of the situation on the frontier and hoped to use the opportunity to their benefit.

A swift campaign could reestablish white control. It could also quell the growth of radical millenarianism in the backcountry. As Grant's army marched to the Cherokee country, authorities captured the leader of a religious cult—a Swiss man named Jacob Weber. Hoping to bring about millennial change, Weber fashioned himself as the messiah and his wife, Hannah, as the Virgin Mary. The "Weberites" practiced nudity, polyamory and ritualized murder. They also recruited African American adherents. Millenarianism spread anti-Anglican sentiment and class conflict. As Richard Clarke and Philip John had proven in 1759, it encouraged slaves to slip their bonds and overthrow their masters. In April, Lieutenant Governor Bull issued the order to execute Jacob Weber and pardoned his co-conspirators. But Weber died unrepentant. The fanaticism of the Weberites was discussed long after. The Cherokees had destabilized the frontier. As long as settlers were isolated, neglected, and vulnerable to Indian attack, radical spirituality could take hold. And this challenged established British authority.[22]

Cherokees, meanwhile, turned to Oconostota for leadership. His trip to Fort Toulouse had been a failure; he and forty Cherokees returned home with just eight or nine horse-loads of goods but just a few French soldiers. Oconostota strongly urged peace with the English. He journeyed to Fort Prince George in early May and announced that he hoped "that things might be settled." Attakullakulla, who was also in the party, hoped the troops would halt at Fort Prince George. "He believ'd all would be adjusted," wrote Monypenny. Oconostota offered to escort a British officer through the Cherokee towns "that he may see how their hearts are disposed, & that they are good." This was a generous offer to promote goodwill and understanding. Grant declined. Expecting to be captured for his role in the deaths of Lieutenant Coytmore and the Fort Loudoun soldiers, Oconostota withdrew to the woods. Attakullakulla awaited Grant's arrival. The disgraced leader hoped to restore his reputation by holding off a British-led invasion, and by leading peace negotiations—which he hoped would prove favorable to the Cherokees.[23]

In private, Grant vowed to prop up Attakullakulla's authority to keep the Indians from "despair." Publicly, the lieutenant colonel demanded the return of all the Fort Loudoun captives. His aim was twofold: to prevent the Cherokees from killing them in the event of a British invasion, and to use them in his army. "Ruin & Destruction hangs over your whole Nation," Grant threatened, vowing to attack Cherokee country. The Virginians would march on their nation, he vowed. But Alexander Monypenny noted in his diary, "Such as remain'd quiet in their Houses [would] be protected."[24]

On May 27, Grant's army arrived at Fort Prince George. All but six of the Cherokee leaders waiting there scattered, fearing for their safety. For two days, Attakullakulla spoke for them. He nearly disarmed the British with his warmth and his soft facial features. He "has the Character of being a Man of great Sense," Captain Christopher French believed. The next day, with his formidable Indian allies present to intimidate the Cherokees, Grant conferred with Attakullakulla. The message was clear. To avoid further peril, it was time to make peace. Attakullakulla could not do so, nor could he accept the harsh terms Grant proposed. "I will not lose half an hour waiting for your people," Grant retorted, remembering his orders from Amherst and the challenges of supplying and disciplining such a large army. Their excitement building, Grant's Indian auxiliaries howled with the nearby wolves.[25]

In Cherokee villages far and wide, most Indians, starving and unarmed, wanted peace. The rapid pace of prisoner exchange only reinforced that sentiment. By mid-May, 115 white prisoners, 70 of them Fort Loudoun soldiers, found safety at Fort Prince George. Their captors delivered them in exchange for foodstuffs and clothes. Another three to five dozen remained, many no doubt willingly. Others filled the place of Cherokee dead as adoptees. Cherokees from the Lower Towns streamed into the Fort Prince George refugee camp. Barred from hunting, they gathered acorns and berries until Grant provided peas and corn. Many Cherokees, Major Monypenny believed, were "much inclin'd to Peace." Grant's soldiers were safe. "A Scalp has not been taken as yet," Monypenny wrote on May 30. The Indians must have been tempted. Wagoners and soldiers defied orders and crossed the Keowee to "ramble all round the opposite Hills, picking strawberries unarmed."[26]

While Grant and his men settled in at Fort Prince George, an army of Virginian provincials under Colonel William Byrd III set out from Winchester toward Chota, a march of 460 miles. The previous August, Byrd's estranged wife had died in Virginia. He spent the winter in Philadelphia, where he remarried. Now, Byrd left his new bride and reluctantly returned to the frontier. His orders called for him to march his troops southwest, join up with North Carolina troops, and attack Chota. Byrd lacked the heart for it. He advised Amherst that such a campaign was impractical and unwise. He needed more men and provisions. North Carolina was unreliable; its assembly took until April 26 to fund a regiment of five hundred men. To raise and arm them was another matter.[27]

Virginia lieutenant governor Francis Fauquier also opposed the campaign. Attakullakulla had not rejected Byrd's 1760 terms. "We cannot enter their Country with Fire and Sword, without a most notorious and infamous Breach of Faith," he wrote to Byrd. Violence was imprudent. The Cherokees could "be brought to reason without much bloodshed." Force, he predicted, "will never let them rest" from "taking blood for blood . . . on the back settlements." Instead, "We must make it their convenience to live at peace with us." But the lieutenant governor felt trapped. If the Virginians refused to act, "we shall with Justice be represented at home by Carolina, as having deserted them," he concluded.[28]

At Fort Prince George, Grant determined to press on. On June 7, the largest force assembled by the British on the southern frontier began a thirty-three-day foray into the Cherokee settlements. Three days later, Grant approached the Dividings and headed north toward Echoe village.[29] Grant expected an ambush on June 10 as he approached the narrow pass where warriors had attacked Montgomery's army the year before. Grant's Indian Corps scouted ahead along the steep hills. The redcoat ordered his men to load their weapons. He deployed flankers, and he made the column march in a compact file. The commander took "all the precaution that could be taken against a surprise," he said.[30]

Sure enough, Cherokee riflemen, cognizant of their success the year earlier, fired on the cattle guard at the back of Grant's train. But the shots had little effect over such a distance. The invaders continued north for a few miles. A mile south of where they had engaged Colonel Montgomery's army in 1760, Cherokees waited at a river crossing, at another pinch point. Encroaching ridges and hillocks squeezed the redcoat invaders into a mile-long trap. The only way out was for the invaders to ford the river again and push north.[31]

Cherokees waited on a steep, brushy hill to the east. The Cowhowee River (today known as the Little Tennessee) divided that hill and a sloping plain to the west, where more warriors awaited the invaders. Between 8:30 and 9:00

A.M., Kennedy's Indian Corps detected Cherokees on the eastern hill. Grant's men trained their already-loaded weapons. Cherokee leaders let out the war whoop. It echoed down the line. On Kennedy's command the Indian Corps burst uphill into the brush. Grant ordered Captain William Moultrie's Provincial Regiment light infantry—which reportedly included Lieutenant Francis Marion—to help. The Cherokees soon scattered, leaving one man killed and scalped. However, taking the high ground meant very little; in large battles the Indians simply regrouped and reorganized.[32]

Meanwhile, Indians on the opposite side of the river fired briskly from rising ground, engaging South Carolina's provincial troops. They hoped to create a distraction and perhaps inflict some casualties with their rifles. Major William Thomson and his South Carolina Rangers attempted to get on the other side of these Indians but were apparently driven back. Kennedy's Corps and the light infantry pressed north, forded the river, and helped others do the same. A Frenchman among the Cherokees taunted Kennedy. But Cherokees were sorely disappointed if they expected a greater French turnout. Spotty evidence suggests the presence of no more than a dozen agents or soldiers led by Lantagnac, the former Overhills trader. With Kennedy's Corps out of firing range, the Cherokees who had been driven from the hillock in the Narrows reorganized. Just as in 1760, they targeted the supply convoy. If they could knock out cattle, horses, and flour, they could lessen Grant's potential to press north. As in 1760, Cherokee shots pierced bags of flour, startled and toppled horses, and scattered packhorsemen as the pack train entered the Narrows.[33]

Without Grant's fiercest combatants to oppose them, the reorganized Cherokees wounded four officers and many soldiers and packhorsemen. Grant rebuffed his eager Indian allies' offer to go back to assist the rear. Provincial soldiers would later boast that they rescued the pack train and drove it through the narrow pass.[34]

For three more hours, Cherokee warriors peppered the northward-marching invaders with "an irregular and incessant fire" that trickled off by 2:00 P.M. As the trader and ethnographer James Adair put it, "had the Cheerake been sufficiently supplied with ammunition, twice the number of troops could not have defeated them." Instead, some Indians were firing bows and arrows. The warriors soon "disappeared" to alert the nearby Middle Towns. Cherokees fled to the hills. All hope of stopping Grant was lost.[35] It is impossible to fathom the despair that many must have felt.

Sixty British packhorses lay dead. Fifty-two British troops lay wounded, four of them officers. Eleven were dead, one of them a Catawba. To avenge

IMAGE 9.3 *A Cherokee view of the 1761 battlefield from the west bank of the Little Tennessee River. Author photo.*

the loss of his kinsman, a Catawba warrior viciously tomahawked, scalped, and mutilated the corpse of a Cherokee prisoner. He "blew out his Brains." Not stopping there, Captain French observed, he "cut open his Breast, & Belly, & cut off his privy parts, & otherways mangled him in a most shocking manner."[36] Using their Indian auxiliaries for the most brutal acts of the campaign, Grant's men rubbed salt into the festering wounds that already typified intertribal relations. Indian allies, seen by the British as brave but deranged, won no respect within the British Army. Instead, they unwittingly contributed to native peoples' collective decline within the empire and played a prominent role in Britain's "divide and conquer strategy," sowing future divisions between tribes.

After the initial encounter with Montgomery in 1760, the Cherokees had persisted in their efforts to expel the invading Britons. But in 1761, after their initial encounter with Grant, the Cherokees offered no further resistance. Unlike the year before, they were short on ammunition and vastly outnumbered by a factor greater than two to one. The Indian Corps foiled Cherokee flanking attempts. And Cherokee troop strength was much smaller than historians have reported. An officer estimated—a bit generously—that the Cherokee army was "not less than a thousand." Many had died in the past year in battle, and of disease and starvation. By most accounts, no Overhill warriors were present.[37] These Cherokees now faced a growing threat: attacks from Indian enemies to the north and west. Spurred by northern Indian superintendent Sir William Johnson and his deputy, George Croghan, several parties of Indians had taken to the warpath in 1760 and 1761, and returned with Cherokee scalps.[38] Overhill warriors, then, were guarding the frontier and caring for refugees. Others, seeking peace with Virginia, did not turn out at all. Nonetheless, Grant boasted of his army's performance against the Cherokees in what one soldier recorded in his journal as "The Battle of Cowhowee."[39]

In the days and weeks that followed, Cherokee women mourned the dead, and the sounds of wailing filled villages. According to Grant's Indian allies, twenty-four Cherokees died and thirty-five suffered wounds that day, most of them early in the battle. The Mankiller of Nequassee later put the number higher. He said that at least thirty-three Cherokees had lost their lives. Attakullakulla reported that "some women" and twenty-two men died in battle. Their authority slipping, women fought to regain the respect they once had. And they stepped in, in traditional fashion, to assist their fallen husbands. Cherokee survivors piled "many vast heaps" of stones atop the graves of the dead as offerings to the spirits who haunted the Narrows. Those stones still stood in 1775 when naturalist William Bartram passed by.[40]

Grant had orders to carry out, and he sensed the Cherokees faltering. Grant's soldiers sunk their dead in the Little Tennessee River "to prevent their being dug up . . . and scalped." They marched on to Echoe, passing the 1760 battlefield, and reached the village at midnight. Rather than retreat as Montgomery had the year before, Grant then sent a detachment "to surprise" and destroy Tassee, a village two miles away. He marched everyone else twelve miles north. By 4:00 A.M., Grant's army converted the townhouse at the Cherokee "mother town" of Nequassee to a hospital. Grant had the Indian Corps, "much fatigued," to escort the army's provisions. They completed the task at 1:00 P.M.[41]

Over the next sixteen days, with the Indian Corps at the lead, Grant's troops burned fifteen Indian villages. Grant earned the Cherokee sobriquet of "the Cornpuller." The army destroyed 580 houses and 1,330 acres of Cherokee corn. They felled fruit orchards and cut up bean plants "to a great amount." Many of the residents of the Lower, Middle, and Out Towns had already fled to the Overhills or to the mountains. Others barely escaped the army's wrath, decamping as the Indian Corps pillaged. Provincial Major John Moultrie Jr. was moved by the tears of a Cherokee woman as her home went up in flames. It "melted me and made me sorry," he wrote. Moultrie's emotion marked a change of heart. He had previously admitted—to his girlfriend—that he had been "making free with the Cherokee squaws."[42]

Finding few Cherokees still in their villages, and prohibited by Grant from detaching to scour the woods, some Chickasaws and Catawbas departed.[43] On June 16, Grant's army reached the commercial hub and the largest of the Middle Towns, Cowee. Like a war leader recruiting for battle, Silverheels taunted Cherokees. "With a loud voice," he "three times summoned all the Cherokees, from all their towns and mountains to come and hear the news he had to tell them from the North." Silverheels and Kennedy's Indians, though a mishmash of British allies, some of them with no history of conflict with the Cherokees, gave Cherokees the impression that as long as they opposed the British, they had Indian enemies in all directions. This comforted the South Carolina forces. When they did not appear, Silverheels rallied the army by shouting that "since they would not come and hear him, he must burn and destroy their towns."[44]

On June 22, Grant's remaining Indian allies sought their Cherokee prey in scout parties that transcended tribal lines. These parties returned with a few scalps. But one group had been "oblig'd to run" when they "fell in with" three or four hundred Indians near Stecoe, Captain French reported.[45]

On June 24, Grant returned to the river opposite Cowee. The next day, he left Lieutenant Colonel Henry Laurens at Nequassee with one thousand men to care for the wounded, the provisions, and the camp. Grant and the Indian Corps led the rest on a four-day, fifty-mile march of destruction. They destroyed the five vacant Cherokee Out Towns, including the "mother town" of Kituwah, the holiest of Cherokee sites. By oral tradition, this was the birthplace of the Cherokee people. Grant made a bold statement: a new era had begun. One soldier dubbed it "the most difficult road ever troops passed over."[46]

In a final act of brutality, Grant's "Mohawk" warriors thrust a stick down the throat of an old Cherokee, stabbed him in the neck and sides with arrows, and tomahawked his head. The men were "so much fatigued, that they could hardly crawl." Grant admitted, "Even our Indians were knocked up."[47]

From June 10 to June 29, the invaders captured seven Cherokees and killed another seven. One of the dead was Kituwah headman Ocayulah, a scout in the Fort Duquesne campaign. Cherokees killed just one white packhorseman. They did so as the weary army headed back to Fort Prince George on July 3,

IMAGE 9.4 *The site of the Cowee townhouse. Author photo.*

its work of vengeance complete. On July 4, the army reached the Dividings, where the trail forked east to Fort Prince George or west to the Valley Towns. Grant feigned toward the Valley Towns but for some reason did not attack them. This was enough to scatter the townspeople to the Overhills.[48] On July 9, the army limped into Fort Prince George with just two days' provisions remaining. "Nothing was left to be done," Grant reported. But Amherst ordered Grant to stay on the frontier until peace was "entirely Settled & Concluded."[49]

For the Cherokee Indians, survival depended upon making peace on British terms. After Grant's march of destruction, villagers were dying of starvation and survivors languished on horse flesh. Attakullakulla journeyed not to meet with Grant, who waited at Fort Prince George, but rather to Colonel Byrd with forty-two other Cherokees. Arriving at the camp at Samuel Stalnaker's on July 16, 180 miles northeast of Chota near the source of the Holston River, he proposed to revisit the Virginian's November 1760 terms. Had Amherst allowed it, Virginia's lieutenant governor, Fauquier, would "secur[e] our own settlements from any future inroads" and block Cherokee-French commerce. A peace, he continued, "without hard or oppressive terms . . . may almost probably be lasting," producing security for the colonies and the Cherokee trade for Virginia. Despite what had happened in 1758, Cherokees preferred such terms to South Carolina's tyranny.[50]

Byrd had no desire to attack Chota. His doting mother urged him to "no more I beseech you expose your self among those barbarians the Chirekees, as you have so often hazzard'd your life & been at vast expence to serve an ungreatfull people." His army remained incomplete, and as one officer put it, "encumbered with Stores, Baggage, Sick and diminish'd," with a 10 percent desertion rate. Three hundred unarmed North Carolina troops and fifty Tuscarora Indians from that province had not yet left the piedmont post of Fort Dobbs. Byrd and Fauquier feared the political cost of alienating South Carolina. With a heavy heart, Byrd obeyed Amherst's orders and referred Attakullakulla to Colonel Grant and Lieutenant Governor Bull. "I certainly must appear in a very despicable Light to them, as I real[ly] do to myself," the colonel wrote to General Amherst. On August 1, Byrd resigned his command and set out for Philadelphia. Attakullakulla returned home dejected and unsure where to turn. It would be months before the signing of a treaty.[51]

TO BURY THE HATCHET, AND MAKE
A FIRM PEACE *Terms and Tensions*

10

On July 21, an elderly Indian rode into Lieutenant Colonel James Grant's camp bearing a white flag of truce. He had ridden a week from the Overhills with a message from Oconostota. Captured and enslaved in South Carolina as a youth, he became fluent in English. Since he escaped bondage, he had been a warrior, intermediary, and translator for Great Tellico and Chatuga. Some called Old Caesar, now "Upward of 80" years old, "the triple-nosed warrior" because of two giant warts on either side of his nose. He "describ'd the extreme distress of his Nation to us in Language so moving" that it would have "touch'd the humanity" of even the most ruthless provincials, Lieutenant Colonel Henry Laurens later recalled. Caesar stated that "hunger & hardships" especially afflicted the young and the old. He presented a string of white beads, calling for peace. It was time, he said, to bury the hatchet. Grant insisted on negotiating only with Oconostota, Ostenaco, Standing Turkey, or Attakullakulla.[1]

But the first three feared for their safety. They disliked the terms Grant had unveiled in May before he invaded the Cherokee villages. They feared that Grant would lure them away from the Overhills so Virginia could attack. On July 31 and August 1, more Cherokees arrived with proposals of their own. They offered to join the British in a long-proposed war against the Creeks. Still others, like Tistoe of Keowee and the Slave-Catcher of Tamassee delivered wampum, a pipe, and some tobacco. Grant refused to deal with these headmen. He ignored the decentralized nature of Cherokee leadership. Currying support village by village, by sending redcoats or provincial delegates on a goodwill tour, would have built consensus. But Grant dismissed the traditional Cherokee solutions that transformed mutual disgust into cooperative arrangements. Instead, the Cornpuller vowed only to negotiate with select warriors. As a result, many of the Indians felt trapped. Though bent on peace, they differed among themselves over the best strategy to achieve it. Only when Tistoe requested it did Grant finally send Captain John Watts, a former trader turned South Carolina Ranger, with Tistoe and the Slave-Catcher to tour the Lower Towns. As a "resident alien," Watts's presence indicated that Grant sought peace. Still, the lieutenant colonel pressured the Indians to hurry back with his hand-picked Cherokee diplomats.[2]

Cherokees had forced South Carolinians of all stripes into a corner, bringing latent disputes into the open. Cherokees hesitated to negotiate with Grant in the manner that he expected. Some Cherokees wished to hold out for French aid. Others sought an economic partnership with Virginia. South Carolina's elites, led by Christopher Gadsden, questioned whether Grant had gone far enough in bringing destruction and ruin on the Cherokee people, and charged the commander with ineptitude. In the process they revealed their concept of the ideal Indian policy. The establishment of separate treaties with Virginia and South Carolina shows the differences between the colonies and highlights the challenge of intercolonial competition.

Grant staked his claim for stronger centralized British authority as he defended his actions on the campaign. This widened the rift between colonial elites and the Crown. When the army returned to Fort Prince George on July 10, provincial commander Colonel Thomas Middleton invoked a March 31 letter from Lieutenant Governor Bull granting him permission to take leave if the service became "disagreeable" to him. He left in a huff without notifying Grant.[3] Middleton reached Charles Town a week later. The incensed gentleman consulted with merchant Christopher Gadsden, his friend and colleague in the South Carolina Assembly.

Miffed and defiant, Grant blasted Middleton for leaving and criticized Bull for the "extraordinary" step of granting leave to the provincial commander. Grant, defending royal prerogative, believed he commanded Middleton. The colonel claimed that placing himself under Grant was "altogether a Voluntary Act," and he needed only answer to his fellow provincials.[4] Their war of words played out in the Charles Town newspapers, but interest spread far beyond South Carolina. One Philadelphia resident called it "Extraordinary." Another dubbed it "Scandelous."[5]

John Rattray, a judge on the vice-admiralty court, urged both parties to calm down, but to no avail. "I . . . think not that Envy will ever be silent," Rattray wrote to Grant. "She already whispers. What[?] not gone to the Valley So few Indians killed Surely Colo. Grant will not make a peace with these wretches Now that their Corn is destroyed they will come down upon us like wolves."[6] Despite the destruction and brutality that Grant had unleashed, many believed Grant had done too little. He had not destroyed the Valley Towns. This, Christopher Gadsden wrote, was "a thing then *expected* and *generally and publickly* talked of throughout the army." Grant's critics also grumbled that he had not inflicted enough suffering on the Cherokees. "When you consider what Indian Towns are, and how soon rebuilt," planter Eliza Lucas Pinckney wrote, "you will think we need not be too much elated . . . unless we had killed more Indians." As British troops returned to Charles Town, "The first Countryman I talk'd to," Major Monypenny wrote, "was of opinion that we did nothing unless we kill'd all the Indians." For many, the memory of the 1760 Cherokee offensive had solidified racial hatred that could be quenched only by genocide.[7]

Over the next month, the war of words escalated. Middleton and his spokesman, Gadsden, became heroes for colonists slighted by imperial rule. In an anonymous letter in the *South Carolina Gazette*, Middleton alleged that Grant had minimized Middleton's contributions and misrepresented his men's courage under fire. In fact, Grant's orders "proved fatal to" many and "must reflect Dishonour somewhat." In a letter to the lieutenant colonel, Middleton called Grant a "mean Spirited Pusillanimous wretch." He continued: "You never once acquainted me with a Singular Plan you had form'd." Then he raised the stakes. He learned "before I left the Camp that you Intended to make a Serious Affair of it, which I Assure you Sir I am as much inclined to do as you are."[8] Grant fired back with a three-thousand-word diatribe. Developing seven points, he refuted Middleton's claims. He blamed the provincial for failing to "observe Established Rules." His next words foreshadowed conflicts to come. "I never do Consult any Body," he said. Rejecting the democratic approach of provincial militias and regiments, he stated that a commander "should think for himself . . . the Sanction of the Advice & Opinion of a hundred People is not worth a Shilling." If Middleton wished to make a "serious affair" of it all, Grant would meet "Any body who calls upon [me]" when he reached town.[9]

Lieutenant Governor Bull was appointed by the Crown, yet he was born in South Carolina and had always been popular with the assembly. He attempted to play both sides. He blocked the publication of inflammatory material in the city's newspapers. He reminded Grant that provincial officers were "gentlemen who had become officers of a season," offering invaluable service to Crown and province. They were "not gentlemen who followed war as a profession." At the same time he assured Grant that the citizens of Charles Town were sympathetic to his own point of view.[10] Rattray paid three visits to Middleton's Charles Town home. He also attempted to talk to the ex-provincial officer on the floor of the assembly. But Middleton ignored Rattray. Instead, he wrote yet another angry letter to Grant, a rebuttal to the lieutenant colonel's seven position points. Grant, he argued, "did not understand the meaning of ye word Concert." Moreover, Middleton alleged, "you acted Hypocritically and Deceitfully." Intensifying the dispute, he added defiantly: "I shall be in Town" upon your return, "and tho' I will not be at home to Every body, yet I most certainly will be to you." No closing salutation followed. The issue was not dead.[11]

It took four months—from late August to late December 1761—to settle peace terms. First, Grant and Attakullakulla drafted preliminaries at Fort Prince George. Next, the assembly and the Cherokee delegation reworked them at Ashley Ferry. Attakullakulla brought those revisions home. He then journeyed to Charles Town to finalize the articles of peace.

On August 28, preliminary peace negotiations took place at Fort Prince George with a select minority of Cherokees. None of the Cherokees present were from the Lower Towns. Nor were Cherokee favorites—Oconostota, Ostenaco, and Standing Turkey—among them. Attakullakulla, Grant's hand-picked diplomat, presented a string of beads representing the peaceful intentions of several villages. The beads did not stand in for the Cherokees as a whole. But Grant affirmed, as if saying it made it so, that the Cherokee came with the assent of "the whole Nation."[12]

Two days later, on August 30, Grant presented the terms of peace. He struck an article proclaiming Attakullakulla as "emperor." Influential headmen would not accede to his authority. "Those head men are not good enough Patriots to Sacrifice their private Interest and Power to the publick Good," he mumbled. Attakullakulla, he admitted, did not represent all Cherokees. He "neither has nor pretends to have Influence enough" to act without their consent, Grant concluded. But Grant would not wait—or work—to win the trust of the rest. Provisioning his troops was becoming difficult. The provincial army dwindled by desertion. Grant wished to push a peace, however imperfect, and get out of Carolina; his troops were needed in the Caribbean. With this in mind, the redcoat struck an article constraining Cherokees to Twenty-Six-Mile Creek (twenty-six miles southeast of Keowee). The stipulation would have limited Indian hunting grounds and promoted white settlement, testing Cherokee pacifism. Bull agreed.[13]

Attakullakulla did not accept all of Grant's terms. He did not want to turn over four Cherokees for execution. He held that whites who killed Cherokees should face Cherokee justice. When he balked, the Cornpuller referred the delegates to the provincial capital to negotiate. As they packed, former Settico trader Charles McGunningham returned from Charles Town. He warned the Cherokees of South Carolina's treachery and of smallpox and other fatal diseases. "If they went to Charles Town they would never come back," McGunningham announced. Only six or seven Cherokees and their "attendants" set out for the city with Attakullakulla on September 2, including the lone representative from the Valley Towns.[14] The Cherokee negotiators represented fewer Cherokees than ever.

Five provincial officers, all of them assemblymen and all of them loyal to Grant, escorted the Cherokees. Grant hoped that these loyal servants of the Crown would sway hardliners in the Commons House. They did so with the hostile climate created by the Grant-Middleton dispute weighing heavily on people's minds. Major John Moultrie Jr. of Middleton's provincial regiment, a Grant defender, wrote to his girlfriend: "It is a naughty world, where falsehood pride & envy are too often much supported, & the best deeds & intentions, are slander'd, misrepresented & abused." He continued, "As you are in Charlestown I imagine you can guess why I say this." Grant's backers would not sway opinion without further drama. The delegation and its escort reached the outskirts of Charles Town after a twelve-day journey. They bypassed the yellow fever–infested capital and continued to Edward Legge's house at Shem Town, also called Ashley Ferry.[15]

Attakullakulla met first with the South Carolina Council. If the translation was accurate, he represented the "great distress" of his people. He then flattered the gentlemen, reportedly calling the white people "superior to us," appealing to their belief in "God almighty," and proclaiming a desire to "live together as brothers."[16]

Several days of fierce debate unfolded as the assemblymen discussed peace terms. Grant's critics, led by Thomas Middleton and Christopher Gadsden, charged Grant with weakness and ineptitude in both 1760 and 1761. They blasted his arrogance, particularly toward Middleton. And they demanded Cherokee scalps as part of a crippling treaty. Henry Laurens and Grant's loyal coterie of provincials fought for a moderate settlement. They defended the redcoat commander and portrayed Gadsden as a bit unhinged. Over a two-year period, Gadsden and Laurens subsequently wrote, circulated, and later published their respective views in letters and pamphlets.

Grant's critics charged the colonel with arrogance and "gross misrepresentation" toward South Carolina's rangers and provincials. Consistent with his past behavior, Grant had maligned colonial forces. According to Gadsden, Grant had characterized the "whole corps" as inept and cowardly. Laurens countered, arguing that Middleton had been glorified "beyond all bounds of modest pretension . . . to Soil & deprecate the merit of an able & experienced officer."[17]

Gadsden also charged Grant with weakness and incompetence and feared a third campaign might be necessary. In 1760, Grant had essentially run Montgomery's campaign, Christopher Gadsden argued. He had unnecessarily ordered the hasty retreat from Echoe after the battle several hours earlier. Gadsden wondered, "Had he no feeling for our back-settlers" or for the Fort Loudoun garrison? Critics also alleged that Grant had not gone far enough in 1761. Grant "might have gone to the Valley [Towns] with ease," but failed to do so. Gadsden later facetiously claimed that Grant's troops could surely have survived for six months "upon strawberries, Chesnuts & Indian potatoes" in order to continue their assault on the Cherokee towns. Laurens remarked snarkily, "I have inform'd them, that the Cherokee Country produces Walnuts & Acorns too."[18]

In contentious assembly debates on September 18, Laurens defended Grant and the 1761 campaign. Laurens cited "impassible" rivers, and blamed the assembly for the barefoot, sick, and poorly supplied provincial soldiers. He offered to debate anyone on this "before 12 Impartial men." As the session adjourned, Laurens and Middleton confronted each other in a shouting match. On Bull's orders, Captain John Stuart, the South Carolina officer who survived the Fort Loudoun siege, arrested and confined the two bickering legislators until they pledged "that they would not terminate their disspute by a duel." But the damage had been done. Stuart proclaimed publicly that "much pains have been taken to Blacken Lauren's Character." With Gadsden on his side, Middleton and Grant edged closer to a duel. Would-be mediator John Rattray contracted yellow fever. He died before the end of the month.[19]

On September 23, Attakullakulla accepted preliminary peace terms bearing the assembly's modifications. The Gadsden faction had acquiesced—for now. The Commons struck two articles. No Cherokee murderers or scalps would be delivered up. The treaty would not name Attakullakulla "emperor." But the terms would do little to win Attakullakulla popularity at home or to ensure a long lasting peace. The legislators declined to garrison Fort Loudoun, yet they claimed the right to do so.[20] The peace terms also blatantly violated Cherokee sovereignty and land rights. The treaty required the Chero-

IMAGE 10.1 *Christopher Gadsden, by Jeremiah Theus, 1760–70. Courtesy of the Charleston Museum, Charleston, S.C.*

kees to put to death or deliver the scalps of any of their villagers accused of murdering white people. It required Cherokees to return the African American adoptees among them—some of them runaway slaves—to British authorities. This reflected white fears of interracial mixing and military alliance, let alone the worry that Cherokee country might become a safe haven for blacks. Against Grant's wishes and contrary to the understanding he had with Bull, the assembly reinserted the article making Twenty-Six-Mile Creek the new Cherokee-Carolina boundary. The Indians could neither hunt nor travel without a white escort beyond it. Bull worried that "they may indeed think the new Limits . . . an encroachment on their Antient possession." Cherokees might have wondered if the British wished to exterminate them altogether. The Lower Towns especially faced the further effects of hunting limits: more starvation and the decline of the deerskin trade. The trade might shift to the Overhills, where Virginians, following the newly widened road toward Chota, would swoop in. The provision banning Cherokees from traveling across the border without a white escort discouraged the friendly, informal exchanges between Cherokees and whites that often took place at Ninety Six. The terms Attakullakulla accepted also required Cherokees to deliver both French and British incendiaries and to respect farmland and pasturage at British forts. These terms would no doubt lead to disagreements in the future.[21]

Attakullakulla promised to return British prisoners. Some, like Fort Loudoun's carpenter John Stevens, wished to return. But others, like Corporal John Bench, had willingly assimilated into Cherokee society. The British offered to return Cherokee prisoners with no strings attached. This was long overdue, and it would regain some popularity for Attakullakulla among his people. A half dozen or more of the forty or fifty taken during the war had died of starvation, disease, and mistreatment. The council journals from the previous winter revealed that British soldiers had raped Cherokee women detainees with impunity. Attakullakulla and his delegation, with copies of the terms in hand, ventured from Ashley Ferry to Charles Town to smoke from a ceremonial peace pipe that the Cherokees had given to Governor Glen a decade earlier. Then they went home, promising to return to Charles Town to confirm the treaty after holding a national referendum at Chota.[22] Given Attakullakulla's limited influence among his people, the promise would be difficult to keep. Indeed, he may never have intended to do so.

Despite an escort of provincial officers, frontiersmen "insulted & threatnd" Attakullakulla "oftner than once" on the road back to Fort Prince George. It was a sign of things to come. These settlers, still stinging from the 1760 Cherokee offensive, viewed all Indians with disdain. Even Grant, typically sympathetic, thumbed his nose at the de facto puppet emperor. The Carpenter, he wrote, referring to the Cherokee's moniker, was so desperate for power that he "would have agreed" to virtually anything. John Stuart, the Indian's friend and confidant, agreed. Stuart believed that Attakullakulla fashioned himself as a hero and dreamt of "regaining his wonted influence and weight with

His countrymen." The Indian carried strings of wampum from just five villages.[23] In July, a trader with reliable information learned of a Cherokee-led plot to assassinate the headman, though he did not elaborate on who the conspirators were.[24]

Attakullakulla and the Cherokees reached Fort Prince George on October 12. Two days later, "without Arms or an Escort," Grant and several officers toured the ruins of the Lower Towns. Lower Townspeople had begun to resettle and rebuild and seemed "much pleased" to put the chaos behind them. Grant was convinced of their "Sincerity." But the proposed treaty jeopardized their hunting grounds, and therefore placed the long-term survival of the Lower Towns in doubt.[25]

An additional two hundred Cherokees camped near the fort, ready to resettle the Lower Towns in the spring. Tistoe and the Wolf of Keowee danced all night on October 31 to celebrate. They were eager to "make Stores, & to Plant, as soon as we can." This was home, and they would not have it any other way: "I have been Lost over the Hills: I am come down to hunt on my own Land," Tistoe announced. He and the Keowees had endured much. Many were starving. As a sign of good faith, they stored their possessions and their corn at Fort Prince George. Tistoe sent a pipe for McIntosh, Grant, and Bull to smoke. Eager to resume a semblance of "ordinary" life, he requested a trader for his people. He also made a symbolic statement. Concerned about the pending treaty and hopeful of ensuring future prospects, he sent a bag of soil to Lieutenant Governor Bull "to put him in mind" of the 1755 meeting at Saluda. There, the headman said, all agreed "we was to hunt this Side Long Canes to Tugala [Tugaloo]." The Long Canes settlers had violated that accord. Tistoe called for limits on white hunting grounds to protect the survival of the Lower Towns. He advocated a vast hunting preserve east of that to be shared by natives and colonists alike. His plan fell on deaf ears. Its reception did not bode well for the Lower Towns.[26]

In the period between preliminary articles and the formal treaty signing, however, Grant learned that the Gadsden-Middleton coterie in the Commons House had set the Cherokee-Carolina boundary at Twenty-Six-Mile Creek. He was incensed. Bull claimed that a clerical mistake had occurred. Grant blamed Bull for allowing South Carolina's assemblymen too much power to overrule the Crown's interests. He worried that the alteration might undo the peace. Grant fretted that "the Intended Encroachment . . . upon the Indian Country, must inevitably produce another War in a few Months." The Indian inhabitants "cannot Subsist" upon smaller hunting grounds, he said. And if Virginia tried to impose her own limits on Cherokee territory, Grant noted,

Cherokees would starve.[27] Laurens, smeared by the opposition in the Commons House, confessed that the actions of the Gadsden-Middleton faction filled him with "grief & shame." Grant scoffed at the notion of allowing an elected colonial assembly to manipulate a treaty.[28]

Grant believed that Bull had intentionally deceived him. He complained to Amherst that Bull's behavior was "so irregular and so unprecedented, that I cannot put up with it." Bull defended his actions, claimed to be sick, and retreated to his country estate. "He knows well how to play with both hands," Stuart wrote, accusing the lieutenant governor of "Dissengenuity & Rotten heartedness." But this is exactly what made Bull so successful. He was a masterful politician, able to balance the interests of both colony and metropole. The dispute nevertheless forced the lieutenant governor and the council to again alter the treaty terms without the assembly's knowledge. The struggle between royal and provincial prerogative was fully in play.[29]

On November 14, after a month in the villages, Attakullakulla passed through the rebuilding Lower Towns and arrived at Fort Prince George with a few pro-British Cherokee leaders. With enlistments expiring, Lieutenant Colonel Laurens disbanded the desertion-plagued South Carolina Regiment. Seven white prisoners were redeemed. Without government sanction, traders from Augusta, Georgia, once again commenced business with Seroweh. Life was returning to normal, and the Cherokees had no resources with which to fight.[30]

If a national referendum took place, no record of it has been found. Cherokee confidence in the proposed peace was not high. The Indians, Grant noted, "in speaking of Charles-town . . . have for many Years been accustomed to call it the Town of Lyes." Cherokee women, fearful for their husbands' safety, believed that Grant had built a jail at Ninety Six to confine the diplomats and "drive" them "like a parcel of Sheep" to Charles Town. Attakullakulla claimed that he had the consent of the "Nation." But he could not gather a large group of pro-British headmen. He blamed this on the hunting season. If Attakullakulla's assertions are true, hunting superseded arranging formal peace terms. If his claims are false, many Cherokees failed to accept the Anglo-European obsession with formal "terms." Or perhaps they disliked the articles and did not accede to the authority the chief claimed. In fact, no Valley Townsmen came to the conferences. Along the way several Cherokees in Attakullakulla's retinue "quarreled" with him and returned home. The Indians reached Charles Town as Grant's British troops sailed for the Caribbean.[31]

News of the South Carolina negotiations surprised Virginian observers. "We catch the reports of Peace with gaping Mouths," planter George Washington wrote.[32] But how would the Cherokees position themselves with Virginia? By early September, Colonel Adam Stephen's army of Virginia provincials pushed closer to Chota. The men built a large fort on the Great Island (Long Island) of the Holston River. Fort Robinson, named after the speaker of the Virginia House of Burgesses, stood just 130 miles from the beloved Cherokee town. This put pressure on Overhills leaders, including Standing Turkey, Ostenaco, and Oconostota, who were already disenchanted with Attakullakulla's proceedings. Fort Loudoun adoptee Corporal John Bench assisted them as secretary and translator. The proud "opposite faction," as Stephen described the men, wanted to establish an economic partnership with Virginia, without assigning guilt or dwelling upon past "mischief done on Both sides." Virginia could also protect the Cherokees from their Shawnee enemies. The men defended Cherokee sovereignty, vowing to enforce law and order without white interference by constructing a Cherokee-run jail in Chota. In a symbolic gesture of goodwill, Standing Turkey's young son delivered a pipe and a message of peace to Fort Robinson.[33]

In mid-November, Attakullakulla went to South Carolina to confirm an unpopular peace. Grant sent his most loyal officers, both provincial and redcoat, to accompany Attakullakulla to Charles Town. These soldiers snubbed Lieutenant Governor Bull during their welcome ceremony. At the same time, Overhill leaders, too proud to concede defeat to South Carolina, went to Virginia to attempt a separate, less humiliating peace. Along the way they met Lieutenant Colonel Hugh Waddell, with his North Carolina provincials, and several dozen Tuscarora Indians, working with the Virginians to widen a road leading from the Great Island to Chota. Virginia, with North Carolina's meager and late-arriving aid, was positioning itself for postwar prosperity and dominance.[34]

Waddell accompanied these two or three hundred Overhill Cherokees back to the Great Island to meet with Colonel Stephen. One hundred Cherokees already camped nearby under Virginia protection. The visitors secured the simple accord they wanted. The treaty signed on November 20 on the Great Island of the Holston included just two articles. First, the Cherokee warriors present agreed "to bury the Hatchet, and make a Firm Peace" with Virginia, North Carolina, and the North Carolina Tuscaroras. Second, Cherokees would deliver the persons, or the scalps, of their people who had murdered British subjects to the Virginia post on the Great Island. This term gave the Cherokees leeway. It stipulated no time limits or conditions, and any Indian scalp might suffice. The officers of the Virginia Regiment had always been reasonable. Virginia wanted the Cherokee trade. And

Stephen gave no indication that Virginia would garrison the post during peacetime. Ostenaco spoke optimistically: "Now our Chain will Certainly be bright."[35]

At the treaty signing, Standing Turkey presented a vision of hope for fellow Cherokees. The Cherokees were neither defeated nor demoralized: "My People will hunt & Plant their fields at Pleasure, and the Young People will grow up, flourish, and Replenish their Towns, and we shall be as numerous & Powerfull as formerly." This would become possible with "suitable goods to traffick for their skins." Willenawa of Toqua, a key figure in the Fort Loudoun siege, agreed. Stephen signed the treaty. But he expressed his doubts to the delegates. As a people with no central authority and with "rash young men [who] can do whatever they Please," he wondered, "how can you be answerable for their Performing the Conditions upon which the Peace is granted to them?" No response was recorded. But filled with hope for a peaceful, prosperous future, the Cherokees invited some Virginia soldiers—among them Lieutenant Henry Timberlake and Sergeant Thomas Sumter, back to their villages on a goodwill tour of peace.[36]

The process of finalizing the South Carolina treaty began in the council chamber on December 14. To be safe, Cherokees brought their own interpreters. Lieutenant Governor Bull was ill.[37] Christopher Gadsden later scoffed, "Of the Cherokees" present, one or two "might have some influence, in his or their own particular town, but not one of any *general* weight in their settlements, much less throughout the nation, not even [Attakullakulla]."[38]

The final treaty resembled the preliminary articles. "Blood revenge"—Cherokee law and custom—became a capital felony, punishable under British law. The British claimed the right to build and garrison forts among the Cherokees and to farm adjacent fields. The trade would reopen, but only after the Cherokees returned English prisoners (now adoptees), horses, and cattle. The final treaty differed in a few ways from the preliminaries. First, no Cherokees were to be delivered up or executed. Second, at the assembly's urging, Cherokees were to hand over all white men who assisted them during the war. The legislators would not entertain the possibility of rogue traders or French agents remaining in the Cherokee villages. The assembly also feared that African American runaway slaves might flock to Appalachia, possibly joining with the Cherokees in a race war. Therefore, it required the Indians to surrender all African Americans among them. Fourth, Bull slipped in a revision on the sly, setting the Cherokee-Carolina boundary at forty miles southeast of Keowee, rather than twenty-six. None of these last three provisions were enforceable. The treaty signed on December 18 addressed few of the underlying problems that had caused the war.[39]

To confirm the peace, Cherokees and councilmen smoked an Indian pipe. Attakullakulla swept the ground with eagle feathers. He produced a string of wampum and an eagle tail. He also delivered several strings of beads from Cherokee villages and headmen. Other Cherokees presented gifts. Councilman and Charles Town militia commander Colonel Othniel Beale, speaking for the ill and absent lieutenant governor (who was also his son-in-law), gave the Cherokees only a stern reminder that "the English had a right to their prisoners" and they would withhold the trade until their return. Though Attakullakulla brought nine British captives, the South Carolinians released just two Cherokees. As formalities concluded in the council chamber, it became clear that the relationship would not be reciprocal.[40]

Cherokee defense and diplomacy had excited the struggle between provincial and crown authority. Grant returned to Charles Town on December 19 to angry partisans and an incensed Colonel Middleton. Jeering mobs heckled the lieutenant colonel, the embodiment of British arrogance, "every Time [he] appeared in the Streets." Indeed, "the Spirit of Prejudice & Party has run higher than it ever did in any part of the World," Grant wrote. Then, Middleton accosted Grant on Vendue Range, striking him with a cane. This was a formal challenge to duel. Grant accepted. "I was under a sort of necessity of doing it," he said.[41]

Four days later, on December 23, at an unknown location, tensions came to a head. Events culminated "to the honour of both parties, and the satisfaction of all the friends of each," the *Gazette* reported. According to Laurens, Middleton's friends were "alledging" that "a G . . . was at 12¼ Yards distance when he fired over an M's Calabash." Middleton's supporters implied that Grant, the accused, had unintentionally missed Middleton's large head, and that Middleton had then reserved fire. The Grant-Laurens faction thought that Grant had lured Middleton into the duel to humble the provincial. The redcoat "played the Old Soldier & seduced the Latter notwithstanding his full presence of mind." Having sufficiently embarrassed Middleton, the redcoat deliberately misfired, sparing the challenger Middleton's life. Grant claimed as much: "I gave him his life, when it was absolutely in my power [to take it]," he informed Amherst. With all parties in the duel sworn to secrecy, public speculation fueled further discord among the merchant-planter aristocracy. Folks were still buzzing about the duel six weeks later.[42]

Whatever the truth was, the duel stood in for a widening rift between white colonists and Crown authority. It also raised contention between different groups of colonists as they sorted out their allegiances, their interests, their friends, and their prospects for the future.

Grant sailed out of Charles Town the day after the duel. Sympathetic to the Cherokees' plight, he thought that the peace would "be a lasting one, If the People of this Province do not, by bad Treatment, force those poor Savages to break out again." But "bad Treatment" was not the only variable. The Cherokees were starving, Grant observed, and could only "Subsist 'till March or April"—well short of the corn harvest.[43]

THE TURBULENT SPIRIT OF GADSDEN
The Origins of Independence

11 With copies of the finalized treaty in hand, Attakullakulla and his warriors returned through the bitter cold to their villages. The lieutenant governor had provided only "a small quantity of powder and ball" for them to hunt with during the journey. Worse, the Indians "were most vilainously handled upon their return," Henry Laurens reported. They were "way laid & rob'd at different places within fourscore Miles of Town of more than 20 Horses by a gang" of lawless frontiersmen. Laurens found the perpetrators "rather viler than any Cherokees." These events jeopardized the "good Accounts" and "good effects" of the peace. Cherokees, white ruling elites, and British authorities all faced a growing threat. "Those Mountaineers," Laurens predicted, "may be again troublesome to us." The settlers, often squatters, defied British authority and encroached on Cherokee hunting grounds.[1]

Yet the war had shown colonial elites how useful frontiersmen could be. In 1760 alone, Cherokees had killed nearly two hundred Carolinians and had captured at least as many. The number of runaway slaves increased each year from 1759 to 1761. And the enslaved population expanded rapidly each year, especially in neighboring Georgia. Settlers buffered coastal elites from the Indians and apprehended runaway slaves. Elites and frontiersmen needed each other. So long as the frontier expanded and farming thrived there, both remained happy. This clashed with the interests of Cherokees and slaves. And it clashed with the interests of the British Crown, responsible for maintaining troops and providing Indian "presents" to prevent the fallout of unbridled expansion: Indian war.

As Attakullakulla returned to the Overhills in January 1762, he saw frontier families building homes and preparing to plant. Entering the Cherokee villages, he saw the effects of war, disease, and starvation. In this weakened state, Cherokees looked to the British Crown and its Indian agents for protection against both frontiersmen and elites.[2]

By early 1762 some members of South Carolina's ruling class had galvanized against the divergent aims of Crown policy. While this discontent was not unprecedented, the Cherokee War had inflamed tensions, and those tensions did not subside. As Grant's friend wrote from Charles Town on January 13, "Prejudice, & resentment, have operated pretty extremely after your departure from thence last summer." In 1779, a Presbyterian pastor and former resident of Charles Town, Alexander Hewatt, directly linked the fallout from the Grant campaign and the Grant-Middleton duel to the coming of the Revolution. After the Grant-Middleton dispute, he wrote, "a party-spirit appeared in Carolina." He added, "Malicious aspersions and inflammatory accusations [were] greedily swallowed . . . and industriously propagated. Prejudices were contracted, cherished, and unhappily gained ground." Invective "poured indiscriminately" on both sides, he said, "with the most pernicious consequence."[3]

When he arrived in South Carolina, just days after the signing of the treaty, the province's new governor, Thomas Boone, observed that the colonists were "warriours and enemies" to each other, and had battled in Charles Town. Animosity lingered; he perceived "wounds skinned over, but I doubt not healed." Boone, thirty-one, was a distant relative of the frontiersman Daniel Boone. He had inherited a plantation in South Carolina and lived there briefly in the 1750s. He now faced a disgruntled assembly. Representatives led by Christopher Gadsden were inflamed by Grant's handling of the expedition and were emboldened by Gadsden's vociferous dissent. Grant's "Enemies in what they say of him," Boone opined, "affect little Moderation at all." The legislators greeted Britain's new top official cordially, but they viewed him with distrust. The treaty, they felt, had been too lenient. They criticized "the manner & Terms different from those recommended by this House." And they were enraged that the previous summer, the council had interfered with provincial sovereignty by thwarting a bill to limit slave importation. The defeated proposal would have driven prices up and lined the pockets of slave traders and planters with surplus slaves to sell. It also would have eased elite fears of revolt. While he refrained from commenting on the Grant-Middleton duel, the new governor vowed to take a stand on new "Topick[s] of Dispute." Boone's

IMAGE 11.1 *Peter Manigault and His Friends, by George Roupell, 1757–60.*
Courtesy, Winterthur Museum, Drawing, Museum Purchase, 1963.73.

instructions called on him to assert royal prerogative, and he did not hesitate to do so.[4]

Moderates in the Commons House predicted a clash of wills and feared the disruption of public business in the province. Alexander Garden, now apparently swayed by the Crown faction, and Henry Laurens, one of Grant's leading supporters, for example, hoped that the "surly, ill-tuned minds" in the Gadsden faction would "not attempt to revive a joke" that they had already "carried too far."[5] The "joke" they referred to was the Grant-Middleton controversy.

General Amherst believed that the peace of Charles Town would establish "a firm and Lasting friendship with those lately misguided Indians, and thereby Secure to the Inhabitants of the Province a perfect tranquility." He was sorely mistaken.[6] Instead, Cherokee affairs set the stage for Revolution.

In early 1762, Virginia and Overhill Cherokee delegates formally reaffirmed the peace terms they had reached in November 1761. An Overhill delegation visited Williamsburg in January. In March, Settico men and women sent wampum and beads to Virginia. Lieutenant Governor Fauquier issued a proclamation "requiring all people in this government to behave with the most perfect amity" toward the delegates on their return. He ordered "two hundred pounds" to any person providing evidence against a Virginian accused of murdering a Cherokee. At the same time, the Overhills hosted Virginia provincial Lieutenant Henry Timberlake, Sergeant Thomas Sumter, their interpreter, and an African slave on a goodwill tour to confirm the accord. Timberlake's journal, later published, offers a remarkable glimpse of eighteenth-century Cherokee life. It also reveals the division, disillusionment, and doubt that swept through the Overhills after the war. Cherokees pursued a full range of options to ensure their immediate and long-term survival.[7]

According to North Carolina's governor, Arthur Dobbs, "upon account of the War Sickness and famine," the Cherokee population had been cut by a third from 1758 to 1761.[8] Stores of weapons and ammunition ran low. British settlers and enemy Indians swarmed over Cherokee hunting grounds. Hopeful of reviving the French and angered at the stinginess and unresponsiveness of British Indian policy, Indians in the Ohio Valley, Illinois Country, and Great Lakes region took to the warpath. Most were Cherokee enemies: Iroquois, Ottawas, Miamis, Delawares, and Shawnees, among others. They sought to replenish their war-depleted populations by taking captives and scalps. If the Cherokees joined the others against mutual enemies—or even against the British—they could not rebuild their villages. Their population would decline further through war, disease, and hardship. And war drew off warriors and hunters, so they also risked attacks from the Creeks to the south or the Chickasaws to the west if they sent their men off to war. Settlers continued to encroach from the east, including from Virginia. Cherokee villages, many of them in ruins, were vulnerable on all sides, with no simple solution available.[9]

For the Cherokees, recent events took precedence. War with the British—in this case Virginia or South Carolina—was no longer an option. Most Cherokees gradually adopted a defensive posture. The first event to prompt this policy was a shock wave of Shawnee raids against the Overhills early in 1762. Willenawa led forty Cherokees to the Virginia frontier to strike back against the attackers. Though his men took four scalps, they lost a key warrior, the Raven of Toqua. Soon thereafter, "for want of arrows," the Shawnees routed another revenge-seeking party of Cherokees. Eight of the thirty Cherokees in the

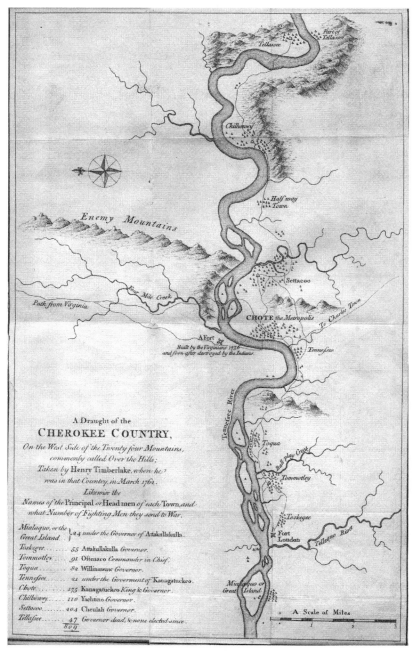

IMAGE 11.2 *"A Draught of the Cherokee Country," by Henry Timberlake, 1762, printed 1765. Map image courtesy of the Norman B. Leventhal Map Center at the Boston Public Library/Richard H. Brown Collection.*

battle died. Cherokees recognized that offensive war was not viable. Moreover, they needed British support to defend themselves against their Indian enemies while they rebuilt their villages and recouped their population losses.

Second, citing high costs and the conclusion of a Cherokee-Virginia peace, Fauquier withdrew the provincial garrison from the fort on the Great Island and disbanded it. Thus Cherokee villagers now faced a dual threat in the 1760s: Indian attacks from the north and settler violence from the northeast.[10] To make matters worse, the safety of the Lower Towns on the Carolina frontier remained unclear. So insecure were the Cherokees that even Seroweh vowed "not to go to war himself unless the white people should begin first." He resisted Creek overtures and now criticized more militant Cherokees. If South Carolina launched a punitive invasion, the reeling Lower Towns would be the first to feel its effects.[11]

The recent disruption of village life was a third reason offensive war was unappealing. Most Cherokee men were out hunting so they could get skins to trade for weapons, blankets, and household items. Displaced villagers had to rebuild or find new places to live. Of the roughly forty Cherokee towns in existence in the mid-1750s, only about twenty remained. Some villagers had reoccupied the Lower Towns by early 1762, but the Lower Towns and the Out Towns, hampered by military vulnerability and shrunken hunting grounds, never recovered. Keowee never rebuilt. Only two Out Towns persisted, and they merged politically with the Middle Towns. In the Middle Towns, Tassee and Nequassee lay empty for several years. Displaced Cherokees thought not of war but of relocation and recovery. They built new villages in defensible locations, including Seneca (today Clemson) in the Lower Towns, and Mialoquo in the Overhills. The occupants of these refugee villages fumed bitterly about their situation. They were angry with the British frontiersmen who had started the Cherokee War, and they were also angry with their elders for mishandling it.[12]

On April 2, 1762, the thirty white and black prisoners "willing" to leave Cherokee country remained in Cherokee hands. It took three months to collect them. The struggle to do so revealed important realities. First, Cherokees had little incentive to free their prisoners. Because unlicensed Virginia and Georgia traders still circulated the Cherokee villages, South Carolina's embargo had no effect. Second, as one redeemed captive put it, "some of the prisoners both old and young had no inclination to leave the nation and chose to remain there." They had developed close relationships and family ties with the Overhill Cherokees at Fort Loudoun. South Carolina officials pressed for the prisoners' return, fearing interracial mixing and envisaging the possibility of Christian Gottlieb Priber's society. Third, not all village clusters agreed on the importance of returning their prisoners. Unlike the Overhills, Lower Townspeople suffered from food shortages and feared a military response from South Carolina, so they surrendered their captives quickly. Each settlement cluster and each village had to look out for its own interests.[13]

The attacks by Shawnees and other northern enemies continued through the spring of 1762, further reducing Cherokee resources. As late as May, northern Indians killed five Cherokees in the Middle Town of Watauga. They also surprised an encampment of warriors, killing fourteen. They left one survivor "to tell the warriors what had been done." Attakullakulla informed the commander of Fort Prince George, Lachlan McIntosh, that the enemy threat kept Cherokees from hunting and rebuilding and hampered their ability to provide food and shelter to their prisoners.[14]

Much like South Carolina elites, the Overhills were split into factions, "between whom there is often great animosity," Timberlake wrote. While Attakullakulla had made his peace with South Carolina, Ostenaco had sided with Virginia, seeing that colony as the best bet for a more equitable future. Both men expected too much.[15]

At the same time, a third group of Cherokees remained "much attached to the French," Timberlake said. Oconostota was one of them. His role in the killing of Lieutenant Coytmore at Fort Prince George and his leadership during the Fort Loudoun siege and aftermath had enhanced his reputation among the Cherokees. But after that he reached too far, starting an unpopular war with the Upper (Western) Chickasaws later that year. Moreover, he was not a charismatic speaker. And he produced little aid from the French. He journeyed often to Fort Toulouse, Mobile, and New Orleans, but he extracted only empty promises from French military and political brass. Whatever his flaws, Frenchmen and Cherokees alike still admired him. "In all his expeditions," Timberlake marveled, Oconostota never lost a man in battle.[16]

The French could live peacefully among the natives. They repaired Indian weapons, offered fair prices, and at times respected and appreciated native cultures. Louisiana governor Louis Billouart, Chevalier de Kerlérec, said all the right things. But for the last five years, he had been cut off from regular supplies and reinforcements. He had little but promises to offer the Indians of the Southeast. On April 28, 1762, he wrote to Paris that he had sent couriers—one of them a Creek headman—to the Choctaws and Cherokees. Kerlérec recruited a dozen prominent Cherokees from the Overhills—some of them from Chota—to plan "operations" against the British. What that meant remains unclear. Oconostota was one of the delegates. He journeyed to New Orleans but returned empty handed and "naked." Kerlérec also dispatched Antoine Adhémar de Lantagnac, the French agent and former Chota resident, to the Overhills "to redouble their hostility and courage against the English." Finally, the Louisiana governor ordered the soldiers at Fort Toulouse to cultivate a Creek-Cherokee alliance. Because the French had no supplies to offer, these efforts did not bear fruit. Oconostota's hopes waned.[17]

For South Carolinians, years of war put Crown and province at odds. Raising provincial regiments and rangers, funding Lyttelton's campaign, provisioning the frontier forts, providing Indian presents, and subsidizing the Grant campaign had proven costly. White elites resented the "load of Taxes" that they "must Struggle with for years to come," House Speaker Benjamin Smith observed. "We never was so taxed in our lives," planter Eliza Lucas Pinckney wrote to a friend in England, and "our Seas does not throw up sands of gold, as surely the British does." Indeed, South Carolina's male landowners, taxed on land and slaves, paid the highest taxes anywhere in the British North American colonies. These taxes had increased to new all-time highs. Parliament provided the colony the third-lowest percentage of wartime reimbursement.[18]

In the Commons House elections of January 1762, as in the two elections before it, radicals prevailed at the polls, defeating more moderate candidates. Henry Laurens was one of the losers. Yet in the new session of the assembly in March, Governor Boone demanded that the legislature reinterpret, or rewrite, the Election Act of 1721 in a way that would reduce the power of the Commons House. He signaled that he would push his instructions to the limit, despite the growing predominance and assertiveness of radicals in the Commons House. It was this concerted British postwar inflexibility and unwillingness to accommodate and adapt that furthered the Revolutionary crisis in years to come.[19]

Gadsden, sensing a threat to colonial rights, resumed his assault on British authority. He had not run in January 1762, but he did not bow out of the public arena. Putting pen to paper, he again targeted his scapegoat, James Grant. Captain John Dunnet, an officer in the Independent Companies, wrote Grant from Fort Augusta. He reported that "the turbulent Spirit of Gadsden pursued You still farther" in March, and "usher'd itself forth" in a second pamphlet criticizing Grant's decisions in 1760 and 1761. The assemblymen were so swayed that they declared publicly on May 28 that the war had provided no "Real advantages" to the province. Again they met with resistance. Governor Boone blocked Peter Timothy from printing articles in his *South Car-*

olina Gazette that criticized the Crown. A rival publication, meanwhile, publicly supported the Crown. In his *South-Carolina Weekly Gazette*, printer Robert Wells gloated that Grant had been promoted to colonel "for Services done in America." Partisanship was further inflamed.[20] Incidentally, General Amherst sent Grant back to Charles Town in May in an ultimately unsuccessful attempt to recruit more men for British campaigns in the Caribbean. Grant kept a low profile. But his mere presence—and fears that he might draw away the white men that kept slaves in check—drew the ire of lowcountry elites.[21]

In September 1762, voters in St. Paul Parish elected Gadsden in a special campaign to fill a vacant seat in the Commons House. Boone targeted his enemy and tried to undercut his election. Gadsden was not only a firebrand. The merchant attracted a following among the white masses. For a political leader who prided himself on his business acumen, not his landed estates, to have an influence over landless men, and to be shaped by them, was anathema to British conservatives at home and abroad. And it flew in the face of British tradition. Boone refused to administer the state oaths and swear in Gadsden. Citing technicalities in election procedure, the governor pointed out that the churchwardens of St. Paul Parish had not taken oaths before a magistrate before conducting the election in which Gadsden had triumphed. The governor claimed to be merely complying with his royal instructions. Assemblymen argued that Gadsden had won by a wide margin—80 percent of the vote. Churchwardens did not need to be sworn in before elections; their oaths were implied. Neither Boone nor the legislators would give an inch. Boone dismissed the assembly and called for new elections. The move backfired: Gadsden won reelection. And so did many of the fiery merchant's friends.[22]

A well-known struggle, detailed by several historians, followed. The origins of this conflict, and the seeds of Revolutionary fervor, date to the tensions unleashed by the Cherokee War and its conclusion. In December 1762, a committee of future patriots excoriated the governor. Not only had Boone denied the assembly the authority to judge and certify the validity of their own elections, but he had also gone a step further in declaring that colonial assemblies existed not as a right of the colonists, but at the pleasure of the Crown. A majority of representatives in the Commons House refused to do business and withheld the province's share of Boone's salary. Their government shutdown lasted for eighteen months. It ended only when imperial authorities recalled Governor Boone. He snuck out of the province without fanfare—and with a married woman.[23]

While the assembly dispute unfolded, Ostenaco, "with two followers and an interpreter," as Fauquier described them, were in England. In April 1762, seventy Cherokees journeyed with Timberlake and Sumter to Williamsburg. Hoping to unseat Attakullakulla, Ostenaco begged Fauquier and the Virginia Council to go to England "to see the great King his Father, and judge whether the little Carpenter [Attakullakulla] had not told them Lies." Was cooperation with the whites the only option? Could Ostenaco supplant Attakullakulla's influence among both the British and the Cherokees? Ostenaco persisted in his machinations despite the "Inconveniences and Dangers he would be exposed to." On his final evening in Williamsburg, Ostenaco addressed the Cherokee encampment as a crowd of white observers watched in wonder. College student Thomas Jefferson recalled years later that the Indian's "sounding voice, distinct articulation, animated action, and the solemn silence of his people at their several fires, filled me with awe and veneration, although I did not understand a word he uttered." The next morning the delegation sailed to England.[24]

The Cherokees appeared in public on numerous occasions. Wherever they went, enormous crowds of enthralled Britons followed. The trio of Indians toured the Woolwich Dockyards, the Tower of London, Parliament, Westminster Abbey, and Vauxhall Gardens. They attended plays and musical performances. Two of the Cherokees posed for portraits. And the Cherokees met the king at St. James Palace. Because their interpreter had died on the passage, the Cherokees could not communicate, which must have been a bitter disappointment. The Indian visitors dined with Colonel Montgomery's cousin, with Lord Egremont—now the Secretary of State—and with former Georgia governor Henry Ellis. Alexander Cuming, the Scottish adventurer who had escorted a different Cherokee delegation to England in 1730, was released briefly from Fleet Street debtor's prison to interpret. The Cherokees were a public curiosity and an instant sensation.[25]

The last prisoners—fewer than a dozen on each side—returned home in the spring and summer of 1762. Governor Boone then reopened the Cherokee trade on new terms. Passed by the assembly on May 19, the Act to Regulate the Trade with the Cherokee Indians (Indian Trade Act) established a public monopoly of the Cherokee trade under five directors. The quintet fixed prices and coordinated shipments. The act prohibited private trade from South Carolina. And it established a factory at Fort Prince George, where a commissary oversaw the exchange of Cherokee deerskins and other items for British manufactures.[26]

IMAGE 11.3 The Three Cherokee Chiefs, 1762. *Hand colored copy of wood engraving. Registration #3576.429, L.B. 88. Courtesy of Gilcrease Museum Archives, Tulsa, Okla.*

The trade remained far from fair. Because the law could not "Operate beyond the Limits of the Province," unscrupulous traders from Virginia, Georgia, and North Carolina—which had no regulations on traders—competed with each other by spreading unfounded rumors. Some of the traders charged exorbitant prices, extended credit too freely, or cheated the Indians, as they had done before the war. Colonial officials had no way to hold the illicit traders accountable, especially those from other colonies. To paint Virginia traders as untrustworthy, Carolina's traders threatened that Virginia troops would attack the Cherokees.[27]

For the Cherokees, the biggest problem was an ongoing shortage of goods. This hampered Cherokee recovery efforts and imperiled Cherokee lives as winter approached. In November, Kettagusta of Chota complained to Governor Boone, but to no effect. As the Cherokees saw it, South Carolina had broken its promises yet again. It was 45 miles from the Middle Towns to the factory at Fort Prince George, 60 miles from the Out Towns, 90 miles from the Valley, and 180 from the Overhill Towns.[28]

For women, the Indian Trade Act was devastating. The new trade stipulations eliminated the informal exchanges that had given women economic and political power. Cherokee women found that the new arrangements cut them out of the trade, save for scraping and preparing the skins. The Cherokees saw the Indian Trade Act as a failure. But the council took no action. Despite its flaws, the Trade Act kept prices fair for the Cherokees, but it decreased the profits of South Carolina merchants. Over the next several years, these men abandoned the Indian trade and turned instead to the cultivation and exportation of lowcountry indigo and backcountry wheat, cattle, hogs, and tobacco. South Carolina's Cherokee deerskin trade waned in importance as Georgia and British West Florida instead turned to Creek hunters. Cherokee concerns dropped lower on the list of provincial priorities. For both elites and frontiersmen, the Cherokees became an obstacle to progress and independence. Once allies, then enemies, Cherokees were now a nuisance.[29]

Because Lieutenant Timberlake had fallen into debt during the junket to England, the Cherokees sailed back to Charles Town with Sumter, arriving there in early November. The tour solidified British support for the Cherokees. It gave Ostenaco political influence and further convinced him to maintain peace with the British. When he landed and met with Governor Boone, he promised "no more bad Talks" among the Cherokees, "no more disturbances," and "no more war." He vowed to bring to justice any Cherokee who killed an Englishman. The population, grandeur, and military capabilities of Britain had awed Ostenaco. When Boone pressed the Indian to recall exactly what convinced him to maintain peaceful intentions, Ostenaco was "astonishingly reserved and silent." Boone wrote to Lord Egremont, British Secretary of State, that the headman "apparently aims at influence with his nation, this seems his chief, and almost only concern." Boone missed the mark. In reality, Ostenaco now believed, as Attakullakulla had all along, that Cherokee survival depended upon peaceful coexistence. If only more of the headman's white contemporaries felt the same way. Instead, Tom Hatley believes, some South Carolinians were offended by the fanfare surrounding the Cherokee visit to England. They wondered whether Indians were more important to the Crown than colonists.[30]

Sumter escorted the trans-Atlantic travelers back to the Overhills. He lived in these villages from November 1762 to March 1763. "The majority" of Cherokees listened alertly and "seemed much delighted with" the accounts Ostenaco and his companions provided. Some Cherokees remained dissatisfied. Around January 1, 1763, Oconostota led fifty followers and six Frenchmen to Fort Toulouse. He met with French soldiers, Choctaws, Creeks, and others. The Upper Creeks and the Fort Toulouse commandant spewed anti-British invective. Oconostota and the Cherokees then ventured to Mobile and New Orleans. No French accounts of the early 1763 conferences have been found. But reliable sources claimed that the French hoped to build forts at Toqua in the Overhills and at Hiwassee in the Valley. While Oconostota visited the French, disaffected Creeks combed the Valley Towns for recruits.[31]

While Sumter was living in the Overhills, Ostenaco's party returned from a hunting trip with a guest: Baron des Jonnes, a French lieutenant who had fought against Braddock in 1755 and against Forbes in 1758. If des Jonnes and the French-leaning Cherokees had any designs against the British, they were soon foiled. Sumter apprehended the Frenchman in a legendary wrestling match in Toqua. He led the prisoner to Fort Prince George and later to Charles Town for interrogation. White observers said that des Jonnes sought to stir up anti-British Cherokees. Others claimed he was just an aspiring French hero. Still others thought he was just passing through the Overhills "to return to Canada." Stuart thought that des Jonnes aimed to "seduce those savages and detach them from the Brittish Interest." Regardless, French and pro-French Cherokee hopes of an alliance died with the capture of des Jonnes.[32]

In February 1763 the British and French governments signed peace terms. The French government and military promised to withdraw from Louisiana permanently by November. Governor Kerlérec reported that the Indians told him "they are not yet all dead; that the French have no right to give them away," and "they know what they have to do when the time comes." For five years, he had tried to keep hopes alive for both Cherokees and French officials in Louisiana and Paris. Now, the embattled chevalier prepared to leave New Orleans and face charges of embezzlement.[33] The impending French departure dealt a crushing blow to any leverage the southeastern tribes had against the English. Most Cherokees sensed the end of the French Empire in North America.

With Cherokee fortunes shifting, Oconostota sought a creative solution that bypassed Virginia and South Carolina, the two colonies that had caused his people so much suffering: he reached out to Georgia. He sent white wampum to the new governor, Sir James Wright, on May 21 and asked for a trade alliance. Wright, South Carolina's former attorney general, and its colonial agent in London during the 1759 campaign, was hardly sympathetic to Cherokee concerns. He had once hoped that Lyttelton would "destroy their

Towns, & Seize upon their Women & Children." Georgia already enjoyed a profitable trade with the populous Creek people. Wright did not wish to alienate these longstanding economic allies. Wright also feared the costs of hosting delegations of Cherokee leaders in Savannah for years to come. He declined Oconostota's invitation to engage. With no other viable alternative, the chief now realized that to ensure his peoples' survival, he had to cultivate military and economic common ground with the British.[34]

In February 1763, the closure of the South Carolina Commons House entered month three of eighteen.[35] In a lengthy open letter to his voting constituents, published in the *South Carolina Gazette*, Gadsden complained that a British subject "bid farewell to the *dearest*" of his liberties upon stepping foot "on American ground." He attacked Parliamentary representation, and he argued for the powers of colonial assemblies, especially the right to oversee their elections.[36]

The shutdown jeopardized the finances of the faction led by Henry Laurens and William Wragg, a stalwart Loyalist recently elected to the assembly. Many of these men had lent money to the provincial government to pay for the war. Now they expected repayment. That could not happen with the legislature closed for business. Laurens and Wragg were eager to restore harmony to South Carolina politics. The two politicians believed that Gadsden was unwisely and illogically challenging the Crown. In late February 1763, Laurens launched a personal attack on Gadsden in the *Weekly Gazette*. The only surviving copy appears in Laurens's papers. Weeks later, writing as "Philolethes," a "Lover of Obscurity," Laurens revisited the debate that had started during peace negotiations in 1761. This fanned the flames of partisanship in the lowcountry.[37]

Expressing great sympathy for the Cherokee Indians and unabashed praise for Colonel Grant, Laurens labeled Gadsden as a "poor rash headlong gentleman . . . a ringleader in popular quarrels." He sided with Governor Boone on the election dispute. Laurens called Gadsden a "Brazen Trumpeter" who had subverted all "Order and Decency." He went on to invoke transatlantic implications. Gadsden aimed, he alleged, "to set the whole province in a flame of civil discord & personal hatred, as well to bring it under the censure of its Mother Country & into contempt with all impartial men abroad."[38]

With the cession of French lands imminent, the northern Indian tribes were more unsettled than ever. British policy disenchanted them, and they hoped to spark the French to return. Nativist religion took root. Indians in the Ohio Valley, Illinois Country, and Great Lakes region launched attacks on white settlers and British forts in the region in 1763. The uprising became known as Pontiac's Rebellion. The disaffected tribes also attacked their traditional enemies, the Cherokees and Catawbas. They did so to punish those southern Indians for their pacifism. And they did so opportunistically: by attacking vulnerable enemies, the chances of taking scalps, and thus proving one's manhood, increased substantially.[39]

After attempting to drive back Virginia frontiersmen in July 1763, Shawnees raided the Cherokee villages repeatedly over a three-month period and killed fifty residents, Stuart wrote. Two of Attakullakulla's sons were reported dead. If the Shawnees expected to build an Indian coalition against white settlers, the Cherokees and their neighbors were hardly swayed.[40] The Cherokees determined to postpone blood revenge if attacked, and to retaliate only when success seemed likely.[41]

The Cherokees' Catawba neighbors, who also declined participation in Pontiac's Rebellion, were not spared. July brought an attack in which northern Indians captured five Catawba women. In September, Shawnee warriors murdered the Catawba headman King Hagler as he returned home from the Waxhaws.[42] To protest corruption in the trade, Upper Creeks murdered five British traders between May and October 1763. But if Cherokees joined forces with disaffected Creeks against the British, the Lower Towns would be the first to feel the effects of a punitive strike from South Carolina. Therefore, Seroweh vigorously opposed any hostile measures against the British.[43]

He did so though settlers were arriving "in great numbers" and were infringing on Cherokee hunting grounds. In December 1761, the king issued a royal proclamation banning the purchase, settlement, or possession of Indian lands without permission or license from the Crown. Governor Boone, for some reason, did not publish it. Virginia did, in April 1762, but it hardly mattered. In all the southern colonies, western expansion continued at unprecedented levels, with the support of coastal elites. Settlers built private forts for their own protection, and their homes, livestock, and hunting trips inched closer to Indian villages.[44] Settlers showed their disgust with the Crown in the spring of 1762 by renaming Goudey's Fort Ninety Six. They now called it Fort Middleton in honor of the provincial who defied Crown authority.[45]

Lord Egremont and Henry Ellis had already planned a conference in Augusta, Georgia, with Cherokee, Catawba, Chickasaw, Choctaw, and Creek leaders. It now became urgent. Southern Indian superintendent John Stuart, who had replaced the late Edmond Atkin in 1762, reassured tribal leaders that the conference aimed to preserve "pacific and Friendly Intentions" between the British and the southeastern Indians. He sent a copy of the king's Proclamation of 1761 to "The Principal Warriors of the Cherokee Nation."

Stuart stalled any alliance they might wish to make with northern Indians or against the British.[46]

In October 1763, seven hundred Indians gathered near the rough frontier town of Augusta. For a few weeks, they smoothed out disputes between themselves. No record of these proceedings has been found. On November 5, Stuart, with southern governors Boone, Dobbs, Wright, and Fauquier, officially opened the British-Indian conference at Fort Augusta. The Lower Cherokees and Lower Creeks dominated the proceedings. Their villages lay nearer to the British, so they had the most at stake. In addition to Attakullakulla, Ostenaco and Seroweh were present and spoke for peace.[47]

British authorities, including those present, feared the effects of a continental Indian war should Pontiac's Rebellion spread south. They attempted to assuage the Indians' fears and to address their concerns. Several days of discussions culminated in a November 10 accord. White and Indian signatories agreed to forgive "all past offences and injuries."[48]

The Crown would supply "all sorts of Goods" provided the warriors did not antagonize British traders. The Indians pledged to "do full and ample justice to the English." They also vowed to prevent their people from stealing cattle and horses or otherwise clashing with colonial settlers.[49]

The British dignitaries promised that the king had ordered his subjects to respect tribal lands and to "always give due attention" to the Indians' interests. Stuart and the governors pledged that Indian lands would "not be taken." This policy pleased the Indians, but it did not appeal to white South Carolinians. Wealthy whites benefitted from land and slave sales and by shipping the fruits of their labor of backcountry farmers.[50] Backcountry farmers served military and police purposes as well. They protected easterly regions from Indian attack and deterred runaway slaves. Predictably, settlers who had traveled hundreds of miles in search of land and opportunity, sometimes escaping debt or religious intolerance to do so, respected no restraints.

Despite earlier promises, Indian lands *were* taken. To make amends for the killing of white traders earlier that year, Lower Creeks ceded Georgia a tract of land between the Savannah and Ogeechee Rivers. They also agreed to return runaway slaves. Attakullakulla and his Cherokees had done the same in 1761. This was a coup for the white delegates and for the expansion of Georgia. France had just agreed to evacuate its military and governmental personnel from southeast North America. Spain had ceded East Florida to the British. Runaway slaves now had nowhere to go. The Catawbas had just lost King Hagler. Poor, surrounded by squatters, and vulnerable to northern Indian enemies, they reluctantly accepted the bounds of their small reservation in exchange for a survey line to delineate those lands. They remained military allies of South Carolina, and they remained on the public dole. The Choctaws and Chickasaws exchanged promises of peace for promises of British traders and goods.

The treaty appeared to assure British security in the Southeast. The guns of Fort Augusta roared to mark the moment, and Stuart distributed a bounty of trade goods to the Indians in attendance.[51]

King George III's Royal Proclamation of 1763 arrived in the colonies at the end of the year. The proclamation restated the 1761 proclamation's ban on purchasing, settling, or possessing Indian lands without royal permission or license. It delineated the Appalachian Divide as the colonial-Indian border beyond which colonists could not settle. It also opened the Indian trade "to all our Subjects whatever" who could pay a bond and secure a license. In one stroke, the proclamation rendered South Carolina's Indian Trade Act moot. White South Carolina had taken a loss. But for the colony's slaveholders, there was a final gesture. The proclamation authorized all public and military officials to apprehend accused white and black felons and to extradite them to their respective colonies. The treaty violated Indian sovereignty. And it eliminated Indian country as an interracial safe haven for criminals and runaways of different races.[52]

Now that the Crown had made its ruling, was it enforceable? The British had sided with Cherokee Indians. Whether or not settlers and coastal elites would respect British policy remained to be seen.

CONCLUSION *Revolutionary Implications*

Scholars have explored the origins of the American Revolution in the South. Some have described the war's outbreak. But no one has fully linked the Cherokee Indians to the turmoil that followed in the era of American independence. African American, Indian, and white actors—each with wide-ranging interests and alliances— seethed in dissatisfaction and reeled from the war and its conclusion. The long-term consequences were dramatic.

For some black South Carolinians, the Anglo-Cherokee War had provided opportunities, however limited. Bondsmen and bondswomen tried to capitalize on white divisions and distractions. Runaways proliferated from 1759 to 1761.[1] Some, like Philip, found adventure and high wages in the army. Others, like the freeman Thomas Jeremiah, amassed wealth during the war years. Jeremiah made his money by working as a firefighter, boatman, and harbor pilot. He shuttled soldiers around Charles Town's waterways on his boat, and he guided British warships through the harbor. Abram was the last slave manumitted by the assembly during the colonial period. In 1762, he appeared in the council chamber as an emergency interpreter during a Chickasaw conference with the governor and council. Because no other Indian interpreters were available, Abram spoke in Cherokee to a Chickasaw diplomat who understood the language. Then, the former deerskin trader faded from the documentary record. In January 1761, the assembly awarded "a free Negro" surgeon of the rangers—whom the clerk neglected to name—a thirty-pound reward for "great service" to the sick and wounded. But it promptly replaced him with a white surgeon. African Americans, it seemed, could merely fill in for whites in emergencies. Joe Fleming of Berkeley County, another veteran of the 1760 campaign, saw the Commons House deny his 1761 petition for freedom. Peace thereafter shut down the opportunities for meritorious service of the kind that could lead to legally sanctioned freedom.[2]

Abram the messenger and Thomas Jeremiah the harbor pilot were exceptions. For most black South Carolinians, the war years brought misery. Some were forced into military camps as laborers and herdsmen or saw combat in frontier forts alongside their white neighbors. About 12 percent of Charleston's African American community died of smallpox, and many never received a decent burial. The Philip John conspiracy shows how black colonists tried to turn the chaos of the war to their own advantage. In a province already in upheaval and vulnerable to Indian attack, slaves looking for an opportunity for freedom—and white fears of slave unrest—had threatened social stability, undermined military readiness, and added to white anxieties.

White Carolinians slammed the doors of opportunity on black provincials. They needed slaves to work the backcountry lands taken from the Indians. By the early 1770s, two-thirds of all slave imports went to the backcountry. Slaves composed 19 percent of the backcountry population, a twofold increase from prewar numbers. With indigo cultivation expanding and lowcountry rice still the dominant export, in the years that followed the war, slavery expanded throughout the colony.[3] The African American population of South Carolina increased from its prewar total of about 60,000 or 70,000 to over 107,000 in 1775.[4] Persistent resistance from black Carolinians only heightened white fears and brutality. As merchants and planters regained their economic footing in the postwar recovery period, African Americans bore a disproportionate share of the burden.

In 1764, to address the inherent instability their labor system created, members of the assembly halted slave importations temporarily from 1766 to 1768. The goal was twofold. First, higher slave prices benefited the wealthiest Carolinians—those eager to sell bondsmen to backcountry settlers. Second, the importation ban curbed the risk of revolt by keeping black numbers in check. Slavers, however, anticipated the embargo. In 1765 alone, ships carried eight thousand new slaves into Charles Town, William Bull II reported. Bull, again South Carolina's acting governor after the recall of Thomas Boone, reported that this was three times the typical annual average. In fact, 8,000 was not only the most ever, it was quadruple the annual average of 1,999 per year from 1753 to 1764.[5]

As Henry Laurens observed, bondsmen applied whites' rhetoric of British mistreatment and tyranny to their own situation. They became, he said, "apprehensive of an Odious Load falling upon their Shoulders." As white Carolinians touting liberty protested the Stamp Act that same year, black Carolinians challenged oppression at home. They, too, took to the streets shouting "Liberty! Liberty!"—albeit with different tyrants in mind.[6] Hundreds of Carolina slaves fled coastal plantations to join or establish maroon communities in the postwar years. They did so in the largest numbers in half a century. Lieutenant Governor Bull reported that in December 1765 alone, 107 freedom seekers had joined "several large parties" of maroons in coastal Colleton County. In late 1765 and early 1766, maroons launched raids on plantations along the Savannah River. Whites feared a massive insurrection and responded with a brutal show of force.[7] As South Carolina used the Catawba Indians as slave catchers, an uneasy quiet reigned during the early 1770s.

The Anglo-Cherokee War was more cataclysmic in the Indian high country, where it left an entire nation in disarray. Cherokees fought and bled alongside British troops in the early stages of the French and Indian War. Then frontiersmen indiscriminately killed them. The ensuing Cherokee blood revenge raids on the frontier led Governor Lyttelton to take hostages. Mutual "pressuring" violence on the frontier continued and escalated until the final crisis of the soldiers at Fort Prince George murdering them. Many white South Carolinians called for extermination, and successfully pressured the British military command to send troops on two devastating expeditions. After two years of war, the Indians struggled to reconstitute life as they knew it. From 1758 to 1761, at least one-third of the Cherokees had died from combat and disease. Smallpox, measles, and mumps had become ubiquitous with the movement of Indian and white troops. The resulting dislocation was social, cultural, and physical. Cherokee towns broke apart, recombined, and relocated. The Out Towns largely emptied. Generational and geographical divisions widened. And longstanding patterns of authority collapsed. Indeed, the rivalry between Oconostota and Attakullakulla foreshadowed the internecine strife that would again divide the tribe during the Revolutionary era.

In spite of all that had happened, the "Chain of Friendship" that once linked the Cherokees to the British actually regenerated after 1763. The Cherokees looked to British metropolitan authorities for help in protecting their lands from colonists. The Crown could not afford another Indian war, so it had a vested interest in placating native peoples. But in spite of the Proclamation of 1763 and the Treaty of Augusta, lawless white settlers overran Cherokee hunting lands. Northern Indian superintendent Sir William Johnson encouraged Iroquois and Ohio Valley Indians to attack southern Indians. This imperiled the sovereignty, survival, and dignity of Indian peoples throughout the Appalachian region.

Many white interlopers, like the Long Canes settlers, were evangelical Protestants from the northern colonies, and were pushed southward from Pennsylvania and Virginia by war and population growth. These migrants had arrived in large numbers during the Anglo-Cherokee conflict, often bringing with them their hatred of Indians. The fighting did nothing to improve their lives. It worsened their material conditions and widened the gulf between the rich and the poor. It launched a dreadful refugee crisis. And it added to their resentment of lowcountry elites, who never supplied sufficient military assistance.

At the war's end, impoverished, starving whites turned into bandits, marauders, and horse thieves. Some sought their living by duping vulnerable Cherokees and carving out homesteads on Indian lands. None of the Cherokee settlement clusters was immune from these intrusions. As a British officer at Fort Prince George wrote in 1765: "numbers of vagrants" came "from all parts" and "Contrary to all orders, goe a Hunting on the Indians Land and Steal their Horses." Bothersome "crackers" hunted beaver illegally, much to the consternation of British civil and military officials. Rum flowed freely, and traders swindled inebriated Cherokees.[8]

The South Carolina Commons House of Assembly only encouraged the white assault on Cherokee lands. Eager to form new partnerships and to keep slaves from fleeing westward, the legislators lured immigrants with free land and economic incentives in 1764 and 1765. As early as 1764, squatters took up lands within fifteen miles of the Lower Towns. South Carolina's non-Indian backcountry population increased from seven thousand to eleven thousand within five years of the war's close. In seven years, nine thousand new settlers occupied the Carolina-Cherokee borderlands.[9]

The frontiersmen, old and new, found safety and confidence in their growing numbers. They targeted their Indian neighbors in a transcolonial backlash against Pontiac's Rebellion, an uprising in which the Cherokees had played no part. In May 1765, backcountry whites in Augusta County, Virginia, ambushed and killed six Cherokees headed to war against Indians in Ohio. Lieutenant Governor Fauquier blamed a "profligate and abandon'd mob," who were "worse than Indians themselves."[10] Try as they might after 1763, Parliament, the southern governors, Superintendent John Stuart, and Indian Commissioner Alexander Cameron (who married Seroweh's daughter) could not restrain the settlers' rapid advance, wanton violence, and seething disdain for Indians.[11]

Not surprisingly, South Carolina's Commons House of Assembly and representatives of the Crown—including Lieutenant Governor Bull—were at odds over these developments. The settlers buffered coastal regions from the Cherokees. Their crops, livestock, and timber propped up the fortunes of coastal merchants and planters—the very men who served in the colonial assembly. Bull expelled the encroaching frontiersmen with force in 1764. White Carolinians, rich and poor, argued that British policy favored Cherokees. Bull's efforts were futile. And when Britain imposed revenue measures in the years that followed, tensions between the executive and the assembly escalated.[12]

Despite British efforts, the deerskin trade never again rose to Cherokee expectations. Virginia traders arrived in Cherokee villages after the war ended. But Virginia no longer coveted Cherokee deerskins and warriors as it had in the mid-1750s. Not until 1765—after the Augusta County frontiersmen had murdered Cherokees—did the House of Burgesses pass legislation to regulate the deerskin trade. As the Cherokee land base shrank and white gunmen invaded, Cherokee men struggled to hunt and thus to hold up their end of the trade. They became debtors. And they began to starve. The British post at Pensacola tapped the Creek deerskin trade, bypassing the Cherokee brokers who had once profited from British commerce. And South Carolina's inland economy shifted to more lucrative ventures: grain, fruit, timber, hogs, and cattle. No longer valued as trading partners, the Cherokees became all the more expendable to coastal planters and hardscrabble farmers alike.[13] What remained of the deerskin trade was as corrupt as ever. Other than five "half-breeds," Alexander Cameron could not find "one honest man" among forty-six traders in 1765.[14]

In 1768, the Crown abandoned most of its frontier outposts, including Fort Prince George, in a cost-cutting measure. Settlers, particularly from Virginia, stormed onto Cherokee lands. As white encroachment and its ill effects became more apparent, elder Cherokees ceded more and more land to colonial authorities. They hoped to avert war and to pays off debts. Treaties and agreements in 1766, 1768, 1770, 1772, and 1773 diminished the Cherokee land base to an unsustainable scrap of its prewar extent. At one conference, angry Georgia frontiersmen—so-called crackers—heckled Cherokee delegates, which must have been insulting and terrifying to the Indians.[15]

Moreover, the actions of northern Indians brought the Cherokees themselves under suspicion. While the Cherokees abstained from making war on their white and black neighbors, the northerners did not. In fact, the policies of Britain's northern superintendent of Indian affairs, Sir William Johnson, promoted Indian violence against the Cherokees for several years, despite the outcry by colonial governors, southern superintendent Stuart, and southern Indians. Johnson reasoned that to stop the attacks was "impolitic." He believed that Iroquois raids would keep all Indians from allying against the British, weaken the Cherokees, and keep "Turbulent Spirits . . . employed." Besides, he argued, the Indians could not be restrained. With the French defeated, historian Theda Perdue explains, the British encouraged the Indians to destroy each other.[16] By 1766, Stuart reported, "The Cherokees by their Sufferings in their War with us, and the perpetual Incursions of the Northern Tribes are much reduced, and at this time do not exceed two thirds the Number they consisted of about ten Years [ago]."[17]

Any Indian violence, regardless of its victims, stirred up white discontent. In 1774, the Shawnee Cornstalk led an intertribal offensive along the Virginia frontier. The attacks reawakened colonial apprehensiveness about the Cherokees, and other Indians, encouraging the brutal American campaigns of the Revolutionary era.[18]

Members of the merchant-planter class emerged victorious at the end of the Anglo-Cherokee War, but this merely meant they had lost the least.

The conflict had tapped into the deepest fears of the coastal gentry. It also exposed internal divisions within South Carolina. Events such as the debate over funding the Lyttelton campaign, the Montgomery and Grant campaigns, and the Gadsden election controversy fully revealed these divides. Afterward, South Carolinians had burdensome war debts to pay off. When the British imposed new assessments of their own, taxpayers objected, arguing that the levies were debilitating and unconstitutional. Finally, the postwar settlement brought a new, centralized Indian policy that seemed to institutionalize Britain's disregard for her colonial subjects. Well-to-do coastal politicians like Christopher Gadsden accused the British of disrespect and abandonment. They charged that arrogant politicians and bureaucrats from the metropole were trying to burden them by forcing them to assume high costs that inevitably raised the provincial tax burden. They sharpened arguments that they had used in the era of war with the Cherokees.[19]

The war gave a generation of young men from all backgrounds military experience and social standing. Some of these men gained prominence for supporting Lieutenant Colonel James Grant. John Moultrie Jr., for example, became Grant's deputy governor in British East Florida. Other men gained renown for their wartime service and their role as Indian fighters. Included among them were the revolutionaries Christopher Gadsden, "Swamp Fox" Francis Marion, William Moultrie, Owen Roberts, "The Gamecock" Thomas Sumter, William "Danger" Thomson, and Andrew Williamson. Another veteran, Andrew Pickens, married a Long Canes refugee, Rebecca Calhoun, and settled on Cherokee lands ceded in the postwar era. For some, the passage of time distorted past realities. By 1775, when the naturalist William Bartram visited Charles Town, proud provincial veterans led him to believe that Colonel Middleton and the provincials had "vanquished" the Indians. These men—and their counterparts in North Carolina and Virginia—leveraged their wartime connections for postwar gain.[20]

In 1775, tensions came to a head. South Carolina's former governor William Henry Lyttelton was by this time a Member of Parliament. In a 1775 speech to the House of Commons, after news of the first bloodshed in Massachusetts reached Britain, he warned his colleagues that he saw an ominous new "Chain of Friendship" forming. The colonies were now linked together against Great Britain. But South Carolina, he observed, was a distinctive place. The colony's racial demography meant that its future was up for grabs. Slaves and Indians, he believed, might serve the British in putting down the colonial "insurrection" in the South.[21]

By the winter of 1775, the Cherokees were on tenterhooks, racked by internal divisions and pressured by the British, by land-hungry colonists, and by other Indian peoples. In March, with the Treaty of Sycamore Shoals, the elder statesmen Attakullakulla and Ostenaco ceded a massive swath of land in present Tennessee and Kentucky to the North Carolina speculator Richard Henderson. Soon thereafter, the northern Indians who had attacked the frontier the previous year came to Chota. The visitors vowed to smash the Cherokees if they refused to help attack the frontier interlopers. At the same time, patriots reached out and sent arms to Cherokees in an effort to forge an alliance against the British. But Loyalists seized the weapons before they reached their destination.[22]

With war looming, South Carolina patriots feared that black resentment and numerical strength would manifest itself. They sent Thomas Jeremiah to the gallows in August 1775 in an effort to keep black ambition in check. On slim evidence, a court convicted the entrepreneurial harbor pilot of conspiring to help the British capture Charles Town by starting a slave revolt. Many African Americans took their chances during the years of fighting that followed. They fled to British lines rather than continue to suffer on their plantations as they had in the Anglo-Cherokee War.[23]

Some Cherokees made similar calculations. Attakullakulla's son, Dragging Canoe, had fought in the siege of Fort Loudoun. In time, he became the leader of the village of Mialoquo in the Overhills. Mialoquo—or "the Great Island"—was settled by refugees displaced during the war. In 1775, when fighting erupted between Britain and her colonists, Dragging Canoe broke with his father and other elders. Angered by endless concessions and bolstered by British agents, the fiery young chief dared his people to take up the hatchet to preserve their traditions and independence. But when Dragging Canoe led disaffected Cherokees against the frontier in July 1776, the Virginians swiftly defeated them. This allowed colonial elites to resume what they had started in 1761: a campaign of genocide.[24]

William Henry Drayton, a prominent patriot leader in South Carolina, vowed in 1776 to "never give my voice for a peace with the Cherokee Nation upon any other terms than their removal beyond the mountains." Virginia's Thomas Jefferson chimed in as well. He hoped "that the Cherokees will now be driven beyond the Mississippi" as "the invariable consequences of their beginning a war."[25]

Patriots then launched four coordinated expeditions against the Cherokee towns in 1776 and 1777. Six thousand troops from Virginia, North and South Carolina, and Georgia rampaged through Cherokee country, leaving desolation in their wake. These expeditions were led by veterans of the conflict a decade and a half earlier. In so doing, white elites perpetuated the very brutality they "abhorred" in the British. When Cherokee elders ceded more lands to save themselves from famine, the nation divided against itself. Dragging Canoe and four Overhill Towns seceded in 1777, determined to fight for Cherokee traditionalism. That same year they moved down the Tennessee River and set up the Chickamauga Towns. They launched raids on Americans for another fifteen years, thus saving the Cherokee people from complete extermination.[26]

As plantations proliferated in the South Carolina backcountry, the new United States negotiated a treaty with the Cherokees at Andrew Pickens's South Carolina estate in 1785. Pickens, a grizzled veteran of the Grant campaign and of the bitter contest for the South Carolina frontier during the Revolution, lived on Cherokee lands. By the terms of the settlement, South Carolina took over what remained of the Lower Towns. The United States took more lands from the Cherokees during the next fifty years. Then, in the 1830s, it forcibly expelled most of them—including the descendants of Dragging Canoe's Chickamaugas—from their lands in the Southeast.[27]

During the French and Indian War, the Cherokee Indians had forced elites to confront their deepest fears and to assert their strongest desires. The Cherokee War laid bare the essential divisions of Carolina society. In many ways it foreshadowed the contentiousness and division of the Revolutionary era, and makes it all the more understandable and apparent. The Cherokees had exposed underlying tensions between colonists and the Crown, and they had lost their lives to enemies who soon put their newfound military experience to use in the Continental army. Fifteen years after the Anglo-Cherokee War, when white South Carolinians severed their ties with Britain, they also broke free of Crown restraints on western expansion. The Cherokees impeded their economic opportunities. The Indians also stood in the way of the postwar economic partnership between the coast and the interior.

Conclusion : 193

The Anglo-Cherokee conflict taught the merchant-planter class that a powerful Native American military presence did more than endanger white lives on the frontier. By drawing resources westward, it emboldened black resistance and endangered white lives and livelihoods on the coast. So long as the Cherokees commanded the frontier, the westward expansion of race slavery was in jeopardy. For Carolina planters, the solution was independence. Independence allowed them to clear away the Cherokees and expand their brutal and inescapable system of African slavery, enabling them to overthrow British rule, but not to create a government truly based on equality and opportunity for all.

NOTES

ABBREVIATIONS

BPRO-SC   William Noel Sainsbury, ed., *Records in the British Public Record Office Relating to South Carolina, 1663–1782*, 37 vols. Microfilm ed. South Carolina Department of Archives and History, Columbia, S.C.

CDFA   Cherokee Documents in Foreign Archives. Microfilm. Hunter Library, Special Collections, Western Carolina University, Cullowhee, N.C.

CLON   James Edward, Smith, ed., *A Selection of the Correspondence of Linnaeus and Other Naturalists*, 2 vols. (London, 1821)

CO   Colonial Office Records, The National Archives, Kew, UK

CRG   Allen D. Candler, Kenneth Coleman, and Milton Ready, eds., *The Colonial Records of the State of Georgia*, 32 vols. (Atlanta, 1904–1916; Athens, 1974–1979)

CSR-NC   William L. Saunders and Walter Clark, eds., *The Colonial and State Records of North Carolina*, 26 vols. (Raleigh, 1886–1907)

CTWB   William Byrd, William Byrd II, and William Byrd III, *The Correspondence of the Three William Byrds of Westover, Virginia, 1684–1776*, 2 vols. Edited by Marion Tinling. (Charlottesville, 1977)

DLAR   David Library of the American Revolution, Washington Crossing, Pa.

DRIA, 1:   William L. McDowell Jr., ed., *Documents Relating to Indian Affairs, May 21, 1750–August 7, 1754* [Vol.1] (Columbia, 1958)

DRIA, 2:   William L. McDowell Jr., ed., *Documents Relating to Indian Affairs, 1754–1765* [Vol. 2] (Columbia, 1970)

EJC   H. R. McIlwaine, ed., *Executive Journals of the Council of Virginia, 1758–1761* (Richmond, 1966)

GPAS   Thomas Gage Papers, 1754–1807. American Series. William L. Clements Library, Ann Arbor, Mich.

JCHA   J. H. Easterby, R. Nicholas Olsberg, and Terry W. Lipscomb, eds., *The Journal of the Commons House of Assembly* [1736–1757], 14 vols. (Columbia, 1951–1989)

JCHA,   Terry W. Lipscomb, ed., *The Journal of the Commons House of
1757–1761 Assembly, October 6, 1757–January 24, 1761* (Columbia, 1996)

JCHA   Journals of the Commons House of Assembly, 1692–1775. South Carolina Department of Archives and History, Columbia, S.C.

JHB   H. R. McIlwaine and John P. Kennedy, eds., *Journals of the House of Burgesses of Virginia, 1619–1776*, 13 vols. (Richmond, 1905–1915)

LPCD   William Henry Lyttelton Papers, 1730–1806, Series I: Correspondence and Documents. William L. Clements Library, Ann Arbor, Mich.

LPLB   William Henry Lyttelton Papers, 1730–1806, Series II: Letter Books and Account Book. William L. Clements Library, Ann Arbor, Mich.

MPA   Dunbar Rowland, A. G. Sanders, and Patricia Kay Galloway, eds. *Mississippi Provincial Archives, 1701–1763: French Dominion*, 5 vols. (Baton Rouge, 1927–1984)

ORRD   Robert Dinwiddie, *The Official Records of Robert Dinwiddie, Lieutenant-Governor of the Colony of Virginia, 1751–1758*, 2 vols. Edited by R. A. Brock (Richmond, 1883–1884)

PFF   Francis Fauquier, *The Official Papers of Francis Fauquier, Lieutenant Governor of Virginia, 1758–1768*, 3 vols. Edited by George Henkle Reese (Charlottesville, 1980–1983)

PGW   George Washington, *The Papers of George Washington: 1748–1775. Colonial Series*, 10 vols. Edited by W. W. Abbot et al. (Charlottesville, 1983–1995)

PHL   Henry Laurens, *The Papers of Henry Laurens*, 16 vols. Edited by George C. Rogers et al. (Columbia, 1968–2003)

PRO   Public Record Office Records, The National Archives, Kew, UK

SCCJ   Journals of His Majesty's Council. Early State Records reel E1p/7, 1754–1756 (3 units); E1p/8, 1757–1762 (6 units); E1p/9, 1763–1767 (4 units). Microfilm. South Carolina Department of Archives and History, Columbia, S.C.

SCG   *South Carolina Gazette*

SCL   South Caroliniana Library, University of South Carolina, Columbia, S.C.

SWJP   William Johnson, *The Papers of Sir William Johnson*, 14 vols. Edited by Alexander Clarence Fick. (Albany, 1921–1965)

WHL   William Henry Lyttelton

WO   War Office Records, The National Archives, Kew, UK

INTRODUCTION

1. Glen, *Description*, 59; James Glen to Robert Dinwiddie, June 1, 1754, *DRIA*, 1:525; Milling, *Colonial South Carolina*, xvi; Piker, *Okfuskee*, 11, 212.

2. Adair, *History of the American Indians*, 268.

3. Arthur Dobbs, "The Colony, Its Climate, Soil, Population, Government, Resources, &c.," *CSR-NC*, 6:617.

4. Anderson, *Crucible of War*; Cave, *French and Indian War*; Fowler, *Empires at War*; Borneman, *French and Indian War*.

5. Ephraim Biggs to William Pitt, Apr. 2, 1759, Chatham Papers, PRO 30/8/96, fol. 203.

6. Wood, *Black Majority*; Olwell, *Masters, Slaves, and Subjects*; Berlin, *Many Thousands Gone*; Morgan, *Slave Counterpoint*; Littlefield, *Rice and Slaves*.

7. Nash, *Forgotten Fifth*; Frey, *Water from the Rock*.

8. Ryan, *World of Thomas Jeremiah*, 8; Egerton, *Death or Liberty*, 41–64.

9. Weir, *"A Most Important Epocha"*; Mercantini, *Who Shall Rule*.

10. Brown, *South Carolina Regulators*, 1–9; Edgar, *Partisans and Redcoats*, xii–xiii; Klein, "Ordering the Backcountry"; Klein, *Unification of a Slave State*; Kars, *Breaking Loose Together*.

11. Mercantini, *Who Shall Rule*, 166.

12. Piecuch, *Three Peoples, One King*, 7–12.

13. Blackmon, *Dark and Bloody Ground*.

14. Griffin, *American Leviathan*, 276.

15. Lee, *Barbarians and Brothers*, 2; Boulware, *Deconstructing the Cherokee Nation*, 105–7.

16. Milling, *Red Carolinians*; Corkran, *Cherokee Frontier*; Hatley, *Dividing Paths*; Oliphant, *Peace and War*.

17. Boulware, *Deconstructing the Cherokee Nation*; Kelton, "British and Indian War," 765, 771, 791.

18. Adair, *History of the American Indians*; De Brahm, *Report*; Timberlake, *Memoirs*; Calloway, *American Revolution in Indian Country*, 182–212; Boulware, "Effect of the Seven Years' War"; Hatley, *Dividing Paths*; Merrell, *The Indians' New World*; Brown, *Catawba Indians*; Lee, "Peace Chiefs and Blood Revenge"; Abram, "Souls in the Treetops."

19. Milling, *Colonial South Carolina*, xvi.

20. On the transformative power of the French and Indian War, see Anderson, *Crucible of War*, xvii–xxiv.

CHAPTER ONE

1. Sir Alexander Cuming's Memoir, British Museum, Add. Mss. 39855, 9–11, in CDFA, reel 172; Steele, *Cherokee Crown of Tannassy*, xiii, 4, 139–42.

2. Sadosky, *Revolutionary Negotiations*, 14–18; Grant, "Historical Relation of Facts," 55.

3. "Account of the Cherokee Indians, and of Sir Alexander Cuming's Journey amongst them," and "Some Heads of Sir Alexander Cumings's Journey to the Cherokee Mountains," *Historical Register* (1731), 2–3, 8; Grant, "Historical Relation of Facts," 56.

4. Alexander Cuming to the Duke of Newcastle, [ca. Sept. 1730], CO 5/4, fols. 217, 222, in CDFA, reel 197.

5. "East Barnet—Sir Alexander Cuming," *Monthly Epitome*, Feb. 1797, 83.

6. Reid, *Law of Blood*, 37.

7. Ibid., 12; Perdue, "Cherokee Relations," 136.

8. Reid, *Law of Blood*, 12–14. The Lower dialect went extinct by the late 1800s. Mooney, *Myths of the Cherokee*, 17.

9. Reid, *Law of Blood*, 12, 15.

10. Ibid., 12–14; Mooney, *Myths of the Cherokee*, 17.

11. Reid, *Law of Blood*, 12.

12. Ibid., 12, 16; Mooney, *Myths of the Cherokee*, 11–17, 506; Wilkes, "Cherokee Dialects," http://voices.yahoo.com/cherokee-dialects-made-easy-least-easier-822353 .html.

13. Wilkes, "Cherokee Dialects," http://voices.yahoo.com/cherokee-dialects -made-easy-least-easier-822353.html.

14. "Account of the Cherokee Indians" and "Some Heads of Sir Alexander Cumings's Journey," *Historical Register* (1731), 3, 6–9; Grant, "Historical Relation of Facts," 56–57; Calloway, *White People, Indians, and Highlanders*, 3–4, 6–7, 9–10, 12, 135–36, 230.

15. Traditionally, each clan had a "peace town," where weapons, fighting, and bloodshed were banned. Rozema, *Footsteps of the Cherokees*, 260; Mooney, *Myths of the Cherokee*, 207, 330–33, 336–37, 477.

16. "Account of the Cherokee Indians," *Historical Register* (1731), 2.

17. Ibid., 2–4; Grant, "Historical Relation of Facts," 56; Sadosky, *Revolutionary Negotiations*, 22–24.

18. Grant, "Historical Relation of Facts," 65–66.

19. Ibid., 65; Kelly, "Attakullakulla," 2–3.

20. Brown, *Old Frontiers*, 6–9, 47; Oatis, *Colonial Complex*; Ramsey, *Yamasee War*.

21. Calloway, *White People, Indians, and Highlanders*, 152, 177.

22. Brown, *Old Frontiers*, 47–48; Rothrock, "Carolina Traders," 15–16; Holland-Braund, *Deerskins and Duffels*, 68, 121–26.

23. Rothrock, "Carolina Traders," 13–14, 17; Brown, *Old Frontiers*, 47–48.

24. "Proceedings of the Council Concerning Indian Affairs," *DRIA*, 1:453.

25. Report from John Cary on the Cherokees, Sept. 18, 1728, CO 5/1337, fol. 128, in CDFA, reel 456; Thomas, *Fort Toulouse*.

26. Holland-Braund, *Deerskins and Duffels*, 87–88; Meriwether, *Expansion of South Carolina*, 191.

27. Kelly, "Attakullakulla," 2; "Account of the Cherokee Indians," *Historical Register* (1731), 5; Admiralty Secretary's Department: Captain's Logs: 1730, Adm. 51/376, in CDFA, reel 191.

28. Kelly, "Attakullakulla," 2–4; Vaughan, *Transatlantic Encounters*, 142–49; Foreman, *Indians Abroad*, 45–46. August and September issues of several British newspapers chronicle the Cherokees' travels. See, for example, *Grub-Street Journal*, July 30, Aug. 5, Sept. 10, 1730; *Daily Post*, Aug. 18, 20, 28, 29, Sept. 5, 7, 24, 1730.

29. Sir Alexander Cuming's Memoir, British Museum, Add. Mss. 39855, p. 26, 27, in CDFA, reel 172; Kelly, "Attakullakulla," 4; Grant, "Historical Relation of Facts," 54n–55n. Appearing to the far right, Attakullakulla holds a pebble-filled gourd in one hand and a knife in the other. Foreman, *Indians Abroad*, 47–50, 52.

30. Kelly, "Attakullakulla," 4; Foreman, *Indians Abroad*, 47–50, 52; *Grub-Street Journal*, July 30, Sept. 10, 17, 24, 1730; *London Journal*, Aug. 15, 29, 1730; J[ames] Crowe to Alexander Cuming, July 15, 1730, CO 5/4, fol. 218, in CDFA, reel 197. See also fols. 198, 209, 211, 215, 217, 218, 219, 222; Vaughan, *Transatlantic Encounters*, 142–44.

31. *Daily Journal*, Oct. 3, 1730; Board of Trade to the Duke of Newcastle, Aug. 20, 1730, Official Approval for Forming a Treaty with the Cherokees, Sept. 1, 1730, Vaughan,

Early American Indian Documents, 13:134–35, 136; *Grub-Street Journal*, Sept. 10, 1730; *London Journal*, Aug. 15, 1730; Kelly, "Attakullakulla," 4.

32. *London Journal*, Sept. 12, 1730; "Articles of Friendship and Commerce," Sept. 7, 1730, LPCD.

33. Ledward, *Journals*, 6:135–40 (Aug. 20, 1730), http://www.british-history.ac.uk/source.aspx?pubid=874; Boulware, *Deconstructing the Cherokee Nation*, 48–49, 95–96.

34. "Articles of Friendship and Commerce," Sept. 7, 1730, LPCD; *London Journal*, Sept. 12, 1730; Answer of the Cherokees to the Proposed Treaty, Sept. 9, 1730, *Early American Indian Documents*, 13:139.

35. Grant, "Historical Relation of Facts," 67–68; Adair, *History of the American Indians*, 103–4; Kelly, "Attakullakulla," 4.

36. Vaughan, *Transatlantic Encounters*, 146; *Daily Journal*, Sept. 30, Oct. 1, 1730; "Articles of Friendship and Commerce," Sept. 7, 1730, LPCD; Sir Alexander Cuming's Memoir, British Museum, Add. Mss. 39855, 28, in CDFA, reel 172.

37. *Daily Journal*, Oct. 3, 1730; *Grub-Street Journal*, Oct. 8, 1730; *The Court Magazine*, Aug. 1762, in Foreman, *Indians Abroad*, 79–80; Alexander Cuming to Alured Popple, Sept. 30, 1730, CO 5/361, fol. 168, in CDFA, reel 327; Kelly, "Attakullakulla," 4.

38. Brown, *Old Frontiers*, 45; Vaughan, *Transatlantic Encounters*, 148.

39. Extract of a letter from South Carolina, Feb. 1733/4, *CRG*, 20:49–50; "Renewal of the Treaties by Upper Cherokees," May 12, 1733, *Early American Indian Documents*, 13:154.

40. Mellon, "Christian Priber and the Jesuit Myth," 75; Grant, "Historical Relation of Facts," 59; Adair, *History of the American Indians*, 240, 243; Abstract of William Bull to the Board of Trade, Oct. 5, 1739, CO 5/406, fol. 22, in CDFA, reel 369; Mellon, "Christian Priber's Cherokee Kingdom of Paradise," 320–22; *SCG*, Aug. 15, 1743.

41. Antoine Bonnefoy, "Journal of Antoine Bonnefoy's Captivity among the Cherokee Indians, 1741–1742," in Mereness, *Travels in the American Colonies*, 247; Adair, *History of the American Indians*, 240; *SCG*, Aug. 15, 1743; Grant, "Historical Relation of Facts," 60. Priber built on existing Cherokee practices of redistribution and places of refuge. Strickland, "Christian Gotelieb Priber," 272, 276–77.

42. Grant, "Historical Relation of Facts," 59–60; Adair, *History of the American Indians*, 240–42; Rozema, *Footsteps of the Cherokees*, 14.

43. *SCG*, May 30, 1743; Grant, "Historical Relation of Facts," 61; Adair, *History of the American Indians*, 243.

44. Kelly, "Attakullakulla," 9; Corkran, *Cherokee Frontier*, 16–49.

45. James Glen to the Board of Trade, Sept. 29, 1746, July 27, 1752, *BPRO-SC*, 22:200, 25:70–71; Stumpf, "James Glen," 23–25.

46. Copy of Deed of Sale by the Cherokee Indians, Feb. 12, 1746, CO 5/373, fol. 200; Meriwether, *Expansion of South Carolina*, 194; Corkran, *Cherokee Frontier*, 16–19.

47. Meriwether, *Expansion of South Carolina*, 193–203; *DRIA*, 1:17–15, 18–20, 28–29, 29, 31, 32–33, 41–60, 61–84, 90–91, 100–102, 107–8, 109, 112–18, 129–33; Maness, *Forgotten Outpost*.

48. Dowd, "Panic of 1751," 528; Meriwether, *Expansion of South Carolina*, 200–202.

49. Kelly, "Attakullakulla," 6; Talk of Tassite of the Lower Towns, July 30, 1751, Peter Timothy to James Glen, [Excerpts] from the *Virginia Gazette*, Lewis Burwell to James Glen, Oct. 26, 1751, *DRIA*, 1:108, 151–54, 159–61.

50. Dowd, "Panic of 1751," 538–39; *DRIA*, 1:33–35, 92–99, 103–7, 108–9, 110–12, 138–46; Meriwether, *Expansion of South Carolina*, 204–5.

51. Stumpf, "James Glen," 26; Lee, "Fortify, Fight, or Flee," 757; Hatley, *Dividing Paths*, 95–98.

52. *JCHA, November 14, 1751–October 7, 1752* [Vol. 11], xi; James Glen to the Board of Trade, Aug. 25, 1754, *BPRO-SC*, 26:108–9; Ivers, *Colonial Forts*, 70–72; *SCG*, Dec. 17, 1753; Sheriff, *Cherokee Villages*, 93–103; Cherokee Deed for Fort Prince George Tract, *DRIA*, 1:519–21; Wallace, *Life of Henry Laurens*, 503–10.

CHAPTER TWO
1. Robert Dinwiddie to James Glen, Jan. 29, 1754, *DRIA*, 1:472–74; Salley, *Independent Company*, 4–7; Washington, *Journal*, 16–17; Anderson, *Crucible of War*, 42–49.

2. *JCHA, November 21, 1752–September 6, 1754* [Vol. 12], 395–96, 410–11, 489, 490, 524–27 (Mar. 5, 9, May 7, 10, 1754); Anderson, *Crucible of War*, 50; Foote, "American Independent Companies."

3. *SCG*, Oct. 17, 1754.

4. Harden, "James Mackay"; *SCG*, Apr. 2–9, June 20–27, July 18–25, 1754; Salley, *Independent Company*, 8, 11, 13; Washington, *Journal*, 45–46.

5. James Glen to Robert Dinwiddie, June 1, 1754, to Sir Thomas Robinson, Aug. 15, 1754, *DRIA*, 1:524–28, 532.

6. Independent Companies' officer Lieutenant Peter Mercier, commander of Fort Congaree II, was among the dead. Robert Dinwiddie to James Glen, *DRIA*, 1:528–32; *SCG*, Aug. 22, 1754; MacLeod, *Canadian Iroquois and the Seven Years' War*, 44.

7. Boulware, *Deconstructing the Cherokee Nation*, 10–31.

8. *JCHA, November 12, 1754–September 23, 1755* [Vol. 13], xxxiii, 559–61, 563–70, 571–72 (Sept. 2, 6, 1755); Robert Dinwiddie to Arthur Dobbs, July 23, 1755, *ORRD*, 2:112; Lower Assembly Minutes, *CSR-NC*, 5:224–25, 227 (Dec. 18, 21, 1754).

9. *SCG*, June 5–12, July 24–31, 1755.

10. Hewatt, *Historical Account*, 2:203.

11. "An Account of Monies paid for the Publick by James Glen, Esqr.," CO 5/377, fol. 104r–v.

12. *SCG*, July 24–31, 1755; Kelly, "Attakullakulla," 10, Corkran, *Cherokee Frontier*, 60–61.

13. Hewatt, *Historical Account*, 2:203; Milling, *Red Carolinians*, 285.

14. Hatley, *Dividing Paths*, 76–79; Robert Dinwiddie to Arthur Dobbs, Sept. 18, 1755, *ORRD*, 2:203. Glen also censored press coverage. Peter Timothy to Benjamin Franklin, June 8, 1755, Franklin, *Papers of Benjamin Franklin*, 6:69.

15. Anderson, *Crucible of War*, 86–107.

16. Robert Dinwiddie to James Abercromby, Aug. 7, 1755, to James Glen, July 28, 1755, to Arthur Dobbs, Sept. 18, 1755, *ORRD*, 1:123–24, 125, 203.

17. Robert Dinwiddie to Arthur Dobbs, Sept. 18, 1755, Minutes of a Council with the Cherokees, Sept. 4, 1755, Robert Dinwiddie to James Glen, Sept. 25, 1755, *ORRD*, 2:203, 187–88, 212–14.

18. *SCG*, Mar. 4, 1756; Evans, "Ostenaco," 41–43.

19. Robert Dinwiddie to Henry Fox, May 24, 1756, *ORRD*, 2:413; William Preston, Diary of Sandy Creek Expedition, Feb. 9–Mar. 13, 1756, Lyman C. Draper Manuscripts, 1QQ96–123; Wood, "I Have Now Made a Path," 39–43; Brown, *Old Frontiers*, 58.

20. *Maryland Gazette*, May 6, 1756; Evans, "Ostenaco," 45; Francis Fauquier to the Board of Trade, May 1, 1762, *PFF*, 2:728.

21. *A Treaty Held with the Catawba and Cherokee Indians*, iii, v–ix, xiii–xiv, xi–xii, 1–8, 9–15.

22. Ibid., 15–17, 20–22.

23. *SCG*, Mar. 11, 1756.

24. Waddell, *Colonial Officer*, 30, 34–35; *CSR-NC*, 5:xlvii–xlix; Maass, *French and Indian War in North Carolina*, 62–63.

25. James Glen to the Duke of Newcastle, Dec. 1748, Letterbook of James Glen, John Forbes Papers in the Dalhousie Muniments, 45/2/1, 65–71; James Glen to the Board of Trade, 1756, Charles Pinckney to the Board of Trade, Feb. 4, 1756, *BPRO-SC*, 26:42–43, 46, 48–49, 27:17–21; Robert Dinwiddie to Sir Thomas Robinson, Nov. 24, 1755, to WHL, Sept. 18, 1756, *ORRD*, 2:282, 508–9; Stumpf, "James Glen," 25–30.

26. Lee, "Fortify, Fight, or Flee," 758–60; Fabel, *Colonial Challenges*, 27–28; Andrew Lewis to Raymond Demere, Sept. 11, 1756, *DRIA*, 2:204.

27. James Glen to the Board of Trade, Apr. 14, 1756, *BPRO-SC*, 26:50.

28. *SCG*, Feb. 12, 1756; SCCJ, Feb. 16, 1756, in *BPRO-SC*, 26:147.

29. Kelly, "Fort Loudoun," 72–75; Correspondence between Glen and Dinwiddie, *ORRD*, 2:369, 379, 392, 484–88, 508, 2:24, 26, 28, 214; *SCG*, May 6, 13, June 5, 1756; Alden, *John Stuart*, 47–50, 57–58; James Glen to the Board of Trade, Apr. 14, 1756, *BPRO-SC*, 26:40–64.

30. Attig, "William Henry Lyttelton," 1–8; Board of Trade Minutes, Jan. 23, 1755, *BPRO-SC*, 26:132.

31. WHL, "Account of the Capture of HMS *Blandford* by the French, and Lyttelton's Subsequent Movements and Return to England," Aug. 3–Sept. 1755, LPCD.

32. Davis, *Good Lord Lyttelton*, 251, 253, 261; Hewatt, *Historical Account*, 2:210.

33. Fenning, *New System of Geography*, 2:671; Milligen-Johnston, *Short Description*, 24–25, 32; Adam Gordon, "Journal of an Officer's [Lord Adam Gordon's] Travels in America and the West Indies, 1764–1765," in Mereness, *Travels in the American Colonies*, 397; Webster, "Journal of a Voyage to Charlestown," 136.

34. De Brahm, *Report*, 91; Milligen-Johnston, *Short Description*, 32, 36–37; *SCG*, June 5, 1756; May, "His Majesty's Ships on the Carolina Station," 166.

35. Milligen-Johnston, *Short Description*, 33–35, 36, 41; *London Magazine*, June 1762, 296; Webster, "Journal of a Voyage to Charlestown," 134–35; De Brahm, *Report*, 90.

36. *SCG*, Mar. 20–27, 1755, June 5, 1756, Dec. 29–Jan. 1, 1759, Jan. 9–16, 1762.

37. Milling, *Exile without an End*. By spring 1756, 1,200 Acadians were in Charles Town. James Glen to the Board of Trade, Apr. 14, 1756, *BPRO-SC*, 27:57–61; *JCHA, November 20, 1755–July 6, 1757* [Vol. 14], xxx–xxxvi.

38. SCCJ, 1754–56, 3:271–73 (June 2, 1756); WHL to the Board of Trade, June 19, 1756, *BPRO-SC*, 27:105–14; *SCG*, June 5, 1756.

39. *A Treaty Held with the Catawba and Cherokee Indians*, 23–25; Robert Dinwiddie to Andrew Lewis, Apr. 14, 1756, *ORRD*, 2:389–90; *SCG*, Apr. 1, 1756.

40. Andrew Lewis to Raymond Demere, July 7, 1756, Raymond Demere to WHL, July 10, 30, 1756, *DRIA*, 2:138, 132, 151; *SCG*, July 29, 1756; Robert Dinwiddie to WHL, Sept. 18, 1756, *ORRD*, 2:510; Henry Bouquet to the Earl of Loudoun, Aug. 25, 1757, Bouquet, *Papers of Henry Bouquet*, 1:174; Alden, *John Stuart*, 59; WHL to the Board of Trade, Aug. 11, 1756, *BPRO-SC*, 27:133.

41. Andrew Lewis to Raymond Demere, Aug. 13, 1756, *DRIA*, 2:167.

42. *SCG*, June 24, 1756; Hodson, *Acadian Diaspora*, 55; WHL to the Board of Trade, Dec. 6, 1756, June 11, 1757, At the Court of St. James, Dec. 6, 1757, *BPRO-SC*, 27:201–2, 280, 338; Mercantini, *Who Shall Rule*, 115–19.

43. *SCG*, July 15–22, 1756; WHL to the Board of Trade, Aug. 11, 1756, *BPRO-SC*, 27:138–39; Milling, *Exile without an End*, 20.

44. *SCG*, Nov. 27–Dec. 4, 1755; Instructions to Gov. Lyttelton, Nov. 4, 1755, CO 5/403, fols. 20–151, in CDFA, reel 366.2; WHL to Henry Fox, June 16, 1756, to the Board of Trade, June 19, 1756, *BPRO-SC*, 27:102–4, 105–16.

45. WHL to the Board of Trade, Aug. 11, 1756, *BPRO-SC*, 27:133; De Brahm, *Report*, 7–19.

46. Raymond Demere to WHL, Oct. 13, 1756, *DRIA*, 2:214–20; De Brahm, *Report*, 18–20, 77–83, 100–102; correspondence in *DRIA*, 2:169–70, 214–18, 225, 232–33, 240, 250–51, 260, 261, 271–75, 281, 284–86, 286–89, 301–2, 365–66, 375; *SCG*, Nov. 4, 1756.

47. Raymond Demere to WHL, July 30, 1757, *DRIA*, 2:396; WHL to the Board of Trade, July 12, 1757; SCCJ, 1757–1762, 1:69 (July 12, 1757).

48. Pargellis, *Lord Loudoun in North America*; Raymond Demere to WHL, Nov. 7, Dec. 27, 1756, *DRIA*, 2:241, 289; Kelly, "Fort Loudoun," 78.

49. De Brahm, *Report*, 102; Raymond Demere to WHL, Jan. 31, Mar. 1, 1757, Paul Demere to WHL, Aug. 18, 1757, *DRIA*, 2:327, 345, 403. Two corn houses, a guardroom, and a house for the commander were added later. Kelly, "Fort Loudoun," 78, 83.

50. Paul Demere to WHL, July 30, Aug. 10, 18, 1757, *DRIA*, 2:396, 399, 404; Brown, *Old Frontiers*, 76; Stone, "Captain Paul Demere," 18–20.

51. De Brahm, *Report*, 101; Raymond Demere to WHL, Nov. 28, 1756, *DRIA*, 2:259–60.

52. Boulware, *Deconstructing the Cherokee Nation*, 77–80; Raymond Demere to WHL, Aug. 10, 1757, *DRIA*, 2:400; Stone, "Captain Paul Demere," 19, 20–21.

53. Kerlérec to De Machault d'Arnouville, [Oct. 1, 1755], Petition of Lantagnac to Kerlérec, translated in *MPA*, 5:159–61, 162–65, 164n; Lachlan McGillivray to James Glen, [Feb. 1755], Raymond Demere to WHL, Oct. 16, 1756, Lachlan McGillivray to James Glen, Feb. 1, 1755, *DRIA*, 2:140, 225.

54. *MPA*, 5:166n.

55. Arthur Dobbs to Hugh Waddell, [Alexander Osborne], and [Nathaniel] Alexander, July 18, 1756, *CSR-NC*, 5:604.

56. Thomas, *Fort Toulouse*, xli–xlii; Alden, *John Stuart*, 52n, 61, 63, 128–29; Raymond Demere to WHL, Nov. 26, 1756, WHL to the Board of Trade, Dec. 31, 1756, Apr. 22, 1757, *BPRO-SC*, 27:225–27, 253, 260; *SCG*, Nov. 18, 1756; Boulware, *Deconstructing the Cherokee Nation*, 77–90.

57. Paul Demere to WHL, Aug. 18, 1757, *DRIA*, 2:403; Paul Demere to WHL, Oct. 11, 1757, LPCD; Kelly, "Fort Loudoun," 84, 84n; SCCJ, 1757–1762, 1:56 (Feb. 12, 1757).

58. Old Hop and Attakullakulla to Paul Demere, summary of talks, Aug. 30, 1757, Raymond Demere to WHL, July 11, 1757, Paul Demere to WHL, Aug. 31, 1757, LPCD; Milling, *Red Carolinians*, 283–84.

59. Raymond Demere to WHL, Dec. 23, 1756, Feb. 7, 1757, *DRIA*, 2:282, 334.

60. Ludovick Grant to James Glen, Mar. 27, 1755, *DRIA*, 2:41–45; Raymond Demere to WHL, July 11, 1757, LPCD; Ingram, *Indians and British Outposts*, 34.

61. James Beamer to James Glen, Feb. 21, 1756, *DRIA*, 2:104–6.

62. The Little Carpenter's Speech to Captain Raymond Demere, July 13, 1756, Raymond Demere to WHL, Dec. 11, 1756, Talk of the Mankiller of Great Tellico to Raymond Demere, Jan. 15, 1757, *DRIA*, 2:137, 267, 320.

63. Raymond Demere to WHL, Jan. 15, 1757, [Report of Lieutenant Wall to Captain Raymond Demere], Jan. 13, 1757, *DRIA*, 2:315, 324.

64. Raymond Demere to WHL, Feb. 5, 1757, *DRIA*, 2:334.

65. *SCG*, Feb. 3, 24, 1757; *SCG*, Postscript, May 26, 1757.

66. Paul Demere to WHL, Aug. 8, 1757, *DRIA*, 2:402; WHL to the Board of Trade, Oct. 17, Dec. 25, 1756, *BPRO-SC*, 27:158, 254–59.

CHAPTER THREE

1. Ward, *Breaking the Backcountry*, 145; Robert Dinwiddie to Clement Read, Apr. 12, 15, 1757, *ORRD*, 2:609–10, 612–13; Clement Read to Robert Dinwiddie, Apr. 5, 1757, Amherst Papers, WO 34/47, fols. 150–51.

2. Ward, *Breaking the Backcountry*, 145; George Mercer to George Washington, Apr. 24, 26, 1757, *PGW*, 4:139–41, 142–43; Preston, "Make Indians of Our White Men," 295.

3. Wood, "I Have Now Made a Path," 43–44, 50; Preston, "Make Indians of Our White Men," 282, 290–91. On these Indian allies, see *EJC*, 6:38 (Mar. 29, 1757); Speech to the Tuscarora Indians, Aug. 1, 1756, *PGW*, 3:308–9; Robert Dinwiddie to William Pitt, June 18, 1757, Pitt, *Correspondence of William Pitt*, 1:80; *SCG*, Aug. 18, 1757; Brown, *Catawba Indians*, 183–215.

4. George Washington to Robert Dinwiddie, Apr. 24, 1756, *PGW*, 3:45. See also William Fairfax to George Washington, Apr. 26–27, 1756, ibid., 3:56.

5. Wood, "I Have Now Made a Path," 50–51; Preston, "Make Indians of Our White Men," 295, 298. On Cherokee diplomacy, see Kelton, "British and Indian War," 771–784, 790–91; Perdue, "Cherokee Relations," 140; correspondence in *SWJP*, 9:945–46, 946–51, 955–961, 967–68.

6. Robert Dinwiddie to George Washington, Sept. 13, 1756, *PGW*, 3:426. See Dinwiddie's letters in *ORRD*, 1:61–63, 205–7; 2:60–61, 76, 168–69, 391, 445–47, 548–49, 550.

7. George Mason to George Washington, Sept. 13, 1756, *PGW*, 3:407.

8. George Washington to Robert Dinwiddie, May 24, 1757, James Baker to George Washington, June 10, 1757, *PGW*, 4:163, 200; Wood, "I Have Now Made a Path," 45–48.

9. John Dagworthy to George Washington, June 14, 1757, George Washington to William Fairfax, June 25, 1757, John Stanwix to George Washington, July 18, 1757, *PGW*, 4:212; 4:261.

10. George Washington to John David Wilper, June 7, 1757, to Robert Dinwiddie, June 12, 1757, to John Stanwix, July 8, 15, 1757, Edmond Atkin to George Washington, July 20, 1757, *PGW*, 4:186–87, 209, 285, 306–7, 321–22; Ward, *Breaking the Backcountry*, 144–45.

11. George Washington to John Stanwix, June 28, 1757, to Robert Dinwiddie, Nov. 5, 1757, *PGW*, 4:270, 5:44–46.

12. Paul Demere to WHL, Apr. 2, 1758, *DRIA*, 2:455; Paul Demere to WHL, July 30, 1758, LPCD.

13. "Captn. Bosomworth's Proceedings with the Indians at Fort Loudoun in Virginia," Apr. 21, 1758, Forbes Headquarters (HQ) Papers, File #132.

14. "Talk of Ohatchie, and the Young Warrior of Estatoe," Sept. 18, 1758, LPCD; Ward, *Breaking the Backcountry*, 143; Dowd, "Insidious Friends," 116, 131.

15. "A Return of the Southern Indians Winchester 21st Apr. 1758," Forbes HQ Papers, File #133; John Forbes to William Pitt, May 1, 1758, to Sir William Johnson, [May 4, 1758], to William Pitt, May 19, 1758, Forbes, *Writings of General John Forbes*, 77–78, 82, 92.

16. SCCJ, 1757–1762, 1:136–38, 139, 141 (Mar. 13, 14, 15, 1758); *JCHA, 1757–1761*, 132–33, 135–36 (Mar. 17, 18, 1758).

17. Robert Dinwiddie to Edmond Atkin, July 18, 1757, to Cherokees, Sept. 24, 1757, *ORRD*, 2:672, 700; *EJC*, 6:49–50 (May 24, 1757); "An Act for Establishing a Trade with the Indians in alliance with His Majesty," June 8, 1757, Edmond Atkin to Nathan Walhoe, Jan. 26, 1758, Amherst Papers, WO 34/47, fols. 185–86, 187–89.

18. WHL to the Earl of Loudoun, Mar. 21, 1758, to James Abercromby, May 15, 1758, Amherst Papers, WO 34/35, fols. 81–83, 91–92; WHL to John Forbes, May 21, 1758, John Forbes Papers in the Dalhousie Muniments, 2/49/3.

19. Thomas H. Beemer [Beamer] et al., "To the Head men and Warriors of the Cherokee Nation at Winchester," "Letter Col: Byrds Indians to the Cherokees at Winchester," May 21, 1758, "Letter Colo. Byrd Bedford in Virginia 21st May," Forbes HQ Papers, File #238, 239.

20. Lachlan McIntosh to WHL, Mar. 4, 1758, *DRIA*, 2:443; William Byrd to WHL, May 1, 1758, *CTWB*, 2:650; Memorandum of James Beamer, Apr. 20, 1758, Memorandum of Ambrose Davis, Apr. 13, 1758, George Turner to WHL, July 2, 1758, *DRIA*, 2:451–52, 453, 473.

21. Cashin, *Henry Ellis*, 131–35; WHL to John Forbes, May 21, 1758, LPLB, 1:134–35; John Forbes, "Plan of Operations on the Mississippi, Ohio & Ca," [1758], *Writings of General John Forbes*, 25; WHL to Jeffery Amherst, Mar. 16, 1759, LPLB, 3:40.

22. "Captn. Bosomworth's Proceedings with the Indians at Fort Loudoun in Virginia," Apr. 21, 1758, Forbes HQ Papers, #132.

23. Tistoe of Keowee and the Wolf to WHL, July 12, 1758, LPCD.

24. George Washington to John Blair, Apr. 9, 1758, *PGW*, 5:113-15.

25. John Forbes to the Earl of Loudoun, Apr. 23, [1758], *Writings of General John Forbes*, 70-71; Cubbison, *British Defeat of the French*, 28-29, 31, 38-39, 46, 81-84.

26. Paul Demere to WHL, June 24, 1758, LPCD; "Depositions Concerning Indian Disturbances in Virginia," *DRIA*, 2:463-70.

27. Hening, *Statutes at Large*, 6:550-52, 564-65, 7:121-23; "Depositions Concerning Indian Disturbances in Virginia," *DRIA*, 2:463-70; Ward, *Breaking the Backcountry*, 165-66.

28. Samuel Wyly to WHL, Oct. 5, 1758, Lachlan McIntosh to WHL, Oct. 22, 1758, Arthur Dobbs to WHL, Aug. 27, 1758, LPCD; Attakullakulla to William Byrd, May 27, 1758, *CTWB*, 2:656; "The Talk of the Emperor Old Hop & the Head Men of the Upper Cherokee Nation" to WHL, July 28, 1758, *BPRO-SC*, 28:86-87; Thomas Beamer to Edmond Atkin, [Sept. 1758], James Beamer to WHL, Sept. 16, 1758, LPCD.

29. "Sir Jno St. Clair Winchester May 19th 1758," Forbes HQ Papers, File #234; "Depositions Concerning Indian Disturbances in Virginia," *DRIA*, 2:463-70; *EJC*, 6:91-94, 101-5 (May 20, June 15, 1758).

30. "Mr. Hoops Lancaster May 2d," Forbes HQ Papers, File #171; Francis Halkett to George Washington, May 4, 1758, John Forbes to James Abercromby, May 4, 1758, *Writings of General John Forbes*, 84, 85.

31. George Washington to Francis Halkett, May 11, 1758, to Sir John St. Clair, May 11, 1758, *PGW*, 5:175-77, 177-79.

32. Allan MacLean to John Forbes, May 2, 1758, John Forbes Papers in the Dalhousie Muniments, 2/51/1; "Copy of Sr. John St Clairs Letter to Mr. Prest. Blair the 31st of May 1758," Forbes HQ Papers, File #277; William Byrd to Lachlan McIntosh, May 12, 1758, LPCD.

33. John Forbes to William Pitt, May 19, 1758, *Writings of General John Forbes*, 91-92; "Sir Jno St. Clair Winchester May 19th 1758," Forbes HQ Papers, File #234.

34. John Forbes to John Stanwix, May 29, 1758, *Writings of General John Forbes*, 102; "Sr John St Clair Winchester 21st May 1758," "Letter Mr. Hoops Lancaster 29th May," Forbes HQ Papers, File #240, 264; Cubbison, *British Defeat of the French*, 83-84.

35. "Copy of Sr. John St Clairs Letter to Mr. Prest. Blair the 31st of May 1758," Forbes HQ Papers, File #277; Sir John St. Clair to Henry Bouquet, May 31, 1758, *Papers of Henry Bouquet*, 1:402-4.

36. "Copy letter to G: Abercromby Ph: Aprile 22d," Forbes HQ Papers, File #135; Oliphant, *Peace and War*, 57; John Forbes to John Stanwix, May 29, 1758, *Writings of General John Forbes*, 103; Cubbison, *British Defeat of the French*, 82-84, 199-211.

37. Henry Bouquet to George Washington, June 14, 1758, *PGW*, 6:286-88; Henry Bouquet, Speech to Cherokee and Catawba Indians, ca. June 16, 1758, *Papers of Henry Bouquet*, 2:98-100; Abraham Bosomworth, "Indian intelligence Camp at Rays Town 20th July 1758," Forbes HQ Papers, File #398; Cubbison, *British Defeat of the French*, 115-22.

38. "Capt. Bosomworth Winchester June 9th," "Letter Colo. Byrd Winchester 23d June," Forbes HQ Papers, File #303, 327.

39. George Washington to John Forbes, June 19, 1758, *PGW*, 5:224–26.

40. Attakullakulla to Paul Demere, Jan. 4, 1758, *DRIA*, 2:434; SCCJ, 1757–1762, 1:115–16 (Feb. 4, 1758); Paul Demere to WHL, Feb. 20, 1758, William Byrd to WHL, Mar. 31, 1758, LPCD; SCCJ, 1757–1762, 1:148–52, 152–59, 159–65 (Apr. 10, 11, 12, 1758); Attakullakulla to William Byrd, May 27, 1758, *CTWB*, 2:656.

41. "Fort Loudoun, Upper Cherokees, George Turner," [June 23, 1758], Forbes HQ Papers, File #326; [Attakullakulla] to WHL, June 3, 1758, *BPRO-SC*, 28:70–72.

42. Lee, "Peace Chiefs and Blood Revenge," 721, 723; William Fyffe to John Fyffe, Feb. 1, 1761, Fyffe Collection.

43. "Fort Loudoun, Upper Cherokees, George Turner," [June 23, 1758], Forbes HQ Papers, File #326; Paul Demere to WHL, June 24, 1758, LPCD; George Turner to WHL, July 2, 1758, *DRIA*, 2:471–73.

44. "Fort Loudoun, Upper Cherokees, George Turner," [June 23, 1758], Forbes HQ Papers, File #326; [Attakullakulla] to WHL, July 29, 1758, *BPRO-SC*, 28:90–93.

45. "Copy Letter to Sir J: St Clair Philad: June 16th 1758," Forbes HQ Papers, File #318; John Forbes to William Pitt, June 17, July 10, 1758, *Correspondence of William Pitt*, 1:279–80, 294–97; James Glen to John Forbes, July 13, 1758, [ca. 1758], John Forbes Papers in the Dalhousie Muniments, 2/44/3, 2/44/22.

46. Cubbison, *British Defeat of the French*, 11, 96, 148, 167; Arthur Dobbs to WHL, Aug. 27, 1758, LPCD; Henry Bouquet to John Forbes, June 28, July 11, 1758, *Papers of Henry Bouquet*, 2:143, 179–80; Shippen, *Memoir of Henry Bouquet*, 7.

47. Cubbison, *British Defeat of the French*, 199; "Copy Letter to Gover. Fauquier Shippensbourg 16th Augt. 1758," "Copy Letter to Governr. Dobbs Shippensbourg 16th Augt. 1758," "Letter to Governr. Littleton Shippensburg 16th Augt. 1758," Forbes HQ Papers, File #473, 474, 475.

48. Francis Fauquier to John Forbes, July 20, 1758, *PFF*, 1:52; John Forbes to Edmond Atkin, Aug. 16, 1758, Tistoe of Keowee and the Wolf to WHL, July 12, 1758, LPCD; George Washington to Henry Bouquet, July 16, 1758, *PGW*, 5:291–93.

49. "Letter Capt. Bossomworth Fort Cumberland 15th July 1758," Forbes HQ Papers, File #375; Paul Demere to WHL, June 24, 1758, LPCD; Lachlan McIntosh to WHL, June 5, 1758, *DRIA*, 2:462; Abraham Bosomworth to George Washington, July 7, 1758, *PGW*, 5:270; John Forbes to Henry Bouquet, Carlisle, July 17, 1758, *Papers of Henry Bouquet*, 2:224–25.

50. Henry Bouquet to John Forbes, July 11, 1758, *Papers of Henry Bouquet*, 2:180; George Washington to Francis Fauquier, July 10, 1758, *PGW*, 5:275–76.

51. "Letter Mr. Glenn Raystown July 26th 1758," "Letter Colo. Byrd Fort Cumberland 3d Augt. 1758," Forbes HQ Papers, File #421, 440; George Washington to Henry Bouquet, July 28, 1758, *PGW*, 5:377–78.

52. John Forbes to James Abercromby, [Aug. 11, 1758], *Writings of General John Forbes*, 174–75; "Letter Major Grant Fort Loudoun 16th August 1758," Forbes HQ Papers, File #476.

53. Calloway, *White People, Indians, and Highlanders*, introduction, 101–2; John Forbes to William Pitt, June 17, 1758, *Writings of General John Forbes*, 117.

54. Thomas Beamer to Edmond Atkin, [Sept. 1758], James Beamer to WHL, Sept. 16, 1758, Lachlan McIntosh to WHL, Sept. 18, 1758, LPCD.

55. Thomas Beamer to Edmond Atkin, [Sept. 1758], James Beamer to WHL, Sept. 16, 1758, Lachlan McIntosh to WHL, Sept. 18, 1758, LPCD; John Echols, "An Extract of a journal," Palmer, *Calendar*, 1:254–57.

56. Thomas Beamer to Edmond Atkin, [Sept. 1758], LPCD.

57. Adair, *History of the American Indians*, 186, 376; John Philip Reid, "A Perilous Rule: The Law of International Homicide," in King, *Cherokee Indian Nation*, 33–45; Abram, "Souls in the Treetops," 21; William Richardson, "An Account of My Proceedings," 16 (Jan. 11, 1759), William Richardson Davie Papers.

58. "The Talk of Tiftoe [Tistoe], the Wolf, and the rest of the Head-men of the Lower Towns," "The Talk of the Emperor Old Hop & the Head Men of the Upper Cherokee Nation," July 28, 1758, *BPRO-SC*, 28:84–86, 86–87.

59. Black Dog and Long Dog to WHL, Oct. 15, 1758, Thomas Beamer to Edmond Atkin, [Sept. 1758], James Beamer to WHL, Sept. 16, 1758, LPCD; Boulware, *Deconstructing the Cherokee Nation*, 113–16; Abram, "Souls in the Treetops," 21–22; Raymond Demere to WHL, Apr. 2, 1757, *DRIA*, 2:361.

60. Lachlan McIntosh to WHL, Sept. 18, 1758, "The Talk of Ohatchie, and the Young Warrior of Estatoe," Sept. 18, 1758, Lachlan McGillivray to WHL, Oct. 17, 1758, LPCD; George Croghan to Sir William Johnson, Jan. 30, 1759, *SWJP*, 10:90–91.

61. Lachlan McIntosh to WHL, Sept. 18, 1758, James Beamer to WHL, Sept. 19, 1758, "The Talk of Ohatchie, and the Young Warrior of Estatoe," Sept. 18, 1758, LPCD.

62. James Beamer to WHL, Sept. 16, 1758, Thomas Beamer to Edmond Atkin, [Sept. 1758], LPCD.

63. Francis Fauquier to WHL, June 16, 1758, *PFF*, 1:28–29; WHL to Francis Fauquier, Sept. 26, 1758, LPLB, 1:220.

64. WHL to "the Lower and Middle Cherokee Headmen and Warriours," Sept. 26, 1758, *DRIA*, 2:481; Lee, "Peace Chiefs and Blood Revenge," 714; Reid, *Law of Blood*, 171–72.

65. *JHB, 1758–1761*, 30, 45 (Sept. 28, Oct. 12, 1758); Hening, *Statutes at Large*, 7:241; Francis Fauquier to WHL, Virginia Council Journal, [Oct. 12, 1758], LPCD; Francis Fauquier to John Buchanan, Nov. 14, 1758, *PFF*, 1:105, 105n.

66. Henry Ellis to the Board of Trade, Nov. 9, 1758, *CRG*, 28, pt. 1:171; James Beamer to WHL, Oct. 20, 1758, Lachlan McGillivray to Henry Ellis, Oct. 17, 24, 1758, LPCD.

67. Black Dog and Long Dog to WHL, Oct. 15, 1758, James Beamer to WHL, Oct. 20, 1758, Cherokee Headmen to WHL, Oct. 20, 1758, LPCD; WHL to Edmond Atkin, Oct. 14, 1758, LPLB, 1:246.

68. Paul Demere to WHL, Sept. 30, Oct. 15, 1758, LPCD.

69. John Forbes to Richard Peters, Oct. 16, 1758, *Writings of General John Forbes*, 234–37; Paul Demere to WHL, Sept. 30, 1758, LPCD.

70. John Forbes to Henry Bouquet, Oct. 10, 15, 1758, *Writings of General John Forbes*, 228, 230; Kelly, "Attakullakulla," 17.

71. Attakullakulla to WHL, Mar. 20, 1759, LPCD; John Forbes to William Pitt, Oct. 30, 1758, *Correspondence of William Pitt*, 1:373.

72. John Forbes to Henry Bouquet, [Oct. 21, 1758], to James Abercromby, Oct. 24, 1758, *Writings of General John Forbes*, 241, 244, 248–49; Kelly, "Attakullakulla," 17–18; Kelton, "British and Indian War," 771–784, 790; Perdue, "Cherokee Relations," 140.

73. George Washington to Francis Fauquier, Nov. 28, 1758, *PGW*, 6:158–60; John Forbes to [James] Burd, Nov. 19, 1758, *Writings of General John Forbes*, 256–58; WHL to the Board of Trade, Feb. 21, 1759, *BPRO-SC*, 28:149; Attakullakulla to WHL, Mar. 20, 1759, LPCD.

74. [Edward] Boscawen to WHL, July 5, 1758, LPLB, 3:51. See Kerlérec to Minister, correspondence in CDFA, reels 142–46.

75. Edward [Edmond] Atkin to James Abercromby, May 20, 1758, Amherst Papers, WO 34/47, fols. 203–6; Henry Ellis to the Board of Trade, Oct. 25, 1758, *CRG*, 28, pt. 1:167; Henry Ellis to WHL, Nov. 5, 1758, Mar. 13, 1759, LPCD.

76. WHL to Edmond Atkin, Oct. 14, 1758, WHL to William Pitt, Nov. 4, 1758, LPLB, 3:246, 29–37; Alexander Garden to John Ellis, Aug. 11, 1757, *CLON*, 1:427.

77. For a list of visitors see SCCJ, 1757–1762, 2:34–37, 39–40 (Nov. 14, 15, 1758).

CHAPTER FOUR

1. Christopher Gist to Francis Fauquier, [Dec. 27, 1758], Francis Fauquier to William Byrd, Jan. 23, 1759, Attakullakulla to Francis Fauquier, Mar. 15, 1759, *PFF*, 1:135, 158–59, 185; *EJC*, 6:124–30, 135–36 (Jan. 19, 20, 23, Apr. 17, 1759); Attakullakulla to WHL, Mar. 20, 1759, Lachlan McIntosh to WHL, Mar. 21, 1759, LPCD.

2. De Brahm, *Report*, 112; Lee, "Peace Chiefs and Blood Revenge," 738, 741; Adair, *History of the American Indians*, 415–16; Perdue, "Cherokee Relations," 135.

3. Adair, *History of the American Indians*, 281.

4. Ibid., 186, 376; Reid, *Law of Blood*, 168; Abram, "Souls in the Treetops," 21.

5. William Fyffe to John Fyffe, Feb. 1, 1761, Fyffe Collection; Adair, *History of the American Indians*, 186; Perdue, *Cherokee Women*, 38–40; Timberlake, *Memoirs*, 122; De Brahm, *Report*, 109.

6. *SCG*, May 18, 1745; Deed of Sale by the Lower Cherokees to the King, CO 5/373, fols. 200r–201r; William Richardson, "An Account of My Proceedings," 24–25 (Jan. 30, 1759); *SCG*, Sept. 15–22, 1759.

7. Tistoe of Keowee and the Wolf to WHL, Mar. 5, 1759, LPCD; Richardson, "An Account of My Proceedings," 20–21 (Jan. 23, 1759).

8. Raymond Demere to WHL, Mar. 26, 1757, *DRIA*, 2:348–49; Richardson, "An Account of My Proceedings," 12, 30 (Dec. 25, 30, 1758). On John Chavis, see Richard Coytmore to WHL, May 17, 1759, James Beamer to WHL, Feb. 25, 1759, LPCD.

9. Milligen-Johnston, *Short Description*, 77–78.

10. Paul Demere to WHL, Feb. 27, Mar. 26, Apr. 6, 1759, Lachlan McIntosh to WHL, Mar. 31, Apr. 2, 1759, LPCD; WHL to the Board of Trade, Apr. 14, 1759, *BPRO-SC*, 28:177, 180–82; Lee, "Peace Chiefs and Blood Revenge," 737.

11. SCCJ, 1757–1762, 2:77–80, 81–82 (Apr. 7, 11, 1759); WHL to the Board of Trade, May 8, 1759, *BPRO-SC*, 28:190–91; *SCG*, Apr. 21–28, 1759.

12. SCCJ, 1757–1762, 2:83–86 (Apr. 21, 1759); *SCG*, Apr. 21–28, 1759.

13. Arthur Dobbs to WHL, May 25, 1759, "Extracts of Letters &ca. to [WHL], relative to the Murders & Outrages committed by the Cherokees, 1759," LPCD; *SCG*, May 5–12, 1759; "Memorabilia of Bethabara, 1759," and "Bethabara Diary, 1759," Fries, *Records of the Moravians*, 1:206, 209–11 (Apr. 24, May 6, 7, 8, 9, 1759).

14. Richard Coytmore to WHL, May 8, 1759, LPCD; SCCJ, 1757–1762, 2:92–93 (May 21, 1759); WHL to the Emperor Old Hop and the Little Carpenter, May 22, 1759, LPLB, 1:354; Lee, "Peace Chiefs and Blood Revenge," 737, 737n; Richter, *Ordeal of the Longhouse*, 40, 44–45; Boulware, *Deconstructing the Cherokee Nation*, 105–7; Adair, *History of the American Indians*, 264.

15. WHL to King Hagler, to Pyamingo, [ca. May 1759], LPLB, 1:358. On Captain Johnny and the Catawbas, see SCCJ, 1757–1762, 2:93–94 (May 30, 1759).

16. "Cherokee Lower Towns to Governor Lyttelton," May 11, 1759, "Tistoe to Governor Lyttelton," May 13, 1759, "Thirteen Cherokee Towns to Governor Lyttelton," May 13, 1759, *DRIA*, 2:491–92, 492, 494–95; Cherokee Headmen to WHL, May 16, 1759, LPCD.

17. WHL to Edmond Atkin, May 21, 1759, LPLB, 1:310.

18. Paul Demere to WHL, June 1, 1759, LPCD; *SCG*, June 2–9, 1759.

19. *SCG*, June 2–9, 1759; SCCJ, 1757–1762, 2:101 (June 6, 1759); Richard Coytmore to WHL, June 11, 1759, Paul Demere to WHL, June 1, 1759, LPCD.

20. "Statement of the Requests to the King of the Colony," translated in *MPA*, 5:227–40. The French gave the Indians clothing, boots, paint, guns, ammunition and knives, and promised much more in four months. "August 1, 1759 An Indian Woman called the Buffolow Skin," LPCD.

21. Tyler, "The Gnostic Trap," 146–50.

22. WHL to the Board of Trade, Sept. 1, 1759, *BPRO-SC*, 28:213. In the Judea wilderness, John the Baptist preached, "Repent ye: for the kingdom of heaven is at hand." Matthew 3:1–2, *King James Bible*.

23. Tyler, "The Gnostic Trap," 152, 159–61; Clarke, *Prophetic Numbers*; *SCG*, Mar. 3–10, 1759; St. Philip's Vestry Minutes, 1756–1774 (Oct. 2, 16, 17, 1758).

24. WHL to the Board of Trade, Sept. 1, 1759, *BPRO-SC*, 28:213–14; Duncan, "Servitude and Slavery," 2:813–19.

25. Simpson, *South Carolina Diary*, 143 (June 17, 1759).

26. SCCJ, 1757–1762, 2:105–6, 110–13 (June 20, July 9, 1759).

27. Ibid., 2:110–11 (July 9, 1759); Wood, "Liberty Is Sweet," 155–56. Robert Wright to John Broadbelt, May 1, 1749, Secretary of State. Recorded Instruments, Miscellaneous Records (Main Series), 21:159.

28. WHL to the Board of Trade, Sept. 1, 1759, *BPRO-SC*, 28:214; *SCG*, Aug. 11–18, 1759.

29. *SCG*, Aug. 27–Sept. 1, Sept. 22–29, 1759; WHL to the Board of Trade, Sept. 1, 1759, *BPRO-SC*, 28:214; Alexander Garden to Philip Bearcroft, Oct. 31, 1759, Selected Pages Relating to South Carolina, SPG Papers, Series B, Vol. 4, Pt. II:284.

30. Youctanah carried them to the wife of "half breed Jemmy," nine miles from the fort. Richard Coytmore to WHL, July 23, 1759, LPCD.

31. WHL to Paul Demere, July 31, 1759, LPLB, 1:378; *SCG*, July 11–14, 1759; Nathaniel Alexander to WHL, June 27, 1759, Arthur Dobbs to WHL, Aug. 22, 1759, LPCD; Maass, *French and Indian War in North Carolina*, 85–88.

32. Paul Demere to WHL, July 10, 1759, *BPRO-SC*, 28:223; *SCG*, July 28–Aug. 4, 1759.

33. *JCHA, 1757–1761*, 422–23, 424–25 (July 12, 13, 1759); Lee, "Peace Chiefs and Blood Revenge," 718–20.

34. "Extract from a Letter from Capt. Paul Demere," July 22, 1759, *BPRO-SC*, 28:224–25. For Attakullakulla's journey, see Richard Coytmore to WHL, Oct. 28, 1759, Attakullakulla to WHL, Nov. 2, 1759, Paul Demere to WHL, Nov. 3, 1759, LPCD.

35. William Atkin and Billy Germany, Conference, Aug. 20, 1759, Richard Coytmore to WHL, Aug. 23, 1759, Paul Demere to WHL, Aug. 28, 1759, LPCD.

36. Paul Demere to WHL, Aug. 28, 1759, Richard Coytmore to WHL, Aug. 23, 1759, LPCD.

37. WHL to the Board of Trade, Sept. 1, 1759, *BPRO-SC*, 28:210–11; WHL to the [Cherokees], Aug. 29, 1759, LPLB, 1:393.

38. Henry Ellis to WHL, Aug. 27, 1759, LPCD; Cashin, *Henry Ellis, 136*; Lee, "Peace Chiefs and Blood Revenge," 737.

39. SCCJ, 1757–1762, 2:116 (Aug. 14, 1759); WHL to John Stewart [Stuart], Aug. 15, 1759, LPLB, 1:385–86. This augmented the force sent on Mar. 21. WHL to the Board of Trade, Apr. 14, Sept. 6, 1759, *BPRO-SC*, 28:177, 209; *SCG*, Mar. 17–24, Aug. 11–18, 1759; John Stuart to WHL, Nov. 15, 1759, LPCD.

40. Richard Coytmore to WHL, Sept. 8, 1759, Paul Demere to WHL, Sept. 13, Oct. 1, 1759, LPCD.

41. Francis planned forts for the northwestern Carolina frontier. James Francis to WHL, Aug. 29, 1759, Lachlan Shaw to WHL, Aug. [1759], LPCD.

42. James Beamer to WHL, Sept. 10, 1759, Richard Coytmore to WHL, Sept. 8, 1759, LPCD; *SCG*, Sept. 15–22, 1759.

43. Patrick Calhoun to WHL, Sept. 21, 1759, Maurice Anderson to Richard Coytmore, Sept. 12, 1759, Paul Demere to WHL, Jan. 26, Sept. 13, Oct. 1, 1759, LPCD; *SCG*, Sept. 29–Oct. 6, 1759; Wood, "I Have Now Made a Path," 49.

44. SCCJ, 1757–1762, 2:116 (Aug. 14, 1759); WHL to Francis Fauquier, Aug. 15, 1759, LPLB, 1:387; Francis Fauquier to WHL, Sept. 5 and 14, 1759, to Richard Smith, Sept. 14, 1759, to WHL, Oct. 21, 1759, LPCD; *EJC*, 6:144–45 (Sept. 3, 1759).

45. John Stuart to WHL, Sept. 26, 1759, LPCD.

46. Richard Coytmore to WHL, Sept. 26, 1759, Amherst Papers, WO 34/35, fol. 129; *SCG*, Sept. 29–Oct. 6, 1759.

47. Colonels John Chevillette, Richard Richardson, and George Gabriel Powell. *SCG*, Sept. 29–Oct. 6, 1759; WHL correspondence, LPLB, 1:420, 426, 426–27, 427, 428–

30, 430, 431–32, 432–33; WHL to Francis Fauquier, ibid., 1:421–23; *JCHA, 1757–1761*, 430, 431–34 (Oct. 1, 5, 1759); SCCJ, 1757–1762, 2:122–23, 124–25 (Oct. 1, 4, 1759).

48. Paul Demere to WHL, Oct. 1, 1759, LPCD.

49. *SCG*, Oct. 27–Nov. 1, 1759; John Stuart to WHL, Oct. 6, 13, 1759; Richard Coytmore to WHL, Oct. 7, 1759, LPCD.

50. Simpson, *South Carolina Diary*, 143–44 (Oct. 12, 1759); SCCJ, 1757–1762, 2:126 (Oct. 6, 1759); WHL to Richard Richardson, Oct. 6, 1759, LPLB, 1:433–34; McMaster, *Soldiers and Uniforms*, 20–21. Lyttelton asked the assembly to provide for 1,500 men. *JCHA, 1757–1761*, 434–35 (Oct. 6, 1759); *SCG*, Oct. 6–13, 1759.

51. Oliphant, *Peace and War*, 44, 69–71; Declaration of War against the Cherokees [two versions, Oct. 1759], South Carolina Assembly to WHL, Oct. 12, 1759, LPCD; SCCJ, 1757–1762, 2:128 (Oct. 11, 1759); WHL to the Board of Trade, Oct. 16, 1759, BPRO-SC, 28:245; *JCHA, 1757–1761*, 444–49 (Oct. 11–13, 1759).

52. John Savage to WHL, Nov. 13, 1759 with copy of a subscription list for financing an expedition against the Cherokees, Nov. 1759, LPCD.

53. *Maryland Gazette*, Nov. 22, 1759; Edmond Atkin to WHL, Oct. 2, 1759, to Creek Headmen, Sept. 28–29, LPCD; *SCG*, Extraordinary, Oct. 13–17, 1759; *SCG*, Oct. 17–20, 1759.

54. Henry Ellis to WHL, Oct. 11, 16, 1759, LPCD; Council Minutes, *CRG*, 8:166–67, 168–70 (Oct. 10, 11, 1759); *SCG*, Oct. 27–Nov. 1, 1759. In 1758 Ellis and Lyttelton halted land encroachment on the Altamaha: "Minutes of my proceedings pursuant to a Commission and Instructions," SCCJ, 1757–1762, 2:66–67 (Mar. 19, 1759).

55. Edmond Atkin to John Cleland, Dec. 23, 1759, to WHL, Nov. 30, 1759, LPCD; Treaty of Waulyhatchy, July 18, 1759, Amherst Papers, WO 34/40, fols. 85–87. For Atkin's expenses, see Amherst Papers, WO 34/47, fol. 209.

56. *SCG*, Extraordinary, Oct. 13–17, 1759; *SCG*, Oct. 17–20, 1759; WHL, "A List of the Cherokees in Charles Town," Oct. 19, LPCD; SCCJ, 1757–1762, 2:132–33 (Oct. 18, 19, 1759).

57. SCCJ, 1757–1762, 2:134 (Oct. 19, 1759); Adair, *History of the American Indians*, 263. The *Gazette* dismissed Cherokee grievances, prefacing them with words like "alleged" and "pretended." *SCG*, Oct. 27–Nov. 1, 1759; Daniel Pepper to WHL, May 7, 1757, *DRIA*, 2:371; Oliphant, *Peace and War*, 84–87.

58. Hatley, *Dividing Paths*, 148–52.

59. SCCJ, 1757–1762, 2:134 (Oct. 19, 1759); Cherokee Headmen to WHL, Oct. 20, 1758, LPCD. Apparently under duress, Oconostota named some of the accused. "Memorandum of the Offenders . . . 21 Oct. 1759," ibid.

60. The governor pointed out that Tistoe (Nov. 16, 1758) and Attakullakulla (Apr. 18, 1758) had promised "in the name of the Nation" to resolve their differences with Virginia. Each had also received goods in Charles Town. SCCJ, 1757–1762, 2:135–36, 136–37 (Oct. 20, 21, 1759); "21 Oct 1759 List of Cherokee Murderers," "Extracts of Letters &ca. to William Henry Lyttelton, relative to the Murders & Outrages committed by the Cherokees, 1759," LPCD.

61. SCCJ, 1757–1762, 2:137–39 (Oct. 22, 1759); Milligen-Johnston, *Short Description*, 79–80; *SCG*, Oct. 27–Nov. 1, 1759. See also WHL to Ellis, to the Board of Trade, to Dobbs,

to Fauquier, and to Amherst, LPLB, 2:15-18, 18-20, 20-22, 22-25, 25-27; William Bull to James Grant, May 15, 1760, Grant Papers, DLAR reel 31, frame 27.

62. Adair, *History of the American Indians*, 265. Historians have written of "a collision of military cultures" to describe the origins of Indian wars. Lee, "Peace Chiefs and Blood Revenge," 738-40.

63. Lyttelton had his supporters. See Eliza Lucas Pinckney to Mr. Morly, Nov. 3, 1759, to [Mrs. Onslow], Pinckney, *Letterbook*, 125, 128; Sir James Wright to WHL, Dec. 29, 1759, LPCD; *SCG*, Nov. 1-3, 1759.

64. Adair, *History of the American Indians*, 266; *SCG*, Oct. 27-Nov. 1, Nov. 1-3, 1759; Calmes, "Lyttelton Expedition," 14-17; G[eorge] G[abriel] Powell to WHL, Oct. 20, 29, 1759, John Chevillette to WHL, Oct. 27, 1759, LPCD; Fabel, *Colonial Challenges*, 49-54. On the volunteer cavalry unit, see Christopher Gadsden et al. to WHL, Oct. 31, 1759, LPCD. For a list of staff officers, see *SCG*, Oct. 27-Nov. 1, 1759.

65. Peter Timothy to WHL, Nov. 3, 1759, LPCD; SCCJ, 1757-1762, 2:139-40 (Oct. 30, 1759); Alexander Garden to Philip Bearcroft, Oct. 31, 1759, Selected Pages Relating to South Carolina, SPG Papers, Series B, Vol. 4, Pt. II:284.

66. "Names of the Indian Desarters from Congarees, Novr.," LPCD; *SCG*, Extraordinary, Oct. 13-17, 1759; *SCG*, Supplement, Nov. 10-17, 1759.

67. SCCJ, 1757-1762, 2:141-42 (Nov. 10, 1759); *SCG*, Supplement, Nov. 17-24, 1759; Hewatt, *Historical Account*, 2:217-18; Mercantini, *Who Shall Rule*, 145.

68. John Chevillette to WHL, Oct. 27, 1759, LPCD; *SCG*, Supplement, Nov. 17-24, 1759; *SCG*, Dec. 1-8, 1759.

69. Greene, *Historic Resource Study*, 4-5. Dudgeon described the fort: "of the Star kind with four angles, the Exterior side Ninety feet, a simple stockade without a Ditch Erected." Inside the palisade, a firing step gave marksmen a better view. New sheds served as barracks. There was a powder magazine inside. Ibid., 25; Richard Dudgeon to Jeffery Amherst, Aug. 16, 1760, CO 5/59, fol. 293, in CDFA, reel 222; *SCG*, Dec. 1-8, 1759.

70. *SCG*, Dec. 1-8, 1759; Ulrich Tobler to WHL, Nov. 7, 1759, LPCD. On the Savannah River Chickasaws, see James Parris to David Douglass, Oct. 21, 1759, Council Minutes, Oct. 30, *CRG*, 8:172-73, 175; Cashin, *Guardians of the Valley*.

71. Lieutenant John Maine and ten men from the Royal Train of Artillery joined the army. *SCG*, Dec. 1-8, Dec. 22-29, 1759, Jan. 8-12, 1760; "Extracts from Letters rec'd from the Speaker of the House of Assembly in So. Carolina," BPRO-SC, 28:267 (Dec. 14, 1759); McMaster, *Soldiers and Uniforms*, 22; Adair, *History of the American Indians*, 267; Richard Coytmore to WHL, Nov. 14, 1759, LPCD.

72. *SCG*, Dec. 22-29, 1759.

73. WHL to the Board of Trade, Dec. 10, 1759, BPRO-SC, 28:280-81; *SCG*, Nov. 17-24, Dec. 15-22, 1759, Jan. 8-12, 1760; Francis Fauquier to the Board of Trade, Dec. 17, 1759, *PFF*, 1:281-83; Hugh Waddell to WHL, Nov. 21, Dec. 20, 1759, Jan. 1, 1760, LPCD; Maass, *French and Indian War in North Carolina*, 90-92.

74. Paul Demere to WHL, Nov. 3, 1759, LPCD; Alden, *John Stuart*, 156-75; Ivers, *Colonial Forts*, 60.

75. John Stuart to WHL, Oct. 25, Nov. 15, 22, 1759, LPCD.

76. Paul Demere to WHL, Nov. 2, Dec. 12, 1759, Attakullakulla to WHL, Nov. 2, 1759, John Stuart to WHL, Dec. 3, 7, 1759, LPCD.

77. Hewatt, *Historical Account*, 2:219.

78. *SCG*, Jan. 8–12, 1760; First Conference with Attakullakulla . . . , Dec. 18, 1759, Second Conference with Attakullakulla . . . , Dec. 19, 1759, LPCD; Lee, "Peace Chiefs and Blood Revenge," 717.

79. *SCG*, Jan. 8–12, 1760.

80. Ibid.

81. Board of Trade to WHL, Nov. 14, 1759, the Earl of Halifax to WHL, Nov. 15, 1759, LPCD.

82. *SCG*, Jan. 8–12, 1760.

83. WHL to Jeffery Amherst, Dec. 27, 1759, Amherst Papers, WO 34/35, fol. 136.

84. "Treaty of Peace and Friendship," *SCG*, Extraordinary, Jan. 5–8, 1760; *SCG*, Jan. 8–12, 1760; Kelly, "Oconostota," 224–25; Milligen-Johnston, *Short Description*, 85–86.

85. *SCG*, Dec. 22–29, 1759, Jan. 12–19, 1760; WHL to His Majesty's Council, Dec. 29, 1759, SCCJ, 1757–1762, 2:152–54, 155–56 (Jan. 7, 1760).

86. *SCG*, Dec. 29, 1759–Jan. 5, 1760; William Fyffe to John Fyffe, Feb. 1, 1761, Fyffe Collection.

CHAPTER FIVE

1. When the infected troops returned, the disease was already in the city. *SCG*, Jan. 8–12, 1760; SCCJ, 1757–1762, 2:152 (Jan. 7, 1760); WHL to Richard Coytmore, Jan. 18, 1760, LPLB, 2:30.

2. Alexander Garden to John Ellis, Mar. 13, 1760, *CLON*, 1:473.

3. *SCG*, Jan. 8–12, 1760; Ramsay, *History of South Carolina*, 42–43; Alexander Garden to John Ellis, Mar. 13, 1760, *CLON*, 1:473; WHL to the Board of Trade, Jan. 21, 1760, *BPRO-SC*, 28:295.

4. McCandless, *Slavery, Disease, and Suffering*; "Whether or not the Governor merited such a reception," Milligen continued, "I leave to the Reader's Judgment." Milligen-Johnston, *Short Description*, 85.

5. Krebsbach, "Great Charlestown Smallpox Epidemic," 30; McCandless, *Slavery, Disease, and Suffering*.

6. Smallpox hit South Carolina in 1698, 1700, 1711–12, 1717–18, and 1732. The colony had a serious outbreak in 1738. Duffy, *Epidemics in Colonial America*, 23–34, 74–77, 82–83.

7. Henry Bouquet to Thomas Stanwix, June 23, 1757, *Papers of Henry Bouquet*, 1:121; *SCG*, June 23, 1757; Greene, "South Carolina Quartering Dispute."

8. WHL to John Stewart [Stuart], July 11, 1758, LPLB, 1:152–53; *SCG*, Nov. 10–17, 1758.

9. *SCG*, Mar. 15–22, 1760.

10. *SCG*, Jan. 12–19, Jan. 26–Feb. 2, Feb. 2–9, 1760; Ramsay, *History of South Carolina*, 43.

11. *SCG*, Dec. 8–15, 1759; Catawba Headmen to WHL, [Oct. 1759], Samuel Wyly to WHL, Nov. 5, 1759, LPCD; William Richardson to J[ohn] F[orfitt], May 6, 1760, *Letters from the Rev. Samuel Davies*, 23.

12. Adair, *History of the American Indians*, 246; Richard Richardson to WHL, Feb. 26, 1760, LPCD; *SCG*, Apr. 26–May 3, 1760; *JCHA, 1757–1761*, 737 (July 19, 1760).

13. Merrell, *Indians' New World*, 203–4.

14. *SCG*, Jan. 12–19, 1760; Richard Coytmore to WHL, Dec. 6, 1759, Jan. 7, 1760, LPCD.

15. *SCG*, Apr. 12–19, 1760.

16. Kelton, "Avoiding the Smallpox Spirits," 60–61; Richard Coytmore to WHL, Jan. 7, 1760, LPCD; *Pennsylvania Gazette*, Sept. 4, 1760.

17. Adair, *History of the American Indians*, 152, 252–53; William Fyffe to John Fyffe, Feb. 1, 1761, Fyffe Collection; Kelton, "Avoiding the Smallpox Spirits," 62.

18. Adair, *History of the American Indians*, 90, 253; White Outerbridge to WHL, May 17, 1759, LPCD.

19. "Plain Instruction for Inoculation in the Small-pox," *SCG*, Apr. 19–26, 1760; McCandless, *Slavery, Disease, and Suffering*, 151–67, 213–19.

20. Eliza Lucas Pinckney to [Mrs. Evance], Mar. 15, 1760, *Letterbook*, 148; *SCG*, Feb. 23–Mar. 1, Mar. 15–22, Apr. 19–26, 1760; Alexander Garden to John Ellis, Mar. 13, 1760, Smith, *CLON*, 1:473; McCandless, *Slavery, Disease, and Suffering*, 204–20.

21. Ramsay, *History of South Carolina*, 44; *Boston Gazette*, Apr. 21, 1760; Edgar, *Biographical Directory*, 2:627.

22. Fraser, *Charleston!*, 93–94; Eliza Lucas Pinckney to [Mrs. Evance], Mar. 15, 1760, *Letterbook*, 148; McCandless, *Slavery, Disease, and Suffering*, 168–87.

23. Hutson, "A Faithful Ambassador," 82, 83 (Feb. 10, 14, 1760).

24. Eliza Lucas Pinckey to [Mrs. Evance], Mar. 15, 1760, *Letterbook*, 147–48; *SCG*, Mar. 15–22, Apr. 12–19, Nov. 29–Dec. 6, 1760; Robert Raper to John Colleton, May 22, 1760, Robert Raper Letterbook. For poetry, see *SCG*, Apr. 7–12, Apr. 19–26, 1760. For mourning apparel and jewelry, see ads by merchant John Scott and silversmith John Paul Grimke, *SCG*, Mar. 15–22, Aug. 2–9, 1760.

25. Krebsbach, "Great Charlestown Smallpox Epidemic," 35. For the death toll by ethnicity and race, see *SCG*, Mar. 15–22, Apr. 12–19, 1760.

26. *SCG*, Mar. 29–Apr. 2, 1760.

27. Brown, "Spiritual Terror and Sacred Authority."

28. Alexander Garden to John Ellis, Apr. 12, 1760, *CLON*, 1:483.

29. *SCG*, Apr. 2–7, 1760.

30. *SCG*, Feb. 2–9, 1760; *JCHA, 1757–1761*, 453 (Feb. 7, 1760); Morgan, "Black Life in Charleston," 217–18; Tobler, "John Tobler's Descriptions," 146.

31. Alexander Garden to John Ellis, Mar. 13, June 1, July 16, 1760, *CLON*, 1:474, 490, 492, 495.

32. Simpson, *South Carolina Diary*, 151 (Feb. 23, 1760).

33. *SCG*, Mar. 15–22, 1760; *Boston Gazette*, Apr. 21, 1760; Simpson, *South Carolina Diary*, 149–50, 152–53 (Feb. 12, Mar. 27, 1760).

34. Milling, *Exile without an End*; Hodson, *Acadian Diaspora*.

35. *JCHA, 1757–1761*, 453, 460, 460n, 462–64 (Feb. 7, 9, 12, 1760); South Carolina Assembly to WHL, Feb. 12, 1760, LPCD.

36. *JCHA*, 1757–1761, 583, 673–74, 712–13 (May 27, June 27, July 17, 1760); McCandless, *Slavery, Disease, and Suffering*, 55–56.

37. *JCHA*, 1757–1761, 583, 673–74, 693, 712–13 (May 27, June 27, July 15, 17, 1760).

38. On May 30, legislation went into effect banning inoculations, requiring homeowners to post signs where sick residents lived, and creating a board of "smallpox commissioners" to keep tabs on the epidemic. On August 9, it remained in only three homes. Krebsbach, "Great Charlestown Smallpox Epidemic," 36; *JCHA*, 1757–1761, 497–98, 504, 507, 511, 546, 561–63, 589–90 (Apr. 16, 18, 19, 23, May 6, 13–15, 28, 30, 1760); *SCG*, Aug. 2–9, 1760.

39. Simpson, *South Carolina Diary*, 150 (Feb. 12, 1760).

40. WHL to the Board of Trade, Feb. 22, 1760, *BPRO-SC*, 28:314. Neither the Board of Trade nor the secretary of state ever commented on Cherokee affairs.

41. *BPRO-SC*, 28:268–79, 29:51–60, 93–94, 130–81.

42. SCCJ, 1757–1762, 2:169, 183 (Feb. 14, Mar. 27, 1760); WHL to the Board of Trade, Feb. 22, 1760, *BPRO-SC*, 28:317; Alexander Garden to John Ellis, Mar. 21, 1760, *CLON*, 1:479.

43. Alexander Garden to John Ellis, Mar. 13, 21, 1760, *CLON*, 1:473, 479; *SCG*, Apr. 2–7, 1760; SCCJ, 1757–1762, 3:103–4 (Apr. 5, 1760).

CHAPTER SIX

1. Timberlake, *Memoirs*, 17; Bartram, *Travels*, 366–69; Gerald F. Schroedl, "Overhill Cherokee Architecture and Village Organization," in Rogers and Duncan, *Culture, Crisis, and Conflict*, 69–70; Boulware, *Deconstructing the Cherokee Nation*, 14–15.

2. John Stuart to Archibald Montgomery, May 2, 1760, Grant Papers, DLAR reel 31, frames 18–19.

3. Richard Coytmore to WHL, Jan. 7, 1760, LPCD.

4. Ibid.

5. Richard Coytmore, Alexander Miln, and John Bell, A copy of a journal kept at Fort Prince George, Jan. 13–Feb. 7, 1760 [hereafter FPG Journal] (Jan. 13), LPCD.

6. Ibid. The traders were Cornelius Dougherty of Hiwassee, James Baldridge of Settico, and Henry Lucas.

7. *SCG*, Feb. 2–9, 1760; FPG Journal (Jan. 19), LPCD. Minutes earlier, traders Isaac Atwood and Thomas Hayley arrived from Hiwassee. Setticos and Great Tellicos had chased them.

8. *SCG*, Feb. 2–9, 1760; FPG Journal (Jan. 19), LPCD.

9. FPG Journal (Jan 19), LPCD.

10. Isaac Atwood Affidavit, Jan. 31, 1760, FPG Journal (Jan. 19–21), LPCD.

11. *SCG*, Feb. 2–9, 1760; Richard Coytmore to WHL, Jan. 23, 1760, *PFF*, 1:316.

12. Atwood continued south to Long Canes settlement. Isaac Atwood Affidavit, Jan. 31, 1760, LPCD.

13. *SCG*, Feb. 2–9, 1760; Isaac Atwood Affidavit, Jan. 31, 1760, Paul Demere to WHL, Jan. 26, 1760, Affidavit of John Downing, James Butler, and Barnet Hues [Hughes], Jan. 29, 1760, FPG Journal (Jan. 28, Feb. 4, 14), LPCD.

14. Bartram, *Travels*, 485; Walker, "Narrative of a Kentucky Adventure," 150–51; William Fyffe to John Fyffe, Feb. 1, 1761, Fyffe Collection.

15. Brice Martin to Lyman Draper, May 18, 1854, Lyman C. Draper Manuscripts, 14DD16, 2; "Narrative of William Martin," 1782, ibid., 3XX44, 7–9.

16. Paul Demere to WHL, Jan. 26, 1760, LPCD.

17. Ibid.

18. Ibid.

19. Ibid.; *JCHA, 1757–1761*, xvii.

20. Cooper and McCord, *Statutes*, 3:332, 523, 768; Corkran, *Cherokee Frontier*, 77–78, 140. Three years earlier, "Benn's Negro" had witnessed a confrontation between the trader and some Nottely warriors. The slave had the opportunity to escape but instead reunited with his master. *DRIA*, 2:106–7, 109–12, 123.

21. FPG Journal (Feb. 4), LPCD.

22. Paul Demere to WHL, Jan. 26, 1760, LPCD.

23. FPG Journal (Feb. 4), LPCD.

24. Ibid.; Kelly, "Oconostota," 227.

25. WHL to Richard Coytmore, Jan. 18, 1760, LPLB, 2:29–30; John Stuart to WHL, Jan. 29, 1760, FPG Journal (Feb. 4), LPCD.

26. The Warrior of Stecoe, Ousanaletah of Joree, Skalitoskee, Tony of Chota, and Chisquatalone died. FPG Journal (Jan. 25–28), Richard Coytmore to WHL, Feb. 7, 1760, LPCD.

27. FPG Journal (Jan. 23, 31, Feb. 4), Richard Coytmore to WHL, Feb. 7, 1760, LPCD.

28. Ibid.; South Carolina Assembly to WHL, Feb. 13, 1760, LPCD; *JCHA, 1757–1761*, 462 (Feb. 10, 1760).

29. WHL to Paul Demere, Feb. 14, 1760, LPLB, 2:19–20; *SCG*, Jan. 8–12, Feb. 2–9, Feb. 9–16, 1760; Krebsbach, "Great Charlestown Smallpox Epidemic," 30–37. Abram may have contracted the virus at Fort Prince George.

30. FPG Journal (Feb. 14), LPCD.

31. Ibid., (Feb. 16).

32. Ibid.

33. Ibid.; Fort Prince George muster roll, Mar. 15, 1761, Grant Papers, DLAR reel 32, frame 444; Williams, *Memoir*, 61–63.

34. FPG Journal (Feb. 14), LPCD.

35. *SCG*, Feb. 28–Mar. 1, 1760.

36. Alexander Garden to John Ellis, May 26, 1760, *CLON*, 1:489.

37. Milligen-Johnston, *Short Description*, 86.

38. Adair, *History of the American Indians*, 267; William De Brahm to WHL, Aug. 25, 1756, LPCD.

39. Milligen-Johnston, *Short Description*, 86.

40. Williams, *Memoir*, 16, 63; Alexander Miln to WHL, Feb. 28, 1760, LPCD.

CHAPTER SEVEN

1. Snyder, "Captives of the Dark and Bloody Ground," 112–59; Antoine Bonnefoy, "Journal of Antoine Bonnefoy's Captivity among the Cherokee Indians, 1741–1742," in Mereness, *Travels in the American Colonies*, 246; Marrant, *Narrative*; Richter, *Ordeal of the Longhouse*, 35–38, 48, 60.

2. Adair, *History of the American Indians*, 382–85; De Brahm, *Report*, 109.

3. Adair, *History of the American Indians*, 186, 188, 383–85, 390; Snyder, "Captives of the Dark and Bloody Ground," 102–11; Lee, "Peace Chiefs and Blood Revenge," 730, 732, 741; "A True Relation of the Unheard-of Sufferings of David Menzies," *Royal Magazine*, July 1761, 27–29; De Brahm, *Report*, 108.

4. *SCG*, Feb. 2–9, Feb. 9–16, 1760; Alexander Miln and John Bell to WHL, journal at Fort Prince George, Feb. 8–24, 1760 [hereafter FPG Journal] (Feb. 12), LPCD. These numbers are derived from reports in the *South Carolina Gazette*, LPCD, Council Journals, Mante, *History of the Late War*, 284, and Meriwether, *Expansion of South Carolina*, 222–25.

5. Simpson, *South Carolina Diary*, 149–50 (Feb. 6, 12, 1760); William Richardson to John Forfitt, May 6, 1760, *Letters from the Rev. Samuel Davies*, 21; Meriwether, *Expansion of South Carolina*, 222–25.

6. Snyder, "Captives of the Dark and Bloody Ground," 98–99; Lee, "Peace Chiefs and Blood Revenge," 722.

7. Ephraim Biggs to William Pitt, Apr. 2, 1759, Chatham Papers, PRO 30/8/96, fol. 204.

8. James Francis, Thomas Bell, Robert Gouedy, and Samuel Benn to WHL, Feb. 6, 1760, LPCD; *SCG*, Feb. 2–9, Feb. 16–23, 1760; "Memoirs of Mrs. Ann Mathews," in Burns, *Life of Anne Calhoun Mathews*, 5–6, 26–30.

9. Edmonds, *Making of McCormick County*, 23–27.

10. De Vorsey, *Indian Boundary*, 115–16; "Aunt Ann—How She Treated Her Bashful Lover," *Abbeville Press and Banner*, May 3, 1876, in Burns, *Life of Anne Calhoun Mathews*, 12–13.

11. Burns, *Life of Anne Calhoun Mathews*, 23–24; Hatley, *Dividing Paths*, 86, 89, 91; Calhoun, "Account"; Edmonds, *Making of McCormick County*, 12–13.

12. William Richardson, "An Account of My Proceedings," 49–50 (Jan. 30, 1759); WHL to the Board of Trade, Sept. 1, 1759, *BPRO-SC*, 28:211; *SCG*, Jan. 8–12, 1760.

13. The "Indian Massacre Site" lays nearly hidden from view. A historical marker and an iron bridge lie in the piney woods off an old dirt road three miles from the tiny hamlet of Troy, South Carolina. There one can find the mass grave with the remains of twenty-three settlers. Calhoun, "Account," 441; Conaway, "Ghosthunting," http://www.youtube.com/watch?v=aYsRHoAI9vU.

14. *SCG*, Apr. 12–19, May 17–24, 1760; Burns, "Memoirs of Mrs. Ann Matthews," 6, 28n–29n, 30n–31n; Calhoun, "Journal of William Calhoun," 194–95; One hundred settlers had already reached safety: Isaac Tobler Affidavit, Jan. 31, 1759, LPCD; *SCG*, Feb. 2–9, 1760.

15. Edmond Atkin to WHL, Feb. 16, 1760, LPCD.

16. White Outerbridge to WHL, Feb. 2, 1760, FPG Journal (Feb. 14), LPCD; *SCG*, Feb. 2–9, Feb. 16–23, 1760; Edmonds, *Making of McCormick County*, 17–19.

17. *SCG*, Mar. 1–8, Mar. 8–15, Mar. 15–22, 1760. Mary Calhoun never returned home. Ann lived two and a half years with the Cherokees. Burns, *Life of Anne Calhoun Mathews*, 30–31; *SCG*, May 17–24, 1760; Meriwether, *Expansion of South Carolina*, 224.

18. *SCG*, Feb. 9–16, 1760; Ivers, *Colonial Forts*, 74.

19. Henry Ellis to WHL, Mar. 5, 1760, Edmond Atkin to WHL, Mar. 5, 1760; White Outerbridge to WHL, Feb. 6, 1760, LPCD.

20. *SCG*, Feb. 9–16, 1760; FPG Journal (Feb. 14), LPCD. One of the slaves escaped. *SCG*, Mar. 8–15, 1760. On Williamson, see Bass, *Ninety Six*, 38.

21. James Francis, Thomas Bell, Robert Gouedy, and Samuel Benn to WHL, Feb. 6, 1760, LPCD; *SCG*, Feb. 2–9, 1760; Meriwether, *Expansion of South Carolina*, 127.

22. *SCG*, Feb. 2–9, 1760; White Outerbridge to WHL, Feb. 6, 1760, James Francis, Thomas Bell, Robert Gouedy, and Samuel Benn to WHL, Feb. 6, 1760, John Pearson to WHL, Feb. 8, 1760, LPCD; Ivers, *Colonial Forts*, 74; Meriwether, *Expansion of South Carolina*, 130, 133.

23. Edward Musgrove and Samuel Aubrey to WHL, Feb. 6, 1760, LPCD.

24. *SCG*, Feb. 2–9, Mar. 15–22, 1760.

25. Edward Musgrove and Samuel Aubrey to WHL, Feb. 6, 1760, LPCD; Howe, *Scotch-Irish*, 18.

26. John Pearson to WHL, Feb. 8, 1760, LPCD; Ivers, *Colonial Forts*, 66; Meriwether, *Expansion of South Carolina*, 156.

27. Henry Gallman to WHL, Feb. 12, 1760, LPCD.

28. Peter Crim to WHL, Feb. 11, 1760, ibid.

29. "Bethabara Diary, 1760," Fries, *Records of the Moravians*, 1:229.

30. A black slave was among the Fort Dobbs casualties. Hugh Waddell to Arthur Dobbs, Feb. 29, 1760, *CSR-NC*, 6:229–30; *SCG*, Apr. 7–12, 1760.

31. John Stuart to Allan Stuart, May 15, 1760, Grant Papers, DLAR reel 31, frame 23.

32. White Outerbridge to WHL, Feb. 6, 1760, Henry Ellis to WHL, Feb. 4, 1760, John Williams and John Fitch to Mssrs. Rae, Barnard, Douglass and Maccartan [McCartan], Feb. 6, 1760, Henry Harden to David Douglass, Feb. 12, 1760, LPCD.

33. Assembly minutes, *CRG*, 8:228, 248 (Feb. 3, 9, 1760); Henry Ellis to WHL, Feb. 4, 1760, LPCD; *SCG*, Feb. 9–16, 1760; Henry Ellis to William Pitt, Feb. 16, Mar. 5, 1760, *Correspondence of William Pitt*, 1:255–66, 259–60. Ellis offended Lyttelton. Cashin, *Henry Ellis*, 139–40.

34. Henry Ellis to WHL, Feb. 4, 1760, Edmond Atkin to WHL, Mar. 5, 1760, John Pearson to WHL, Mar. 5, 1760, Lachlan McGillivray et al. to Mssrs. Rae, Barnard, Douglass and Maccartan [McCartan], Feb. 6, 1760, Lachlan Shaw to WHL, Feb. 21, 1760, LPCD; *SCG*, Feb. 9–16, Mar. 15–22, 1760.

35. Snyder, "Captives of the Dark and Bloody Ground," 131; Wood, *Black Majority*, 129; Henry Ellis to William Pitt, Feb. 16, 1760, *Correspondence of William Pitt*, 1:255; Henry Ellis to the Board of Trade, Feb. 15, 1760, *CRG*, 28, pt. 1:227.

36. Lachlan Shaw to WHL, Feb. 21, 1760, LPCD; *SCG*, Mar. 15–22, 1760.

37. Henry Ellis to WHL, Feb. 4, 1760, LPCD; Henry Ellis to the Board of Trade, Feb. 15, 1760, *CRG*, 28, pt. 1:227–28.

38. Edmond Atkin to WHL, Feb. 13, Mar. 5, 1760, Edmond Atkin to the Creeks, Feb. 5, 1760, Henry Ellis to WHL, Feb. 4, 1760, LPCD.

39. Henry Ellis to WHL, Feb. 16, 27, 1760, LPCD; *Pennsylvania Gazette*, Apr. 3, 1760; *SCG*, Feb. 16–23, Feb. 23–Mar. 2, Mar. 15–22, 1760.

40. Lachlan Shaw to WHL, Mar. 6, 1760, Edmond Atkin to WHL, Feb. 13, 1760, LPCD; Henry Ellis to the Board of Trade, Feb. 15, 1760, *CRG*, 28, pt. 1:226.

41. In late February, Cherokees brought fifty prisoners to Conasatchee, Estatoe, Nequassee, Watauga, Settico, and Keowee, and took some to French Louisiana. *SCG*, Apr. 12–19, 1760.

42. *London Magazine*, Apr. 1760, 219–20; James Francis to WHL, Mar. 6, 1760, *DRIA*, 2:504; *SCG*, Mar. 1–8, Mar. 8–15, 1760. Gouedy rushed to Fort Prince George. Francis begged Lyttelton for reinforcements. John Chevillette to WHL, Mar. 3, 1760, LPCD.

43. Very few casualties, and sometimes the first letting of blood, sufficed to end battles. Some battles "only served to uphold their collective prestige." Lee, "Peace Chiefs and Blood Revenge," 727.

44. James Francis to WHL, Mar. 6, 1760, *DRIA*, 2:504; John Chevillette to WHL, Mar. 3, 1760, LPCD; *SCG*, Mar. 8–15, 1760; Abram, "Souls in the Treetops," 29, 32–35, 40; Adair, *History of the American Indians*, 390.

45. *SCG*, Mar. 8–15, 1760; Lee, "Peace Chiefs and Blood Revenge," 729–30; Hatley, *Dividing Paths*, 161–62.

46. *SCG*, Mar. 15–22, 1760.

47. *SCG*, Mar. 8–15, 1760; Ivers, *Colonial Forts*, 66, 74; John Grinnan to WHL, Mar. 6, 1760, LPCD; Lee, "Peace Chiefs and Blood Revenge," 724–27.

48. *SCG*, Mar. 15–22, 1760.

49. On Mar. 30, Cherokees attacked the Virginia frontier including William Bryan's trading post near present-day Salem. Robert Stewart to George Washington, Apr. 14, 1760, *PGW*, 6:412–14.

50. *SCG*, Mar. 8–15, Mar. 15–22, 1760; Henry Ellis to William Pitt, Mar. 5, Apr. 16, 1760, *Correspondence of William Pitt*, 1:259, 277; Henry Ellis to the Board of Trade, Apr. 16, 1760, *CRG*, 28, pt. 1:246; Henry Ellis to WHL, Mar. 7 and 13, 1760, LPCD; *Pennsylvania Gazette*, Apr. 3, 1760; Cashin, *Henry Ellis*, 139–40.

51. Abraham Maury to Francis Fauquier, Mar. 28, 1760, *PFF*, 1:339; Maass, "All This Poor Province Could Do," 71; "Part II: Bethabara and Bethania, 1760, Summary from Wachovia Church Book," and "Bethabara Diary, 1760," Fries, *Records of the Moravians*, 1:227–29, 229–31; *SCG*, Apr. 7–12, 1760.

52. White Outerbridge to WHL, Feb. 6, 1760, LPCD; Meriwether, *Expansion of South Carolina*, 234–35.

53. Edmond Atkin to WHL, Feb. 1, 5, 1760, White Outerbridge to WHL, Feb. 6, 1760, LPCD; *SCG*, Feb. 23–Mar. 1, Mar. 15–22, 1760; Simpson, *South Carolina Diary*, 150, 153 (Feb. 13, Mar. 29, 30, 1760); Bernheim, *History of the German Settlements*, 147.

54. Christopher Rowe to WHL, Feb. 8, 1760, Benjamin Waring to WHL, Feb. 15, 1760, George Pawley to WHL, Feb. 27, 1760, LPCD.

55. Robert Raper to unknown, Mar. 19, 1760, to John Colleton, Mar. 23, 1760, Robert Raper Letterbook; Milligen-Johnston, *Short Description*, 25; Alexander Garden to John Ellis, June 1, 1760, *CLON*, 1:493; Ivers, *Colonial Forts*, 37.

56. Milligen-Johnston, *Short Description*, 85; Edmond Atkin to WHL, Feb. 16, 1760, LPCD.

57. Simpson, *South Carolina Diary*, 150–51, 154 (Feb. 13, 17, 23, Apr. 15, 1760).

58. *SCG*, Feb. 9–16, Feb. 16–23, Mar. 1–8, Mar. 8–15, 1760; Silver, *Our Savage Neighbors*, xix, 80–82, 94–99, 115, 225–26.

59. White Outerbridge to WHL, Feb. 15, 1760, LPCD.

60. Alexander Garden to John Ellis, Mar. 21, 1760, *CLON*, 1:479; Milligen-Johnston, *Short Description*, 85.

61. Alexander Garden to John Ellis, Mar. 21, Apr. 12, 1760, *CLON*, 1:480, 484–85.

62. Alexander Garden to John Ellis, Apr. 12, 1760, *CLON*, 484.

CHAPTER EIGHT

1. John Stuart to Archibald Montgomery, May 2, 1760, Grant Papers, DLAR, reel 31, frames 18–19; Perdue, *Cherokee Women*, 49; Lee, "Peace Chiefs and Blood Revenge," 735; [James] M[ark] Prevost to Thomas Gage, May 20, 1764, GPAS 15.

2. Timberlake, *Memoirs*, 35; Lee, "Peace Chiefs and Blood Revenge," 735, 735n.

3. *SCG*, Apr. 26–May 3, 1760; John Stuart to Archibald Montgomery, May 2, 1760, to Allan Stuart, May 15, 1760, Grant Papers, DLAR reel 31, frames 18–19, 22; Robert Raper to John Beswicke, Mar. 27, 1760, Robert Raper Letterbook.

4. *SCG*, May 3–10, 1760.

5. James Glen to [Jeffery Amherst], Apr. 28, 1760, Amherst Papers, WO 34/47, fol. 11r-v; Jeffery Amherst to James Glen, May 31, 1760, Amherst Papers, WO 34/48, fol. 25.

6. WHL to Jeffery Amherst, Feb. 2, 9, 1760, Amherst Papers, WO 34/35, fols. 148, 155; Jeffery Amherst to Archibald Montgomery, Feb. 24, Mar. 6, to James Grant, Mar. 3, 1760, Amherst Papers, WO 34/48, fols. 1, 2, 3, 4–6; Jeffery Amherst to William Pitt, Mar. 8, 1760, *Correspondence of William Pitt*, 1:260; McCulloch, *Sons of the Mountains*, 2:51–52.

7. Archibald Montgomery to Jeffery Amherst, May 24, 1760, Amherst Papers, WO 34/47, fol. 12v.

8. Charles Pinckney to the Board of Trade, Dec. 2, 1756, *BPRO-SC*, 27:193; Philopatrios, *Observations*, 7–13, 19; Henry Laurens, *A Letter Signed Philolethes*, [Mar. 2, 1763], *PHL*, 3:333.

9. *SCG*, Apr. 2–7, 1760; Archibald Montgomery to Jeffery Amherst, Apr. 12, 22, May 24, 1760, Amherst Papers, WO 34/47, fols. 4–5, 7, 12r, 12v; James Grant to Jeffery Amherst, Apr. 17, 1760, Grant Papers, DLAR reel 47, frames 140–41; Henry Bouquet to the Earl of Loudoun, Aug. 25, 1757, *Papers of Henry Bouquet*, 1:172; Greene, "South Carolina Quartering Dispute"; Jeffery Amherst to WHL, Feb. 26, 1760, LPCD.

10. Robert Raper to Thomas Boone, Apr. 15, 25, 1760, Robert Raper Letterbook; James Grant's Order Book of the Montgomery Expedition, Apr. 3–June 1760, Grant Papers, DLAR reel 31, frames 138–60.

11. *SCG*, Apr. 12–19, May 3–10, May 10–17, 1760; William Bull to Archibald Montgomery, May 23, 1760, Grant Papers, DLAR reel 31, frames 29–30.

12. Philopatrios, *Observations*, 76.

13. *SCG*, May 24–31, 1760; Archibald Montgomery to [Jeffery Amherst], May 24, 1760, Amherst Papers, WO 34/47, fol. 12r; Philopatrios, *Observations*, 76; William Bull to James Grant, Apr. 29, 1760, John Stuart to Allan Stuart, May 15, 1760, Grant Papers, DLAR reel 31, frames 15, 20; William Bull to the South Carolina Assembly, July 7, 1760, *JCHA, 1757–1761*, 684–86 (July 9, 1760).

14. William Bull to Arthur Dobbs, May 31, 1760, *CSR-NC*, 6:260; Archibald Montgomery to Jeffery Amherst, May 24, 1760, Amherst Papers, WO 34/47, fol. 12v.

15. Philopatrios, *Observations*, 77–79; *SCG*, June 10–14, 1760.

16. Philopatrios, *Observations*, 79, 80. One soldier suggested that those who burned alive were near death from smallpox. *SCG*, June 10–14, 1760.

17. *SCG*, Supplement, June 14–21, 1760; Philopatrios, *Observations*, 79, 80; Grant reported "60 to 80 Cherokees killed, with about 40 prisoners." *SCG*, June 10–14, 1760.

18. SCCJ, 1757–1762, 3:125–26 (May 24, 1760); William Bull to Archibald Montgomery, May 23, 1760, Grant Papers, DLAR reel 31, frames 29–30.

19. Archibald Montgomery to William Bull, June 23, 1760, SCCJ, 1757–1762, 3:149 (June 30, 1760); Philopatrios, *Observations*, 81, 87.

20. *SCG*, Supplement, June 14–21, 1760; *SCG*, June 28–July 5, 1760.

21. George Washington to Richard Washington, Aug. 10, 1760, *PGW*, 452–54; Alexander Garden to John Ellis, Apr. 12, 1760, *CLON*, 1:484.

22. Archibald Montgomery to William Bull, June 23, 1760, SCCJ, 1757–1762, 3:149 (June 30, 1760); Philopatrios, *Observations*, 15; Archibald Montgomery to Jeffery Amherst, June 23, 1760, Amherst Papers, WO 34/47, fol. 16.

23. *SCG*, May 24–31, 1760; Francis Fauquier to the Board of Trade, June 2, 30, 1760, *PFF*, 1:371–72, 385; *JHB, 1758–1761*, xv, 171, 176, 178 (May 19, 23, 24, 1760); *EJC*, 6:159, 161 (May 8, June 11, 1760), William Byrd to James Abercromby, Sept. 16, 1760, *CTWB*, 2:703; Maass, *French and Indian War in North Carolina*, 94–96.

24. *SCG*, May 24–31, May 31–June 7, 1760; Piker, *Okfuskee*, 52–63.

25. *SCG*, Supplement, June 14–21, 1760; Simpson, *South Carolina Diary*, 155 (June 7, 1760); William Bull to Jeffery Amherst, June 12, 1760, Amherst Papers, WO 34/35, fol. 17or; William Bull to the Board of Trade, June 17, 1760, *BPRO-SC*, 28:359–60; *SCG*, July 5–12, 1760; William Bull to James Grant, June 2, 1760, Grant Papers, DLAR reel 31, frames 37–38.

26. Henry Ellis to Jeffery Amherst, May 30, 1760, Amherst Papers, WO 34/34, fols. 216–17; SCCJ, 1757–1762, 3:131 (June 2, 1760); Alexander Garden to John Ellis, May 26, June 1, July 16, 1760, *CLON*, 1:499, 492–93, 495–98; Philopatrios, *Observations*, 13; William Bull to the Board of Trade, May 29, 1760, *BPRO-SC*, 28:348, 352–54, 356.

27. William Bull to Archibald Montgomery, May 23, 1760, Grant Papers, DLAR reel 31, frame 32; William Bull to the Board of Trade, May 8, 1760, *BPRO-SC*, 28:336–37; SCCJ, 1757–1762, 4:2 (July 3, 1760); Lockley, *Maroon Communities*; Price, *Maroon Societies*; *SCG*, May 24–31, 1760.

28. *SCG*, Supplement, June 14–21, 1760; Archibald Montgomery to William Bull, June 23, 1760, Paul Demere to William Bull, June 6, 1760, SCCJ, 1757–1762, 3:149–50 (June 30, 1760).

29. John Stuart to James Grant, June 6 and 9, 1760, Grant Papers, DLAR reel 31, frame 39; Paul Demere to William Bull, June 6, 1760, SCCJ, 1757–1762, 3:149–50 (June 30, 1760).

30. John Stuart to James Grant, June 6 and 9, 1760, Grant Papers, DLAR reel 31, frames 39–40.

31. Paul Demere to William Bull, June 6, 1760, SCCJ, 1757–1762, 3:149–50 (June 30, 1760); *SCG*, Supplement, June 14–21, 1760.

32. SCCJ, 1757–1762, 3:150 (June 30, 1760); *SCG*, July 12–19, 1760; Philopatrios, *Observations*, 81.

33. Grant believed that some Overhill warriors were present. Ostenaco and Oconostota were not among them; both were near Fort Loudoun. *SCG*, July 5–12, July 12–19, 1760; Philopatrios, *Observations*, 81–82, 86. Cherokee accounts reported 630 warriors present. The Mankiller of Nequassee said 617 warriors were there. *SCG*, Aug. 13–20, Aug. 16–23, 1760; Eid, "A Kind of Running Fight," 148–52.

34. *SCG*, July 5–12, July 12–19, Aug. 13–20, 1760; Philopatrios, *Observations*, 24, 83; William Fyffe to John Fyffe, Feb. 1, 1761, Fyffe Collection.

35. *SCG*, July 5–12, July 12–19, 1760; Abram, "Souls in the Treetops," 31, 31n; Adair, *History of the American Indians*, 381.

36. *SCG*, July 12–19, 1760.

37. Philopatrios, *Observations*, 84; Eid, "A Kind of Running Fight," 148–49, 154, 163–64; *SCG*, July 5–12, July 12–19, Oct. 18–25, 1760.

38. "Return of the Killed and Wounded," Amherst Papers, WO 34/47, fol. 19; Archibald Montgomery to Jeffery Amherst, July 2, 1760, Amherst Papers, WO 34/47, fol. 16r; McCulloch, *Sons of the Mountains*, 2:39, 62–63, 67, 73; Philopatrios, *Observations*, 84, 86; *SCG*, July 5–12, 1760; Mante, *History of the Late War*, 293; William Bull to the Board of Trade, July 20, 1760, *BPRO-SC*, 28:373.

39. John Stuart to James Grant, Oct. 17, 1761, Grant Papers, DLAR reel 32, frame 334; Archibald Montgomery to Jeffery Amherst, July 2, 1760, Amherst Papers, WO 34/47, fol. 17v; Philopatrios, *Observations*, 85, 87; *SCG*, July 5–12, 1760.

40. *SCG*, July 5–12, July 12–19, 1760; James Grant's Order Book of the Montgomery Expedition, Apr. 3, 1760–June 1760, Grant Papers, DLAR reel 31, frame 160; Philopatrios, *Observations*, 84; Archibald Montgomery to Jeffery Amherst, July 2, 1760, Amherst Papers, WO 34/47, fol. 18r.

41. Archibald Montgomery to Jeffery Amherst, July 2, 1760, Amherst Papers, WO 34/47, fols. 17v–18r; Philopatrios, *Observations*, 84–85, 87; *SCG*, July 12–19, 1760; William Bull to the Board of Trade, June 17, July 20, 1760, *BPRO-SC*, 28:358, 373–74.

42. *SCG*, July 12–19, 1760.

43. *SCG*, July 5–12, July 12–19, 1760; Mante, *History of the Late War*, 293; Philopatrios, *Observations*, 87–88; Archibald Montgomery to Jeffery Amherst, July 2, 1760, Amherst Papers, WO 34/40, fol. 18r.

44. *SCG*, July 12–19, July 19–26, July 26–Aug. 2, 1760; Archibald Montgomery to Jeffery Amherst, July 2, 1760, Amherst Papers, WO 34/47, fol. 18r; Philopatrios, *Observations*, 22, 80, 87.

45. *SCG*, July 5–12, 1760; William Bull to the Board of Trade, July 20, 1760, *BPRO-SC*, 28:374–75; William Fyffe to John Fyffe, Feb. 1, 1761, Fyffe Collection.

46. SCCJ, 1757–1762, 4:5 (July 11, 1760); *JCHA, 1757–1761*, 690–92 (July 12, 1760); William Bull to Archibald Montgomery, July 12, 1760, *BPRO-SC*, 28:381–87.

47. Archibald Montgomery [actually James Grant] to William Bull, July 19, 1760, Grant Papers, DLAR reel 31, frame 210.

48. Jeffery Amherst to Archibald Montgomery, June 18, 29, 1760, Amherst Papers, WO 34/48, fols. 26r–26v, 28r–28v. Bull later publicly defended Montgomery. William Bull to Archibald Montgomery, July 30, 1760, Grant Papers, DLAR reel 31, frames 62–63.

49. Archibald Montgomery [actually James Grant] to William Bull, July 19, 1760, Archibald Montgomery to Jeffery Amherst, Sept. 11, 1760, Grant Papers, DLAR reel 31, frames 56–60, reel 47, frames 144–45; *SCG*, July 19–26, July 26–Aug. 2, Aug. 2–9, 1760; Isaac Barré to Jeffery Amherst, Jan. 10, 1761, Amherst Papers, WO 34/86, fol. 23.

50. *SCG*, Aug. 16–23, Oct. 18–25, 1760; De Brahm, *Report*, 103; William Bull to the Board of Trade, Aug. 31, 1760, *BPRO-SC*, 28:396.

51. *SCG*, Extraordinary, Aug. 9–13, 1760; *SCG*, Aug. 13–16, Aug. 16–23, 1760; "Destruction of Fort Loudoun by the Cherokees, 1760," Lyman C. Draper Manuscripts, 2DD12–13.

52. William Byrd to Francis Fauquier, [July 4, 1760], to Robert Monckton, May 26, 1760, *CTWB*, 2:694, 695n, 697–98; Francis Fauquier to the Board of Trade, Sept. 17, 1760, *PFF*, 1:411.

53. William Byrd to Francis Fauquier, [July 11, 1760], Francis Fauquier to William Byrd, [July 24, 1760], *PFF*, 1:391, 392; William Byrd to Robert Monckton, May 26, July 18, 1760, Maria Taylor Byrd to William Byrd, July 13, 18, 1760, *CTWB*, 2:690–92, 692–94, 696–97, 698–99; Adair, *History of the American Indians*, 269; "Laws of North Carolina, [Apr. 24–June 26], 1760," *CSR-NC*, 23:517–18; Maass, *French and Indian War in North Carolina*, 97–98, 101–3.

54. "Articles of Capitulation," Aug. 7, 1760, *SCG*, Aug. 16–23, 1760; William Bull to the Board of Trade, Aug. 31, 1760, *BPRO-SC*, 28:394.

55. *SCG*, Aug. 16–23, Aug. 30–Sept. 6, Sept. 6–13, 1760; John Stuart to Allan Stuart, May 15, 1760, Grant Papers, DLAR reel 31, frame 23; "Council of War," Paul Demere to William Bull, Aug. 8, 1760, *London Magazine*, Nov. 1760, 605.

56. "Destruction of Fort Loudoun by the Cherokees, 1760," Lyman C. Draper Manuscripts, 2DD18; Kelly, "Fort Loudoun," 89.

57. *SCG*, Sept. 13-20, Sept. 20-27, Oct. 11-18, 1760; SCCJ, 1757-1762, 4:43 (Oct. 22, 1760); William Bull to Jeffery Amherst, Oct. 19 and 24, 1760, Amherst Papers, WO 34/35, fols. 174r, 174v; Kelly, "Fort Loudoun," 89.

58. *SCG*, Sept. 20-27, Sept. 27-Oct. 4, 1760. For Stevens's account, see *SCG*, Oct. 11-18, 1760; De Brahm, *Report*, 103-4; William Fyffe to John Fyffe, Feb. 1, 1761, Fyffe Collection. Bull had just promoted Adamson to captain. William Bull to James Grant, June 11, 1760, Grant Papers, DLAR reel 31, frame 43.

59. *SCG*, Sept. 27-Oct. 4, 1760; Calloway, *White People, Indians, and Highlanders*, 149-52; Jean-Bernard Bossu to the Marquis de l'Estrade, Jan. 10, 1760 [actually 1761], translated in Bossu, *Bossu's Travels*, 183-84; SCCJ, 1757-1762, 4:43 (Oct. 22, 1760); John Stuart to Allan Stuart, May 15, 1760, Grant Papers, DLAR reel 31, frame 23; William Byrd to James Abercromby, Sept. 16, 1760, *CTWB*, 2:705.

60. Abram, "Souls in the Treetops," 38, 38n; Adair, *History of the American Indians*, 380, 384-85; Lee, "Peace Chiefs and Blood Revenge," 732; Reid, *Law of Blood*, 188; SCCJ, 1757-1762, 4:43 (Oct. 22, 1760).

61. William Bull to Jeffery Amherst, Oct. 19 and 24, 1760, Amherst Papers, WO 34/35, fol. 174r; William Bull to the Board of Trade, Oct. 21, 1760, *BPRO-SC*, 28:409. For the death toll, see *SCG*, Aug. 30-Sept. 6, Sept. 13-20, Sept. 20-27, Oct. 4-11, Oct. 11-18, 1760.

62. *SCG*, Sept. 27-Oct. 4, Oct. 11-18, 1760; William Fyffe to John Fyffe, Feb. 1, 1761, Fyffe Collection.

63. SCCJ, 1757-1762, 4:43 (Oct. 22, 1760); Hewatt, *Historical Account*, 2:240.

64. *SCG*, Sept. 20-27, Sept. 27-Oct. 4, Oct. 4-11, 1760; Andrew Lewis to William Byrd, [Sept. 9, 1760], *BPRO-SC*, 28:405-6; William Byrd to Francis Fauquier, Sept. 10, 1760, to James Abercromby, Sept. 16, 1760, *CTWB*, 2:702-3, 702n, 703-5; William Bull to Jeffery Amherst, Oct. 19 and 24, 1760, Amherst Papers, WO 34/35, fol. 174v; *EJC*, 6:170-71 (Oct. 6, 1760).

65. "Articles of Peace proposed to the Cherokees," Sept. 17, 1760, Amherst Papers, WO 34/37, fols. 54-55; William Byrd to James Abercromby, Sept. 16, 1760, to Francis Fauquier, Sept. 19, 1760, *CTWB*, 2:704-5, 705-6.

66. William Byrd to James Abercromby, Sept. 16, 1760, *CTWB*, 2:704-5.

67. William Byrd to the Cherokees, [Sept. 16, 1760], *PFF*, 1:413; *SCG*, Oct. 11-18, 1760.

68. William Byrd to James Abercromby, Sept. 16, 1760, *CTWB*, 2:705; William Bull to the Board of Trade, Sept. 9, 1760, *BPRO-SC*, 28:402; *SCG*, Aug. 16-23, Sept. 6-13, Sept. 20-27, 1760.

69. William Bull to the Board of Trade, Oct. 21, 1760, *BPRO-SC*, 28:414-16.

70. *SCG*, Aug. 16-23, Sept. 6-13, Sept. 20-27, 1760; Francis Fauquier to Jeffery Amherst, Oct. 5, 1760, *PFF*, 1:418.

71. *SCG*, Sept. 20-27, Sept. 27-Oct. 4, Oct. 11-18, Oct. 18-25, 1760; *JCHA, 1757-1761*, 770-71, 774-75 (Oct. 10, 13, 1760).

72. SCCJ, 1757-1762, 4:43 (Oct. 22, 1760); *SCG*, Oct. 11-18, Oct. 18-25, 1760.

73. *SCG*, Oct. 11-18, 1760. This was probably Nancy Butler, employed at Fort Loudoun as an intelligence agent, but may have been the war woman later known as Nancy Ward.

74. Ibid.

75. *SCG*, Oct. 18–25, Nov. 22–29, 1760; William Bull to the Board of Trade, Oct. 21, 1760, *BPRO-SC*, 28:419–20.

76. *SCG*, Oct. 4–11, Oct. 18–25, 1760.

77. Extract of William Bull to Jeffery Amherst, Nov. 18, 1760, Grant Papers, DLAR reel 31, frames 84–85; William Bull to the Board of Trade, Nov. 18, 1760, *BPRO-SC*, 28:434–36. On Lantagnac's mission, see *SCG*, Nov. 22–29, Nov. 29–Dec. 6, 1760.

78. Atkin planned to resign his position. Edmond Atkin to Jeffery Amherst, Nov. 20, 1760, Amherst Papers, WO 34/47, fols. 218–21.

79. *SCG*, Nov. 29–Dec. 6, 1760; William Byrd to Francis Fauquier, [Nov. 3, 22, Dec. 3, 1760], *PFF*, 1:431, 434–35, 438, 442; *EJC*, 6:174 (Nov. 12, 1760); *PGW*, 6:470n; Guy Johnson to Sir William Johnson, Feb. 2, 1761, *SWJP*, 10:209.

80. William Bull to Jeffery Amherst, Oct. 19 and 24, Nov. 18, 1760, Amherst Papers, WO 34/35, fols. 174–78, 182–83; *SCG*, Nov. 8–15, 1760; William Bull to the Board of Trade, *BPRO-SC*, 28:436; SCCJ, 1757–1762, 4:56 (Dec. 2, 1760); Extract of Jeffery Amherst to William Bull, Nov. 27, 1760, Grant Papers, DLAR reel 31, frame 89.

81. *JCHA*, *1757–1761*, 747–48, 750 (Aug. 1, 1760); Duncan, "Servitude and Slavery," 2:475–76. On slaves in the militia, see Cooper and McCord, *Statutes*, 4:119; JCHA, 26 Mar. 1761 to 9 July 1761; 13 July–26 Dec. 1761, 14, 16, 76, 79, 87, 92, 168–71 (Apr. 2, May 20, 22, June 23, 1761).

82. William Bull to Jeffery Amherst, Oct. 19 and 24, Nov. 18, 1760, Amherst Papers, WO 34/35, fols. 176v, 183r.

83. SCCJ, 1757–1762, 4:51–53 (Nov. 15, 1760); *SCG*, Nov. 29–Dec. 6, Dec. 6–16, Dec. 16–23, 1760.

84. *SCG*, Dec. 16–23, 1760; Lee, "Peace Chiefs and Blood Revenge," 732–33; Adair, *History of the American Indians*, 427.

85. *SCG*, Dec. 16–23, 1760.

CHAPTER NINE

1. *SCG*, Jan. 24–31, Feb. 28–Mar. 7, May 2–9, June 20–27, 1761; William Bull to Jeffery Amherst, Jan. 24, 1761, Amherst Papers, WO 34/35, fol. 189v; James Grant to Jeffery Amherst, Mar. 15, 1761, Amherst Papers, WO 34/47, fol. 54v; Jeffery Amherst to James Grant, Jan. 14, 1761, Grant Papers, DLAR reel 32, frame 44. Miln was later transferred to Fort Augusta. *SCG*, Apr. 4–11, 1761.

2. James Grant to Jeffery Amherst, Jan. 17, 1761, Amherst Papers, WO 34/47, fol. 37r.

3. *SCG*, Feb. 14–21, Apr. 4–11, 1761; "A Talk from the Young Warrior of Estatoe to Mr. Mackintosh," Apr. 1, 1761, Lachlan McIntosh to William Bull, Apr. 2, 1760, "From Ostenaco of Tomotl[e]y," Apr. 19, 1761, James Grant to William Bull, Apr. 11, 1761, Grant Papers, DLAR reel 32, frames 99, 100–101, 130, 405.

4. *SCG*, May 13–16, June 13–20, June 27–July 4, 1761; Francis Fauquier to Jeffery Amherst, Apr. 17, 1761, Amherst Papers, WO 34/37, fols. 63–65; Instructions to the Commissioners to the Cherokees, *EJC*, 6:184–86 (Apr. 13, 1761); William Byrd to Jeffery Amherst, Apr. 19, 1761, Amherst Papers, WO 34/47, fols. 92, 262–63.

5. Grant's troops consisted of two battalions of Independents from England, formed into Burton's 95th Regiment; and two light infantry companies, each of the 17th and 22nd Regiments. They arrived on Jan. 6 and landed on Jan. 12. French, "Journal," 276 (Jan. 6, 9, 12); Jeffery Amherst to James Grant, Dec. 15, 1760, Feb. 13, Apr. 3, 1761, Amherst Papers, WO 34/48, fols. 39–44, 60–61, 72–73.

6. George Washington to Richard Washington, Oct. 20, 1761, *PGW*, 7:80.

7. Monypenny, "Diary," 321 (Mar. 23–24).

8. James Grant to Jeffery Amherst, Jan. 17, 1761, Amherst Papers, WO 34/47, fol. 36v. The Cherokees must be "punished . . . severely too, before Peace is Granted them." Jeffery Amherst to James Grant, Feb. 13, 1761, Amherst Papers, WO 34/48, fols. 60–61; Philopatrios, *Observations*, 40–57.

9. *SCG*, Apr. 11–18, 1761; Eliza Lucas Pinckney to Mrs. King, Apr. 13, 1761, *Letterbook*, 165; Stephen, "The Ohio Expedition of 1754."

10. French, "Journal," 277 (Mar. 20–Apr. 14); Monypenny, "Diary," 320 (Mar. 20–Apr. 14); James Grant to Jeffery Amherst, Apr. 25, 1761, Amherst Papers, WO 34/47, fol. 64v.

11. Monypenny, "Diary," 323 (Apr. 15); French, "Journal," 278 (Apr. 22); *SCG*, Apr. 25–May 2, 1761; James Grant to Jeffery Amherst, Apr. 25, 1761, Amherst Papers, WO 34/47, fol. 64r.

12. *SCG*, May 16–23, May 23–30, June 13–20, 1761. At Ninety Six, there were 1,300 redcoats, 520 provincial privates, and 400 rangers. *South-Carolina Weekly Gazette*, Apr. 29–May 6, 1761, in CO 5/377, fol. 76.

13. Monypenny, "Diary," 324 (May 3); *SCG*, May 2–9, 1761; *South-Carolina Weekly Gazette*, Apr. 29–May 6, 1761, in CO 5/377, fol. 76; Laurens, *Philolethes, PHL*, 3:342.

14. French, "Journal," 279 (May 6).

15. *SCG*, May 2–9, May 16–23, 1761; French, "Journal," 279 (Apr. 30).

16. Monypenny called the structure "a true American Fort, a pitiful Palisade thrown round a Barn." Monypenny, "Diary," 325–26 (May 14, 16); *SCG*, Apr. 4–11, 1761; James Grant to Jeffery Amherst, Mar. 30, 1761, Amherst Papers, WO 34/47, fols. 57v–58r; James Grant to William Moultrie, Mar. 27, 1761, John Moultrie Jr. to James Grant, Apr. 10, 12, and [April] sketch, 1761, Grant Papers, DLAR reel 33, frames 392–93, 109, 117–18; Anderson, *A People's Army*.

17. Monypenny, "Diary," 325–26, 329 (May 14, 18, 28); French, "Journal," 279 (May 16, 18); *SCG*, May 23–30, June 13–20, 1761; James Grant to Jeffery Amherst, June 2 and 5, 1761, Amherst Papers, WO 34/47, fol. 82r.

18. *SCG*, Jan. 10–17, June 27–July 4, Oct. 3–10, 1761; Duncan, "Servitude and Slavery," 2:659–61, 680–81; Proclamation of William Bull, Dec. 3, 1761, Secretary of State. Recorded Instruments. Miscellaneous Records (WPA Transcripts), II:421; Laurens, *Philolethes, PHL*, 3:311. Slave runaway ads in the *South Carolina Gazette* increased from 62 in 1759 to 77 in 1760 and 114 in 1761. Windley, *Runaway Slave Advertisements*, 3:168–79, 179–91, 191–209.

19. Duncan, "Servitude and Slavery," 1:391–93; JCHA, 26 Mar. 1761 to 9 July 1761; 13 July–26 Dec. 1761, 45, 49–50, 57 (Apr. 23, 29).

20. Duncan, "Servitude and Slavery," 1:172-73; *SCG*, May 23-30, June 4-6, June 6-13, 1761.

21. JCHA, 26 Mar. 1761 to 9 July 1761; 13 July-26 Dec. 1761, 112 (May 28); SCCJ, 1757-1762, 5:132 (June 17, 1761); *SCG*, June 13-20, 1761.

22. Moore, "Religious Radicalism"; *SCG*, Apr. 18-25, May 9-16, 1761; William Bull to the Board of Trade, Apr. 26, 1761, *BPRO-SC*, 29:80-82.

23. "A Talk from Oconostota, & the Little Carpenter, to Lieut. Mackintosh," May 22, 1761, William Bull to James Grant, May 29, 1761, Grant Papers, DLAR reel 32, frames 164, 168-69; William Bull to Jeffery Amherst, June 6, 1759 [actually 1761], Amherst Papers, WO 34/35, fol. 201; *SCG*, June 13-20, 1761; Monypenny, "Diary," 327-28 (May 23); "The Little Carpenter's Talk to Col. Grant," May 23, 1761, Amherst Papers, WO 34/47, fol. 89.

24. Monypenny, "Diary," 328 (May 23); "Lieut. Colonel Grant's Talk to the Little Carpenter," May 23, 1761, Amherst Papers, WO 34/47, fol. 88; William Bull to Jeffery Amherst, Jan. 24, 1761, Amherst Papers, WO 34/35, fol. 189v.

25. Twenty more Chickasaws and twenty more Catawbas joined the army on May 28. French, "Journal," 280-81 (May 27-29); Monypenny, "Diary," 328, 329 (May 27, 28); *SCG*, June 13-20, 1761. By June 12 there were six "Mohawks," ten Stockbridges, three Yuchis, twenty Upper (Western) Chickasaws, eleven Lower (Savannah River) Chickasaws, and forty Catawbas.

26. French, "Journal," 280 (May 29); *South-Carolina Weekly Gazette*, Apr. 29-May 6, 1761, in CO 5/377, fol. 76; James Grant to William Bull, June 2, 1761, Grant Papers, DLAR reel 33, frame 418; James Grant to Jeffery Amherst, June 2 and 5, Amherst Papers, WO 34/47, fols. 81-83; Monypenny, "Diary," 329, 330 (May 27, 28, 30); *SCG*, June 13-20, 1761.

27. *SCG*, Feb. 16-23, 1760; William Byrd to Jeffery Amherst, Mar. 10, May 30, 1761, Amherst Papers, WO 34/47, fols. 256-58, 265; Jeffery Amherst to John Robinson, Mar. 25, 1761, to William Byrd, May 11, 1761, Amherst Papers, WO 34/37, fols. 223-24, 227; *South-Carolina Weekly Gazette*, Apr. 29-May 6, 1761, in CO 5/377, fol. 76; *EJC*, 6:187 (May 6, 1761); Maass, "All This Poor Province Could Do," 79-81. Neither Grant nor Monypenny expected the Virginians to attack. Monypenny, "Diary," 327 (May 21).

28. Francis Fauquier to William Byrd, Feb. 16, 1761, *CTWB*, 2:712; Francis Fauquier to William Byrd, [Apr. 28, 1761], to the Board of Trade, May 12, 1761, *PFF*, 2:515-16, 524-26.

29. "A Return of His Majesty's Forces in South Carolina commanded by Lt. Coll Grant," June 1, 1761, Amherst Papers, WO 34/47, fol. 85; French, "Journal," 282-83 (June 7-8); "Journal of the March & Operations of the Troops . . . ," Grant Papers, DLAR reel 28, frames 5-8; *Scots Magazine*, Aug. 1761, 429-30; King, "Powder Horn," 32.

30. "American Affairs: Charles-Town, July 15," "Col. Grant's head-quarters, near Fort Prince George, July 10, 1761," *Royal Magazine*, Sept. 1761, 153; James Grant to Jeffery Amherst, July 10, 1761, Amherst Papers, WO 34/47, fols. 94-95; Grant, "Journal," 27 (June 10).

31. French, "Journal," 283 (June 10); Grant, "Journal," 27 (June 10).

32. Grant, "Journal," 28 (June 10); *Scots Magazine*, Aug. 1761, 429; King, "Powder Horn," 32; Hewatt, *Historical Account*, 2:248; Weems and Horry, *Life of Gen. Francis*

Marion, 21–26; Monypenny, "Diary," 330 (May 31); "Extract of a letter from an officer of the regulars, dated July 10," *Scots Magazine*, Oct. 1761, 543.

33. French, "Journal," 283–84 (June 10); Philopatrios, *Observations*, 43; *Scots Magazine*, Aug. 1761, 429; William Bull to the Board of Trade, *BPRO-SC*, 29:114–28; Grant, "Journal," 28 (June 10); Hewatt, *Historical Account*, 2:249, 250–51.

34. *Scots Magazine*, Aug. 1761, 429; *SCG*, July 18–25, Sept. 5–12, 1761.

35. Hewatt, *Historical Account*, 2:249–50; Adair, *History of the American Indians*, 269.

36. Grant, "Journal," 29 (June 10); "Return of the Killed & Wounded on the 10th June 1761," Amherst Papers, WO 34/47, fol. 97; William Bull to the Board of Trade, July 17, 1761, *BPRO-SC*, 29:125. For casualty reports, see: "American Affairs," *Royal Magazine*, Sept. 1761, 154; *Scots Magazine*, Aug. 1761, 429; French, "Journal," 283–84 (June 10, 11); *SCG*, July 11–18, 1761.

37. Boulware, *Deconstructing the Cherokee Nation*, 125; William Bull to James Grant, July 17, 1761, Grant Papers, DLAR reel 32, frame 206; Adam Stephen to Francis Fauquier, Sept. 7, 1761, *PFF*, 2:570.

38. George Croghan to Horatio Gates, May 20, 1760; George Croghan: Indian Conference at Detroit, Dec. 3–5, 1760, Indian Conference at Fort Pitt, Mar. 1–3, 1761, *Papers of Henry Bouquet*, 4:567, 5:152, 325–26; "At a Meeting held at the Huron Village near D'etroit," Oct. 17, 1761, Sir William Johnson, Journal to Detroit, [July 4–Oct. 30, 1761], *SWJP*, 3:497–98, 13:246, 260 (Aug. 27, Sept. 1).

39. Grant, "Journal," 28–29 (June 10); French, "Journal," 283 (June 10).

40. John Stuart to James Grant, Sept. 25, 1761, Grant Papers, DLAR reel 32, frame 306; Perdue, *Cherokee Women*, 38–40; French, "Journal," 283–84, 292 (June 10, Aug. 31); *SCG*, July 4–11, July 25–Aug. 1, 1761; *Scots Magazine*, Aug. 1761, 431; Bartram, *Travels*, 348, 348n.

41. "Extract of a letter from an officer in Col. Middleton's regiment, dated July 10," *Scots Magazine*, Aug. 1761, 431; Grant, "Journal," 28, 29 (June 10, 11); "American Affairs," *Royal Magazine*, Sept. 1761, 153; French, "Journal," 285 (June 10); Hewatt, *Historical Account*, 2:250; King, "Powder Horn," 34, 40n.

42. Philopatrios, *Observations*, 89; *Scots Magazine*, Aug. 1761, 430; "From the *South-Carolina Weekly Gazette*, July 15," *Scots Magazine*, Aug. 1761, 430; John Moultrie Jr. to Eleanor Austin, July 10, 1761, Moultrie Family Papers.

43. *SCG*, Sept. 5–12, 1761; French, "Journal," 288 (June 28); Grant, "Journal," 34 (June 28).

44. Grant, "Journal," 30 (June 16); *Scots Magazine*, Aug. 1761, 431; King, "Powder Horn," 35.

45. Grant, "Journal," 31 (June 22, 23); French, "Journal," 285, 288 (June 22, 23, July 7); King, "Powder Horn," 40n; Corkran, *Cherokee Frontier*, 251–52.

46. "American Affairs," *Royal Magazine*, Sept. 1761, 153–54; Grant, "Journal," 31, 32 (June 24, 25); French, "Journal," 285, 286 (June 24, 25, 26); "From the *South-Carolina Weekly Gazette*, July 15," *Scots Magazine*, Aug. 1761, 430; "Return of Troops to go," June 25, 1761, Grant Papers, DLAR reel 32, frame 449.

47. Grant, "Journal," 34 (June 28); French, "Journal," 288 (June 28).

48. French, "Journal," 283–89 (June 12, 14, 16, 22, 26–29, July 3); *SCG*, July 4–11, July 25–Aug. 1, 1761; King, "Powder Horn," 34.

49. James Grant to Jeffery Amherst, July 10, 1761, Amherst Papers, WO 34/47, fol. 94r-v; Jeffery Amherst to Francis Fauquier, July 2, 1761, Amherst Papers, WO 34/37, fol. 234.

50. Francis Fauquier to William Byrd, July 1, 1761, Attakullakulla to William Byrd, July 7, 1761, *CTWB*, 2:741, 743–45; Robert Stewart to George Washington, July 18, 1761, *PGW*, 7:56–58.

51. Maria Taylor Byrd to William Byrd, Feb. 17, 1761, *CTWB*, 2:714; William Byrd to Jeffery Amherst, July 1, Aug. 1, 1761, "A General Return of the Virginia Regiment . . . July 31, 1761," Amherst Papers, WO 34/47, fols. 268, 271–72, 274; Robert Stewart to George Washington, July 7, 20, 1761, *PGW*, 7:51, 56–58; Ward, *Breaking the Backcountry*, 198.

CHAPTER TEN

1. French, "Journal," 290 (July 21, 23); Laurens, *Philolethes*, *PHL*, 3:342; "Lieutenant Colonel Grant's Talk to Oconostota & the Standing Turkey," July 22, 1761, Grant Papers, DLAR reel 28, frame 11.

2. "Nothing but the fear of their Persons, can prevent their coming." James Grant to William Bull, Aug. 7, 1761, Grant Papers, DLAR reel 28, frame 15; French, "Journal," 291 (July 31, Aug. 1, 9, 10); *SCG*, Aug. 29–Sept. 3, 1761; Lee, "Peace Chiefs and Blood Revenge," 737–38.

3. Thomas Middleton to William Bull, Mar. 31, 1761, William Bull to Thomas Middleton, Mar. 31, 1761, James Grant to William Bull, Apr. 3, 1761, Grant Papers, DLAR reel 32, frames 91, 93–94, 402.

4. William Bull to James Grant, July 8 [actually 18], 1761, Thomas Middleton to James Grant, July 10, 1761, James Grant to Thomas Middleton, [July 10, 1761], Grant Papers, DLAR reel 32, frames 200–201, 202, reel 28, frames 3–4.

5. Thomas Barnsley to Henry Bouquet, Sept. 24, 1761, James Dow to Henry Bouquet, Sept. 24, 1761, *Papers of Henry Bouquet*, 5:771–73, 774–75.

6. John Rattray to James Grant, July 18, 1761, Grant Papers, DLAR reel 32, frame 208.

7. Eliza Lucas Pinckney to Mr. Morly, [1761], *Letterbook*, 173; Alexander Monypenny to James Grant, Nov. 14, [ca. 1762] [actually 1761], Grant Papers, DLAR reel 33, frame 115.

8. *SCG*, July 4–11, July 18–25, Aug. 1–8, 1761; Thomas Middleton to James Grant, July 19, 1761, Peter Timothy to John Gray, July 29, 1761, William Bull to James Grant, Aug. 19, 1761, Grant Papers, DLAR reel 32, frames 215–16, 229, 265; Philopatrios, *Observations*, 47–53, 57.

9. James Grant to Thomas Middleton, July 30, 1761, Grant Papers, DLAR reel 28, frames 12–14.

10. William Bull to James Grant, July 25, Aug. 19, 1761, John Rattray to James Grant, Aug. 20, 1761, Grant Papers, DLAR reel 29, frames 226, 264–66, 267–68.

11. John Rattray to James Grant, Aug. 16, 1761, Thomas Middleton to James Grant, Aug. 17, 1761, Grant Papers, DLAR reel 32, frames 255-57, 258-63.

12. Journal of the Conferences with the Cherokee Deputies, Amherst Papers, WO 34/47, fols. 103-4; French, "Journal," 290, 291-92 (Aug. 28, 29-31).

13. William Bull to James Grant, Apr. 14, 24, 1761, James Grant to William Bull, Sept. 2, 1761, Grant Papers, DLAR reel 32, frames 120-21, reel 28, frames 16-18; "Col. Grant's Talk to the Cherokee Deputies," Aug. 30, 1761, Amherst Papers, WO 34/37, fol. 104r; Dennis, "American Revolutionaries and Native Americans," 100-101.

14. Journal of the Conferences with the Cherokee Deputies, Amherst Papers, WO 34/47, fols. 104v-105; French, "Journal," 291 (Aug. 28); James Grant to William Bull, Sept. 2, 1761, to Messrs. Smith and Nutt, Sept. 11, 1761, Grant Papers, DLAR reel 28, frames 16-18, 24.

15. John Moultrie Jr. to Eleanor Austin, Sept. 1, 1761, Moultrie Family Papers; James Grant to William Bull, Sept. 2, 1761, Henry Laurens to James Grant, Sept. 9, 1761, William Bull to James Grant, Sept. 11, 1761, Grant Papers, DLAR reel 28, frames 16-18, reel 32, frames 278, 280-81; Dennis, "American Revolutionaries and Native Americans," 101.

16. SCCJ, 1757-1762, 5:159-61 (Sept. 15, 1761); Hewatt, *Historical Account*, 2:253-54.

17. Philopatrios, *Observations*, 3, 20-22; Laurens, *Philolethes*, PHL, 3:276-77, 290-99.

18. Philopatrios, *Observations*, 7-8, 27-36, 40-54, 58-59, 66-67; Henry Laurens to James Grant, Oct. 1, 1761, Grant Papers, DLAR reel 32, frames 309-10.

19. JCHA, 26 Mar. 1761-9 July 1761; 13 July-26 Dec. 1761, 237-39, 243-45, 247-56 (Sept. 15, 16, 18, 1761); John Stuart to James Grant, Sept. 18, 26, 1761, Grant Papers, DLAR reel 32, frames 287-89, 306-7; *SCG*, Sept. 26-Oct. 3, 1761.

20. SCCJ, 1757-1762, 5:162-66, 167-69 (Sept. 22, 23, 1761); JCHA, 26 Mar. 1761-9 July 1761; 13 July-26 Dec. 1761, 247-56 (Sept. 18); McCandless, *Slavery, Disease, and Suffering*, 74-75.

21. JCHA, 26 Mar. 1761-9 July 1761; 13 July-26 Dec. 1761, 247-56 (Sept. 18); William Bull to Jeffery Amherst, Sept. 24, 1761, Amherst Papers, WO 34/35, fol. 206r-v.

22. William Bull to the Board of Trade, Sept. 23, 1761, *BPRO-SC*, 29:183-85; SCCJ, 1757-1762, 5:63, 67 (Jan. 8, 20, 1761); Henry Laurens to James Grant, Oct. 1, 1761, Grant Papers, DLAR reel 32, frame 310.

23. John Stuart to James Grant, Sept. 26, 1761, Grant Papers, DLAR reel 32, frame 306; SCCJ, 1757-1762, 5:160 (Sept. 15, 1761).

24. William Bull to James Grant, July 17, 1761, Grant Papers, DLAR reel 32, frame 206.

25. Henry Laurens to James Grant, Oct. 1, 1761, Grant Papers, DLAR reel 32, frame 139; James Grant to Jeffery Amherst, Nov. 5, 1761, Amherst Papers, WO 34/47, fol. 111r.

26. James Grant to Jeffery Amherst, Nov. 5, 1761, Amherst Papers, WO 34/47, fol. 111r; Lachlan McIntosh to William Bull, [Nov. 1], 1761, "A Talk from Tiftoe [Tistoe], & the Wolf to Capt. Mackintosh," Nov. 1, 1761, Lachlan McIntosh to William Bull, Nov. 6, 1761, Grant Papers, DLAR reel 32, frames 343-44, 345-46.

27. James Grant to William Bull, Sept. 28, 1761, Grant Papers, DLAR reel 28, frames 26–28; James Grant to Jeffery Amherst, Oct. 6, Nov. 5, 1761, Amherst Papers, WO 34/47, fol. 108r.

28. Henry Laurens to James Grant, Oct. 14, 1761, James Grant to William Bull, Nov. 4, 1761, Grant Papers, DLAR reel 32, frames 330–31, reel 28, frames 36–39.

29. James Grant to Jeffery Amherst, Oct. 6, 1761, Amherst Papers, WO 34/47, fol. 108r; SCCJ, 1757–1762, 5:176–77 (Nov. 13, 1761); William Bull to James Grant, Nov. 13, 1761, Grant Papers, DLAR reel 32, frames 351–52; Mercantini, *Who Shall Rule*, 150, 161–62.

30. Henry Laurens to James Grant, Nov. 10, 1761, to John Grinnan, Nov. 15, 1761, Grant Papers, DLAR reel 32, frames 350, 357–58; SCCJ, 1757–1762, 5:175 (Nov. 13, 1761); *SCG*, Nov. 28–Dec. 5, 1761.

31. French, "Journal," 293 (Oct. 16, 26, 30), 299; "A Talk from the Little Carpenter to Mr. Mackintosh," [Nov. 15, 1761], Lachlan McIntosh to James Grant, Nov. 16, 1761, "A Talk From the Little Carpenter," Nov. 16, 1761, James Grant to William Bull, Nov. 19, 1761, Grant Papers, DLAR reel 32, frames 355–56, 361, 363, reel 28, frames 44–45; James Grant to Jeffery Amherst, Nov. 5, 19, 1761, Amherst Papers, WO 34/47, fols. 111r–v, 116; *SCG*, Oct. 31–Nov. 7, Nov. 14–21, Nov. 28–Dec. 5, 1761; JCHA, 26 Mar. 1761–9 July 1761; 13 July–26 Dec. 1761, 263 (Dec. 4).

32. George Washington to Richard Washington, Oct. 20, 1761, *PGW*, 7:80.

33. Adam Stephen to Jeffery Amherst, Oct. 5, 24, 1761, with copies of letters from Cherokee Warriors to Stephen, Amherst Papers, WO 34/47, fols. 277–78, 284–85, 279–81; "A Talk from the great Warrior and all the other head Men of the whole Nation to Colonel Grant," Grant Papers, DLAR reel 28, frames 31–32; Williams, "Fort Robinson," 28–30.

34. Alexander Monypenny to James Grant, Nov. 14, [1761], Grant Papers, DLAR reel 33, frames 111–15; *SCG*, Nov. 21–28, 1761; Adam Stephen to Jeffery Amherst, Nov. 24, 1761, Amherst Papers, WO 34/40, fol. 99; Arthur Dobbs to Jeffery Amherst, Jan. 19, 1762, Amherst Papers, WO 34/35, fol. 19; Williams, "Fort Robinson," 28. Waddell arrived October 8 at Fort Chiswell. On October 23, he listed 225 men, including 34 Indians and 14 slaves. *EJC*, 6:199 (Oct. 26, 1761); "A Return of a Detachment of the North Carolina Regiment Encamped at Bigg Island on Houlstons River 23d October 1761," Amherst Papers, WO 34/47, fol. 287; Maass, *French and Indian War in North Carolina*, 105–7, 111–14.

35. "Occonostota or the Great Warrior's Answer," Oct. 17, 1761, "A Copy of Jud Friend's Letter," Oct. 17, 1761, Treaty with the Cherokees, [Nov. 20, 1761], *PFF*, 2:587, 593; "Colo. Stephen's Speech . . . ," Nov. 20, 1761, Amherst Papers, WO 34/40, fol. 100.

36. "A Speech of the Governor of the Cherokees," Nov. 21, 1761, "The Speech of Willinawa," Nov. 21, 1761, Amherst Papers, WO 34/40, fols. 101, 102; Treaty with the Cherokees, [Nov. 20, 1761], *PFF*, 2:593; Timberlake, *Memoirs*. Stephen dismissed Waddell's troops. Adam Stephen to Jeffery Amherst, Nov. 24, 1761, Amherst Papers, WO 34/40, fol. 99.

37. SCCJ, 1757–1762, 5:186–87 (Dec. 16, 1761); James Grant to Jeffery Amherst, Dec. 24, 1761, Amherst Papers, WO 34/47, fol. 119v.

38. Philopatrios, *Observations*, 54, 58.

39. SCCJ, 1757–1762, 5:187–89, 190–91, 191–97 (Dec. 16, 17, 18, 1761).

40. SCCJ, 1757–1762, 5:190, 191–97 (Dec. 17, 18, 1761).

41. James Grant to Jeffery Amherst, Dec. 24, 1761, Amherst Papers, WO 34/47, fol. 119r–v; Simms, *History of South Carolina*, 133–35.

42. James Grant to Jeffery Amherst, Dec. 24, 1761, Amherst Papers, WO 34/47, fol. 119r.

43. *SCG*, Dec. 19–26, 1761.

CHAPTER ELEVEN

1. *SCG*, Jan. 2–9, Jan. 23–30, Jan. 30–Feb. 6, 1762; Henry Laurens to James Grant, Feb. 11, 1762, Grant Papers, DLAR reel 33, frames 8–9; Thomas Boone to Jeffery Amherst, Jan. 12 and 18, 1762, Amherst Papers, WO 34/35, fol. 210r; SCCJ, 1757–1762, 6:449, 450–51, 462 (Jan. 11, 12, Feb. 24, 1762).

2. *SCG*, Jan. 2–9, Jan. 23–30, Jan. 30–Feb. 6, 1762; Henry Laurens to James Grant, Feb. 11, 1762, Grant Papers, DLAR reel 33, frames 8–9.

3. Hewatt, *Historical Account*, 2:255; Unknown to James Grant, Jan. 13, 1762, Grant Papers, DLAR reel 33, frames 3–5.

4. Thomas Boone to unknown, Jan. 17, 1762, SCL; JCHA, 26 Mar. 1761 to 9 July 1761; 13 July–26 Dec. 1761, 271, 273 (Dec. 24); Gerlach, "Thomas Boone"; McCrady, *History of South Carolina*, 353–66.

5. Thomas Boone to unknown, Jan. 17, 1762, SCL; Henry Laurens to James Grant, Mar. 2, 1762, Grant Papers, DLAR reel 33, frame 111; Alexander Garden to John Ellis, Feb. 26, 1762, *CLON*, 1:514.

6. Jeffery Amherst to Thomas Boone, Feb. 4, 1762, Amherst Papers, WO 34/36, fol. 85.

7. *EJC*, 6:205, 206, 208, 209–10 (Jan. 16, 21, Mar. 11, 1762); Timberlake, *Memoirs*.

8. Arthur Dobbs, "The Colony, Its Climate, Soil, Population, Government, Resources, &c.," *CSR-NC*, 6:617.

9. Perdue, "Cherokee Relations," 144; Indian Intelligence, Sept. 28, 1762, Sir William Johnson to Jeffery Amherst, July 24, 1763, Journal of Indian Affairs [Oct. 4–17, 1763], and Indian Congress, Oct. 20, 1763, *SWJP*, 10:534–35, 755, 891, 903.

10. Timberlake, *Memoirs*, 37, 42–43, 45–46, 47; Francis Fauquier to Jeffery Amherst, Feb. 3, 1762, Amherst Papers, WO 34/37, fols. 109–10.

11. *SCG*, Mar. 20–27, May 15–22, 1762.

12. Boulware, *Deconstructing the Cherokee Nation*, 131, 137–38; Laurens, *Philolethes, PHL*, 3:337; *SCG*, Mar. 6–13, 1762; George Price to Benjamin Franklin, Mar. 7, 1764, *Papers of Benjamin Franklin*, 11:93; Anne Frazer Rogers, "Archaeology at Cherokee Town Sites Visited by the Montgomery and Grant Expeditions," in Rogers and Duncan, *Culture, Crisis, and Conflict*, 37–39; Cashin, *William Bartram*, 142, 147; Milling, *Red Carolinians*, 310–11.

13. *SCG*, Mar. 27–Apr. 3, Apr. 24–May 1, June 12–19, 1762; SCCJ, 1757–1762, 6:468, 484–85, 505 (Mar. 11, Apr. 2, May 25, 1762).

14. *SCG*, Apr. 24–May 1, May 22–29, June 12–19, 1762.

15. Timberlake, *Memoirs*, 37.

16. Ibid., 37.

17. Minister to Kerlérec, Jan. 25, 1762, in CDFA, reel 105; Kerlérec to Choiseul, Apr. 28, 1762, to M. Accaron, June 24, 1762, translated in *MPA*, 5:276–77, 279–80; *SCG*, July 24–31, 1762.

18. Eliza Lucas Pinckney to [Mrs. King], Feb. 27, 1762, *Letterbook*, 176; South Carolina Assembly to Thomas Boone, Mar. 30, 1762, Amherst Papers, WO 34/47, fol. 221; JCHA, 6 Feb. 1762–13 Sept. 1762, 47–48, 49 (Mar. 23, 30); Philopatrios, *Observations*, 45, 65; Mercantini, *Who Shall Rule*, 188.

19. JCHA, 6 Feb. 1762–13 Sept. 1762, 45 (Mar. 19).

20. Philopatrios, *Observations*; John Dunnet to James Grant, Dec. 4, 1762, Grant Papers, DLAR reel 33, frames 97–98; JCHA, 6 Feb. 1762–13 Sept. 1762, 138 (May 28).

21. James Grant to Jeffery Amherst, June 28, 1762, William Ramsay to Jeffery Amherst, Aug. 10 and 13, 1762, Amherst Papers, WO 34/47, fols. 122–23, 129r.

22. See #12 in Instructions from the King to Governor Boone, Nov. 11, 1761, CO 5/404, fol. 79; JCHA, 6 Feb. 1762–13 Sept. 1762, 41 (Mar. 19); Thomas Boone to the Board of Trade, Sept. 14, 1762, *BPRO-SC*, 29:238–41.

23. *A Full State of the Dispute*; Godbold and Woody, *Christopher Gadsden*, 22–49; Mercantini, *Who Shall Rule*, 22, 167–86; Edgar, *South Carolina*, 188.

24. Francis Fauquier to the Board of Trade, May 1, 1762, to the Earl of Egremont, May 1, 1762, *PFF*, 2:727–28, 729; Thomas Jefferson to John Adams, June 11, 1812, Jefferson, *Writings of Thomas Jefferson*, 13:160.

25. Timberlake, *Memoirs*, 56–97; *Emissaries of Peace*, 44–68; Evans, "Ostenaco," 47–54; Oliphant, "Lord Egremont and the Indians," in Rogers and Duncan, *Culture, Crisis, and Conflict*, 121–38.

26. *SCG*, June 26–July 3, July 3–10, July 31–Aug. 7, 1762; JCHA, 6 Feb. 1762–13 Sept. 1762, 146 (June 29); SCCJ, 1757–1762, 6:505, 522–23 (May 25, June 1, 1762); Thomas Boone to Francis Fauquier, [June 15, 1762], *PFF*, 2:758; Cooper and McCord, *Statutes*, 4:168–73.

27. SCCJ, 1757–1762, 6:468 (Mar. 11, 1762); Jeffery Amherst to Thomas Boone, Feb. 4, 1762, Amherst Papers, WO 34/36, fol. 85; *SCG*, Feb. 27–Mar. 6, May 29–June 5, 1762; Jeffery Amherst to John Stuart, Apr. 16, 1763, Amherst Papers, WO 34/48, fol. 103. The *South Carolina Gazette* spread rumors that Cherokees would not keep the peace. *SCG*, May 15–22, May 22–29, 1762.

28. SCCJ, 1757–1762, 6:566 (Nov. 19, 1762).

29. John Stuart to Jeffery Amherst, Mar. 15, 1763, Amherst Papers, WO 34/47, fols. 233r-v, 234r; Meriwether, *Expansion of South Carolina*, 247.

30. SCCJ, 1757–1762, 6:489, 557–63 (May 5, Nov. 3, 1762); "A Talk between His Excellency Thomas Boone . . . and Judd's Friend . . . ," Nov. 3, 1762, *BPRO-SC*, 29:251–58; Thomas Boone to the Earl of Egremont, Nov. 11, 1762, *BPRO-SC*, 29:249–50; Tom Hatley,

"An Epitaph for Henry Timberlake and the First Cherokee and American 'Greatest Generation'," in Rogers and Duncan, *Culture, Crisis, and Conflict*, 21.

31. *SCG*, Mar. 19–26, Apr. 16–23, Apr. 30–May 7, 1763; John Stuart to Jeffery Amherst, Mar. 15, 1763, Amherst Papers, WO 34/47, fols. 232r–33r.

32. Thomas Boone to the Earl of Egremont, Apr. 21, 1763, *BPRO-SC*, 29:327–28; *SCG*, Mar. 19–26, Apr. 16–23, Apr. 30–May 7, 1763; John Stuart to Jeffery Amherst, Mar. 15, 1763, Amherst Papers, WO 34/47, fol. 233r; SCCJ, 1763–1767, 1:34–39 (Mar. 21, 1763); Gregorie, *Thomas Sumter*, 20–22.

33. Kerlérec to Choiseul, May 2, 1763, translated in *MPA*, 5:83–84.

34. Council Minutes, *CRG*, 9:78–79 (July 14, 1763); Sir James Wright to WHL, Dec. 29, 1759, LPCD.

35. *SCG*, Dec. 4–11, 1762; JCHA, 25 Oct. 1762–28 Dec. 1762, 18–20, 30, 35–37, 38–45, 48, 49 (Nov. 30, Dec. 4, 7, 9, 16, 24), JCHA, 24 Jan. 1763–6 Oct. 1764, 8, 11 (Mar. 28, Aug. 18, 1763); Thomas Boone to the Board of Trade, May 31, 1763, *BPRO-SC*, 29:332–35.

36. Christopher Gadsden, "To the Gentleman Electors of the Parish of St. Paul, Stono," *SCG*, Jan. 29–Feb. 5, 1763.

37. *PHL*, 3:270–71; Laurens, *Philolethes*, ibid., 273–355.

38. Christopher Gadsden to Peter Timothy, Mar. 12, 1763, Gadsden, *Writings of Christopher Gadsden*, 50; Laurens, *Philolethes*, PHL, 3:305, 350.

39. Jeffery Amherst to John Stuart, June 15, 17, 1763, Amherst Papers, WO 34/48, fols. 104, 105; Dowd, *War under Heaven*.

40. Thomas Boone to the Earl of Egremont, June 1, 1763, *BPRO-SC*, 29:339; John Stuart to Jeffery Amherst, June 2, Oct. 4, 1763, Amherst Papers, WO 34/47, fols. 241v, 247r; *SCG*, May 28–June 4, 1763; Extract of Sir James Wright to John Stuart, July 20, 1763, Amherst Papers, WO 34/47, fol. 245.

41. Francis Fauquier to Jeffery Amherst, Aug. 2, 1763, Amherst Papers, WO 34/37, fol. 177; Henry Laurens to Willis Martin, Aug. 29, 1763, *PHL*, 3:552–53, 553n.

42. John Stuart to Jeffery Amherst, July 30, 1763, Amherst Papers, WO 34/47, fol. 244r; *SCG*, July 9–16, 1763.

43. John Stuart to Jeffery Amherst, Oct. 4, 1763, Amherst Papers, WO 34/47, fol. 247r–v; *SCG*, Oct. 15–22, 1763; Cashin, *Henry Ellis*, 174; Council Minutes, *CRG*, 9:70–77 (July 14, 1763).

44. King George III, Additional Instructions to Jeffery Amherst, Dec. 9, 1761, *PFF*, 2:607–9, 609n; Lord Egremont to Jeffery Amherst, Jan. 27, 1763, CO 5/214, fol. 308; Cashin, *Henry Ellis*, 170–71, 177–82, 186, 192–93; *SCG*, May 15–22, 1762, June 18–25, 1763.

45. *SCG*, July 24–31, 1762.

46. Hagy and Folmsbee, "Lost Archives," 115–18. Adam Stephen and Robert Rogers had also wanted to be superintendent. Francis Fauquier to the Board of Trade, Feb. 24, 1762, *PFF*, 2:692; Robert Rogers to Jeffery Amherst, Oct. 24, 1761, Amherst Papers, WO 34/47, fol. 224. See also Snapp, *John Stuart*, ch. 4.

47. *Journal of the Congress*, 22–25.

48. Ibid., 38.

49. Ibid., 38–39.

50. Thomas Boone, Arthur Dobbs, and Francis Fauquier, "Copy of the Talk inclosed to Mr Stuart for the Indians at Augusta, Oct. 18, 1763," ibid., 14–15.

51. Cashin, *Henry Ellis*, 175–76; *Journal of the Congress*, 38, 39–41; James Wright et al., to the Earl of Egremont, Nov. 10, 1763, ibid., 42–43.

52. George Rex, [The Royal Proclamation of 1763], [Oct. 7, 1763], *SCG*, Extraordinary, Dec. 31, 1763; Meriwether, *Expansion of South Carolina*, 247.

CONCLUSION

1. Windley, *Runaway Slave Advertisements*, 3:168–79, 179–91, 191–209.

2. Duncan, "Servitude and Slavery," 1:391–93; Ryan, *World of Thomas Jeremiah*; Lord William Campbell to the Earl of Dartmouth, Aug. 31, 1775, *BPRO-SC*, 35:196, 202; William Bull to the South Carolina Assembly, Jan. 15, 1761, *JCHA, 1757–1761*, 790, 792 (Jan. 17, 1761); SCCJ, 1757–1762, 6:506 (May 28, 1762).

3. Klein, "Ordering the Backcountry," 663–67; Henry Laurens to Richard Oswald & Co., Feb. 15, 1763, *PHL*, 3:260.

4. Alexander Garden to John Ellis, July 16, 1760, *CLON*, 1:494; Wood, "The Changing Population of the Colonial South," 38, 72.

5. William Bull to the Board of Trade, Dec. 17, 1765, *BPRO-SC*, 30:300; "Table IX: Importation of Negroes at Charlestown, 1706–1776," in Duncan, "Servitude and Slavery," 1:105.

6. Cooper and McCord, *Statutes*, 4:187–88; Henry Laurens to John Lewis Gervais, Jan. 19, 1766, *PHL*, 5:53–54; William Bull to the Board of Trade, Jan. 25, 1766, *BPRO-SC*, 30:20–21.

7. Lockley, *Maroon Communities*, 16–38; William Bull to the Board of Trade, Dec. 17, 1765, *BPRO-SC*, 30:300; JCHA, Oct. 28, 1765–Oct. 12, 1768, 34–35, 76–77, 88 (Jan. 14, Feb. 28, Mar. 15, 1766); *Boston Evening Post*, Feb. 10, 1766.

8. Gavin Cochrane to George Price, Dec. 19, 1764, GPAS 29; William Bull to Thomas Gage, Apr. 9, 1765, Gavin Cochrane to Thomas Gage, Apr. 9, 1765, GPAS 33; Ralph Phillips to Thomas Gage, Nov. 26, 1765, GPAS 46; George Price to Gavin Cochrane, Jan. 24, 1765, GPAS 36; John Stuart to John Pownall, Aug. 24, 1765, Shelburne Papers, 60:56–64.

9. Meriwether, *Expansion of South Carolina*, 259; Hatley, *Dividing Paths*, 168.

10. *JHB, 1761–1765*, xx–xxiii, lxviii; *EJC*, 6:600 (May 13, 1765); Francis Fauquier to Andrew Lewis, May 14, 1765, to the Board of Trade, Aug. 1, 1765, *PFF*, 3:1238, 1266; McConnell, *A Country Between*, 240, 319n.

11. Charles Montagu to the Board of Trade, Jan. 16, 1767, to the Earl of Shelburne, Mar. 5, Apr. 14, 1767, "Regulations for the better carrying on the Trade with the Indian Tribes in the Southern District," Oct. 4, 1769, William Bull to the Earl of Hillsborough, Nov. 30, 1770, *BPRO-SC*, 31:184, 297, 314–15, 318, 319, 32:108–9, 403; Calloway, *White People, Indians, and Highlanders*, 152.

12. Hatley, *Dividing Paths*, 168.

13. *JHB, 1761–1765*, 66 (Nov. 2, 1762); Francis Fauquier to the Board of Trade, June 5, 1765, *PFF*, 3:1250–51; William Bull to the Earl of Hillsborough, Nov. 30, 1770, *BPRO-SC*, 32:403.

14. Alexander Cameron, "A Return of the Traders in the Cherokee Nation," May 1, 1765, CO 323/23, fol. 254; Hatley, *Dividing Paths*, 180, 182–85, 212–14.

15. De Vorsey, *Indian Boundary*, 64–78; Kelly, "Oconostota," 227–34; Silver, *Our Savage Neighbors*, 75.

16. Perdue, "Cherokee Relations," 145; Sir William Johnson to Francis Fauquier, Dec. 30, 1762, to John Stuart, Sept. 17, 1765, *SWJP*, 3:988, 4:848.

17. John Stuart to Sir William Johnson, Mar. 30, 1766, *SWJP*, 12:56.

18. Holton, *Forced Founders*, ch. 2.

19. Mercantini, *Who Shall Rule*, 251–57.

20. "Officers of the South Carolina Regiment in the Cherokee War, 1760–61"; Bartram, *Travels*, 330, 348; Andrew Pickens to Henry Lee, Aug. 28, 1811, Thomas Sumter Papers, Lyman C. Draper Manuscripts, 1VV107; Weems and Horry, *Life of Gen. Francis Marion*, 24–25. North Carolina Patriots with Anglo-Cherokee War experience included Griffith Rutherford and Robert Howe. Virginia Patriots included William Christian and Adam Stephen.

21. William Lyttelton's Speech, Oct. 26, 1775, quoted in Ryan, *World of Thomas Jeremiah*, 16.

22. Kelly, "Attakullakulla," 24–26; Piecuch, *Three Peoples, One King*, 14–122.

23. Ryan, *World of Thomas Jeremiah*.

24. Evans, "Dragging Canoe"; Henry Stuart to John Stuart, Aug. 25, 1776, *CSR-NC*, 10, pt. 2:763–85.

25. William Henry Drayton to Francis Salvador, July 24, 1776, Gibbes, *Documentary History*, 2:29; William Hooper, Joseph Hewes, and John Penn to the North Carolina Council of Safety, *CSR-NC*, 10, pt. 2:730–32; Hatley, *Dividing Paths*, 192–99; Thomas Jefferson to Edmund Pendleton, Aug. 13, 1776, *Writings of Thomas Jefferson*, 4:280.

26. Evans, "Dragging Canoe," 183–89; Boulware, *Deconstructing the Cherokee Nation*, ch. 8; Calloway, *American Revolution in Indian Country*, ch. 7.

27. Milling, *Red Carolinians*, 334.

BIBLIOGRAPHY

MANUSCRIPT SOURCES
Archives Nationales, Paris, France
  Archive des Colonies
David Library of the American Revolution, Washington Crossing, Pa.
  General John Forbes Headquarters Papers, 1729–1758. Microfilm.
  John Forbes Papers in the Dalhousie Muniments, 1748–1759. Microfilm.
  Papers of James Grant of Ballindalloch, 1720–1805. Microfilm.
  War Office Records (WO 34) Sir Jeffery Amherst Papers, 1717–1797. Microfilm.
Hunter Library, Special Collections, Western Carolina University, Cullowhee, N.C.
  Cherokee Documents in Foreign Archives, 1632–1909
  Cherokee Maps, 1540–1863. Microfilm.
Library of Congress, Washington, D.C.
  Christopher French Papers, 1756–1778
Manuscript Collection, Gilcrease Museum Archives, Tulsa, Okla.
  William Fyffe to John Fyffe, Feb. 1, 1761. William Fyffe Collection, Registration
    3825.1653.
The National Archives, formerly Public Record Office, Kew, UK
  Colonial Office Records (CO)
  Public Record Office Records (PRO)
  War Office Records (WO)
Perkins Library, Duke University, Durham, N.C.
  Lyman C. Draper Manuscripts. Microfilm.
South Carolina Department of Archives and History, Columbia, S.C.
  Journals of His Majesty's Council, 1721–1774. Microfilm.
  Journals of the Commons House of Assembly, 1692–1775
  Secretary of State. Recorded Instruments. Miscellaneous Records
    (WPA Transcripts), 1692–1779. Microfilm.
  Secretary of State. Recorded Instruments. Miscellaneous Records (Main
    Series), 1732–1981. Microfilm.
  Selected Pages Relating to South Carolina from the Library of Congress
    Transcripts of the Papers of the Society for the Propagation of the Gospel
    in Foreign Parts [SPG Papers], 1702–1769. Microfilm.
  St. Philip's Vestry Minutes, 1756–1774. Microfilm.
South Carolina Historical Society, Charleston, S.C.
  Robert Raper Letterbook, 1759–1770
  Transcripts and Abstracts of Moultrie Family Papers, 1746–1965
South Caroliniana Library, University of South Carolina, Columbia, S.C.

James Glen Papers, 1738–1777
Thomas Boone to unknown, Jan. 17, 1762
William L. Clements Library, Ann Arbor, Mich.
Thomas Gage Papers, 1754–1807
American Series
William Henry Lyttelton Papers, 1730–1806
Series I: Correspondence and Documents
Series II: Letter Books and Account Book
William Petty, 1st Marquis of Lansdowne, 2nd Earl of Shelburne Papers, 1665–1885
Wilson Library, University of North Carolina, Chapel Hill, N.C.
William Richardson Davie Papers, 1758–1819

NEWSPAPERS AND PERIODICALS

Boston Evening Post	*Maryland Gazette*
Daily Journal	*Monthly Epitome*
Daily Post	*Pennsylvania Gazette*
Grub-Street Journal	*Royal Magazine*
Historical Register	*Scots Magazine*
London Journal	*South Carolina Gazette*
London Magazine; or,	
Gentleman's Monthly Intelligencer	

PUBLISHED PRIMARY SOURCES

A Full State of the Dispute Betwixt the Governor and the Commons House of Assembly of His Majesty's Province of South Carolina. . . . Charles Town: n.p., 1763.

A Treaty Held with the Catawba and Cherokee Indians, at the Catawba-Town and Broad-River in the Months of February and March 1756. Williamsburg: W. Hunter, 1756.

Adair, James. *The History of the American Indians.* Edited by Kathryn E. Holland-Braund. Tuscaloosa: University of Alabama Press, 2005.

Atkin, William. *The Appalachian Indian Frontier: The Edmond Atkin Report and Plan of 1755.* Edited by Wilbur R. Jacobs. Columbia: University of South Carolina Press, 1954.

Bartram, William. *Travels through North Carolina, Georgia, East and West Florida, the Cherokee Country, the Extensive Territories of the Muscogulges, or Creek Confederacy, and the Country of the Chactaws.* . . . Philadelphia: James & Johnson, 1791.

Bossu, Jean-Bernard. *Jean-Bernard Bossu's Travels in the Interior of North America, 1751–1762.* Edited and translated by Seymour Feiler. Norman: University of Oklahoma Press, 1962.

Bouquet, Henry. *The Papers of Henry Bouquet.* 6 vols. Edited by S. K. Stevens, Donald H. Kent, and Autumn L. Leonard. Harrisburg: The Pennsylvania Historical and Museum Commission, 1951–1994.

Burns, Hobert W., ed. *The Life of Anne Calhoun Mathews (18 May 1755–19 December 1830)*. Palo Alto, Calif.: Hobert W. Burns, 1988.

Byrd, William, William Byrd II, and William Byrd III. *The Correspondence of the Three William Byrds of Westover, Virginia, 1684–1776*. 2 vols. Edited by Marion Tinling. Charlottesville: University Press of Virginia, 1977.

Calhoun, John C. "Account of the Settlement of the Calhoun Family in South Carolina." *Gulf States Historical Magazine* 1 (July 1902): 439–41.

Calhoun, William. "Journal of William Calhoun, June 10, 1769." Edited by Alexander S. Salley. *Publications of the Southern History Association* 8 (May 1904): 179–95.

Candler, Allen D., Kenneth Coleman, and Milton Ready, eds. *The Colonial Records of the State of Georgia*. 32 vols. Atlanta: Franklin Printing and Publishing Company, 1904–1916; Athens: University of Georgia Press, 1974–1979.

Clarke, Richard. *The Prophetic Numbers of Daniel and John Calculated*. Charles Town: Robert Wells, 1759.

Cooper, Thomas, and David J. McCord, eds. *Statutes at Large of South Carolina*. 10 vols. Columbia, S.C.: A. S. Johnston, 1836–1841.

Davies, Samuel. *Letters from the Rev. Samuel Davies*. London: J. and W. Oliver, 1761.

De Brahm, John Gerar William. *Report of the General Survey in the Southern District of North America*. Edited by Louis De Vorsey Jr. Columbia: University of South Carolina Press, 1971.

Dinwiddie, Robert. *The Official Records of Robert Dinwiddie, Lieutenant-Governor of the Colony of Virginia, 1751–1758*. 2 vols. Edited by R. A. Brock. Richmond, Va.: The Society, 1883–1884.

Easterby, J. H., R. Nicholas Olsberg, and Terry W. Lipscomb, eds. *The Journal of the Commons House of Assembly* [1736–1757]. 14 vols. Columbia: Historical Commission of South Carolina, 1951–1989.

Fauquier, Francis. *The Official Papers of Francis Fauquier, Lieutenant Governor of Virginia, 1758–1768*. 3 vols. Edited by George Henkle Reese. Charlottesville: University Press of Virginia, 1980–1983.

Forbes, John. *Writings of General John Forbes Relating to His Service in North America*. Edited by Alfred Procter James. Menasha, Wis.: Collegiate Press, 1938.

Franklin, Benjamin. *The Papers of Benjamin Franklin*. 37 vols. Edited by Leonard W. Labaree et al. New Haven: Yale University Press, 1959–2011.

French, Christopher. "Journal of an Expedition to South Carolina." *Journal of Cherokee Studies* 2 (Summer 1977): 275–96.

Fries, Adelaide L., ed. *Records of the Moravians in North Carolina*. 13 vols. Raleigh: Edwards & Broughton, 1922–2006.

Gadsden, Christopher. *The Writings of Christopher Gadsden, 1746–1805*. Edited by Richard Walsh. Columbia: University of South Carolina Press, 1966.

Gibbes, Robert Wilson, ed. *Documentary History of the American Revolution*. 3 vols. Columbia, S.C.: Banner Steam Power Press, 1853–1857.

Glen, James. *A Description of South Carolina*. London: R. and J. Dodsley, 1761.

Grant, Lt. Col. James. "Journal of Lieutenant-Colonel James Grant, Commanding an Expedition against the Cherokee Indians, June–July, 1761." *Florida Historical Quarterly* 12 (January 1933): 25–36.

Grant, Ludovick. "Historical Relation of Facts Delivered by Ludovick Grant, Indian Trader, to His Excellency the Governor of South Carolina." *South Carolina Historical and Genealogical Magazine* 10 (January 1909): 54–68.

Hagy, James William, and Stanley J. Folmsbee, eds. "The Lost Archives of the Cherokee Nation, Part 1, 1763–1772." *East Tennessee Historical Society's Publications* 43 (1971): 115–18.

Hening, William Waller. *The Statutes at Large; Being a Collection of all the Laws of Virginia.* 12 vols. Richmond: Samuel Pleasants, 1810–1823.

Hutson, William. " 'A Faithful Ambassador': The Diary of Rev. William Hutson, Pastor of the Independent Meeting in Charleston, 1757–1761." Edited by Daniel J. Tortora. *South Carolina Historical Magazine* 108 (January 2007): 32–100.

Jefferson, Thomas. *The Writings of Thomas Jefferson.* 20 vols. Edited by Andrew A. Lipscomb and Thomas Ellery Bergh. Washington, D.C.: Thomas Jefferson Memorial Association of the United States, 1903–1904.

Johnson, William. *The Papers of Sir William Johnson.* 14 vols. Edited by Alexander Clarence Fick. Albany: University of the State of New York, 1921–1965.

Journal of the Congress of the Four Southern Governors with the Five Nations . . . at Augusta, 1763. Charles Town: Peter Timothy, 1764.

Laurens, Henry. *The Papers of Henry Laurens.* 16 vols. Edited by George C. Rogers et al. Columbia: University of South Carolina Press, 1968–2003.

Ledward, K. H., ed. *Journals of the Board of Trade and Plantations, Volume 6: January 1729–December 1734*, http://www.british-history.ac.uk/source.aspx?pubid=874. September 1, 2014.

Lipscomb, Terry W., ed. *The Journal of the Commons House of Assembly, October 6, 1757–January 24, 1761.* Columbia: South Carolina Department of Archives and History, 1996.

Marrant, John. *A Narrative of the Lord's Wonderful Dealings, with John Marrant. . . .* In *Held Captive by Indians: Selected Narratives, 1632–1836*, edited by Richard VanDerBeets, 177–201. Knoxville: University of Tennessee Press, 1983.

McDowell, William L., Jr. *Documents Relating to Indian Affairs, May 21, 1750–August 7, 1754* [Vol. 1]. Columbia: South Carolina Department of Archives and History, 1958.

———. *Documents Relating to Indian Affairs, 1754–1765* [Vol. 2]. Columbia: South Carolina Department of Archives and History, 1970.

McIlwaine, H. R., ed. *Executive Journals of the Council of Colonial Virginia.* 6 vols. Richmond: Virginia State Library, 1925–1966.

———, and John P. Kennedy, eds. *Journals of the House of Burgesses of Virginia, 1619–1776.* 13 vols. Richmond: Virginia State Library, 1905–1915.

Mereness, Newton D., ed. *Travels in the American Colonies.* New York: Macmillan, 1916.

Milligen-Johnston, George. *A Short Description of the Province of South-Carolina.* London: John Hinton, 1763.

Monypenny, Alexander. "Diary of Alexander Monypenny: March 20–May 31, 1761." *Journal of Cherokee Studies* 2 (Summer 1977): 320–31.

———. "Order Book of the Grant Expedition by Major Alexander Monypenny." *Journal of Cherokee Studies* 2 (Summer 1977): 302–19.

Palmer, William P., ed. *Calendar of Virginia State Papers and Other Manuscripts.* 11 vols. Richmond: R. F. Walker, 1875–1893.

Philopatrios [Christopher Gadsden]. *Some Observations on the Two Campaigns against the Cherokee Indians, in 1760 and 1761.* Charles Town: Peter Timothy, 1762.

Pinckney, Eliza Lucas. *The Letterbook of Eliza Lucas Pinckney, 1739–1762.* Edited by Elise Pinckney. Columbia: University of South Carolina Press, 1997.

Pitt, William. *Correspondence of William Pitt, When Secretary of State, with Colonial Governors and Military and Naval Commissioners in America.* 2 vols. Edited by Gertrude Selwyn Kimball. New York: Macmillan, 1906.

Rowland, Dunbar, A. G. Sanders, and Patricia Kay Galloway, eds. *Mississippi Provincial Archives, 1701–1763: French Dominion.* 5 vols. Baton Rouge: Louisiana State University Press, 1927–1984.

Sainsbury, William Noel, ed. *Records in the British Public Record Office Relating to South Carolina, 1663–1782.* 37 vols. Microfilm ed. Columbia: South Carolina Department of Archives and History, 1973.

Saunders, William L., and Walter Clark, eds. *The Colonial and State Records of North Carolina.* 26 vols. Raleigh: P. M. Hale, 1886–1907.

Simpson, Archibald. *The South Carolina Diary of Reverend Archibald Simpson, Part I, May 1754–April 1770.* Edited by Peter N. Moore. Columbia: University of South Carolina Press, 2012.

Smith, James Edward, ed. *A Selection of the Correspondence of Linnaeus and Other Naturalists.* 2 vols. London: Longman, Hurst, Rees, Orme, and Brown, 1821.

Stephen, Adam. "The Ohio Expedition of 1754." *Pennsylvania Magazine of History and Biography* 18 (1894): 46.

Timberlake, Henry. *The Memoirs of Lt. Henry Timberlake: The Story of a Soldier, Adventurer, and Emissary to the Cherokees, 1756–1765.* Edited by Duane H. King. Chapel Hill: University of North Carolina Press for the Museum of the Cherokee Indian Press, 2007.

Tobler, John. "John Tobler's Descriptions of South Carolina (1753)." Edited by Walter L. Robbins. *South Carolina Historical Magazine* 71 (July 1970): 141–61.

Vaughan, Alden T., et al., eds. *Early American Indian Documents: Treaties and Laws, 1607–1789.* 20 vols. Bethesda, Md.: University Publications of America, 1984–2001.

Walker, Felix. "Narrative of a Kentucky Adventure in 1775." Edited by Samuel R. Walker. *DeBow's Review* 16 (February 1854): 150–55.

Washington, George. *The Journal of Major George Washington.* Williamsburg: Colonial Williamsburg Foundation, 1959.

———. *The Papers of George Washington: 1748–1775. Colonial Series*. 10 vols. Edited by W. W. Abbot et al. Charlottesville: University of Virginia Press, 1983–1995.

Webster, Pelatiah. "Journal of a Voyage to Charlestown in So. Carolina by Pelatiah Webster in 1765." Edited by T. P. Harrison. *Publications of the Southern History Association* 2 (April 1898): 131–48.

Windley, Lathan A. *Runaway Slave Advertisements: A Documentary History from the 1730s to 1790*. 4 vols. Westport, Conn.: Greenwood Press, 1983.

SECONDARY SOURCES

Alden, John Richard. *John Stuart and the Southern Colonial Frontier: A Study of Indian Relations, War, Trade, and Land Problems in the Southern Wilderness, 1754–1775*. New York: Gordian Press, 1966.

Anderson, Fred. *Crucible of War: The Seven Years' War and the Fate of Empire in British North America, 1754–1766*. New York: Alfred A. Knopf, 2000.

———. *A People's Army: Massachusetts Soldiers and Society in the Seven Years' War*. Chapel Hill: Published for the Omohundro Institute of Early American History and Culture, Williamsburg, Virginia, by the University of North Carolina Press, 1984.

Anderson, William L., and James A. Lewis. *A Guide to Cherokee Documents in Foreign Archives*. Metuchen, N.J.: Scarecrow, 1983.

Bass, Robert D. *Ninety Six: The Struggle for the South Carolina Backcountry*. Lexington, S.C.: The Sandlapper Store, 1978.

Berlin, Ira. *Many Thousands Gone: The First Two Centuries of Slavery in North America*. Cambridge, Mass.: Belknap Press of Harvard University Press, 1998.

Bernheim, G. D. *History of the German Settlements and of the Lutheran Church in North and South Carolina*. Philadelphia: The Lutheran Book Store, 1872.

Blackmon, Richard D. *Dark and Bloody Ground: The American Revolution along the Southern Frontier*. Yardley, Pa.: Westholme, 2012.

Borneman, Walter R. *The French and Indian War: Deciding the Fate of North America*. New York: HarperCollins, 2006.

Boulware, Tyler W. *Deconstructing the Cherokee Nation: Town, Region, and Nation among Eighteenth-Century Cherokees*. Gainesville: University Press of Florida, 2011.

———. "The Effect of the Seven Years' War on the Cherokee Nation." *Early American Studies* 5 (Fall 2007): 395–426.

Brown, Douglas Summers. *The Catawba Indians: The People of the River*. Columbia: University of South Carolina Press, 1966.

Brown, John P. *Old Frontiers*. Kingsport, Tenn.: Southern Publishers, 1938.

Brown, Richard Maxwell. *The South Carolina Regulators*. Cambridge, Mass.: Belknap Press of Harvard University Press, 1963.

Brown, Vincent. "Spiritual Terror and Sacred Authority in Jamaican Slave Society." *Slavery & Abolition* 24 (April 2003): 24–53.

Brumwell, Stephen. *Redcoats: The British Soldier and War in America, 1755–1763*. New York: Cambridge University Press, 2002.

Bull, Kinloch. *The Oligarchs in Colonial and Revolutionary Charleston: Lieutenant Governor William Bull II and His Family.* Columbia: University of South Carolina Press, 1990.

Calloway, Colin G. *The American Revolution in Indian Country: Crisis and Diversity in Native American Communities.* Cambridge, UK: Cambridge University Press, 1995.

———. *The Scratch of a Pen: 1763 and the Transformation of North America.* Oxford: Oxford University Press, 2006.

———. *White People, Indians, and Highlanders: Tribal Peoples and Colonial Encounters in Scotland and America.* New York: Oxford University Press, 2008.

Calmes, Alan. "The Lyttelton Expedition of 1759: Military Failures and Financial Successes." *South Carolina Historical Magazine* 77 (January 1976): 10-33.

Cashin, Edward J. *Governor Henry Ellis and the Transformation of British North America.* Athens: University of Georgia Press, 1994.

———. *Guardians of the Valley: Chickasaws in Colonial South Carolina and Georgia.* Columbia: University of South Carolina Press, 2009.

———. *William Bartram and the American Revolution on the Southern Frontier.* Columbia: University of South Carolina Press, 2000.

Cave, Alfred A. *The French and Indian War.* Westport, Conn.: Greenwood Press, 2004.

Conard, A. Mark. "The Cherokee Mission of Virginia Presbyterians." *Journal of Presbyterian History* 58 (Spring 1980): 35-48.

Conaway, Andrew. "Ghosthunting—Long Canes Massacre Site." August 29, 2006. http://www.youtube.com/watch?v=aYsRHoAI9vU. September 1, 2014.

Copeland, Peter F., and Fitzhugh McMaster. "South Carolina Regiment of Horse, 1740-1775." *Military Collector and Historian* 25 (Fall 1973): 142-44.

Corkran, David H. *The Cherokee Frontier: Conflict and Survival, 1740-1762.* Norman: University of Oklahoma Press, 1962.

———. *The Creek Frontier, 1540-1782.* Norman: University of Oklahoma Press, 1967.

Cubbison, Douglas R. *The British Defeat of the French in Pennsylvania, 1758: A Military History of the Forbes Campaign against Fort Duquesne.* Jefferson, N.C.: McFarland & Company, 2010.

Cumming, William P. *The Southeast in Early Maps.* 3rd ed. Chapel Hill: University of North Carolina Press, 1998.

Davis, Rose Mary. *The Good Lord Lyttelton: A Study in Eighteenth Century Politics and Culture.* Bethlehem, Pa.: The Times Publishing Company, 1939.

Desmond, Ian. *Arthur Dobbs, Esquire, 1689-1765: Surveyor-General of Ireland, Prospector and Governor of North Carolina.* Chapel Hill: University of North Carolina Press, 1957.

De Vorsey, Louis, Jr. *The Indian Boundary in the Southern Colonies, 1763-1775.* Chapel Hill: University of North Carolina Press, 1966.

Dowd, Gregory Evans. "'Insidious Friends': Gift Giving and the Cherokee-British Alliance in the Seven Years' War." In *Contact Points: American Frontiers from the Mohawk Valley to the Mississippi, 1750-1830,* edited by Fredrika J. Teute and

Andrew Robert Lee Cayton, 114–50. Chapel Hill: University of North Carolina Press, 1998.

———. "The Panic of 1751: The Significance of Rumors on the South Carolina–Cherokee Frontier." *William and Mary Quarterly* 53 (July 1996): 527–60.

———. *War under Heaven: Pontiac, the Indian Nations and the British Empire.* Baltimore: Johns Hopkins University Press, 2002.

Duffy, John. *Epidemics in Colonial America.* Baton Rouge: Louisiana State University Press, 1953.

Dunkerly, Robert M. and Eric K. Williams. *Old Ninety Six: A History and Guide.* Charleston, S.C.: The History Press, 2006.

Edgar, Walter, ed. *Biographical Directory of the South Carolina House of Representatives.* 5 vols. Columbia: University of South Carolina Press, 1974–1978.

———. *Partisans and Redcoats: The Southern Conflict That Turned the Tide of the American Revolution.* New York: William Morrow, 2001.

———. *South Carolina: A History.* Columbia: University of South Carolina Press, 1988.

Edmonds, Bobby. *The Making of McCormick County.* McCormick, S.C.: Cedar Hill, 1999.

Egerton, Douglas R. *Death or Liberty: African Americans and Revolutionary America.* New York: Oxford University Press, 2011.

Eid, LeRoy V. "'A Kind of Running Fight': Indian Battlefield Tactics in the Late Eighteenth Century." *Western Pennsylvania Historical Magazine* 71 (April 1988): 147–72.

Emissaries of Peace: The 1762 Cherokee & British Delegations; Exhibit Catalog. Cherokee, N.C.: Museum of the Cherokee Indian, 2008.

Evans, E. Raymond. "Notable Persons in Cherokee History: Dragging Canoe." *Journal of Cherokee Studies* 2 (Winter 1977): 176–89.

———. "Notable Persons in Cherokee History: Ostenaco." *Journal of Cherokee Studies* 1 (Summer 1976): 41–54.

Fabel, Robin F. A. *Colonial Challenges: Britons, Native Americans, and Caribs, 1759–1775.* Gainesville: University Press of Florida, 2000.

Fenning, Daniel. *A New System of Geography; Or, A General Description of the World.* 2 vols. London: S. Crowder, 1765–1766.

Foreman, Carolyn. *Indians Abroad, 1493–1938.* Norman: University of Oklahoma Press, 1943.

Fowler, William. *Empires at War: The French and Indian War and the Struggle for North America, 1754–1763.* New York: Walker & Co., 2005.

Franklin, W. Neil. "Virginia and the Cherokee Indian Trade, 1673–1752." *East Tennessee Historical Society's Publications* 4 (1932): 3–21.

———. "Virginia and the Cherokee Indian Trade, 1753–1775." *East Tennessee Historical Society's Publications* 5 (1933): 22–38.

Fraser, Walter J. *Charleston! Charleston!: The History of a Southern City.* Columbia: University of South Carolina Press, 1989.

Frey, Sylvia R. *Water from the Rock: Black Resistance in a Revolutionary Age.* Princeton, N.J.: Princeton University Press, 1991.

Gerlach, Larry R. "Thomas Boone." In *The Governors of New Jersey 1664–1974: Biographical Essays,* edited by Paul A. Stellhorn and Michael J. Birkner, 65–69. Trenton: The Commission, 1982.

Godbold, E. Stanly, Jr., and Robert H. Woody. *Christopher Gadsden and the American Revolution.* Knoxville: University of Tennessee Press, 1982.

Greene, Jack P. "The South Carolina Quartering Dispute, 1757–1758." *South Carolina Historical Magazine* 60 (October 1959): 193–204.

Greene, Jerome A. *Historic Resource Study and Historic Structure Report, Ninety Six: A Historical Narrative.* Denver, Colo.: Denver Service Center, U.S. Dept. of the Interior, 1978.

Gregorie, Anne King. *Thomas Sumter.* Columbia, S.C.: R. L. Bryan, 1931.

Griffin, Patrick. *American Leviathan: Empire, Nation, and Revolutionary Frontier.* New York: Hill and Wang, 2007.

Harden, William. "James Mackay, of Strathy Hall, Comrade in Arms of George Washington." *Georgia Historical Quarterly* 1 (June 1917): 77–98.

Hatley, M. Thomas. *The Dividing Paths: Cherokees and South Carolinians through the Era of Revolution.* New York: Oxford University Press, 1993.

———. "The Three Lives of Keowee: Loss and Recovery in the Eighteenth-Century Cherokee Villages." In *American Encounters: Natives and Newcomers from European Contact to Indian Removal,* edited by Peter Mancall and James H. Merrell, 240–260. New York: Routledge, 2000.

Hewatt, Alexander. *An Historical Account of the Rise and Progress of the Colonies of South Carolina and Georgia.* 2 vols. London: A. Donaldson, 1779.

Hodson, Christopher. *The Acadian Diaspora: An Eighteenth-Century History.* Oxford and New York: Oxford University Press, 2012.

Holland-Braund, Kathryn E. *Deerskins and Duffels: The Creek Indian Trade with Anglo-America.* 2nd ed. Lincoln: University of Nebraska Press, 2008.

Holton, Woody. *Forced Founders: Indians, Debtors, Slaves, and the Making of the American Revolution in Virginia.* Chapel Hill: Published for the Omohundro Institute of Early American History and Culture, Williamsburg, Virginia, by the University of North Carolina Press, 1999.

Howe, George. *The Scotch-Irish and Their First Settlements on the Tyger River and Other Neighboring Precincts in South Carolina: A Centennial Discourse.* Columbia, S.C.: Southern Guardian Steam-Power Press, 1861.

Ingram, Daniel. *Indians and British Outposts in Eighteenth-Century America.* Gainesville: University Press of Florida, 2012.

Ivers, Larry E. *Colonial Forts of South Carolina, 1670–1775.* Columbia: University of South Carolina Press, 1970.

Kars, Marjoleine. *Breaking Loose Together: The Regulator Rebellion in Pre-Revolutionary North Carolina.* Chapel Hill: University of North Carolina Press, 2002.

Kelly, James C. "Fort Loudoun: British Stronghold in the Tennessee Country." *East Tennessee Historical Society's Publications* 50 (1978): 72–91.

———. "Notable Persons in Cherokee History: Attakullakulla." *Journal of Cherokee Studies* 3 (Winter 1978): 2–34.

———. "Oconostota." *Journal of Cherokee Studies* 3 (Fall 1978): 221–38.

Kelly, Paul. "Fort Loudoun: The After Years, 1760–1960." *Tennessee Historical Quarterly* 20 (December 1961): 303–22.

———. *Historic Fort Loudoun*. Vonore, Tenn.: Fort Loudoun Association, 1958.

Kelton, Paul. "Avoiding the Smallpox Spirits: Colonial Epidemics and Southeastern Indian Survival." *Ethnohistory* 51 (Winter 2004): 45–71.

———. "The British and Indian War: Cherokee Power and the Fate of Empire in North America." *William and Mary Quarterly* 69 (October 2012): 763–92.

King, Duane H. "A Powder Horn Commemorating the Grant Expedition against the Cherokees." *Journal of Cherokee Studies* 1 (Summer 1976): 23–40.

———, and E. Raymond Evans, eds. "Historic Documentation of the Grant Expedition against the Cherokees: 1761." *Journal of Cherokee Studies* 2 (Summer 1977): 272–73.

Klein, Rachel N. "Ordering the Backcountry: The South Carolina Regulation." *William and Mary Quarterly* 38 (October 1981): 661–80.

———. *Unification of a Slave State: The Rise of the Planter Class in the South Carolina Backcountry, 1760–1808*. Chapel Hill: University of North Carolina Press, 1990.

Koontz, Louis Knott. *The Virginia Frontier, 1754–1763*. Baltimore: Johns Hopkins University Press, 1925.

Krebsbach, Suzanne. "The Great Charlestown Smallpox Epidemic of 1760." *South Carolina Historical Magazine* 97 (January 1996): 30–37.

Kutsche, Paul. *A Guide to Cherokee Documents in the Northeastern United States*. Metuchen, N.J.: Scarecrow Press, 1986.

Kuttruff, Carl, et al. *Fort Loudoun in Tennessee: 1756–1760; History, Archaeology, Replication, Exhibits, and Interpretation*. Walden, Tenn.: Waldenhouse Publishers, 2010.

Lee, Wayne E. *Barbarians and Brothers: Anglo-American Warfare, 1500–1865*. New York: Oxford University Press, 2011.

———. "Fortify, Fight, or Flee: Tuscarora and Cherokee Defensive Warfare and Military Culture Adaptation." *Journal of Military History* 68 (July 2004): 713–70.

———. "Peace Chiefs and Blood Revenge: Patterns of Restraint in Native American Warfare, 1500–1800." *Journal of Military History* 71 (July 2007): 701–41.

Littlefield, Daniel C. *Rice and Slaves: Ethnicity and the Slave Trade in Colonial South Carolina*. Baton Rouge: Louisiana State University Press, 1981.

Lockley, Timothy James, ed. *Maroon Communities in South Carolina: A Documentary Record*. Columbia: University of South Carolina Press, 2009.

Maass, John R. " 'All This Poor Province Could Do': North Carolina and the Seven Years' War, 1757–1762." *North Carolina Historical Review* 79 (January 2002): 50–89.

———. *The French and Indian War in North Carolina: The Spreading Flames of War.* Charleston, S.C.: The History Press, 2013.

MacLeod, D. Peter. *The Canadian Iroquois and the Seven Years' War.* Toronto: Dundurn Press, 1996.

Maness, Harold S. *Forgotten Outpost: Fort Moore & Savannah Town, 1685–1765.* Beech Island, S.C.: Beech Island Historical Society, 1986.

Mante, Thomas. *The History of the Late War in North-America.* London: W. Strahan and T. Cadell, 1772.

May, W. E. "His Majesty's Ships on the Carolina Station." *South Carolina Historical Magazine* 71 (July 1970): 162–69.

McCandless, Peter. *Slavery, Disease, and Suffering in the Southern Lowcountry.* Cambridge, UK: Cambridge University Press, 2011.

McConnell, Michael N. *A Country Between: The Upper Ohio Valley and Its Peoples, 1724–1774.* Lincoln and London: University of Nebraska Press, 1992.

McCrady, Edward. *The History of South Carolina under the Royal Government, 1719–1776.* New York: Macmillan, 1899.

McCulloch, Ian M. *Sons of the Mountains: The Highland Regiments in the French and Indian War.* 2 vols. Toronto: Robin Brass Studio, 2006.

McMaster, Fitzhugh. *Soldiers and Uniforms: South Carolina Military Affairs, 1670–1775.* Columbia: Published for the South Carolina Tricentennial Commission by the University of South Carolina Press, 1971.

Mellon, Knox, Jr. "Christian Priber and the Jesuit Myth." *South Carolina Historical Magazine* 61 (April 1960): 75–81.

———. "Christian Priber's Cherokee Kingdom of Paradise." *Georgia Historical Quarterly* 57 (Fall 1973): 319–31.

Mercantini, Jonathan. *Who Shall Rule at Home? The Evolution of South Carolina Political Culture, 1748–1776.* Columbia: University of South Carolina Press, 2007.

Meriwether, Robert L. *The Expansion of South Carolina, 1729–1765.* Kingsport, Tenn.: Southern Publishers, 1940.

Merrell, James Hart. *The Indians' New World: Catawbas and Their Neighbors from European Contact through the Era of Removal.* New York: W. W. Norton, 1989.

Milling, Chapman J., ed. *Colonial South Carolina: Two Contemporary Descriptions.* Columbia: University of South Carolina Press, 1951.

———. *Exile without an End.* Columbia, S.C.: Bostick & Thornley, 1943.

———. *Red Carolinians.* Chapel Hill: University of North Carolina Press, 1940.

Mooney, James. *Myths of the Cherokee and Sacred Formulas of the Cherokees.* Nashville, Tenn.: Charles Elder, Bookseller, 1972.

Moore, Peter N. "Religious Radicalism in the Colonial Southern Backcountry: Jacob Weber and the Transmission of European Radical Pietism to South Carolina's Dutch Fork." *Journal of Backcountry Studies* 1 (Fall 2006): 1–19.

Morgan, Philip D. "Black Life in Charleston." *Perspectives in American History,* N.S. 1 (1984): 187–232.

———. *Slave Counterpoint: Black Culture in the Eighteenth-Century Chesapeake and Lowcountry.* Chapel Hill: Published for the Omohundro Institute of Early American History and Culture, Williamsburg, Virginia, by the University of North Carolina Press, 1998.

Nash, Gary B. *The Forgotten Fifth: African Americans in the Age of Revolution.* Cambridge, Mass.: Harvard University Press, 2006.

Nelson, Paul David. *General James Grant: Scottish Soldier and Royal Governor of East Florida.* Gainesville: University Press of Florida, 1993.

Oatis, Steven J. *A Colonial Complex: South Carolina's Frontiers in the Era of the Yamasee War, 1680–1730.* Lincoln: University of Nebraska Press, 2004.

O'Donnell, James H. *Southern Indians in the American Revolution.* Knoxville: University of Tennessee Press, 1973.

"Officers of the South Carolina Regiment in the Cherokee War, 1760–61." *South Carolina Historical & Genealogical Magazine* 3 (October 1902): 202–6.

Oliphant, John. "The Anglo-Cherokee War, 1759–1761." In *The Seven Years' War: Global Views*, edited by Mark H. Danley and Patrick J. Speelman, 325–358. Boston: Brill, 2012.

———. "The Cherokee Embassy to London, 1762." *Journal of Imperial and Commonwealth History* 27 (January 1999): 1–26.

———. *Peace and War on the Anglo-Cherokee Frontier, 1756–1763.* Baton Rouge: Louisiana State University Press, 2000.

Olwell, Robert. *Masters, Slaves, and Subjects: The Culture of Power in the South Carolina Lowcountry, 1740–1790.* Ithaca, NY: Cornell University Press, 1998.

Pargellis, Stanley McCrory. *Lord Loudoun in North America.* New Haven: Yale University Press, 1933.

Perdue, Theda. "Cherokee Relations with the Iroquois in the Eighteenth Century." In *Beyond the Covenant Chain: Iroquois and Their Neighbors in Indian North America, 1600–1800*, edited by Daniel K. Richter and James Hart Merrell, 135–49. University Park, Pa.: The Pennsylvania State University Press, 1987, rev. ed., 2003.

———. *Cherokee Women: Gender and Culture Change, 1700–1835.* Lincoln: University of Nebraska Press, 1998.

Piecuch, Jim. *Three Peoples, One King: Loyalists, Indians, and Slaves in the Revolutionary South, 1775–1782.* Columbia: University of South Carolina Press, 2008.

Piker, Joshua. *Okfuskee: A Creek Indian Town in Colonial America.* Cambridge, Mass.: Harvard University Press, 2004.

Preston, David L. "'Make Indians of Our White Men': British Soldiers and Indian Warriors from Braddock's to Forbes's Campaigns, 1755–1758." *Pennsylvania History* 74 (Summer 2007): 280–306.

Price, Richard, ed. *Maroon Societies: Rebel Slave Communities in the Americas.* 3rd ed. Baltimore: Johns Hopkins University Press, 1996.

Ramsay, David. *Ramsay's History of South Carolina from its First Settlement in 1670 to the Year 1808.* Newberry, S.C.: W. J. Duffie, 1858.

Ramsey, William L. *The Yamasee War: A Study of Culture, Economy, and Conflict in the Colonial South.* Lincoln: University of Nebraska Press, 2008.

Reid, John Phillip. *A Law of Blood: The Primitive Law of the Cherokee Nation.* New York: New York University Press, 1970.

Richter, Daniel K. *The Ordeal of the Longhouse: The Peoples of the Iroquois League in the Era of European Colonization.* Chapel Hill: Published for the Omohundro Institute of Early American History and Culture, Williamsburg, Virginia, by the University of North Carolina Press, 1992.

Robinson, W. Stitt. *James Glen: From Scottish Provost to Royal Governor of South Carolina.* Westport, Conn.: Greenwood Press, 1996.

Rogers, Anne F. and Barbara R. Duncan, eds. *Culture, Crisis, and Conflict: Cherokee British Relations 1756-1765.* Cherokee, N.C.: Museum of the Cherokee Indian, 2009.

Rothrock, Mary U. "Carolina Traders Among the Overhill Cherokees, 1690-1760." *East Tennessee Historical Society's Publications* 51 (1979): 14-29.

Rozema, Vicki. *Footsteps of the Cherokees: A Guide to the Eastern Homelands of the Cherokee Nation.* Winston-Salem: John F. Blair, 1995.

Ryan, William Randolph. *The World of Thomas Jeremiah: Charles Town on the Eve of the American Revolution.* Oxford: Oxford University Press, 2012.

Sadosky, Leonard J. *Revolutionary Negotiations: Indians, Empires, and Diplomats in the Founding of America.* Charlottesville: University of Virginia Press, 2009.

Salley, A. S. *The Independent Company from South Carolina at Great Meadows.* Columbia, S.C.: Printed for the Commission by the State Company, 1932.

Sheriff, G. Anne, ed. *Cherokee Villages in South Carolina.* Greenville, S.C.: A Press, 1990.

Shippen, Edward. *Memoir of Henry Bouquet, 1719-1765.* Philadelphia: G. H. Buchanan, 1900.

Silver, Peter. *Our Savage Neighbors: How Indian War Transformed Early America.* New York: W. W. Norton, 2008.

Simms, William Gilmore. *The History of South Carolina: From Its First European Discovery to Its Erection into a Republic.* Charleston: S. Babcock, 1840.

Snapp, J. Russell. *John Stuart and the Struggle for Empire on the Southern Frontier.* Baton Rouge: Louisiana State University Press, 1996.

Steele, William O. *The Cherokee Crown of Tannassy.* Winston-Salem: John F. Blair, 1977.

Strickland, Rennard. "Christian Gotelieb Priber: Utopian Precursor of the Cherokee Government." *Chronicles of Oklahoma* 48 (Autumn 1970): 264-79.

Stone, Richard G., Jr. "Captain Paul Demere at Fort Loudoun, 1757-1760." *East Tennessee Historical Society's Publications* 41 (1969): 17-33.

Strohfelt, Thomas A. "Warriors in Williamsburg: The Cherokee Presence in Virginia's 18th-Century Capital." *Journal of Cherokee Studies* 11 (Spring 1986): 4-18.

Stumpf, Stuart. "James Glen, Cherokee Diplomacy, and the Construction of an Overhill Fort." *East Tennessee Historical Society's Publications* 50 (1978): 21-30.

Thomas, Daniel H. *Fort Toulouse: The French Outpost at the Alabamas on the Coosa*. Tuscaloosa: University of Alabama Press, 1989.

Townsend, Eleanor Winthrop. *John Moultrie, Junior, M.D., 1729-1798, Royal Lieutenant-Governor of East Florida*. New York: Paul B. Hoeber, 1940.

Tyler, Lyon G. "The Gnostic Trap: Richard Clarke and His Proclamation of the Millennium and Universal Restoration in South Carolina and England." *Journal of Anglican and Episcopal History* 58 (June 1989): 146-68.

Vaughan, Alden T. *Transatlantic Encounters: American Indians in Britain, 1500-1776*. New York: Cambridge University Press, 2006.

Waddell, Alfred Moore. *A Colonial Officer and His Times. 1754-1773: A Biographical Sketch of Gen. Hugh Waddell, of North Carolina*. Raleigh: Edwards & Broughton, 1890.

Wallace, David Duncan. *The Life of Henry Laurens with a Sketch of the Life of Lieutenant-Colonel John Laurens*. New York: Russell & Russell, 1915.

Ward, Matthew C. *Breaking the Backcountry: The Seven Years' War in Virginia and Pennsylvania*. Pittsburgh: University of Pittsburgh Press, 2003.

Weems, M. L, and P. Horry. *The Life of Gen. Francis Marion: A Celebrated Partizan Officer in the Revolutionary War against the British and Tories in South-Carolina and Georgia*. Philadelphia: Mathew Carey, 1809.

Weir, Robert M. *Colonial South Carolina: A History*. Millwood, N.Y.: KTO Press, 1983.

———. *"A Most Important Epocha": The Coming of the Revolution in South Carolina*. Columbia: University of South Carolina Press, 1970.

Wilkes, Brian. "Cherokee Dialects Made Easy—Or at Least Easier." January 24, 2008. http://voices.yahoo.com/cherokee-dialects-made-easy-least-easier-822353.html. September 1, 2014.

Williams, Marshall W. *A Memoir of the Archaeological Excavation of Fort Prince George, Pickens County, South Carolina along with Pertinent Historical Documentation*. Columbia: South Carolina Institute of Archaeology and Anthropology, University of South Carolina, 1998.

Williams, Samuel C. "Fort Robinson on the Holston." *East Tennessee Historical Society's Publications* 4 (1932): 22-31.

Wood, Douglas McClure. " 'I Have Now Made a Path to Virginia': Outacite Ostenaco and the Cherokee-Virginia Alliance in the French and Indian War." *West Virginia History*, N.S. 2 (Fall 2008): 31-60.

Wood, Peter H. *Black Majority: Negroes in Colonial South Carolina from 1670 through the Stono Rebellion*. New York: Knopf, 1974.

———. "The Changing Population of the Colonial South: An Overview by Race and Region, 1685-1790." In *Powhatan's Mantle: Indians in the Colonial Southeast*, edited by Peter H. Wood, Gregory A. Waselkov, and M. Thomas Hatley, 35-103. Lincoln: University of Nebraska Press, 1989.

———. " 'Liberty Is Sweet': African-American Freedom Struggles in the Years before White Independence." In *Beyond the American Revolution: Explorations in the History of American Radicalism*, edited by Alfred F. Young, 149–184. DeKalb: Northern Illinois University Press, 1993.

DISSERTATIONS

Abram, Susan Marie. " 'Souls in the Treetops': Cherokee War, Masculinity, and Community, 1760–1820." Ph.D. diss., Auburn University, 2009.

Attig, John Clarence. "William Henry Lyttelton: A Study in Colonial Administration." Ph.D. diss., University of Nebraska, 1958.

Barker, Eirlys Mair. "Much Blood and Treasure: South Carolina's Indian Traders, 1670–1755." Ph.D. diss., The College of William and Mary, 1993.

Dennis, Jeffrey William. "American Revolutionaries and Native Americans: The South Carolina Experience." Ph.D. diss., University of Notre Dame, 2003.

Duncan, John Donald. "Servitude and Slavery in Colonial South Carolina, 1670–1776." 2 vols. Ph.D. diss., Emory University, 1972.

Foote, William Alfred. "The American Independent Companies of the British Army, 1664–1764." Ph.D. diss., UCLA, 1966.

Snyder, Christina Nicole. "Captives of the Dark and Bloody Ground: Identity, Race, and Power in the Contested American South." Ph.D. diss., University of North Carolina–Chapel Hill, 2007.

INDEX

Abram (African American), 96, 98, 121, 128, 129, 145, 186, 216 (n. 29)

Acadians, 34–35, 36–37, 87–88

Act to Regulate the Trade with the Cherokee Indians (Indian Trade Act), 178–80, 185

Adair, James: on "Articles of Friendship and Commerce," 19; on Byrd's Virginia troops, 131; on Fort Prince George Massacre, 100; on Grant campaign, 149; on Lyttelton, 75; on Priber, 21; on prisoners, 138; on rapes, 73; on scalping, 102–3; on smallpox, 83–84; on South Carolina–Cherokee relations, 1; on tyrants, 61

Adamson, James, 132, 133–34

Adoption by Cherokees: Cane Creek attack and, 133, 134; Cherokee attacks and, 112, 116; Cherokee offensive of 1760 and, 105; Cherokee revenge and, 101, 147; Fort Loudoun and, 133, 134, 147, 165; Grant's peace negotiations and, 161; of slaves, 96, 102, 161; treaties and, 166. *See also* Bench, John *and other adoptees*

African American culture, 86

African Americans: Acadians and, 36; backcountry and, 187; British and, 4; Cherokee attacks and, 106, 107, 109, 111, 113–14, 119; Cherokees and, 3, 15, 90–91, 96, 102, 161; Clarke and, 65; Creeks and, 123; Dobbs and, 132; elites and, 25, 184, 187; "English Camp Tennecy River" and, 37; Fort Chiswell and, 231 (n. 34); Fort Dobbs and, 218 (n. 30); free, 123; Grant campaign/treaty and, 145–46, 161, 177; Great Island Treaty and, 166; importation

of, 170, 187; Jamaican, 124; Long Canes and, 104, 105; population statistics, 33–34, 187; as prisoners of Cherokees, 174; Revolutionary implications and, 3, 4, 137, 186–88, 192, 194; Royal Proclamation of 1763 and, 185; runaways, 169, 184, 185, 186; smallpox and, 81, 85–87, 88; South Carolina Assembly and, 86, 130, 137, 145–46, 186, 187; taxes and, 176; trade and, 106; unrest and, 2, 6, 8, 65–67, 75–76, 80, 86–87, 123, 124; Virginia goodwill tour and, 172; white anxiety and, 6, 8, 17, 87, 146, 161, 170, 187–88. *See also* Abram *and other African Americans;* Manumission; Maroons

Alexander, Nathaniel, 63

Alleck of Cussitah, 110

Alliance, treaty of (1756), 39

Allies of British, Indian, 143–44, 149, 150, 152

Amelia, 77 (map), 114 (map), 121

Amherst, Jeffery: attacks on Cherokees and, 141; Bull and Byrd and, 137; Byrd's treaty and, 134; on Cherokee affairs, 171, 226 (n. 8); Fort Loudoun siege and, 123; Grant and, 141–42, 153, 177; Lyttelton and, 98, 118–19; Montgomery and, 129; on troops, 120

Ammunition: Cane Creek attack and, 132; embargoes and, 68–73, 94, 118, 132, 138; French and, 41, 62, 64, 72, 209 (n. 20); Grant campaign and, 149, 150; John/Pendarvis plot and, 66; low stores of, 149, 150, 172; peace negotiations and, 54, 59, 73, 74; Skiagunsta on, 16. *See also* Hunting

Amouskositte, 22

Anderson, Fred, 2, 144
Anderson, Maurice, 124
Anglicans, 8, 65, 75, 146
Anglo-Cherokee War, effects of, 7, 182, 191. *See also* Revolutionary implications
Appalachian Divide, 185
"Articles of Friendship and Commerce" (Treaty of Whitehall) (1730), 18–21, 79, 80
Ashepoo River fort, 114
Ashley Ferry, S.C., 158, 159
Assimilation by Cherokees, 102, 109, 118
Atkin, Edmond, 43, 45, 50–51, 52, 58, 72–73, 110, 122, 128, 224 (n. 78)
Attakullakulla ("Little Carpenter") of Tomotley: accused by governor, 211 (n. 60); Byrd's peace proposal and, 137, 148; captured by Ottawas, 22; Charles Town conferences and, 63, 165, 167; Connecorte on, 78–79; on Cowhowee attack, 151; death threats and, 124; delegation to England and, 14–15, 17–19, 18 (ill.), 20, 198 (n. 29); described, 94; Fort Duquesne campaign and, 50, 51, 57, 58; Fort Loudoun and, 94–95, 118, 122, 124–25; Gadsden on, 166; Grant campaign and, 146, 147, 153, 154; Grant's treaty and, 155, 158–59, 160, 162, 164, 165, 169, 170; Great Island Treaty and, 167; Illinois Country trip and, 68; influence over Cherokees of, 60–61, 68, 79, 95, 97, 118, 134–35, 158, 160, 162–63, 166; Lyttelton and, 75, 78, 79–80; on northern Indian attacks, 175; Oconostota and, 188; Ostenaco and, 178; other names for, 14, 15; Overhills fort and, 30, 33; "Panic of 1751" and, 23; peace and, 139, 140; Saluda Conference and, 28; slaves and, 184; sons of, 183; Stuart and, 78, 134; trade grievances and, 41, 63;

Treaty of Augusta and, 184; Treaty of Sycamore Shoals and, 192; Virginia trade and, 60–61
Atwood, Isaac, 94, 215 (n. 7)
Aubrey, Samuel, 107
Augusta, Ga., 105, 109
Augusta, Treaty of (1763), 183–85, 188
Augusta County frontiersmen, 190
Ayers, Colonel, 144

Backcountry residents. *See* Frontiersmen, farmers, and settlers
Baldridge, James, 215 (n. 6)
Barré, Isaac, 131
Bartram, William, 94, 151, 191
Battle of Cowhowee (1761), 148–50, 150 (ill.)
Battle of Echoe (Battle of Tessentee Old Town; 1760), 126–27
Battle of Echoe (Battle of Cowhowee; 1761). *See* Cowhowee River attack
Beale, Othniel, 167
Beamer, James, 40–41, 46, 49, 53–54, 55, 56, 62
Beamer, Thomas, 49, 53–54, 55, 92, 93
Beaver Creek attack, 108
Bell, John, 73
Bell, Thomas, 141
Bench, John, 162, 165
"Benn's Negro," 216 (n. 20)
Bethabara, 108, 113
"Bethabara Diary," 63
Bethania, 108, 113
Biggs, Ephraim, 2
Black River, 113
Blacks. *See* African Americans
Blood gifts, 54, 55, 61, 64
Board of Trade (Lords Commissioners of Trade and Plantations), 18–19, 79, 88, 89, 214 (n. 40)
Bogges, John, 134
Boone, Thomas, 89, 170–71, 176–77, 178, 180, 182, 183, 184

and, 92, 93, 94; hostages and, 92, 97; as Lyttelton's emissary, 79; Oconostota and, 70, 71, 98, 132, 146; perception of uneasiness of, 91; rape and, 73; "Rascals" and, 97; smallpox and, 83

Creeks: Atkin and, 58, 72–73, 110; as Cherokee allies or enemies, 22, 56, 64–65, 101, 104, 123, 126, 172; Cherokee-British relations and, 62–63, 64–65, 72–73, 155; Confederacy of, 15, 16; deerskin trade and, 15, 58, 180, 190; P. Demere and, 64; Fort Loudoun fall and, 118; Fort Prince George Massacre and, 93–94; French and, 62, 64, 110, 176; Georgia and, 182; Georgia conference and, 183, 184; Lantagnac and, 39; Lower Town meetings with, 70; neutrality of, 109–10; Oconostota and, 181; Overhill Cherokees and, 44; Pontiac's Rebellion and, 183; Priber and, 21; white anxiety and, 123. *See also* Cussitah warriors

Creeks, Lower, 72–73, 94, 110, 135, 184

Creeks, Upper, 56, 135, 181, 183

Crim, Peter, 108

Crises of 1759, 60–70

Croghan, George, 151

Crown of Tanasee, 14, 17

Crucible of War (Anderson), 2

Culture, Cherokee. *See* Cherokee culture

Cuming, Alexander, 10–11, 13–15, 17, 18, 20, 178

Cusabos, 142

Cussitah warriors, 72, 94, 110

Davis, Ambrose, 46, 99

De Brahm, John William Gerar (Gerard), 37–38, 60, 61

Debt, 15–16, 40, 70

Deconstructing the Cherokee Nation (Boulware), 5

Deerskin trade. *See* Trade and traders

Delawares, 43, 172

Demere (Demeré), Paul: Cherokee revenge and, 69; on Cherokees, 39, 40, 41, 52, 62, 98, 125; on Coytmore's embargo, 68; Creeks and, 63, 64; death of, 133; Fort Loudoun and, 37, 38, 39, 125, 130, 132, 133; on Fort Loudoun siege, 131; Fort Loudoun surrender and, 132; Fort Prince George Massacre and, 96; French and, 56–57, 63, 64; negotiations and, 71, 122; Overhill warriors and, 56–57, 95, 96, 98. *See also* Abram

Demere (Demeré), Raymond, 41

DeSaussure plantation, 82

Diaries, 6

Dictionaries, Cherokee, 21

Dinwiddie, Robert, 25, 26, 28, 29, 36, 44, 46

Diplomacy, peace negotiations, and treaties: Attakullakulla's trip to England and, 17–19; Cherokee culture and, 79, 155–56; Cherokee vs. British, 69; Grant campaign and, 7, 142, 146, 147, 151, 153–68; land and, 190; scholarship on, 5; tribe-to-tribe, 44. *See also* Ammunition; Grant, James; Hostages–Lyttelton's; Ostenaco of Tomotley *and other peace negotiators*; Treaties

Disease (illness): Atkin's detainees and, 45; Cherokee population and, 1, 188; Cherokee warriors (1750s) and, 17; depopulation and, 15; disarray and, 136; Grant campaign and, 151; hostages and, 100; Lyttelton's expedition and, 76; omens and, 51; peace and, 138; South Carolina and, 82. *See also* Smallpox

The Dividing Paths (Hatley), 5

Dobbs, Arthur, 1, 49, 67, 131–32, 172, 184

Dougherty, Cornelius, 215 (n. 6)

Fox (naval vessel), 14, 17, 20
France and the French: ammunition
and, 41, 62, 64, 72, 209 (n. 20); appeal
of, 40, 41; attacks on, 61; Attakullakulla and, 68, 134; black unrest and,
67; Cherokee-British relations and,
6, 16–17, 62, 181, 182–83; Cherokee
culture and, 175; Cherokee prisoners
and, 110; Chotas and, 136–37;
Connecorte and, 62; Creeks and, 62,
64, 110, 176; evacuation by, 184; Fort
Loudoun and, 39, 118; Fort Prince
George Massacre and, 95; forts and,
32–33; gifts from to Indians, 221 (n. 20);
Grant and, 129, 153–54, 156; Indian
raids and, 48; Oconostota and, 21, 138,
139, 140 (ill.), 146, 175–76, 181; Ostenaco and, 175; scalp bounties and,
69; Seroweh and, 135, 137; Shawnees
and, 136–37; Slave-Catcher of Chota
and, 68; trade and, 16–17, 20, 41–42;
Virginia and, 25–26. *See also* Acadians; Cherokee-French relations; Fort
Duquesne; French and Indian War;
French-British relations; Lantagnac,
Antoine Adhémar de
Francis, James, 106, 107, 111, 210 (n. 41),
219 (n. 42)
Franklin, Benjamin, 30
French, Christopher, 71 (ill.), 147, 150, 152
French and Indian War era, 27 (map);
beginning of, 25–42; Cherokee-British alliance and, 6–7; Cherokees and,
26, 28; Revolutionary War era com-
pared to, 4; South Carolina and, 2–3
French-British relations, 16–17, 19, 22,
29, 42, 47, 181. *See also* Fort Duquesne
campaigns
French John, 39
Frontiersmen, farmers, and settlers:
Appalachian, 81; attacks by, 45–46, 49,
52–54, 55, 59, 60, 169, 188; attacks on,
39, 48, 63, 67, 68; Attakullakulla and,

162; Bull and, 189; Cherokee attacks
and, 108; Cherokee hunting and, 183;
Cherokee land and, 184, 188; effects of
war and, 174; elites and, 7, 104, 114, 119,
169, 189; Fort Duquesne campaigns
and, 48; Grant on, 144; hunting and,
73, 183; land grabs and, 8; Lyttelton's
expedition and, 76; militia of, 70;
millenarianism and, 146; Ostenaco's
raid and, 30; slaves and, 187; smallpox and, 87; South Carolina Assembly's treatment of, 37; South Carolina-British relations and, 7–8; threat
of, 174; value to South Carolina of, 119.
See also Refugees
Fyffe, William, 61, 84, 129

Gadsden, Christopher: on Anglo-
Cherokee War, 72; on British, 119–20,
182; British and, 176, 177; election
controversy and, 191; Grant cam-
paign/treaty and, 157, 159, 160, 163–64,
166, 170; Middleton and, 156; on
Montgomery's defeat, 128; portrait of,
161 (ill.); Revolutionary implications
and, 191; as soldier, 75
Gallman, Henry, 107–8
Garden, Alexander: on Atkin, 58; on
blacks, 86, 87, 113, 123; on Cherokees,
123; on crisis of 1759, 75; on epidemics, 81, 82, 89; on Gadsden, 171; on
inoculation of blacks, 86; on Lyttelton, 89, 116; on Lyttelton's hostages,
100; Saluda Treaty and, 28
Geographical context, 6, 8, 11, 26
Geopolitical landscape, 5, 17
George II, 13, 14, 17, 19–20
George III, 24, 178, 183, 184, 185
George Town militia, 113
Georgia: Cherokee attacks and, 105,
109–10, 112; Cherokee land and, 190;
Creeks and, 72–73, 182; deerskin trade
and, 180; land and, 184; Oconostota

Nancy (Indian woman), 136
Nanyehi (Nancy Ward), 61
Natchez Indians, 13
Nequassee (Nikwasi; today Franklin, N.C.), 11, 12 (map), 14, 94, 136, 152, 174
New Orleans and Louisiana, 47, 51–52, 58, 175–76, 181. *See also* Kerlérec, Chevalier de
New River (Virginia), 43
New Savannah, Ga., 112
Newspaper accounts, 6, 29, 115, 156, 177. See also *South Carolina Gazette*
North Carolina: attacks by Cherokees on, 39, 63, 67, 112–13; Byrd and, 154; Fort Loudoun siege and, 123, 131–32; Lyttelton's expedition and, 78; recruitment and, 138; Revolutionary implications and, 193; scalp bounties and, 132; trade and, 32, 179; Virginia and, 60, 165. *See also* Broad River; Catawba Town; Dobbs, Arthur; Fort Dobbs
North Carolina Assembly, 148
North Carolina militia, 32
North Carolina Rangers, 63
North Carolina Regiment, 165
Northern and western Indians, 151, 175, 190–91, 192. *See also* Iroquois *and other northern and western Indians;* Pontiac's Rebellion
"Norward" raids, 22–23
Nottely and Nottelies, 12 (map), 56, 70, 94, 216 (n. 20)
Nottoways, 44
Nottowegas, 22
Nunnehi ("the immortals"), 14

Ocayulah of Chota, 79
Ocayulah of Kituwah, 152
Oconoeca, 80
Oconostota (Chota): Attakullakulla and, 188; British and, 182; Cane Creek attack and, 132–33; Coytmore and, 71,

97, 98–99, 146–47, 175; described, 94; Fort Duquesne campaign and, 56–57; Fort Loudoun and, 94, 95, 125, 131, 132; Fort Loudoun fall and, 222 (n. 33); French and, 21, 138, 139, 140 (ill.), 146, 175–76, 181; Georgia and, 181–82; Grant's treaty and, 158; hostages and, 92, 95–96, 97, 98; leadership of, 97, 146–47, 175; Lyttelton and, 71, 74–75, 79, 80; naming of accused and, 211 (n. 59); peace and, 136, 137, 155; Stuart and, 71, 97, 134; trade and, 73; Treaty of Fort Prince George and, 98; Virginia and, 165
Oglethorpe's correspondent, 20–21
Ohio Country and Indians, 6, 25–26, 42, 43, 44, 45, 172, 182
Okfuskee (Creek town), 56
Old Caesar of Chatuga, 136, 155
Old Warrior of Estatoe, 122
Oliphant, John, 5
Onatoy of Toqua, 133, 134
Oonodutu. *See* Stuart, John
Orangeburg, S.C., 77 (map), 113
Ostenaco (Syacust Ukah) of Tomotley: Atkin and, 50–51; British and, 178, 180; Cane Creek attack and, 133; Cherokee revenge and, 56; Fort Duquesne and, 45; Fort Loudoun and, 109, 117, 125, 222 (n. 33); Fort Prince George demands and, 70; French and, 175; Georgia conference and, 184; leadership of, 69–70, 178, 180; peace negotiations and, 71, 136, 139, 141, 155, 158, 166, 180; portrait of, 31 (ill.); Stuart and, 78; Treaty of Sycamore Shoals and, 192; Virginia and, 29–30, 165, 175, 178; visit to Britain of, 180–81
Ottacite, 80
Ottawas, 22, 172
Ounakannowie (Lower Townsman), 17
Ousanaletah of Joree, 216 (n. 26)

Outerbridge, White, 84, 115
Out Towns, 12 (map); Cherokee revenge and, 55, 64; demise of, 188; described, 11–13; effects of war and, 174; French and Indian War and, 26; Grant campaign and, 151, 152; hostages and, 92; hunting and, 174. *See also* Round O of Stecoe *and other Out towns*
Overhill Towns, 12 (map); ammunition and, 69; "Articles of Friendship and Commerce" and, 20; attack on Montgomery and, 131; attacks by, 108, 109; Byrd's proposed treaty and, 134–35; Cane Creek attack and, 134; Cherokee revenge and, 54, 56–57, 64; dictionary and, 21; disease and, 136; effects of war and, 174; factions and, 175; Fort Augusta conference and, 184; Fort Duquesne campaign and, 50; Fort Loudoun and, 38–39, 120, 121, 124, 133; Fort Loudoun fall and, 222 (n. 33); Fort Prince George Massacre and, 96, 98; Fort Prince George Treaty and, 97; forts and, 23, 32, 33, 35, 36, 37, 46; French and, 45, 138, 176; French and Indian War and, 26, 28; geography and, 13; geopolitical considerations and, 44; Grant campaign/ treaty and, 151, 165; horse stealing and, 49; hostages and, 92; Kerlérec and, 175–76; Lantagnac and, 39; Lyttelton and, 70, 71; mistreatment and, 41; North Carolina and, 112–13; Ostenaco and, 70, 180–81; peace and, 136, 138; power struggle and, 22; prisoners and, 174; rivals for power among, 94; Shawnees and, 29, 172, 174; smallpox and, 83; threats to, 122; trade and, 46, 162; trip to England and, 17; Virginia and, 43, 141, 165, 172; warriors, 46. *See also* Attakullakulla of Tomotley; Chota and Chotas *and other Overhill towns;* Oconostota of Chota

"Panic of 1751," 22–23
Paris, Treaty of (1763), 2, 181
Parsell, Thomas, 99
The Patriot (film), 3
Pawley, George, 113
Peace. *See* Diplomacy, peace negotiations, and treaties
Peace and War on the Anglo-Cherokee Frontier (Oliphant), 5
Peace conference, Glen's (1755), 28
"Peace towns," 14, 198 (n. 15)
Pearis, Richard, 36
Pearson, John, 107
Pendarvis, John, 66, 67, 123
Pennsylvania, 58, 83, 115, 120, 188. *See also* Fort Duquesne campaigns
Pennsylvania Gazette, 29
Pepper, Daniel, 73–74
Perdue, Theda, 190
Peter (African American), 145
Philip, 145, 186
Pickens, Andrew, 191, 193
Piecuch, Jim, 4
Pinckney, Eliza Lucas, 84–85, 142, 157, 176
Pitt, William, 33
Pittsburgh, Pa., 25
Planter society, 8. *See also* Frontiersmen, farmers, and settlers
Poisonings, 145
Pontiac's Rebellion, 183, 184
Powell, George Gabriel, 75, 210 (n. 47)
Pownall, Thomas, 89
Preachers, 6
Presbyterians, 115
Preston, David, 43, 44
Prevost, James Mark, 117
Priber, Gottlieb, 21, 175, 199 (n. 41)
Prince of Tanasee, 70
Prince William Parish, 66, 67, 71–72
Prisoners: Cherokee, 122, 132, 136, 137, 162, 167; of Cherokee enemy Indians, 172; exchanges of, 135, 178;

of Cherokees: Cherokee offensive
of 1760 and, 105, 107, 109, 112; Fort
Prince George Massacre and, 93,
110, 219 (n. 41); Fort Prince George
ransoming of, 140; freeing of, 136,
141, 174–75; Grant campaign/treaty
and, 147, 162, 164, 166; Great Island
Treaty and, 167; number of, 169;
Reed Creek talks and, 137 *See also*
Adoption by Cherokees; Hostages–
Lyttelton's; Torture
Proclamation Line (1763), 8
Psychological warfare, 111–12
Pyamingo (Savannah River Chicka-
saw), 64

Quaratchee and Quaratchees, 12 (map),
55, 122
Quebec, 104

Racism, 4. *See also* Interracial mixing
Randolph, Peter, 30
Rape, 73–74, 103, 162
Raper, Robert, 113, 120
Rattray, John, 156–57, 158, 160
"Raven," 61
Raven of Chota, 92
Raven of Estatoe, 126
Raven of Settico, 49
Raven of Toqua, 172
Raven of Toxaway, 51
Reed Creek talks, 137
Refugees: Cherokee, 22, 105, 134, 139,
144, 147, 151, 174, 192; white, 107, 108,
113, 189–90
Regionalism, 5
Regulator movement, 3
Religion, nativist, 182
Reservations, 83, 184–85
Revenge, Cherokee: Adair on, 73;
Beamers and, 54; Cane Creek attack
and, 132; Cherokee attacks and, 110,
111; Cherokee culture and, 54, 55–56,

61, 64, 166; Cherokee unity and, 55,
56; Cherokee women and, 54, 117–18;
Coytmore and Demere and, 69;
Creeks and Chickasaws and, 56;
diplomacy and, 70–71, 74–75; Forbes
on, 50; Fort Prince George Massacre
and, 100, 103, 110; Great Island Treaty
and, 166; Lower Towns and, 54, 55, 56,
58–59, 122; Lyttelton and, 54, 55–56,
63–64, 74–75, 188; Overhills and,
56–57; Shawnee attacks and, 183
Revenge, white, 49, 68, 100
Revolutionary implications: African
Americans and, 3, 4, 137, 186–88,
192, 194; Amherst and, 171; Anglo-
Cherokee War veterans and, 191, 193;
Boone and, 177; Cherokee-British
relations and, 188–91; Cherokee
rivalries and, 188; French and Indian
War and, 2, 4; frontiersmen and, 144;
Grant campaign and, 144, 170;
hunting and, 190; scholarship on, 3–4,
5; South Carolina-British relations
and, 5, 8–9, 176, 180, 192, 193; trade
and, 193–94
Rice, 187
Richardson, Richard, 75, 121, 210 (n. 47)
Richardson, William, 61, 62, 83, 104–5
Roberts, Owen, 191
Rogers, Robert, 234 (n. 46)
Rogers' Rangers, 143
Round O of Stecoe: Atkin and, 45;
Charles Town troops and, 75;
Cherokee revenge and, 55; Coytmore
and, 71, 92; Fort Prince George
Massacre and, 93, 97; Lyttelton and,
71, 76; Stuart and, 71; Virginia and, 30
Royal American Regiment, 120
Royal Proclamation of 1763, 185
Royal Scots (1st Regiment), 119, 128, 129,
142
Royal Train of Artillery, 212 (n. 71)
Rum and spirits, 40–41, 62, 64, 104, 189

St. Clair, John, 49
St. Helena Parish, 145
St. Paul Parish, 177
Saluda, 77 (map), 114 (map)
Saluda Old Town, Treaty of (1755),
  28–29, 30, 40, 41
Saluda River, 23, 69, 105–6, 107, 111
Sandy Creek campaign veterans, 45
Savannah, Ga., 110, 113
Savannah River, 11, 109, 187
Savannah River Chickasaws, 56, 64, 70,
  76, 84, 227 (n. 25)
Savannahs, 39
Saxe-Gotha Township, 112, 113
Sayer, Alexander, 137
Scalping: Attakullakulla and, 57, 64,
  68, 95; bounties and, 48, 49, 54, 56, 69,
  103, 107, 110, 132; Bouquet and, 50; by
  Catawbas, 150; Cherokee culture and,
  14, 17, 50, 61, 64, 91, 102–3, 134, 183; by
  Cherokees, 39, 44, 45, 54, 67, 69, 108,
  112, 116, 124, 128, 130, 132, 149; by
  Creeks, 56; Georgia frontier and, 109;
  Grant campaign/treaty and, 151, 152,
  159, 160–61, 165; Long Canes and,
  105; manumission and, 137, 145; by
  northern Indians, 151, 172; Stevens
  Creek settlement and, 105; by whites,
  49, 54, 103, 111, 112
Scalp Jack of Toxaway, 91
Scots, 15, 128. See also Grant, James;
  Kennedy, Quintin
Scots-Irish Presbyterians, 87, 104, 113
Scott, John, 214 (n. 24)
Scottish Highlanders (Montgomery's
  77th Regiment), 119, 120, 128
Second Man of Conasatchee, 78
Seed of Settico, 138, 139
Seneca Mingos, 142, 152
Seneca (Esseneca; today Clemson,
  S.C.), 11, 12 (map), 174
Seroweh ("Young Warrior of Estatoe"):
  British and, 183; Bull's peace terms

and, 122; Creeks and, 174; daughter of,
  189; Fort Loudoun fall and, 126; at
  Fort Prince George, 55; Fort Prince
  George Massacre and, 92–93; French
  and, 135, 137; peace and, 140–41, 174,
  184; Saluda and, 105–6; trade and, 164
Setticos, 12 (map); attacks by, 63, 69, 70,
  108, 215 (n. 7); Cane Creek attack and,
  133; Chotas and, 132; Fort Prince
  George Massacre and, 97; Lyttelton
  and, 67–68; Virginia and, 64, 172. See
  also Raven of Settico; Seed of Settico;
  Wolf of Settico
Settlers. See Frontiersmen, farmers,
  and settlers
Seven Years' War, 2, 6, 8–9
Shaw, Lachlan, 123
Shawnees: attacks by, 22, 172, 175, 183;
  Fort Duquesne campaign and, 48;
  French and, 136–37; miscommunica-
  tion and, 49; Overhills and, 172;
  Virginia and, 29, 43, 165. See also
  Cornstalk
A Short Description of the Province of
  South-Carolina (Milligen), 100
Silver, Peter, 115
Silverheels (Seneca Mingo), 142, 152
Simmons, Samuel, 70
Simpson, Archibald, 66, 71–72, 87, 88,
  103, 115, 129
Skalitoskee, 216 (n. 26)
Skiagunsta of Keowee, 15
Slave-Catcher of Chota, 64, 68
Slave-Catcher of Conasatchee, 135
Slave-Catcher of Tamassee, 155, 156
Slaves. See African Americans
Smallpox: Abram and, 98, 216 (n. 29);
  African Americans and, 81, 85–87, 88,
  186; Anglo-Cherokee War and, 188;
  burning of Estatoe and, 221 (n. 16);
  Charles Town and, 7, 81, 186, 213 (n. 1),
  215 (n. 38); Cherokee towns and,
  83–84, 118, 127, 128; Fort Ninety Six

and, 110; Fort Prince George siege and, 97–98; frontier and, 103, 113; Keowee and, 78; Lyttelton's expedition and, 80, 88–89, 116; McGunningham's warnings and, 159; Priber on British and, 21; recruitment and, 135; refugees and, 113; social upheaval and, 81–89, 188; South Carolina outbreaks, 213 (n. 6); Upper Creeks and, 135. *See also* Disease

Smith, Anne Loughton, 85

Smith, Benjamin, 72, 85, 137, 176

Smith, Thomas, 124

Social stability/upheaval, 3, 6, 81–89, 187, 188

South Carolina, 77 (map); French and Indian War era and, 2–3; internal divisions and, 8, 191, 193; peace and, 142; recruitment and, 138; slaves and, 34; smallpox and, 81–89, 188, 213 (n. 6); trade and, 179–80; Virginia and, 134, 156. *See also* Charles Town *and other towns;* Elites; Frontiersmen, farmers, and settlers; Glen, James *and other politicians;* South Carolina Assembly; South Carolina–British relations

South Carolina Assembly (Commons House): Acadians and, 35, 36, 87–88; Attakullakulla and, 160; Braddock's campaign and, 28; British relations and, 119–20, 163–64, 176–77, 189–90; Bull and, 157, 189–90; Cane Creek attack and, 133–34; Cherokee-Carolina boundary and, 162; Cherokee land and, 160, 189–90; closure of, 182; elections and, 176, 177; Fort Loudoun and, 46, 98, 137; Fort Prince George and, 98, 158; funding of troops by, 68; Gadsden and, 177; Grant campaign/treaty and, 129, 159–63, 166, 170–71, 176; Lower Towns and, 22–23; Lyttelton and, 34–35, 37, 70, 72, 75,

76, 89, 211 (n. 50); makeup of, 119; Montgomery and, 123, 129; radical members and, 176; Revolutionary War and, 192; Saluda Treaty and, 28; sending of trade goods by, 46; Setticos and, 68; slaves and, 86, 130, 137, 145–46, 186, 187; smallpox and, 83, 87–88. *See also* Gadsden, Christopher *and other members*

South Carolina–British relations: Boone and, 176–77; British military campaigns and, 7; Cherokee attacks and, 104, 114–15; costs of war and, 176, 191; elections and, 182; elites/frontiersmen and, 7–8, 169–70; frontiersmen attacks and, 169; Gadsden and, 191; Garden on, 116; Glen and, 34–35; Grant-Middleton duel and, 167–68; Grant's treaty and, 156, 163, 164; Indian Trade Act and, 178–79; Lyttelton's expedition and, 70, 72; Montgomery's retreat and, 129; Ostenaco's visit to Britain and, 180; Revolutionary implications and, 5, 9, 176, 180, 192, 193; Seven Years' War era and, 7, 9; South Carolina Assembly and, 119–20, 163–64, 176–77, 189–90; Virginia and, 24

South Carolina–Cherokee relations: Adair on, 1; French and Indian War and, 26, 28; Glen's peace conference and, 28; mistreatment of Cherokees and, 61; Revolutionary implications and, 194; Revolutionary War and, 5; Seven Years' War era and, 1; Virginia and, 24

South Carolina Council: Attakullakulla and, 159; Byrd's proposed treaty and, 135–36; Grant treaty and, 164, 166–67; Lyttelton's expedition and, 70, 74, 76; peace terms and, 122; on rapes by British, 162; slave import tax and, 146,

170; South Carolina–British relations and, 129

South Carolina Gazette: on Attakullakulla, 28, 63; on black rebellion, 66–67, 75; on black smallpox, 85–86; Boone and, 176–77; on Cherokee attacks, 69, 107, 111; on Cherokee grievances, 211 (n. 57); on elite fears, 25; on Fort Loudoun siege, 131; on Fort Prince George Massacre, 100; on Grant, 167; Jamaican uprising and, 124; on Lyttelton, 34, 66, 75; on Lyttelton's expedition, 76, 80; Middleton's letter to, 157; on peace, 141, 233 (n. 27); on slave duty, 145–46; on smallpox, 82–83, 85–86, 88; on treatment of Cherokees, 62. *See also* Newspaper accounts

South Carolina militia: Acadians and, 36; Black River and, 113; Broad River and, 112; Cherokee culture and, 49; Cherokee resistance and, 111, 119; Creeks and, 123; Fauquier and, 56; Glen's peace conference and, 28; Grant on, 157; Lyttelton's expedition and, 66, 69, 70, 71–72, 75–76, 78, 80; slaves and, 65, 123, 137; smallpox and, 80, 82, 87; strength of, 123

South Carolina Rangers: at Cowhowee River attack, 149; Fort Ninety Six numbers of, 226 (n. 12); Fort Prince George and, 136, 138, 139; Glen's peace conference and, 28; Grant campaign and, 142, 143, 144, 145, 149; Grant on, 129, 160; Kennedy and, 145; Lyttelton and, 68, 77; Montgomery and, 121–22, 127, 128; Pearson and, 107; Turner's Fort and, 112

South Carolina Regiment (Provincials), 121, 123, 126, 129, 164; Stuart's detachment, 69, 70, 71

South-Carolina Weekly Gazette, 177, 182

South Catawba River, 39

Southeastern colonies, 2

Spain and the Spanish, 13, 19, 184

Speculators, 7–8

Speeches and dictation, 6

Stalnaker, Samuel, 153

Stamp Act, 187

Standing Turkey of Chota (Conocotocko/ Kanagatucko; Chota), 97, 120, 132, 139, 155, 158, 165, 166

Starvation, 138, 139, 151, 153, 164, 168. *See also* Hunting

Stecoe. *See* Round O of Stecoe

Stephen, Adam, 165–66, 231 (n. 36), 234 (n. 46)

Stevens (Stephens), John, 133, 162

Stevens Creek settlement, 105, 114 (map)

Stockbridge Indians, 143, 227 (n. 25)

Stoney Creek, 66

Stono Rebellion, 66

Stuart, John ("Bushyhead"; Oonodutu): Attakullakulla and, 78, 79, 118, 124–25, 134, 162–63; background of, 78; on Bull, 164; Cane Creek attack and, 133; on Cherokee idea of imprisonment, 90; on Cherokee populations, 190–91; on P. Demere, 133; Fort Loudoun and, 134; Fort Loudoun fall and, 132; on Fort Loudoun siege, 97, 117, 121, 124; Georgia conference and, 183–84, 185; on des Jonnes, 181; Laurens and Middleton and, 160; negotiations and, 122; Oconostota and, 97, 109; on Shawnees, 183

Stuart's detachment, 69, 70, 71

Sumter, Thomas, 166, 172, 180, 181, 191

The Swallow (Lower Towns), 43, 44

Swiss people, 113, 146

Syacust Ukah. *See* Ostenaco of Tomotley

Sycamore Shoals, Treaty of (1775), 192

Tackey's War, 124

Tanasee (Tanasi), 12 (map), 13

Tanasee conference, 64

Tassee, 150 (ill.), 151, 174

Tattoos, 61

Taxes, 176

Tellico River, 13

Tellico River attack, 132

Tennessee, 192

Tennessee River, 193

Terron, Samuel, 131, 133, 134

Thomson, William, 136, 138, 149, 191

Three Peoples, One King (Piecuch), 4

Timberlake, Henry, 166, 172, 173 (ill.),
    175, 178, 180

Timothy, Peter, 34

Tistoe (Tiftoe) of Keowee: Cherokee
    unity and, 126; Chickasaw attack and,
    144; Coytmore and, 91–92; Fort Prince
    George Massacre and, 92; Grant
    campaign/treaty and, 155, 156, 163; as
    hostage, 79, 122; Lower Town
    refugees and, 139; Lyttelton and,
    58–59, 73; Virginia and, 211 (n. 60)

Tobacco-Eater (Cussitah), 72

Tomotley, 12 (map), 28, 37, 122, 124. *See
    also* Attakullakulla of Tomotley

Tony of Chota, 216 (n. 26)

Toqua, 12 (map), 124, 181. *See also* Corn
    Tassel of Toqua; Onatoy of Toqua;
    Raven of Toqua; Tullatahee of Toqua;
    Willenawa of Toqua

Torture, 102–3, 110, 112, 136

Townhouses, Cherokee, 90, 91 (ill.)

Toxaway and Toxaway warriors, 51,
    55, 122

Trade and traders: African Americans
    and, 106; Atkin and, 72; attacks on,
    70; Attakullakulla and, 23, 60–61;
    British and, 16, 19; British-Creek, 73;
    Byrd and, 131, 134, 137; Cane Creek
    attack and, 132; Charles Town and, 15;
    Cherokee attacks and, 103, 106, 108,
    109, 113, 119; Cherokee-British
    alliance and, 6–7; Cherokee culture

and, 43; Cherokee dependence on,
15–17, 46, 47, 62, 74; Cherokee women
and, 117; Creeks and, 15, 58, 180, 190;
Cuming and, 10; dishonesty of, 40, 41,
62, 189, 190; embargoes and, 68, 174;
Fort Loudoun and, 40, 41, 139; Fort
Prince George Massacre and, 93,
94; forts and, 23, 32, 33; French and
Indian War and, 26; French-British
relations and, 16–17; Georgia and, 182;
Georgia conference and, 184; Glen
and, 23; goods and, 15–16; Grant
treaty and, 162; Great Island Treaty
and, 166, 167; Indian Trade Act and,
178–80; as informants, 104; Lyttelton
and, 72, 80; Montgomery and, 120;
names for Cherokees and, 13; Nottely
warriors and, 216 (n. 20); Ostenaco
and, 141; "Panic of 1751" and, 22;
Pontiac's Rebellion and, 183; Revolutionary implications and, 193–94;
Royal Proclamation of 1763 and, 185;
Seroweh and, 164; Settico and, 68;
slaves and, 96, 187; smallpox and,
85; South Carolinians and, 17; Tistoe
and, 73, 163; Virginia and, 29, 30, 43,
46, 60, 74, 165, 179, 190. *See also* Adair,
James *and other traders*; Ammunition; Hunting; Rum and spirits

Trading posts, 11

Treaties (chronologically): 1730, of
Whitehall ("Articles of Friendship
and Commerce"), 18–21, 79, 80; 1751,
of Charles Town, 23; 1755, of Saluda
Old Town, 28–29, 30, 40, 41; 1756, at
Catawba Town, 30; 1756, of Broad
River, 30, 32; 1756, of alliance, 39; 1759,
of Waulyhatchy, 73; 1759, of Fort
Prince George, 80, 90, 91, 92, 95, 96,
97, 98, 100; 1761, of Great Island of the
Holston River, 165–67, 172; 1761, of
Charles Town, 155–56, 158–68, 170–71;
1763, of Paris, 2, 181; 1763, of Augusta,

Made in the USA
Columbia, SC
28 December 2019